THE EAST GERMAN ECONOMY

THE EAST GERMAN ECONOMY

Edited by
Ian Jeffries and Manfred Melzer

Advisory Editor
Eleonore Breuning

Translations by
Eleonore Breuning and Ian Jeffries

CROOM HELM
London • New York • Sydney

Croom Helm Ltd, Provident House,
Burrell Row, Beckenham, Kent BR3 1AT
Croom Helm Australia, 44-50 Waterloo Road,
North Ryde, 2113, New South Wales

Published in the USA by
Croom Helm
in association with Methuen, Inc.
29 West 35th Street
New York, NY 10001

British Library Cataloguing in Publication Data

The East German economy.
1. Germany (East)——Economic policy
II. Jeffries, Ian I. Melzer, Manfred
338.9431 HC290.78

ISBN 0-7099-1469-5

Library of Congress Cataloging-in-Publication Data

The East German economy.

Bibliography: p.
Includes index.
1. Germany (East) — Economic policy. 2. Germany (East) — Economic conditions. I. Jeffries, Ian.
II. Melzer, Manfred.
HC290.78.E23 1987 338.9431 87-17163
ISBN 0-7099-1469-5

Typeset in 10pt Times by Leaper & Gard Ltd, Bristol, England
Printed and bound in Great Britain
by Billing & Sons Limited, Worcester.

Contents

Figures

Tables

Acknowledgements

While the whole Department of Economics at the University College of Swansea is to be most warmly thanked for shouldering many of my teaching responsibilities during a year's sabbatical leave, there are two people deserving particular mention.

It is conventional, of course, to thank the typist. I would go much further and say that Miss Siân Davies helped make the book possible. She displayed a constantly willing attitude throughout the long process and the accuracy, speed and style of her work are quite amazing. The equivalent of two chapters was typed when she was quite alone in coping with the heavy general demands of a very busy office.

I am especially grateful also to Dr Karen Williams of the Department of Management Science and Statistics at the University College of Swansea. During a number of critical periods, when Dr Breuning was overwhelmed with University work and editing for the Foreign and Commonwealth Office, Karen collaborated with me on a significant portion of the translations, in the sure knowledge of no greater reward than a 'thank you' in the acknowledgements. The exacting standards needed for an international project of this sort make a partner in translation indispensable. Karen's timely contributions are deeply appreciated.

It must be said, however, that I was left with the final word. I take full responsibility, therefore, for any errors of translation that may occur in this book.

During the latter stages of this project Dr Melzer suffered a major heart attack. It is with great regret that he was unable to finish the chapter on pricing, but all his colleagues recognise his outstanding contribution and wish him a speedy recovery.

Ian Jeffries

1

The GDR in Historical and International Perspective

Ian Jeffries

The main aim of this book is to provide an objective account of how the economic system of the German Democratic Republic (GDR) actually operates. Its industrial past, resource endowment and demographic features need to be looked at briefly in order to understand the changes which have occurred in economic policy since the end of the Second World War. These policy changes have only amended what is still essentially a Soviet-type political and economic system, have been constrained by Soviet domination, but have also been induced in part by the continual comparisons made to the Federal Republic of Germany as regards economic performance.

The GDR is a world-ranking industrial country,[1] with the highest standard of living in the socialist bloc. The problem faced by the Socialist Unity Party (SED), however, is the tendency of consumers to compare their living standards not with their poorer socialist neighbours, but with the West, especially the more affluent Federal Republic. This makes demonstrating the superiority of socialism and the quest for party legitimacy uphill tasks, even amongst those born after the Second World War and despite the general awareness of the progress which has been made. Particular resentment is felt by the inability of GDR citizens normally to travel to the West (the major exception being pensioners), even though 1986 saw a significant increase in permissions for urgent family visits.

Economic reform has been severely constrained by a number of factors. The division of Germany placed the GDR at the frontier between East and West, with an all-pervading Soviet presence. There has simply not been the latitude to depart to any important degree from the Soviet political and economic system (the sort of latitude granted to Hungary especially) and a 'Berlin Spring' has always been unthinkable. The GDR also has a border with Poland, a country with a history of unrest and instability, and the rise (albeit brief) of Solidarity had a traumatic effect on the GDR leadership. Significant economic decentralisation is seen as leading to political devolution. Hence, economic reform is viewed as having to be formulated within tight constraints and needing to be well thought out, with no chance of unexpected results and no danger of instability: effective party control has to be preserved at all costs.

This is in marked contrast to Hungary, whose lesser strategic significance is one factor allowing a relatively high degree of economic (and political) liberalisation. There have been setbacks in the reform process, but the Hungarian Communist Party Congress of March 1985 reaffirmed the main features of the New Economic Mechanism (first introduced in a radical and comprehensive package on 1 January 1968) and further measures have been taken (such as those of 1 January 1985, which allowed for worker influence over the choice of management in medium and small enterprises). Despite economic difficulties, 1986 also witnessed a general reaffirmation of the NEM and on 1 January 1987 a decentralised banking system was introduced. In Hungary the industrial enterprise, within the constraint of a basic production profile, generally takes output and input decisions in the light of post-tax profit and a varying milieu of 'economic levers' and pressures (including informal ones), which the state uses to steer the economy indirectly.

Czechoslovakia shared with the GDR the distinction of being an advanced, industrial country before the start of socialist development, but the GDR, as has already been mentioned, could not even have contemplated the radical political and economic ideas associated with the 'Prague Spring' of 1968 — ideas quickly eradicated by the Warsaw Pact invasion. During the 1960s the GDR's attempt to find solutions to its economic problems revolved around the NES (*Neues Ökonomisches System*: New Economic System), very modest by Hungarian or Czechoslovak standards, but even that was effectively scrapped in 1970.

The relative success of the GDR economy makes radical reform less urgent. Nevertheless, Gorbachev's advocacy of openness (*glasnost'*) and 'democratisation' (such as multi-CPSU candidate elections and secret ballots) and the sweeping personnel changes in the Soviet Union are unsettling to a conservative leadership long used to proclaiming the virtues of its socialist system and extremely fearful of the possible consequences of political relaxation. On the other hand, there is now greater potential room to manoeuvre in the economic sphere, and it will be interesting to see how GDR policy will be affected, particularly in the longer run.

Gorbachev (promoted to General Secretary of the CPSU in March 1985) fully supported Andropov's more candid approach to problems and his call for change. Gorbachev has mentioned the need to increase the decision-making powers of production units, to create a strong link between performance and reward, to emphasise modernisation rather than enlargement of the capital stock, to improve quality, to increase labour effort and discipline, to improve prices and for 'intensification'. These ideas have been given substance in the new 1985 Party Programme, the 1986-90 five-year plan and in measures taken before and after the 27th Congress of the CPSU (25 February-6 March 1986), at which a generally critical tone was adopted (a whole catalogue of problems, such as inertia, bureaucracy and corruption, was openly discussed). In broad terms, improved management of the economy is to take two forms. Firstly, that of increasing the role both of the centre ('strategic' decisions) and of the production units, at the expense of the reform-hindering ministries (in addition to ministerial amalgamations for streamlining purposes, four 'co-ordinating bureaux' having already been set up in the agro-industrial, machine tool, energy and construction sectors). Secondly, retaining tight control over the key heavy and defence industries, while devolving more decision-making authority to light and consumer goods industries (fewer targets to fulfil, for example), where quicker reaction to consumer demand is seen to be necessary.

Specific Soviet measures include numerous personnel changes, the anti-drinking campaign, the loss of bonuses for poor quality or unsaleable goods, industrial price surcharges for good quality products and price reductions for below-standard ones, increased prices for grain and other major agricultural products in excess of the 1981-85 average production levels, and the ability of collective and state farms to sell 30 per cent of the targeted output of fruit and vegetables as they wish. Since 1 January 1987, foreign trade reforms have been introduced in more than twenty ministries and departments as well as in seventy individual and amalgamated enterprises. This involves the right of direct participation in export and import transactions, including those in the markets of capitalist and developing countries. (The recent general stress on direct links between enterprises in different Comecon countries predated this measure.) A new overall body, the State Foreign Economic Commission, has also been set up. (Note that with the Soviet acceptance of joint equity ventures with Western companies since 1 January 1987, the GDR is now isolated among the East European CMEA states in this respect.) Also in 1987 significant concessions to private and co-operative activity were introduced, and a draft law published in February 1987 envisages elected enterprise management. Experiments at the VAZ car plant at Togliatti and the Frunze machine tool enterprise at Sumy (involving, for example, retention of 40 per cent of hard currency earnings and bonuses linked to productivity) were followed by the introduction on 1 January 1987 of 'full' economic and commercial accounting in 7 ministries and 36 enterprises (ministries no longer being allowed to subsidise loss-making enterprises by means of profit transfers from relatively successful enterprises), with the intention of covering the whole of Soviet industry by 1990. A quality control commission has been set up and delivery obligations have become a key indicator.

The Soviet Union has a natural interest in the economic diversification to be found within Comecon. The GDR's relative economic success has attracted particular attention. (Hungary has also come under the microscope, despite its disappointing economic performance of late.) In May 1985 Gorbachev praised the GDR's endeavours to reach international standards in production and in June 1985 what he called 'inter-industry associations' (which suggests that the Soviet Union might well introduce a GDR type of combine). The nature of the Soviet foreign trade reforms and the concessions to private and co-operative activity also suggest GDR influence. Gorbachev personally attended (as with the Polish, but in contrast to the Hungarian, Czechoslovak and Bulgarian congresses) the 11th Congress of the SED (17–21 April 1986), the generally self-congratulatory tone of which contrasted markedly with that of the CPSU. Gorbachev again praised the GDR's economic success and the work ethos of its citizens, although he did not specifically mention the combine.

Honecker, General Secretary of the SED, indulged in some mild criticism (the need to improve service in shops, for instance), listed the GDR's economic achievements (in robotics, for example), stressed the importance of continued 'perfecting' of planning and management, and mentioned specific proposals. The latter included a fully paid year at home for working mothers after the birth of the first child, higher quality non-essential goods to reflect the costs of producing them, increased support for private tradesmen and more allotments for urban dwellers. It is interesting to speculate on the possible influence of the momentous events which have taken place in China since 1978[2] on the Soviet Union and thus, indirectly, on the GDR.

Economic background

The GDR started off in generally worse shape than the Federal Republic:

(1) Although what is now the Federal Republic suffered greater wartime destruction, the GDR fared relatively badly with respect to reparations paid from current production and the large-scale dismantling and removal of plant to the Soviet Union. Reparations and occupation costs accounted for an estimated 25 per cent of social product between 1946 and 1948 (*DIW Handbuch*, 1984, p. 38). In contrast, the Federal Republic fared much better in this respect and actually became a recipient of Marshall Plan aid after 1948 (although it should be noted that the Federal Republic took in many refugees from the eastern provinces of the Third Reich and also paid compensation to Israel).

(2) The economic structure of the GDR was relatively unbalanced, in contrast to that of the Federal Republic. The GDR's industrial structure was relatively strong with respect to machine tools, office machines, textile machinery, optical equipment, electrical engineering, motor vehicles, light industry and aircraft. On the other hand, chemicals and iron and steel were weakly developed, the present area of the GDR producing only 1.3 per cent of the pre-war total of pig iron. In 1938 the share of iron ore was only 1.3 per cent and coal 1.9 per cent (Strassburger, 1984, p. 114). In 1939 *per capita* industrial output was slightly higher than that of the present-day Federal Republic.

As regards transport, the GDR is physically relatively small, but the pre-war road and rail networks ran mainly east–west and the rivers Elbe and Oder end in the present-day Federal Republic and Poland respectively. The GDR is poorly endowed with raw materials, with important exceptions such as brown coal and potash.[3] The rising marginal costs of extraction, and increasing world raw material and energy prices following, with a lag, the 1973-74 oil shock, focused urgent attention on the need to make efficient use of inputs. The quest for economic changes to induce greater efficiency continues to this day.

During the early years after the end of the Second World War various measures were taken to introduce a Soviet-type economic system. There was a major land reform and significant nationalisation. About two-thirds of the land confiscated from those possessing more than 100 hectares (excluding the Church) was distributed in the shape of small farms. There was also confiscation of the land owned by those described as Nazi activists and war criminals. In 1948 nationalised industry accounted for 39 per cent of gross industrial production, SAGs (*sowjetische Aktiengesellschaften*: Soviet joint-stock companies) for 22 per cent, and private industry 39 per cent (McCauley, 1983, p. 38). By 1949 the 'commanding heights' of the economy were in the hands of the state, namely heavy industry, mining and transport (ibid., p. 43). By 1955 nationalised concerns accounted for 85.3 per cent of gross industrial output and private 14.7 per cent (ibid., p. 76).

The last SAGs were returned in January 1954, but while they existed they played a major part in transfers to the Soviet Union out of current production and monopolised uranium and iron ore mining. The SAG was headed by a Soviet director with a German under-manager and workforce (Childs, 1983, p. 13). It should be noted, however, that some investment did take place and this was on German soil (in contrast to the acts of dismantling and transfer), while some goods were sold in the GDR itself (which helped other firms).

Demography and manpower

Labour is a scarce factor of production in the GDR. The population was 16.7 million in 1939 and reached a post-war peak of

19.1 million in 1947 (swollen by refugees). The present population is well below this figure, as Table 1.1 illustrates.

Table 1.1: GDR population (end of year)

Year	Population
1955	17,832,232
1965	17,039,717
1975	16,820,249
1985	16,640,059

Source: *Statistical Pocket Book of the GDR* (East Berlin, 1986), p. 15.

Between 1949 and the building of the Berlin Wall 12-13 August 1961, almost 2.7 million migrants from the GDR were registered by the Federal and West Berlin authorities. They were mainly young (just below a half being less than 25 years of age), skilled workers, professionals and entrepreneurs.

GDR policy has been both to promote an increase in the birth rate (1974 saw an all-time low of 10.6 per thousand) and the participation of women in the workforce (by measures such as the generous provision of crèches and kindergartens, maternity grants and reduced working hours). As a result, the present figure of 88 per cent of women of working age either at work or in training is the highest in the world (Edwards, 1985, p. 10). In 1982 28 per cent of women in employment were in part-time work (ibid., p. 82). In 1983 females accounted for 49.5 per cent of persons employed, excluding apprentices (1950, 40.0 per cent; 1980, 49.9 per cent: *Statistical Pocket Book of the GDR*, 1984, p. 28). The birth rate has risen above its 1974 low, as Table 1.2 illustrates.

At the end of 1985 the 16,640,059 population was divided into females 52.7 per cent and males 47.3 per cent (*Statistical Pocket Book of the GDR*, 1986, p. 145).

Table 1.2: Live births and deaths (per thousand population)

	1950	1960	1970	1980	1985
Live Births	16.5	17.0	13.9	14.6	13.7
Deaths	11.9	13.6	14.1	14.2	13.5

Source: *Statistical Pocket Book of the GDR* (East Berlin, 1986), pp. 148-9.

The GDR has a relatively high dependency ratio. At the end of 1985 the population was divided into those of working age 64.8 per cent, children under 15 18.6 per cent and those of pensionable age 16.6 per cent (ibid., p. 147). Edwards (1985, Chapter 4) discusses the attempts to employ people above pensionable age (60 for women, 65 for men). In the 1978 Labour Code, for example, enterprises are required to provide sheltered workplaces for the elderly and the enterprise is expected to make part-time work available for elderly workers if they want it (ibid., p. 187).

The scarcity of labour as a factor of production has had a profound impact on economic policy in the GDR. Incentives are needed to encourage a high level of commitment and productivity. Compensations for the acute shortage of labour include attempts to increase the amount of shift work and the GDR's on the whole successful efforts to maintain the tradition of a highly skilled workforce (the system of education has a strongly vocational bent). Indeed the German tradition in general has been of benefit (hard work, order, discipline, administrative efficiency, honesty and achievement-orientation). This tradition encourages a relatively greater willingness to work with and within the rules and regulations of a command economy.

The computation of national income

Although this book deals essentially with the way the economy operates, use is made of official statistics such as 'produced national income'. A short digression is in order to explain the main differences between the Western and Eastern concepts of national income. A diagrammatic explanation is given in Figure 1.1.

The GDR uses the Soviet Material Product System, as opposed to the System of National Accounts recommended by the United Nations. The Material Product System excludes so-called 'non-productive' services (such as finance and insurance, public administration and justice, defence and education). 'Productive' services include hotels and the restaurant trade, publishing, architects' and engineers' offices, laboratories and laundries (*DIW Handbuch*; 1984, p. 132). Thus services which are used in material production are counted in national income.

Figure 1.1: Generation of national product in West and East

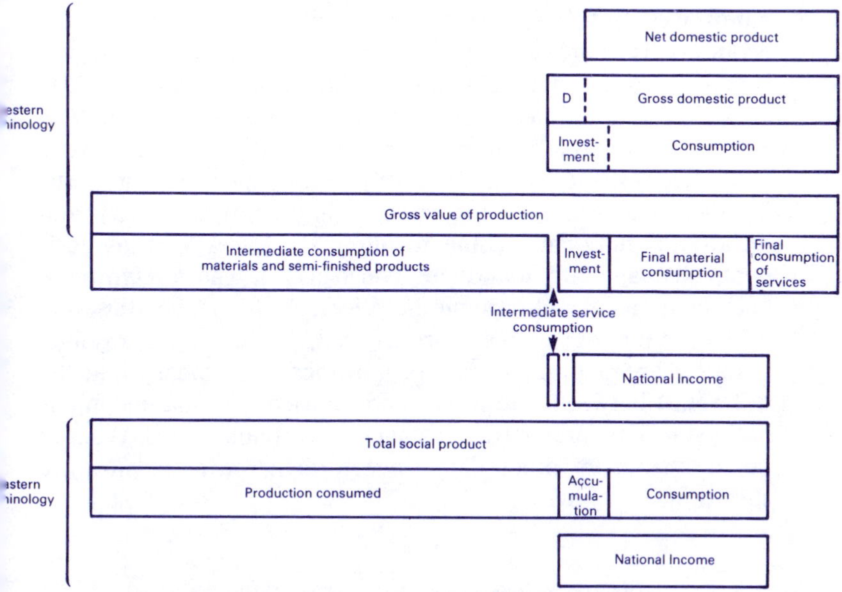

D: capital consumption.
Intermediate consumption of materials and semi-finished products within the producing sector.
Intermediate services to branches of material production.
Investment: includes changes in stocks.
Final material consumption: consumption of material goods and services.
Final consumption of services: consumption by both private households and public institutions.

Source: Wilkens, H., *Sonderhefte des DIW*, 115 (1976), p. 152; *DIW Handbuch* (1984), p. 133.

Wilkens (1981, p. 10) quotes the example of the works doctor generating national income, whereas a doctor working in a hospital does not. There are some differences in practice between CMEA countries, however. The GDR, for example, counts the whole of the transport and communications sector as 'productive' and not merely that part servicing the 'producing' sector, although this is done less on grounds of principle than from practical considerations (*DIW Handbuch*, 1984, p. 132).

The whole economy becomes divided into 'productive' ('producing') and 'non-productive' ('non-producing') sectors. The Western concept of nct national product at market prices, minus the contribution of the 'non-producing' sectors of the economy, is approximately equal to national income calculated according to the Material Product System (ibid., 1984, p. 133).

'Utilised' national income (*verwendetes Nationaleinkommen*) is usually defined as 'produced' national income (*produziertes Nationaleinkommen*) minus exports plus imports, but there may also be a deduction (as in the Soviet Union) from 'produced' national income to allow for losses such as accidental damage and abandoned construction. The foreign trade balance is calculated in domestic prices. As far as the utilisation side of national income is concerned, however, no absolute numbers are published, only proportions. This means that the difference between 'produced' and 'utilised' national income is not given. The foreign trade balance is not published and cannot be derived from other data since foreign trade statistics are shown in valuta marks.

Table 1.3: Official statistics for rates of growth of produced national income (per cent)

1950	22.0	1963	3.5	1975	4.9
1951	21.1	1964	4.9	1976	3.5
1952	13.7	1965	4.6	1977	5.1
1953	5.5	1966	4.9	1978	3.7
1954	8.7	1967	5.4	1979	4.0
1955	8.6	1968	5.1	1980	4.4
1956	4.4	1969	5.2	1981	4.8
1957	7.3	1970	5.6	1982	2.6
1958	10.7	1971	4.4	1983	4.4
1959	8.8	1972	5.7	1984	5.5
1960	4.5	1973	5.6	1985	4.8
1961	1.6	1974	6.5	1986	4.3
1962	2.7				

Source: *Statistisches Jahrbuch der DDR* (1968); *Statistisches Jahrbuch der DDR* (1986).

NOTES

1. International comparisons of *per capita* industrial output are difficult to make, but according to the World Bank it ranks twelfth.

2. Colourful phrases such as 'socialism with Chinese characteristics' and 'building socialism with capitalist methods' (Deng Xiaoping's term) give a flavour of the dramatic changes. These include the 'responsibility' system in agriculture, China's 'open door' policy on foreign and especially Western trade, capital and technology (especially via the four 'special economic zones' and fourteen coastal cities, four of which have been given priority since July 1985), and the gradual extension of reforms to the urban sector (involving a division of the state sector into tight and loose central control, bearing some superficial resemblance to the GDR's 'structure-determining tasks' phase of the NES). Even allowing for the economic restrictions after 1985 (due to foreign trade problems etc.) and the political restrictions at the beginning of 1987, events in Eastern Europe seem rather dull in comparison.

3. Priorities during the first five-year plan (1951-5) included energy, raw materials, iron and steel, chemicals and capital goods, while the second five-year plan (1956-60) again stressed energy and chemical production (Frowen, 1985, pp. 36-7).

2

Command Planning and the Production Unit

Ian Jeffries and Manfred Melzer

Bornstein (1977, pp. 103-4) lists the main features of the traditional command economy as follows: the overwhelming dominance of nationalised means of production in non-agricultural sectors; agriculture dominated by collectives only nominally independent; a hierarchical economic organisation, with decision-making power resting mainly at the top, although vertical bargaining takes place; output and its distribution planned in detail in both physical and value terms; administrative allocation of non-labour inputs, with labour controlled via wage funds; prices mainly centrally determined and infrequently changed; money essentially passive, financial flows being adjusted to physical flows; managerial and worker incentives mainly emphasise quantitative targets; arbitrarily determined exchange rates and a system of taxes and subsidies that separate domestic from foreign prices. Specialised foreign trade enterprises means that production units have no direct contacts with foreign partners.

There are potential advantages in command planning such as the simultaneous achievement of full employment, high growth rates and a relatively stable general price level, the ability rapidly to implement decisions such as a large-scale investment project and the co-ordination of research and production. In reality things have been different in some respects. Under-employment exists, prices do not reflect changing scarcity relationships and innovation is a serious problem. Growth is not an end in itself, there is the danger of a stagnating or inadequately growing level of consumption, the productivity of labour and capital is relatively low by Western standards, a significant amount of scarce manpower is engaged in control mechanisms, and distorted information can adversely affect central decisions. Economic performance has not been free of disturbances and enterprise initiative in decision-making has been hindered by the lack of incentives. Problems such as these have led to economic reforms of various kinds, the type varying between countries and over time, depending on the specific circumstances and limitations.

The present-day economy of the GDR is still easily recognisable as a command economy, with political power lying in the hands of the SED, the dominance of social ownership of the means of production and central guidance of the economy, including foreign trade. Figure 2.1 summarises the GDR economic and political hierarchy as it existed in the mid-1980s.

PARTY ORGANISATION

At the end of 1985 the Socialist Unity Party (*Sozialistische Einheitspartei Deutschlands*: SED) had 2,293,300 full and candidate members. Its General Secretary is Erich Honecker. Real power is exercised by the Politburo and the Secretariat of the Central Committee (whose members belong to the Politburo).

Politburo (Politbüro der SED): 22 full members and five candidates (with no voting rights), representing the party, governmental and mass organisations (trade unions and youth).

Central Committee of the SED (Zentralkomitee der SED): 165 full members and 57 candidates, who are eligible to replace voting members between Congresses of the SED.

Secretariat of the Central Committee: 11 full members. Led by Honecker, the other ten being allocated specific areas of responsibility. Günter Mittag is responsible for economic policy. A powerful means of control is exercised through the nomenklatura, a list containing all important appointments and qualified people. The top appointments appear on the nomenklatura of the Politburo.

The SED Congress: the Congress is nominally the supreme party organ (with the Central Committee exercising this

Figure 2.1: State bodies responsible for planning and decision-making in the GDR

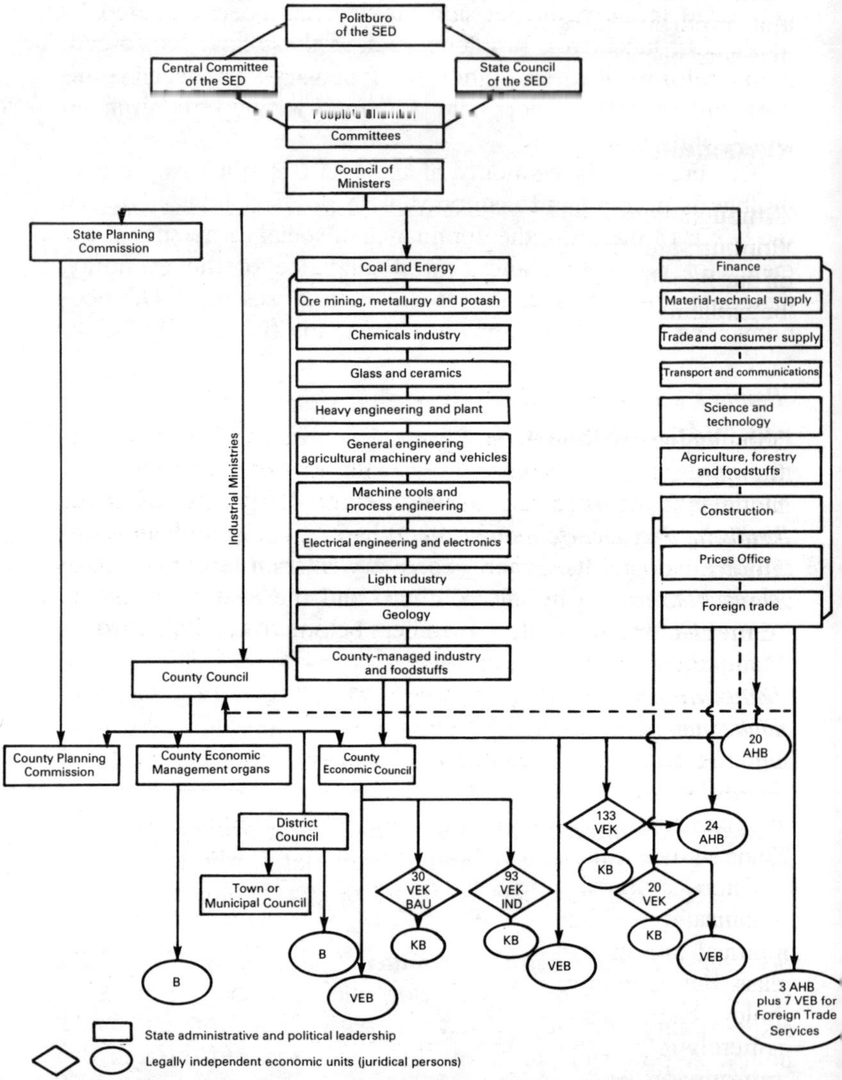

Abbreviations etc: AHB, Volkseigener Aussenhandelsbetrieb (nationally owned foreign trade enterprise); B, Nichtstaatlicher Betrieb (non-state enterprise); BAU, construction; IND, industry; KB, Kombinatsbetrieb (combine enterprise); VEB, Volkseigener Betrieb (nationally owned enterprise); VEK, Volkseigenes Kombinat (nationally owned combine).

Source: Melzer, M., 'Wirtschaftspolitik der administrativen Reformen', in Cassel, D. (ed.), *Wirtschaftspolitik im Systemvergleich* (Verlag Franz Vahlen, Munich, 1984), p. 29.

function in between Congresses[1]), but in reality it rubber-stamps decisions already taken. Nevertheless, it is at Congresses that important announcements of party policy are made, new five-year plans, programmes and strategies, for example.

GOVERNMENTAL ORGANISATION

Although real decision-making power is exercised by the Politburo and the Secretariat of the Central Committee, the role of the People's Chamber and the Council of Ministers needs to be explained.

People's Chamber of the GDR (Volkskammer der DDR)

500 members. This is given the nominal look of a 'parliament' by the representation of other parties and organisations: SED (127 members); Democratic Farmers' Party of Germany (*Demokratische Bauernpartei Deutschlands*: 52); Christian Democratic Union of Germany (*Christlich-Demokratische Union Deutschlands*: 52) Liberal Democratic Party of Germany (*Liberal-Demokratische Partei Deutschlands*: 52) National Democratic Party of Germany (*National-Demokratische Partei Deutschlands*: 52); Free German Trade Union Federation (*Freier Deutscher Gewerkschaftsbund*: 68); Democratic Women's Federation of Germany (*Demokratischer Frauenbund Deutschlands*: 35); Free German Youth (*Freie Deutsche Jugend*: 40); League of Culture of the GDR (*Kulturbund der DDR*: 22). Their statutes acknowledge the leading role of the SED.

There are, of course, many SED members in the mass organisations. Elections themselves are not about providing political alternatives to the SED as the party of the working class, but to involve voters in the realisation of party and state policy. The role of the other 'parties' and the mass organisations is merely to convince their members of SED goals and to act as transmission belts for SED decisions in relation to the social groups they represent. The National Front (*Nationale Front*), which has comprised all the parties and mass organisations since the end of the 1940s, presents a single list of candidates. Within the National Front it is actually the competent SED organ which decides on the nomination and sequences of all the candidates. Voters express their 'approval' with typical 99.6 per cent election results. (Although voters have the formal right to abstain and to cross out the names of candidates, typically voters fold unmarked ballot papers and place them in the box, thus avoiding the attention which using the booth provided would bring and the possible adverse consequences of official displeasure.) Since 1948 there have been fixed quotas of seats in the People's Chamber for the individual parties and mass organisations. Thus the importance of this pseudo-parliament as a decision-making unit (although described as the supreme organ of state power) is practically nil, its main function being to explain and nominally approve party policy.

The Council of Ministers (Ministerrat)

The Chairman is Willi Stoph, who has eleven representatives, each allocated special duties. Formally called the 'Government' since 1974, there are 45 members, ministers and heads of other government bodies, such as the State Bank and the State Planning Commission. In accordance with the recommendations and resolutions of the SED, it deals with fundamental aggregate economic policy goals (structural questions, capital formation and consumption, for example), regional planning, major investment projects, basic questions of foreign trade and payments, reserves and co-operation with other Comecon members. The *Presidium* of the Council of Ministers (15 members under chairman Willi Stoph) is the real centre of decision-making and acts as a sort of 'economic cabinet'.

ECONOMIC ORGANISATION

The Council of Ministers imparts the basic decisions to the economic hierarchy. It should be noted that the party, governmental and economic bodies are closely linked to one another. Party members occupy powerful positions in the economic hierarchy and informal relationships are likely to be important too.

The State Planning Commission (Staatliche Plankommission)

Its essential role is to transform the decisions of the Council of Ministers into concrete plans (the main planning technique being MAK balancing). The SPC draws up plan variants, coordinates plans and guides the work of plan preparation, balancing and supervision of plan implementation.

The eleven industrial ministries

These exercise sectoral control, participating in the drawing up of plans and disaggregating plan targets to the production units under their guidance (for example, centrally guided *Kombinate*). There are also territorial bodies: in 1981 around 5.5 per cent of industrial production was under county level direction.

The VVB (*Vereinigung Volkseigener Betriebe*: association of nationally owned enterprises) played an important role during the NES and the 1970s (see Chapter 3). It disaggregated plan targets received from ministries to the enterprises in their charge and tried to ensure that the enterprises carried out the lines of production desired by the state. There were 85 VVBs in 1967, 53 in 1973 and 13 in 1979. They subsequently disappeared, leaving the *Kombinat* dominant.

The nationally owned combine (Volkseigenes Kombinat)

The years 1979 and 1980 saw a fundamental change in economic organisation with accelerated combine formation. The *Kombinat*, a horizontal and vertical amalgamation of enterprises, is the basic production unit today, exercising unitary management from research right through to sales. As we shall see later, great hopes are placed in the combine to accelerate scientific-technical progress, reap economies of scale, improve information flows, increase exports and improve supply.

The nationally owned enterprise (Volkseigener Betrieb)

Although the enterprise is still a legally and economically independent unit, its decision-making powers have been weakened to the benefit of the *Kombinat*. The Director General of the combine, for example, can now shift capacities and transfer plan tasks between enterprises.

Plan horizons

There are annual, medium[2] (normally five, but sometimes seven years) and long-term plans (including specific programmes, such as that for housing 1976 to 1990 (Junker, 1973, p. 5 ff.); long-term energy and fuel balances; long-term programmes for different sectors of the economy). In the Planning Order for

1981 to 1985 long-term planning is described as the preparatory stage of five-year planning. In principle the five-year plan is the 'main steering instrument' from which the annual plan is derived as 'annual slices'. The Planning Order realistically has to take account of deviations of annual plans from the guidelines (to allow for factors such as changes in demand, new technologies and altered world market circumstances), but the five-year plan itself is now no longer redrawn.

In the drawing up of five-year and annual plans, central drafts are passed down the economic hierarchy for consultation, suggestions and disaggregation, and passed back up for amendment and confirmation. The formal and normal sequence for annual planning is described below.

As soon as the State Planning Commission is given the first preliminary plan fulfilment data by the Statistical Administration (around the end of January or the beginning of February of the pre-plan year), it compares these results with the objectives of the five-year plan and takes into consideration new directives issued by the Council of Ministers. Minimum plan targets (*Aufgaben*) are passed down the hierarchy and increasingly disaggregated. During August and September draft plans are submitted by the lower economic organs. From October to mid-December the State Planning Commission draws up the version which is submitted to the Council of Ministers for confirmation and then to the People's Chamber. The plan is then imposed on the economic units as obligatory targets (*Auflagen*).

Material, Equipment and Consumer Goods (MAK) Balances (Material-, Ausrüstungs- und Konsumgüterbilanzen)

These balances are divided into five groups: energy, raw materials, materials and components; equipment (machines and vehicles); industrial plant and consumer goods. Most production is covered by centrally determined balances. Different bodies are responsible for the confirmation of balances, depending on the importance of various products. For example, the Council of Ministers confirms the state plan balances (S-balances) drawn up by the State Planning Commission, the State Planning Commission confirms the balances determined by the branch ministries (M-balances), while the branch ministries confirm the balances drawn up by the *Kombinate*. The remaining part of production is accounted for by the balances worked out by combines (in former times by the VVBs) on the basis of central targets (a large proportion of these *Kombinat* balances are subordinate to the aggregately balanced S and M balances in a product-specific or assortment-specific sense).

MAK balancing is the principal planning technique, used in the attempt crudely to approximate supply and demand. Typical supply deficiencies are preferably met with demand adjustments (tightening of input norms), rather than supply adjustments (which would necessitate the complex and time-consuming tracing through of the effects on other balances). Input–output tables have been drawn up since 1959 and are used, for example, in variant analysis, but suffer from the problems of too high a level of aggregation (27 sectors in 1959 and 118 today) and reliance on past input coefficients for long planning periods, which fail to reflect scientific and technical progress.

The non-state sector

Åslund (1985) analyses the non-agricultural private sector. He estimates that in 1979 the private sector contributed 3 per cent of net material product outside agriculture and employed 5.2 per cent of the non-agricultural labour force. Following the early nationalisation measures (described in the introduction) there was a falling trend with cycles: a socialist offensive 1952-3; a liberal interlude 1953-7; a second socialist offensive 1958-60; a period of successful competition between the state and private sectors during the period of the NES; a third socialist offensive 1971-5, with the first half of 1972 especially prominent. The period since 1976 has seen the granting of tax

Figure 2.2: Simplified MAK balance

	Supply		Demand
1.	Total production	1.	Domestic utilisation (material utilisation, investment, consumption)
2.	Imports a. socialist countries b. non-socialist countries	2.	Exports a. socialist countries b. non-socialist countries
3.	Stocks and reserves at the beginning of the year	3.	Stocks and reserves at the end of the year

and credit concessions and many new licences for handicrafts, trade and catering. Excluding apprentices, employment in the private trades sector increased by 11,844 to 258,100 between 1980 and 1984 (Brückner, 1985, p. 3). The 1986-90 plan foresees further growth of the sector.

Mention should also be made of the existence of production and trade co-operatives and the semi-state enterprises (*Betriebe mit staatlicher Beteiligung*, which were nationalised in 1972). To date the GDR has not allowed joint equity ventures with Western companies, but it will be interesting to see whether the Soviet acceptance of these organisations in 1987 will lead to a change of policy.

The production unit and the role of plan indicators

In a classic command economy the basic production unit is state-owned, operates on the principle of one-man responsibility and control (*Prinzip der Einzelleitung*: principle of individual management) by a manager (director) appointed by the state and is given the task of fulfilling the state plan expressed in the form of obligatory indicators, output typically predominating (although participating in the drawing up of the plan by providing information and making suggestions/requests to the superior bodies in the vertically organised hierarchy). Given the differing importance of the indicators, their inconsistency with one another and the inevitable room for independent decision-making (given the impossibility of the central authorities generally providing precise details), production units resort to output distortion and lack of adaptation to user need. Gross output, for example, leads to attempts to concentrate on those products containing a high proportion of intermediate products, especially the most expensive, while an indicator expressed in weight encourages unnecessarily heavy goods.

The production unit is a financially separate and accountable unit (the Soviet term for economic accounting is *khozraschyot*), the account being compulsorily kept in the local branch of the State Bank for plan monitoring. Financial flows are transacted in cashless (book-keeping) form (with the important exception of the paying out of wages and salaries).

Investment was mainly determined by the state. In the early model grants covered fixed capital investment and planned working capital (extra-plan working capital requiring credits bearing a low rate of interest), although these came more and more to be replaced by interest-bearing credits. Prices were in principle set by the state on the basis of average cost (excluding a charge for capital) and remained unchanged for long periods of time. They were, therefore, not efficiency prices, but, since the economy was centrally planned, the main function of prices related to control and evaluation, not allocation. Basic wage rates were also set by the state (although there was a market for labour, unlike raw materials, intermediate goods and capital goods, which were administratively allocated). The main role of the trade union organisation was to fulfil the plan, although it also administered the social security system and defended workers' interests in areas such as safety and bonuses (see section below). The state monopoly of foreign trade shielded the production unit from the world economy, foreign trade being handled by separate foreign trade enterprises. Domestic and international prices were divorced from one another, the production unit being paid the domestic price in the case of exports and paying the price of comparable home-produced goods in the case of imports. There was both currency and goods inconvertibility and the foreign trade enterprises made accounting profits and losses at the arbitrarily set, normally overvalued, exchange rates.

This basic model of enterprise organisation was associated with serious problems, which later led to economic reform. There was a tendency to understate productive capacity and aim for a 'soft' plan. There were no bonuses for less than 100 per cent fulfilment, but significant over-fulfilment was avoided because of the 'ratchet effect': the starting point for next period's plan being this period's achievement. There was also a tendency to overindent for, and to hoard, inputs, due to supply difficulties which were often severe and the fact that capital was a free good to the production unit. This led to the phenomenon of 'grey men' (unofficial supply agents, *tolkachi*, in the Soviet Union) and an incentive to self-supply, especially component parts. Labour too was hoarded to meet likely changes in plan. There was an anti-innovation bias at the level of the production unit because of the adverse effects on short-term plan fulfilment and ratchet effect deterrents. This was aggravated by the separation of research and production units. Problems of this kind were particularly serious for the poorly endowed, labour-scarce, trade-dependent, industrial economy of the GDR, and the history of reform demonstrates the continuous attempts to overcome them, while at the same time maintaining effective party control and the essentials of a centrally planned economy.

Trade unions and wage determination

The Free German Trade Union Federation (*Freier Deutscher Gewerkschaftsbund*) is a federated monopoly, which embraces some 97 per cent of eligible members (only those in the armed forces, self-employed people and co-operative farmers are excluded) and is organised along industrial as opposed to craft lines. There are sixteen unions (*Gewerkschaften*), eight of which are industrial (*Industriegewerkschaften*) and eight are for government and public service, food and retail trade, the state sector of agriculture, education, health, science, the arts and civilians employed by the armed forces. All employees, including management, belong to the same union.

The 26 member Presidium of the federal executive of the FDGB is led by Harry Tisch, who is also a member of the Politburo. Below the Presidium is the federal executive itself, which comprises 200 full and 25 candidate members. An FDGB organisation exists in each enterprise and institution, while the FDGB itself is represented on party and government bodies: for example, it is assigned 68 of the 500 seats in the People's Chamber.

The functions of trade unions

(1) To implement party policy. In the economic field this involves carrying out state plans, reducing waste and inefficiency, encouraging technical progress and worker discipline and organising 'socialist competitions' to improve various aspects of worker performance. The trade unions participate in planning, although in reality their impact is marginal. Basic wage rates are formally agreed by the Council of Ministers and the FDGB, real power, however, lying in the former body. The limitations placed on the role of trade unions at the enterprise level are neatly summarised by Strassburger (1985, p. 468).

The right to monitor, criticise and make proposals does not at heart affect the principle of individual management, democratic centralism and the political primacy of the SED at the enterprise level. It is true that pressure can be exerted upon enterprise management by means of discussion and criticism, but, if these recommendations and proposals are not taken into account, there at best remains open to the enterprise trade union executives the path of complaining to the relevant superior management organs.

The trade union leader is the deputy chairman of the enterprise 'production committee' (the chairman being the party secretary), although this only plays a consultative role. The 'enterprise collective contract' (*Betriebskollektivvertrag*), worked out by enterprise management and the trade union executive, on the basis of the confirmed enterprise plan, constitutes an obligation to fulfil the enterprise production tasks and socio-cultural programme for the given plan period. It contains information about labour tasks, plans concerning qualifications, culture and training, the forms of wages to be applied, criteria for the allocation of bonuses and special measures for the promotion of women and youth (Strassburger, 1985, pp. 467-8).

(2) To protect workers by ensuring, for example, management compliance with health/safety and wage/bonus regulations. Also provided are highly subsidised holidays and cultural/sporting activities.

(3) To administer the social security system. The right to strike featured in the 1949 constitution, but not that of 1968, the argument being that strikes make no sense in a workers' state for they would be striking against themselves.

There is a labour market in the GDR so that the wage and salary system is used to allocate manpower and provide incentives to greater effort and qualifications. But during the 1960s and the first half of the 1970s only around 50 per cent of the actual earnings of most employees in the producing sectors were accounted for by basic wage rates. The 'extra-performance wage' (*Mehrleistungslohn*) — that part of earnings linked to performance — was originally introduced, as its name implies, as a means of increasing performance, but came largely to lose that function. It came to be paid merely upon fulfilment of the prescribed norm, additions and deductions in cases of over- and under-fulfilment being rare (Vortmann, 1984, p. 258). Factors such as technical progress led to increased labour productivity and enterprise management were reluctant to raise norms. With wage rates essentially remaining unchanged, increases in actual earnings were basically accounted for by increases in the 'extra-performance wage'. This led to distortion in the labour market, discriminating against those mainly reliant on basic wage rates (individuals like technicians, white collar workers and master craftsmen and those working in sections such as trade and services).

After an announcement at the 8th FDGB Congress in 1972 that the wage system was to be reformed, a 1976 resolution of the Central Committee affected production workers in industry, construction and other branches of the economy such as transport and communications over the course of the 1976-80 five-year plan. The 'basic wage' (*Grundlohn*), which comprised the set wage rate and a substantial proportion of the former 'extra-performance wage', was to constitute some 70 to 80 per cent of actual earnings. The 'basic wage' was to be paid on fulfilment of norms, under-fulfilment being followed by deductions and over-fulfilment by a real 'extra-performance wage' (Strassburger, 1985, p. 849).

In 1982 the wage reform was essentially concluded, having involved around 1.8 million production workers and some 600,000 master craftsmen and employees who had completed college or technical college courses, for whom new, performance-dependent salaries were set (Strassburger, p. 848 and p. 850).

Besides wages and salaries (note there is a minimum wage of 400 marks per month for full-time work), employees also receive bonuses. These bonuses are intended to be paid according to performance, but in practice this is frequently not the case. In particular, end-of-year bonuses are calculated more or less automatically and have developed *de facto* into a 13th month's salary. This bonus is by far the most important one for those who work in industrial enterprises (Vortmann, 1984, p. 260).

Unemployment and social welfare

While there is some frictional and structural unemployment (a recent example being the difficulties in placing lorry drivers affected by the switch from road to rail in the effort to save petrol), the GDR is a labour-scarce economy (albeit with 'under-employment', although this is impossible to quantify). The Labour Code (*Gesetzbuch*) provides protection against unwarranted dismissal. Enterprises which release workers because of rationalisation schemes or structural changes must normally ensure a new situation or retraining for the employees concerned, while loss of earnings is made good for one year by the enterprise. Informal pressure can be employed, including that by the trade unions, to persuade reluctant workers who refuse to change jobs. A form of social welfare relief can be paid out to those adversely affected by structural unemployment (the number of people actually involved is probably very small). Social welfare is paid out in the case of dismissal without notice if no new employment follows immediately thereafter: otherwise unemployment is no longer a branch of the social security system (Vortmann, 1984, pp. 253-4).

NOTES

1. There have been Congresses in 1946, 1947, 1950, 1954, 1958, 1963, 1967, 1971, 1976 and 1981 and 1986.
2. Following plans for the latter half of 1948 and for 1949-50, there were medium-term plans for 1951-55, 1956-60, 1959-65, 1964-70, 1971-80 and 1981-85. The current plan is for 1986-90.

3

The New Economic System of Planning and Management 1963-70 and Recentralisation in the 1970s

Ian Jeffries and Manfred Melzer

THE NEW ECONOMIC SYSTEM (NES)

Economic and political background

The typical micro-economic problems associated with command economies (distorted prices, gross output, 'tonnage ideology', anti-innovation bias, concealment of potential, factor hoarding, striving for 'soft' plans and the 'scattering' of investment resources) were particularly serious in the advanced, industrial, poorly endowed, trade-dependent GDR. The complexities of central planning increase with the level of development, thus involving a greater volume and assortment of goods and more complicated production processes.

The ambitious second five-year plan 1956-60 was firstly revised downwards and then replaced by a seven-year plan 1959-65 (following the Soviet lead). The 'main economic task' adopted at the fifth SED Congress in July 1958, was to catch up with and overtake the Federal Republic in *per capita* production of major foodstuffs and consumer goods by 1961 and in labour productivity by 1965. The reason was to staunch migration to the Federal Republic by holding out the promise of a much higher standard of living. By 1960 it was clear that this strategy was not going to be successful. The attempt to increase consumption rapidly, while maintaining the other items of expenditure, led to inconsistencies, stresses and strains. There arose a 'growth crisis' (*Wachstumskrise*), with produced national income increasing by only 1.6 per cent in 1961 and 2.7 per cent in 1962 and investment stagnating during these two years. The seven-year plan, which collapsed in reality in 1961, was formally annulled at the sixth Congress of the SED early in 1963 with the announcement of a new plan for the period 1963 to 1970. This was the background to the building of the Berlin Wall in August 1961, which directly staunched the labour haemorrhage and meant that the aims of the 'main economic task' were no longer so important.

The combined impact of the growth crisis and other economic problems, especially distorted prices (which led to such consequences as a squandering of scarce raw materials) and over-centralisation of decision-making (which hindered initiative and risk-taking by enterprises), made the party leaders realise that current planning methods had to be improved. At the sixth SED Congress in January 1963 it was resolved to introduce the NES.

Main features of the NES[1]

It must be stressed that the NES did not represent a form of market socialism, as practised in Yugoslavia, pre-1968 Czechoslovakia or post-1968 Hungary, but an attempt to achieve state goals more effectively by a combination of traditional command planning (with its use of directives) and indirect steering of enterprises by means of mainly monetary instruments ('economic levers'), including net profit deductions, taxes, prices, the cost and availability of credit and fund formation. These 'economic levers' were designed to induce enterprise behaviour in line with the state plan. With the NES, indirect steering reached the pinnacle of its importance.

It should be noted that: discussion about economic reform was vigorous after the famous 1962 Liberman article in *Pravda*; there was a limited previous experiment (involving ten enterprises and four VVBs); the Soviet Union approved (indeed started to introduce general reforms itself in 1965); the NES was the first comprehensive, post-Liberman reform and the most radical of its time; and that the NES was only gradually introduced from 1964 onwards (the whole panoply of steering instruments only really operating by 1969-70, when the system was already amended by the introduction of 'structure-determining tasks').

When discussing the aims of the NES it is important to

remember the special characteristics of and circumstances surrounding the GDR. The hope was to bring about a scientific and technical revolution, a highly efficient, dynamic, innovative economy, which would prove the 'superiority' of socialism and, at the same time, maintain effective party control.

The role of the VVB

VVBs (*Vereinigungen Volkseigener Betriebe*: associations of nationally owned enterprises) were first formed at the end of the 1940s as management bodies, but in 1952 were changed into mainly administrative entities when enterprises became economically independent. A transformation of 'chief administrations' into VVBs took place in the late 1950s. In 1964 they were placed on a *khozraschyot* basis, declined in importance during the 1970s and finally disappeared during the 1980s.

The VVB was an intermediate-level institution between ministry and enterprise, put in charge of the major enterprises in a particular branch of industry (other state enterprises coming under the authority of territorial bodies). Primarily administrative (as opposed to operational production) organs, their functions included participation in plan discussion and disaggregating plan targets to enterprises, balancing, initiating cost reductions and the commissioning of product research (including consumer goods).

The VVBs appointed a leading enterprise to carry out the agreed proposals arising from the work of 'product groups' (*Erzeugnisgruppen*), which involved the co-operation of enterprises of different legal form (state, semi-state, private and handicraft producer co-operative). Such proposals could involve, for example, the redistribution of production tasks to allow greater specialisation, standardisation and the use of spare capacity. 'Long-term plan groups' in the VVBs had the task of evaluating domestic and international research and development in order to draw up the 'blueprints of scientific and technical development' for all the main branches of the economy and the most important enterprises.

The neglect of enterprises outside the VVB (possibly inside others), but with which the VVB had important linkages, was one reason for the setting up of *Kombinate* (combines), although *Kombinate* were not established in significant numbers until 1968-9 (to help implement 'structure-determining tasks'). At the end of the 1970s the *Kombinat*, a horizontal and vertical amalgamation of enterprises, became the basic production unit, altogether a more powerful body than the VVB.

Enterprise planning and decision-making

In the economy of the GDR, enterprise behaviour has always been guided both directly and indirectly into implementation of state objectives, but during the NES, as has already been said, indirect steering received its greatest emphasis to date.

The number of compulsory plan indicators was reduced, although still covering the main areas of activity: for example, production (including commodity or gross output — *Warenproduktion* — and product groups), sales (home and abroad), fixed capital, science and technology and the wage fund. Net profit (*Nettogewinn*: gross profit minus the capital charge) was designed to help measure and stimulate enterprise performance, retained profit financing fund formation and investment. Within the framework of the state plan and in order to uncover reserves and release growth potential, there was increased scope for independent decision-making, economic levers providing incentives and indirect guidance. The still-constrained room for such decision-making included investment, product and input mix, composition and organisation of the labour force, contracts and foreign trade. With regard to foreign trade, enterprises could conclude short-term contracts not anticipated in the plan, provided they were approved by the foreign trade organ and did not adversely affect other planned export obligations and other plan targets. Enterprises could also obtain foreign currency credits to finance imports if, for example, subsequent increases in exports were made possible, while they received rights to the use of foreign currency for imports if they over-fulfilled export plans or did not use all the foreign currency granted in the plan (through buying more cheaply or by import substitution). The decentralisation of decision-making is particularly stressed by Granick, who describes the situation in mid-1970 as profit 'satisficing' (Granick, 1975, p. 212) and Keren, who talks of lower bodies deciding on the more routine, operational matters, while major, strategic decisions remained with the state (Keren, 1973, p. 557). In line with the attempt to give greater importance to the medium-term, enterprises were obliged to stick as closely as possible to the enterprise five-year plan in working out their annual plan drafts.

The construction of a new plant remained a central decision, but the remaining investment was to be steered by economic levers (such as differentiated net profit deductions, the capital charge and the availability and cost of credit) and the constraints imposed by plan production targets. Although there were difficulties relating to the supply of capital goods, it was in the interest of the enterprise to increase profit, within plan constraints, using retained profit (and credits) to increase decentralised investment.

Economic levers (*ökonomische Hebel*)

The precondition for an effective system of indirect steering is a set of efficient prices. Although price determination was improved as a result of the reform, imperfections still played a role in the downfall of the NES. It is worth briefly summarising at this point the changes that did take place (see Chapter 9 for details).

It was essential to replace the system of prices based, to a large extent, on those of 1944 — prices which encouraged a wasteful use of scarce raw materials and semi-finished products and which hindered technical progress. The first step taken was the revaluation (in mid-1963) of the gross fixed capital stock of industry, on the basis of 1962 replacement prices (to make depreciation rates and the notion of profitability more meaningful and to enable more efficient investment choices to be made by providing planners with information on existing capacity). Depreciation rates were then to be based on these new values. This also allowed, to a limited extent, that account could be taken of technical and economic obsolescence and not only physical wear and tear. The period 1964 to 1967 saw a three-stage price reform moving time-wise from raw materials and materials, semi-finished products to finished products, the prices rising, on average, by 70 per cent, 40 per cent and 4 per cent for each group respectively. It should be noted, however, that the policy of stable retail prices for consumer goods was retained.

Although generally based on predicted (1967) average cost, not all costs were taken into account and the new prices still neglected demand and lacked flexibility. Depreciation was taken into account, but not the interest rate on long-term credit or imputed interest on retained profit. The capital charge was not counted as a cost as such, although the profit mark-up on cost was adjusted to make allowance for the charge. Despite these deficiencies, however, the new prices provided a better reflection of real performance and enterprises were given the incentive to strive for enhanced profits.

The 'principle of earning one's own resources' (*das Prinzip der Eigenerwirtschaftung der Mittel*) meant not only that enterprises, *Kombinate* and VVBs should cover current expenditure from their own revenue, but that investment was no longer to be financed exclusively from budgetary grants (as previously), but out of profit, depreciation allowances and interest-bearing credits.

Banks were responsible for checking projects from the design stage onwards and implementing state credit policy. Interest rates of 1.8 per cent to 3.6 per cent were charged for credit in the case of investment conforming to plan: in other cases rates of up to 15 per cent were charged or credit simply refused. Additional criteria for credit approval included partial enterprise self-financing and a five-year recoupment period (rate of return of 20 per cent). The banking reform carried out during the NES period transformed the banks into independent, though non-competing institutions, which followed the 'principle of economic accountability'.

The 'unitary enterprise result' (*das einheitliche Betriebsergebnis*) meant that export revenues were added to domestically earned profit through the use of existing exchange rates and (unpublished) 'direction coefficients' (*Richtungskoeffizienten*): these were differentiated by country or groups of countries and commodity groups in order to correct the exchange rates and to promote the politically desired trade flows. The differences from the exchange rate were paid from the state budget, or, where the coefficient was less than one, were paid into the state budget.

The 'production fund levy' or capital charge (*Produktionsfondsabgabe*) was a charge of basically 6 per cent on the gross value of the fixed and working capital of an enterprise, which, as has been stated, was not treated as a cost for accounting purposes, but was paid out of profit. It was brought into operation in nationalised industry from the beginning of 1967, with differentiated rates of 1 per cent, 4 per cent and 6 per cent. With the exception of agriculture, it was made a uniform 6 per cent after 1971. The aim was to encourage efficiency in the use of capital.

With the 'net profit deduction' (*Nettogewinnabführung*) enterprises were required to pay into the state budget a certain *percentage* of net profit (gross profit minus the capital charge) via the VVB. The annual minimum was laid down and deduction rates were differentiated by branches, the intention being to implement the structure of production desired by the state.

Enterprise funds (such as the bonus, socio-cultural, science and technology and depreciation funds) were mainly financed out of profit and linked to the fulfilment of plan indicators. For example, the bonus fund was linked to net profit, but affected by the fulfilment or non-fulfilment of plan indicators, such as centrally planned investment and the wage fund. Fund formation in the VVB was mostly financed out of enterprise profits. Tasks important for the entire branch (an investment project, for example) were financed in this manner.

The contract system between enterprises was improved. For example, penalties for contract violation could mean price discounts and reimbursements for losses incurred (including losses caused by the actions of superiors in the planning hierarchy).

In 1968 the 'capital-related price' was introduced. This involved a percentage profit mark-up (maximum 18 per cent) on the *necessary* (as opposed to actual) capital input (based on the experience of the most efficient enterprises in a product group). The intention of taking account of the economically necessary capital expenditure in price was to make possible the payment of the capital charge by capital-intensive enterprises.

With 'dynamic pricing' the intention was to bring about price reductions by two methods. The first foresaw price reductions down to a floor of permissible profit per 1,000 marks of necessary fixed and working capital once a ceiling had been exceeded (according to the 1969-70 regulations on prices, enterprises were initially allowed to deduct the full amount of the profit loss from net payments due to the state, as an incentive to reduce costs). The second method foresaw the gradual lowering of the prices of what were then new and improved products, in order to encourage enterprises to develop products of a technically higher standard later on. (See Chapter 9 for further details.)

THE AMENDED NES: 'STRUCTURE-DETERMINING TASKS' 1969-70

Before analysing the general reasons for the demise of the NES, it should be noted that the particular cause of the amendment was the state's inability to implement its desired structural developments by means of indirect steering instruments. Although prices were improved, they could not be made to reflect all the many (and frequently changed) targets set by the state. Enterprises, guided by the existing prices, used the room for manoeuvre in decision-making to further their own interests, undertaking, for example, investment projects which were efficient from their point of view, but which diverged substantially from the politically desired goals. There was also the problem that small enterprises were not willing enough to apply or capable of applying modern technologies. The answer to these problems was seen in the so-called 'structure-determining tasks' (*strukturbestimmende Aufgaben*).

These concerned production tasks, processes, investment or basic research projects which exert a revolutionary influence on the scientific and technical level of development of the economy and ensure the achievement of the highest world standards. Included in the (actually unpublished) list were products or technologies necessary for automation and rationalisation of production processes (such as electronic data processing and automated production lines), products which lead to economical substitution processes (such as artificial materials and synthetic fibres) and products which determine progress in processing technology (such as components of semi-conductor technology). The growth industries were electronics, electrical goods and instrument-making, chemicals and the most important branches of engineering and motor vehicles. As well as those aimed at improving the structure of production there were also politically desired tasks which enterprises were required to carry out even at a loss. Note that sometimes a whole enterprise could be covered, others were affected by individual products and tasks, while other enterprises were completely unaffected. The 'structure-determining tasks' were given priority (in material supplies, for example) and planned in precise detail from the centre, thus basically signalling the end of the NES in relation to them.

The amended NES was associated with specific problems

which helped lead to its abandonment. The economy had grown steadily until the end of the 1960s, after recovering from the shaky period at the start of the 1960s, but, at the time when the reformed system was to come fully into operation, the economy was beset with severe supply problems. The relative neglect of the non-priority sectors led to bottlenecks and shortages, which rebounded on the priority sectors. Severe winters in 1968-69 and 1969-70, followed by hot, dry summers, aggravated the situation and had negative effects on power supply, transport, agricultural production, construction and water supply. Keren makes the additional point that plan tautness was important. Indeed, he goes on to suggest that '... tautness can be blamed on the impatience induced by structure-determining planning, not on the method of priority planning as such: less ambitious priority planning within a slacker plan might have worked' (Keren, 1973, p. 582).

General reasons for the ending of the NES

(1) The inefficiency of even the reformed prices was a crucial factor, enterprises producing goods which were at variance with state plans, for example. Price dynamisation actually resulted in price rises, rather than the intended opposite, which hindered the introduction of 'capital-related prices' (a condition for their introduction was that price rises were supposed to be avoided: by the end of 1970 only around a third of industrial production had been affected). A price freeze was subsequently ordered in 1971.

(2) There was a lack of clarity in the delimitation of powers, duties and decision-making rights between enterprises and VVBs and between the latter and their superior organs.

(3) Bank personnel were inadequately trained and enterprise directors had to shift to a more 'entrepreneurial' way of thinking. It was difficult to get used to the instruments provided by the NES. As the price reform was not completed before 1967 enterprises were unable to calculate their costs before that date.

(4) The principle of 'earning one's own resources' was in contradiction to the structure of production desired by the state, as enterprises' decisions were guided by profit (see Leptin and Melzer, 1978, Chapter III).

(5) The construction industry was inundated with orders and unable to cope, with completion dates lengthening and costs rising. The increased enterprise decision-making rights with regard to investment resulted in an exacerbation of the problem of the 'scattering of resources' among too many projects. The introduction of 'structure-determining tasks' only made the problem worse by competing with the already large number of started projects, these projects subsequently suffering from their non-priority status.

(6) To be an efficient steering mechanism, wages not only need to be translatable into goods and services, but also to be related to performance. During the 1960s (and indeed during the first half of the 1970s) only about 50 per cent of the earnings of most employees in the producing sector was accounted for by wage rates. The part of the wage which was supposed to be linked to performance (the 'extra-performance wage' — *Mehrleistungslohn*) had in fact largely become payable merely upon reaching prescribed norms, thus becoming unrelated to under- or over-fulfilment of the plan and thereby losing its stimulatory effect.

(7) When introducing the concept of 'structure-determining tasks' the economic leadership had not realised the high risk of disproportions arising in demarcating high and low priority tasks. The marked departures of decentralised investment from state-desired lines of development had a profound effect and played an important part in the decision to scrap the NES. (See Leptin and Melzer, 1978, for a detailed analysis of the whole NES period.)

RECENTRALISATION, 1971-79

This period (i.e. between the abandoning of the NES and the *Kombinat* reform) has been described as one of 'recentralisation without concept'; that judgement has not been without its critics,[2] but it is argued here that there was a lack of any new theoretical, comprehensive model to replace the NES and that there was a distinct shift back to the sort of command planning which prevailed before 1963 (while accepting that significant reform elements lingered on, such as the capital charge, parts of fund formation and the principle of earning one's own resources). It was at the fourteenth plenum of the Central Committee of the SED in December 1970 that important changes in the planning and guidance system, in the direction of centralisation, were decided upon, after severe criticism of the NES.

It is worth noting that the expression 'management and planning' was used from 1970 onwards, rather than the previous 'planning and management', to underline central control and the idea of planning being an implement of management. The distinction between the two terms is not very clear, but planning essentially involves the drawing up of plans and management the direct and indirect guidance of the economy.

The immediate concern was to correct the supply imbalances which were a feature of the years 1969 to 1970. On 3 May 1971 Erich Honecker replaced Walter Ulbricht as First Secretary of the SED and the eighth Congress of the SED took place 15 to 19 June 1971. Three leading tasks were set during the 1970s, as given below:

(1) The 'chief task' (*Hauptaufgabe*) was a quantitative and qualitative improvement in the supply of consumer goods. This was repeated in the 1976 programme of the SED.

(2) With a given labour force an extensive growth of capital would mean a decrease in the utilisation of capital and an increase in repairs. There was need, therefore, for all-round 'intensification' of production (output increased mainly through the more efficient utilisation of existing factors of production, especially through technical progress).

(3) An active social policy which included:

(a) a massive housing programme, which envisaged the construction or modernisation of 2.8 to 3 million dwellings over the period 1976 to 1990, substantially improving the living standards of approximately ten million inhabitants and increasing incentives and labour mobility (see Melzer, 1983b).

(b) numerous individual measures: for example, pensions were increased (1971-72, 1976 and 1979), reductions in working hours for shift workers (in 1977 the length of the working week was reduced to 40 hours for three-shift workers and 42 for two-shift workers, both groups also being granted an additional three days holiday), measures to help working mothers and young married couples, improved health care and longer maternity leave; the minimum wage was increased in 1976.

The increased stress on an active social policy showed that there was need to correct the distribution of income even in a socialist economy.

The close links between the three leading goals is worth exploring further (indeed the slogan 'unity of economic and social policy' was coined and awarded a prominent place in the party programme at the ninth Congress of the SED in May 1976). This linkage helped compensate for the lack of any new theoretical concept for recentralisation and provide a central idea for the new Honecker era.

The party leadership was careful to make the 'chief task' conditional upon the success of 'intensification', but the 'unity of economic and social policy' showed that the time had come to reward the relatively neglected consumer, to provide incentives for increased effort and to illustrate the virtues of socialism. The disturbances in Poland in 1970 reinforced the importance of the moment.

The deteriorating foreign trade situation in the second half of the 1970s and rising international indebtedness led to a lower priority being given to consumption and a slightly higher one to exports, although the 'chief task' was not formally abandoned. The resort to heavy borrowing from the West, which characterised a number of countries in Eastern Europe besides the GDR, allowed the import of the increasingly expensive raw materials and advanced technologies. This may be interpreted (with the exception of Hungary) as a substitute for the radical economic reform necessary for successful intensification. Rather than contemplating fundamental changes the GDR leadership was concerned with trying to understand what was happening and adopting short-term policies, such as increased borrowing.

The instruments of indirect steering were partially dismantled or modified and balancing recentralised. In 1971 the net profit to be earned by an enterprise became a compulsory plan indicator derived indirectly from other indicators. Impermissible profit (gained by distorting product assortment, for example) was to be surrendered in full to the state budget. If profit exceeded the planned amount, half of the extra profit went into the state budget and the remainder was used for a rather restricted range of possibilities. If the planned profit was not achieved the enterprise could not form the funds according to plan nor finance the anticipated planned investment: recourse to bridging credits could be limited and was expensive. The role of profit changed from being an incentive for new enterprise initiatives, to being merely a means of securing the planned financial needs of enterprises. Net profit deduction (differentiated by branch) was changed into an absolute sum, while the capital charge became fully operational in 1971. Indirect steering was now intended to achieve closer plan implementation and to reduce costs.

Fund formation was changed somewhat. The bonus fund was linked to the fulfilment of the commodity production and net profit indicators,[3] while the performance fund was created in 1972. The latter fund was linked to increases in labour productivity, reductions in material use, improvements in product quality and the introduction of new products, and used to improve the working and living conditions of the workforce (for example, improved provision for shift workers and assistance to employees building their own homes), rationalisation schemes and the construction of holiday accommodation.

The other major enterprise funds were the investment fund and the science and technology fund. Strict regulations governed the use of resources for investment to ensure conformity to plan. New investments could only be initiated if they corresponded to predetermined requirements, had been accepted in the state title lists and if their completion within the anticipated time was assured.

The degree of centralised decision-making was increased (for example, detailed assortment plans and highly controlled investment). The number of obligatory plan targets was expanded, to include, for example, commodity production, production sold, production of major products by quantity and value, quantity of finished consumer goods, number of employees, wage bill, exports and imports. In the second half of the 1970s, supplementary indicators (such as labour productivity and quality standards) were established. The 47 indicators mentioned in 1970 were increased to 100 for annual planning (less for the five-year plan) in the subsequently published planning order. On 1 January 1979 the 'final product' (*Endprodukt*) indicator was established for *Kombinate* (equal to commodity production of a combine less deliveries of intermediate inputs between enterprises in a combine), to stimulate a reduction in material use and prevent commodity production being inflated by intra-combine transactions.[4]

Credit control was tightened up and in 1974 the Industry and Trade Bank was incorporated into the State Bank (in order to prevent banks increasing their profits by granting credits, at the higher interest rates, not in line with the state plan). The banks then took a more active part in the planning process (for example, in investment preparation and control), commented on draft plans, carried out inspections and imposed punitive interest rates or refused credit altogether in cases of severe plan violations. Investment credits were tied to observance of specified data (for example, technical performance, proportion of investment covered by enterprise funds, completion times and rate of return) and fulfilment of material use norms. As a rule, credits were granted for five years at an interest rate of 5 per cent, although for rationalisation measures the minimum interest rate was 1.8 per cent. Plan violations resulted in rates of 8 to 10 per cent.

Dynamic pricing was abandoned, as was probably the further introduction of 'capital-related prices', and a price freeze ordered in 1971. The raw-material-poor GDR was battered by the rapid increases in world energy and raw material prices after the oil shock of 1973-74 (though delayed by the Comecon pricing system until 1975, when the formula of annually moving five-year world averages was adopted, which speeded up the adjustment). The rising import prices, together with deteriorating geological conditions (which, for example, raised the marginal cost of extracting the all-important lignite), led to the decision to raise domestic prices in stages from 1976 onwards. (See Chapter 9 on pricing.)

The recentralisation model of the 1970s did not solve the basic economic deficiencies of the system and even aggravated some of them. The typical micro-economic problems mentioned earlier still persisted. Labour continued to be hoarded (in case of plan changes or input delays and the difficulties anyway of sacking workers, given that enterprises were responsible for finding another job or retraining if necessary) and wasted in insufficiently mechanised processes such as repairs and transport and in obsolete, extremely labour-intensive plant. It should be noted at this point that the GDR equivalent of the Soviet *Shchekino* experiment began in 1978. Between 1978 and October 1981 the Schwedt petro-chemical combine released 2,400 employees for other work in the *Kombinat* (for example, for more shift work, for additional production of consumer goods and for the in-house construction of rationalisation means). In some branches of industry there were also pecuniary benefits in that wage fund savings could be used for one-off bonuses or regrading. Between 1981 and 1983 200,000 employees were affected in industry, construction and transport.

There were continuing problems with investment and the use of capital. Excessive construction times and the 'scattering' of resources over too many projects persisted, as did the phenomenon of unplanned investment (due to the greater ease of obtaining additional resources after the start of initially allegedly modest projects). Much of the capital stock was obsolete, while the level of utilisation of new plant was relatively low. (For more details on the recentralisation period see Melzer, 1982.)

NOTES

1. The NES was renamed the Economic System of Socialism (*Ökonomisches System des Sozialismus*) in April 1967, ironically to indicate permanency.

2. Naor argues that there was conceptual continuity in the wish to achieve a desired balance between centralised and decentralised planning and that, in addition, structure-determining planning continued, though there were changes in priorities (Naor, 1973 and 1980).

3. Increases in the bonus fund above planned level depended on the fulfilment of additional targets and the fund was used as an incentive for special performances and the end-of-year bonus.

4. It is of interest to note that the problem of inefficient subcontracting outside the combine was meant to be tackled in March 1980 by a new indicator called 'net production' (commodity production minus all deliveries of materials, including those from outside the combine). At the same time another new indicator called 'materials costs per 100 marks of commodity production' was introduced.

4

The Economic Strategy of the 1980s and the Limits to Possible Reforms

Ian Jeffries and Manfred Melzer

THE ECONOMIC STRATEGY OF THE 1980s

Problems of foreign trade and payments

The rise in world market prices of energy and raw materials after the mid-1970s was particularly serious for poorly endowed, industrial countries like the GDR. At the beginning of the 1970s rising imports could be financed, to a large extent, by exports, but from the middle of the 1970s onwards, as a delayed consequence of the 1973-74 oil shock, the foreign trade and payments situation and the GDR's commodity terms of trade deteriorated markedly. At first, the GDR resorted to credits from Western countries[1] and the USSR, but the interest rate burden subsequently became apparent. In addition, GDR exports were adversely affected by recession in the West. The GDR already had a deficit in trade with the West in 1970. Trade with the Soviet Union, too, went into deficit after 1975, not returning to surplus until 1984. Net indebtedness with the West increased at an annual rate of more than 20 per cent during the second half of the 1970s. The second oil shock in 1979 made the situation even worse.

The accumulated trade deficit for the years 1976 to 1980 amounted to just under 29 billion valuta marks (25 billion VM with Western countries and 9 billion VM with the Soviet Union, there being surpluses with some East European countries). The GDR was faced with the need to increase exports (especially better quality and more highly finished industrial products) and to reduce imports (such as through improvements in the use of

Table 4.1: GDR foreign trade by groups of countries[a]

	1975	1976	1977	1978	1979	1980[b]	Structure 1975	Structure 1980	1980 compared to 1975[d]
	in billion VM[c]						per cent		
GDR Imports									
Total	39.29	45.92	49.88	50.71	56.43	62.97	100.0	100.0	10.3
Socialist countries[e]	26.16	29.11	34.21	35.45	36.36	39.87	66.6	63.3	9.9
of which: CMEA countries[f]	24.94	27.93	32.70	34.03	34.73	37.90	63.5	60.2	10.0
(of which: USSR)	(14.09)	(14.91)	(17.66)	(18.60)	(19.66)	(22.21)	(35.9)	(35.3)	(9.4)
Western industrial countries[g]	11.41	14.52	13.16	12.90	17.37	19.19	29.0	30.5	10.3
Developing countries	1.72	2.19	2.51	2.36	2.70	3.91	4.4	6.2	15.9
GDR Exports									
Total	35.11	39.54	41.84	46.17	52.42	57.13	100.0	100.0	10.2
Socialist countries[e]	25.69	28.22	31.25	24.40	38.53	39.26	73.2	68.7	9.8
of which: CMEA countries[f]	24.32	26.71	29.54	32.58	36.87	37.39	69.3	65.4	10.0
(of which: USSR)	(12.45)	(12.88)	(14.79)	(16.31)	(19.61)	(20.40)	(35.5)	(35.7)	(10.2)
Western industrial countries[g]	7.88	9.59	8.50	9.10	10.91	13.77	22.4	24.1	9.4
Developing countries	1.54	1.73	1.99	2.67	2.97	4.11	4.4	7.2	19.3
Balance							Sum of balances 1976-80		
In total	−4.18	−6.38	−8.04	−4.54	−4.00	−5.84	−28.80		
Socialist countries[e]	−0.47	−0.89	−2.96	−1.05	+2.18	−0.62	−3.34		
of which: CMEA countries[f]	−0.62	−1.22	−3.16	−1.45	+2.14	−0.52	−4.21		
(of which: USSR)	(−1.64)	(−2.03)	(−2.87)	(−2.29)	(−0.05)	(−1.82)	(−9.06)		
Western industrial countries	−3.53	−5.03	−4.56	−3.80	−6.45	−5.43	−25.27		
Developing countries	−0.18	−0.46	−0.52	−0.31	+0.27	+0.20	−0.20		

Notes: a. In current prices, FOB, exporting and importing countries; b. Provisional data; c. VM: valuta marks: statistical accounting unit used in GDR foreign trade data; exchange rate 4.67 VM = 1 transferable rouble; the rate of exchange with respect to Western currencies fluctuated with the change in par values between the rouble and convertible currencies: in 1980 1 VM = DM 0.597; d. Annual average rate of growth with regard to total volume 1976 to 1980; e. CMEA countries and the People's Republic of China, Yugoslavia, North Korea and also Laos from 19[illegible]; f. Albania, Bulgaria, Cuba, Mongolia, Poland, Romania, Czechoslovakia, Hungary and also Vietnam from 1978 (previously classified as a socialist country); g. All the so-called 'capitalist' countries of Europe, together with Australia, Japan, Canada, New Zealand and the USA.

materials), both requiring changes in the structure of production.

Domestic problems

The increased foreign trade and payments burden exacerbated the already serious domestic problems relating to efficiency (Melzer, 1980, pp. 361-4).

(1) Scarce labour was often wastefully employed in labour-intensive ancillary production (storage, repair and transport) and discontinuous production runs (downtime and overtime followed one another in fluctuating fashion).

(2) Capital had long since been inefficiently used. Production was insufficiently mechanised and equipment frequently not modern. Investment was inadequately prepared, some unplanned projects still took place and capacity utilisation was low.

(3) There was a wasteful use of scarce and expensive materials. With over 70 per cent of production costs in industry comprising expenditure on materials and with over a half of all manpower in the producing sectors used for the production and transport of energy, raw materials and materials, there was obviously considerable scope for economising (Heinrichs, 1978, p. 904).

(4) An acceleration was needed in the slow rate of technical progress. There were problems with research: insufficiently related and applied to practical needs, duplication, research institutions not on an economic accounting basis, and research capacities on the one hand scattered over too many individual projects and, on the other hand, covering too small a number of research topics.

(5) Various weaknesses in management were mentioned by GDR economists, the following being indicative of these weaknesses: the declining rate of growth; inability to meet demand; increasing amounts of both downtime and overtime; the increase in special shifts; stagnation of innovation; growing discontent among employees and a rise in the number of complaints from the lower ranks (Authors' Collective, 1976, p.368).

In addition, there were problems with the information system, which was more concerned with the needs of the centre than the other management levels. There were overlaps in the decision-making powers of central organs, poor co-ordination in the process of planning and inadequate feedback (*Rückkoppelung*).

The 1981-85 five-year plan

Considering that the 1976-80 plan targets were generally not attained, the increasing foreign trade and payments difficulties and the continuing domestic problems, one would have expected lower plan targets for the 1981-85 five-year plan: in fact they were set surprisingly high (produced national income to grow in line with the plans of the 1970s), especially since the other CMEA countries set lower targets than previously.

The tenth Congress of the SED (12-17 May 1981) had to take account of the increasing external problems, which meant that a dramatic increase in exports, together with a reduction in imports, became the decisive 'leading goal' (*Leitziel*). But although the aim of raising consumption had to be scaled down, the planners were not prepared to make any changes in the 'leading idea' (*Leitidee*) of the Honecker era. Its retention is strongly emphasised both in Honecker's report made to the Congress and also in the five-year plan Directive (1981). The Law on the Five-year Plan (*Gesetz zum Fünfjahrplan*, 1981, p. 405) states the five-year plan serves the good of the working class and the whole people. In the centre stands the policy of continuing with the main task in its unity of economic and social policy in the 1980s too. It comprises the further raising of the material and cultural living standards of the people on the basis of a high rate of development of socialist production, of an increase in efficiency, of scientific-technical progress and of the growth of labour productivity.

But there is a considerable difference between the avowed and actual behaviour of the state: in reality, exports became the first priority, while on paper it remained consumption. But since there were limits to restraining the growth of consumption (for party legitimacy, workers' incentives and the backwash of Solidarity in Poland) and since defence spending was not allowed to suffer,[2] the boosting of exports was, to a large extent, at the expense of investment. Nevertheless, as we shall see, this would adversely affect the aims of further developing the domestic

Table 4.2: Plan targets and plan-fulfilment in the GDR: annual average rates of change in per cent

	1971-75		1976-80		1981-85	
	Five-year plan	Actual	Five-year plan	Actual	Five-year plan	Actual
Produced national income	5.0	5.4	5.0	4.1	5.1-5.4	5.1
Industrial commodity production	6.0	6.5	6.0	5.0	5.1-5.4	5.1
Investment[a]	3.0	4.1[b]	5.2	4.8	—	−2.1[c]
Retail trade turnover (nominal)	4.1	5.1	4.0	4.1	3.7-4.1	3.7
Exports (nominal)	9.9-11.1[d]	9.2	8.5[d]	—	—	8.4[e]

Notes: a. Without foreign contributions; b. Including GDR contributions in other countries, especially in the Soviet Union (pipeline construction, for example); c. The planned total sum of 256 billion marks at 1980 prices for the five years was compared to the actual of 1980 (54.5 billion marks); d. Exports to socialist countries; e. Exports to socialist countries; constant plan prices.

Source: Periodic report of DIW.

energy and raw material base, import substitution and replacing obsolete equipment and plant.

The planners were placed in a real dilemma. The need to increase exports substantially, while still allowing consumption to grow, required a high rate of growth, even when no increase in investment was allowed. Since the labour force was only growing by a small amount, this would involve substantially increased labour productivity (with a given stock of capital). At the same time, considerable savings on energy and materials were necessary in order to be able to limit imports.

The new strategy

In view of the ambitious growth targets set for the 1981-85 five-year plan, an 'economic strategy of the 1980s' was developed. It was expounded by Honecker in ten points at the party Congress (Erich Honecker, *Neues Deutschland*, 12 April 1981, p. 3 ff): a fusion of the advantages of socialism with the achievements of the scientific-technical revolution; a significant rise in labour productivity; a higher level of finishing and processing; substantially better utilisation of raw materials and fuel; high quality of products; increased efficiency of labour; all-round socialist rationalisation; new criteria in investment policy; production of more and better consumer goods; a high dynamism in social production and national income; improved economic performance via intensification.

These can be seen in terms of three operational goals (below):

(1) The rapid raising of labour productivity through an increased focus on qualitative growth factors, especially the acceleration of scientific-technical progress (broad application of micro-electronics and robots, for example).

(2) Improvements in the quality of products; above all, better consumer goods and more profitable exports.

(3) Greater 'intensification' (more economical use of raw materials and fuels, especially oil, which was also to be replaced by domestic lignite whenever possible); greater efficiency in the use of labour; higher finishing/processing of products; the limited amount of investment to enlarge the capital stock should be concentrated on a small number of priority projects involving modern technologies, but the overwhelming emphasis should be

on the repair, renovation and modernisation of the existing capital stock, including the use of 'own-produced' means of rationalisation by the *Kombinate.* The amount of scrapping should, therefore, be reduced: since 1983 the aim has been to increase the useful life of equipment by about 30 per cent. Bryson (1984, p. 189) states that during the period 1970 to 1978 72 per cent of investments was for expansion and only the remainder for replacement and modernisation: there was now to be a 'reversal' to modify that strategy.

In other words, the ambitious growth targets were to be attained not on the basis of an increasing capital stock and use of materials, but by the use of qualitative — that is, resource-saving — factors. Production methods should not only be labour-saving, but also energy-, material- and capital-saving. As Nick (1982, p. 3) puts it:

> A multitude of practical conclusions derive from this course of systematic intensification. The most important is certainly not to call for more manpower, investment, energy or material resources. The national economy just does not have at its disposal a large pot out of which all these resources can be drawn at will. On the contrary, it is necessary to consider how rationalisation solutions, linked with the introduction of more effective technologies and organisation of production, can be found, by way of example means for economising on investment. The higher degree of processing of materials and the more effective utilsation of intellectual potential, which has grown rapidly in past years, also bring intensification strongly to the forefront.

Günter Mittag (1982, pp. 472-4) underlines this:

> The growth of production, higher quality and falling costs are three aspects of the task of ensuring the Republic's further economic growth in the 1980s. Cost reduction thereby more and more becomes a source of growth of decisive importance ... Every effort expended to make better use of the existing fixed capital stock, by means both of technical improvements and shiftwork, is ten times more effective than any enlargement of the capital stock through investment.

(With respect to the connection between this policy and

improved utilisation of capital, innovation and technical progress, see Chapter 8.)

Although Günter Mittag considered the whole strategy laid down in the above-mentioned ten points 'to be amongst the most important achievements by our party in the present time' (1981, p. 533), what was needed was a set of instruments to carry out the strategy in practice (see Chapter 7) and a vehicle providing impulses for its success (see Chapter 5). In the meantime it is worth briefly analysing the change in the pattern of growth which took place in the 1980s. This is illustrated in Table 4.3, which contrasts the 1960s and 1970s with the early years of the 1980s.

Table 4.3: Growth of produced national income and growth factors

	1960-65	1965-70	1970-75	1975-80	1980-83
Produced national income[a]	3.5	5.2	5.5	4.1	3.9
Employees[b]	−0.5	0.2	0.1	0.4	0.4
Fixed capital[c]	6.2	4.9	5.9	5.5	5.4
Production consumed (*Produktionsverbrauch*)[d]	6.0	6.4	5.8	4.4	1.3

Notes: a. 1980 prices; b. Employees in the producing sectors, including apprentices; c. In the producing sectors, 1980 prices. Machines, equipment and construction; d. Difference between total social product and produced national income, 1980 prices. It comprises raw materials and intermediate goods used up in the course of production and capital consumption.
Source: DIW, *Handbuch* (1984), p. 137.

During the 1970s the annual average rate of growth of produced national income was very respectable, although declining somewhat during the second half of the decade. It is noticeable that this was achieved with only a slow growth in the number of employees, but rates of growth of fixed capital and 'production consumed' (*Produktionsverbrauch*) faster than output. The 'net ratio' (the ratio of produced national income to total social product, i.e. net to gross output) fell from 39 per cent to 35 per cent between 1960 and 1980. Thus output growth during the 1970s was labour-saving, but energy-, material- and capital-intensive.

Table 4.3 shows that a successful start was made in the period 1980 to 1983 in reducing the growth of 'production consumed' below that of produced national income. This is illustrative of a clear change from the 1970s pattern of growth, with progress being made towards a more efficient use of all factors of production.

THE LIMITS TO POSSIBLE REFORMS

The 1970s recentralisation model proved inadequate to meet the challenge of 'intensification' and, at the very least, some changes were necessary. A return to an NES-type system was out of the question. Reactivation of profit as an important motive force would require both a significant decentralisation of decision-making and a solution of the price problem. The two, both ruled out as options, are interlinked: decentralisation without radical price reform would lead to serious divergences between the lines of development preferred by the state and production units. Reactivation of profit would also need greater tolerance by the centre of production units departing from the lines desired by the state. The state was not prepared to condone this behaviour before and shows no signs of changing its mind.

A radical price reform and a revaluation of the capital stock are necessary preconditions for a better measurement of efficiency and a raising of efficiency in the use of all factors of production. At the beginning of the 1980s, however, a price reform seemed inexpedient to the economic leadership both because of the uncertainties of price developments with regard to energy and raw materials on world markets and within Comecon, and also because of the danger posed to the 'social net' (the relationship between prices, subsidies and wages), as this would imply rises in consumer goods prices. Moreover, with the orientation of prices for new products above all to use value ('price-performance relationship': see Chapter 9) rather than economically necessary expenditure, no unequivocal standard of measurement existed to which a price reform could be related.

A model of decentralisation which preserves price distortions would be even more dangerous, because it could scarcely increase efficiency and yet it would create strong divergences between the lines of development desired by the state and the production units (as in the NES). In particular, there would be the problem of distorted prices inducing lower-level decision-makers to pursue wholly uneconomic micro goals simply because they are 'profitable'. A decentralised economic system with distorted prices, therefore, even when a whole range of indirect steering instruments is introduced, cannot create a 'goal–means structure' (*Ziel-Mittel Gefüge*: implying that means are needed to implement goals) capable of functioning with sufficient efficiency, because prices can function adequately neither as an instrument of plan implementation nor as an instrument of performance measurement.

At the beginning of the 1980s, therefore, after much discussion, the economic leadership was forced into a substitute model, a solution without a radical price reform and without decentralisation of decision-making worth talking about, but one which would hopefully raise productivity. This really amounted to a 'squaring of the circle' (*die Quadratur des Kreises*) and, moreover, this had to be achieved rather quickly. The answer was seen in the formation of *Kombinate* and the 'perfecting' (*Vervollkommnung*) of the (essentially given) economic mechanism.

NOTES

1. The GDR's net external debt with the West reached a peak of $12-13 billion in 1981 (Frowen, 1985, p. 40), falling to approximately $7 billion by the latter half of 1985 (*Financial Times*, 19 December 1985, p. 2).

2. It is interesting to note that in November 1984 it was announced that the defence budget for 1985 was to be increased by 6.7 per cent, this probably largely reflecting the cost of installing Soviet missiles in response to the installation of Cruise and Pershing missiles in Western Europe. In November 1985 a 7.7 per cent increase in defence spending for 1986 was announced.

5

The *Kombinat* in GDR Economic Organisation[1]

Phillip J. Bryson and Manfred Melzer

The economic reforms of the 1960s are currently viewed by GDR specialists as an unfortunate mistake. Since the termination of the reform movement at the end of 1970, some Western specialists have looked back with fond nostalgia upon the reform period (Keren, 1985), but the East Germans have never again shown interest in renewing the effort. They watch with interest the reform experiments of Hungary, but in private many express their disbelief that the Hungarians will be able to match achieved and anticipated GDR economic success. Planning strategies since 1970 have continued to reflect the conviction that acceptable improvement can be derived from the process of continually 'perfecting' the central planning mechanism (*Vervolkommnung der Planung*).

Central control was effectively re-established and the more serious distortions generated in the reform period were overcome after 1970. Nevertheless, as Melzer (1982) observes, the processes of recentralisation failed in the 1970s to achieve the transition to intensive (rather than the classical extensive) economic development. The complex and difficult problems that confronted the GDR in the 1970s convinced the party that determined and imaginative planning initiatives had become imperative. Still, there was no inclination to re-embark on a decentralising course of genuine reform (see Chapter 3). The energy crisis, adverse terms of trade, an international credit crisis, an ageing capital stock, and the usual menu of planning problems have together merely encouraged the GDR to pursue enhanced economic performance through industrial reorganisation via combine (*Kombinat*) formation and through the introduction of a 'flood' (Cornelsen, 1983) of new planning coefficients, directives and improved management techniques (see Cornelsen, Melzer and Scherzinger, 1984). Chapter 7 is devoted to the 'perfecting' of planning, while this chapter will focus on the nature and implications of the reorganisation of industry around the *Kombinat*.

The history and objectives of combine formation

By 1981 combine formation had essentially been completed, with 133 combines in GDR centrally directed industry and each *Kombinat* employing an average of around 25,000 workers in from 20 to 40 enterprises. The present figure is 127 combines (*Beilage der 'Presse-Informationen'*, 47, 27 April 1986, p. 1). These huge production units are under the leadership of a single decision-maker, the Director General.

The process of combine formation began well before the termination of the reforms of the 1960s (Leptin and Melzer, 1978, pp. 68-9). Later, it became the central objective of GDR economic reorganisation to transform the relatively independent associations of nationally owned enterprises (VVBs), which had simply served as an intermediate administrative link between the enterprises and industrial ministries, into today's *Kombinate*. Combine formation was seen as a tool of structural policy, designed to rationalise the management of the whole production process from the conception of a product to its successful marketing domestically or abroad.

For a decade or so the *Kombinat* co-existed with industrial associations of nationally owned enterprises (*Vereinigungen Volkseigener Betriebe*, or VVBs), which were a middle rung in the industrial planning hierarchy. The main function of these associations was to implement central directives and structural-political measures under the direction of the appropriate industrial ministry. Since their decision-making prerogatives extended only to subordinated enterprises within the relevant industry, increasingly complex inter-industrial interaction became increasingly difficult to manage. Actual production decisions were increasingly being made by one state organ, and product planning by another (Burian, 1978). Research and development activities were generally completely removed from the authority and the information centred in actual production. Exporting and domestic marketing organs were separate, and these were also separated by ministries worlds away from the producing agents.

The result of the traditional planning co-ordination was that those engaged in R & D efforts felt no responsibility to meet the specific needs of producers, whilst producers felt little inspiration to pursue the output visions of those planners far removed from the actual production of commodities and services. They likewise felt little motivation to generate products with characteristics capable of satisfying the demands of the international market confronting those seemingly distant agents in the foreign trade ministries who had to 'unload' whatever producers offered them.

To reduce the distance between decision-making and performance, and to increase industrial co-ordination, the *Kombinat* organisational form was adopted for all (not merely centrally directed) industries. At the beginning of the 1980s regionally guided industry also underwent combine formation, 66 new combines being added to the existing ones to give a total of 93 (currently 94), employing, on average, about 2,000 employees. They are mainly occupied with the production of consumer goods (such as textiles, leatherware, furniture, food and beverages). They also include small enterprises, since it is believed that a variety of enterprise sizes increases both flexibility and the product mix (Hensel and Kuciak, 1984).

The combine is both a horizontal and a vertical union of enterprises under the control of a single decision-maker, the Director General. The Director is invested with such broad powers that Western observers have considered this organisational development a furthering of the trend towards economic centralisation. The combine, as indicated, is responsible for (Richter, 1981):

(1) the research and development activity related to the entire industry or industrial branch;
(2) the acquisition or development of the appropriate capital equipment;
(3) construction of equipment and facilities required for new innovations (referred to in the East German literature as *Rationalisierungsmittelbau*, see Wenzel, 1984);
(4) the production of intermediate goods ('inputs');
(5) the production of final goods ('outputs');
(6) the domestic and foreign marketing of the commodity.

Combine formation was intended as a rationalisation of industrial organisation, designed not only to reduce the number of formal, central links in communications processes, but also to free ministries and departments from a multitude of detailed functional responsibilities.

The attempt to achieve economies of scale through the growth of industrial concentration has been ubiquitously treated in socialist and Western literature. Closely related is the fact (observed by Friedrich *et al.*, 1983) that production is very difficult to manage when split into many specialised part-processes utilising complex technologies. Large production units are also seen (ibid., p. 63) as the means of achieving flexible reaction to new market conditions and changes, economical use of production resources, concentrated utilisation of available inputs, and more effective development and use of the specialisation and division of labour within and among the enterprises of any given combine (see also Melzer, Scherzinger and Schwartau, 1979, on this point).

Combines are perceived as the key to concentrating managerial powers in the hands of the Director General, and to consolidating sectors whose outputs had previously been subject to overlapping ministerial jurisdictions.

Additional potential benefits are cited by Krakat (1980), who conceives of combine formation as the attempt to make international economic decisions an integral part of the unified *Kombinat* planning process rather than maintaining the organisational distance that existed between industrial associations and the state foreign trade monopolies. Melzer (1981b) adds the goal of rationalising planned investment through better co-ordination and communication, together with greater concentration of investment responsibility in the combine.

The *Kombinat's* organisational forms

Thiele *et al.* (1982, p. 28) observe that the formation of the combines was designed to make the enterprise groupings a worthy partner of the central planning agency in the performance of both production and planning obligations. If the combines are to co-operate in planning technological developments, investment projects, detailed production processes, and the generation of improved and new commodities, they must be given appropriate organisational forms. As of the inception of the general combine formation drive, several organisational forms suggested themselves and were also adopted. In each form, of course, the *Kombinat* was to retain a substantially greater degree of decision manoeuvrability than had previously been possible for the VVBs. It was intended that the Director General was to gain additional powers pertaining to the internal organisation of the combine and to its constituent enterprises as well.

Originally, four basic organisational types predominated in the combine formation process, each designed to accommodate to specific industrial conditions (Krakat, 1980 and Melzer, 1981a). These included:

(1) enterprises united under the direction of an independent management body, as were such enterprises formerly under the VVB (industrial association) system;

(2) enterprises combined under a 'leading enterprise' (*Leitbetrieb*) producing some commodity in a product group, and joined with other such combinations, with the overall industry directed by a small group of these leading enterprises;

(3) some single enterprises with diverse and large enterprise divisions;

(4) enterprises joined under the leadership of a dominating 'parent enterprise' (*Stammbetrieb*).

Whether the number of enterprises is small or great, whether or not they are geographically dispersed, or whether they produce a small or large number of products, each of these four organisational forms is directed by a single decision-maker, the Director General.

Combines, unlike their industrial association predecessors, link enterprises on other than strictly industrial lines, taking account of organic relationships among enterprises, and also considering profitability, efficiency, and sales turnover (Melzer, 1981b). Important suppliers outside a given industry are absorbed in the most suitable *Kombinat.* It is anticipated that this will result in quantitatively better and more rapid information flows and a reduction of effort necessary to co-ordinate inter-industrial processes. Similarly, information and decision processes in intersectoral co-ordination were to be less frequently necessary and less time-consuming. The objective was to create a more clearly defined and more streamlined system of economic administration and management.

These benefits could be expected to accrue to all four *Kombinat* organisational types, of course. Certain difficulties would also accrue to each type, as Erdmann and Melzer (1980, Part II, pp. 1048-51) have shown. We will have occasion to discuss some of these below. It is important to observe here, however, that some major criticism of the *Kombinat* in Western literature may be due to a lack of perception of more recent developments in East German industry.

Rather early in *Kombinat* history it became apparent that only one of the organisational forms, namely type 4 featuring the parent enterprise or *Stammbetrieb*, would be approved on a long-term basis. At an economic conference in September of 1983, Günter Mittag, secretary for economics of the Central Committee of the Socialist Unity Party (1983, p. 45), announced that this form of combine leadership had proved most effective in terms of management rationality and reduced administrative costs. According to Mittag's quasi-official pronouncement, such management represents a fundamental principle applicable to all industry, and those industries in which other 'transitional solutions' (*Übergangslösungen*) were in effect should create the conditions necessary for the adoption of this management type. This viewpoint was reinforced by Mittag's recent announcement that progress towards universal adoption of the *Stammbetrieb* form would be made (1985, p. 73). He stated that the strengthening of combine organisation through capable parent enterprise leadership was a key question and indicated that, with few exceptions, all combines are to be so managed.

The East Germans cite obvious benefits to this particular organisational form. Through the former industrial associations, leaders were removed from actual management practice and enterprise managers could not identify with them. Their recommendations and plans were too easily identified with the centre and with academic, wishful thinking. After all, even if VVB managers were once practising industrialists who understood the problem of production and management, they were no longer such. They were individuals who could engage in wishful thinking, publish an abundance of directives, threaten to intervene in enterprise functioning, and not really bear any responsibility for their suggestions.

Consider, then, the benefits of *Stammbetrieb* organisation: first, since combine directors are now managers of the largest enterprise in the industry, their leadership is far from merely academic. Their suggestions come from their personal experience in actual operation. Second, the Directors General have direct access to vital planning information bearing on all the production and scarcity relationships in their own industry. They can know very well from the production efforts in their own enterprise the actual costs of production, scarcity values, factor substitute relationships, and so on for their own industry.[2] Third, because combine managers are burdened with very large parent enterprises as a primary function of their overall managerial function, they simply have no time to intervene in the petty affairs (or even major routine tasks) of the juridically independent client enterprises. Their time is fully absorbed in planning general industrial proportions and balances and in day-to-day parent enterprise management.

In the pursuit of their own objectives, enterprises will have intimate knowledge of the real costs and prices that are so essential to (and yet seemingly unattainable by) central agents in the planning process. This information is clearly *not* inherent in the non-market prices established under the central pricing office. Combine formation can be viewed as an attempt to reduce the scope of the information problem growing out of the divergent objectives of the centre and the individual production units (Melzer and Erdmann, 1979; Melzer, 1981a; Hamel, 1981; Klein, 1983). Combines of the *Stammbetrieb* type are particularly suited to accomplish this task, because they put the Director General into the same position as the enterprise managers with respect to accessibility to planning information.

The delegation of some of the planning activities formerly assigned to ministries and/or the State Planning Commission also has the effect of relieving the central planning organs of some of their former burdens, so that they can devote themselves more fully to the challenging question of the basic structural development of the economy. For this reason, perhaps, Honecker (1979) referred to combine formation as 'the most significant step in the perfecting (*Vervollkommnung*) of economic management and planning'.

According to the conception of the 'reform' the production units are simultaneously actors and objects of economic policy. They are an object with respect to their role in implementing central imperatives. They are actors, first, in providing informational inputs from the production level for economic decision processes made at higher levels, and second, in taking independent corrective or other positive action where planning errors, gaps, and inconsistencies leave latitude for them to do so. The *Kombinat* Director General is expected to exercise planning and management powers as well as to perform the entrepreneurial function; he is to follow the plan, achieve a certain harmonisation between enterprise and central planning objectives, and also overcome any bureaucratic constraints in developing new technical and production initiatives.

The role of the Director General: ministerial agent and entrepreneur

The Director General of the *Kombinat* possesses greater authority than did the managers of the former VVBs. As we have seen, ministers can delegate some of their functions to the Director General, whereby the latter can undertake work preparatory to the implementation of planning decisions (*Gesetzblatt*, 1979). Directors General are granted the responsibility for some key decisions pertaining to organisational questions even at the enterprise level. They are, for example, authorised to transfer tasks and functions from one enterprise in their jurisdiction to another, and to hire and fire enterprise managers. They can change middle-level enterprise management, create new enterprise divisions, shift the site of production from one enterprise to another, or effect inter-enterprise transfers of machinery. Directors General determine and establish the principal developmental directions and the long-term goals of the combine (Richter, 1981, p. 100). They set the direction for the branch's research effort, and make decisions pertaining to the development of products and processes within the combine. These decisions will determine the *Kombinat*'s level of concentration and the nature of enterprise and industrial specialisation. The host of additional tasks associated with all phases of the production process from investment to marketing (tasks possibly requiring greater centralisation of the combine or a realignment of the resources and production programme of sibling enterprises) also belong to the combine management.

In actual practice, the 1979 Law on Combines (*Gesetzblatt*, 1979) appears to leave the division of certain rights between

Ministers and Directors General somewhat contestable, and has been interpreted in a manner beneficial to the prerogatives of the combine managers. Honecker (1979) has asked that ministries limit their focus to 'main issues' in establishing the general development of industrial planning, which (as conceded by Kühnau, 1979) is really a matter of interpretation and perspective.

One may naturally expect that ministries will continue to utilise their prerogatives of intervention at both combine and enterprise levels of activity if a given issue is considered sufficiently important. During the height of the export drive of the early Eighties, perceived opportunities to alter production plans in pursuit of windfall foreign exchange earnings were strongly supported from the centre. Recalcitrant enterprise directors unwilling to depart from the plan to pursue such earnings were simply overridden by the office of the Director General, or even of the minister. In normal situations, of course, and where industrial leadership is strong, 'petty tutelage' from the ministry is not really a problem. The tendency under normal conditions is for the ministries to restrict their activities to the preparation of investment decisions and to general legislative concerns (e.g. supplying new norms and planning indicators, and establishing planning framework conditions).

Directors General have also received significant responsibilities with respect to foreign trade and 'socialist economic integration'. Usually this responsibility is shared with foreign trade enterprises; sometimes it is directly within the jurisdiction of the combine. The former industrial associations were not empowered to participate directly in international transactions. They were, as a result, rather disinterested in the headaches that marketing their own products inflicted upon the foreign trade monopoly. The *Kombinate* have now been confronted with the world market, with basically all of them being expected to produce commodities that sell beyond national frontiers. The combines producing final products especially are expected to enter into international trade contracts. Additionally, combines participate in presenting alternative solutions for economic, scientific and technological co-operation; they can exchange information and experience; they can enter into specialisation and production co-operation contracts with CMEA partners (Klinger, 1980).

In 1981 and 1982 organisational changes were also implemented in the foreign trade system. To facilitate the export drive that at that time was the regime's top economic priority, the attempt was made to unite the production, development and international trade functions in the hands of combine leadership. Twenty-four foreign trade enterprises are no longer strictly under the jurisdiction of the Ministry for Foreign Trade, but simultaneously under a *Kombinat* as well. The export asssortment of these enterprises basically corresponds to the production profile of the related combine. It is hoped that this arrangement will provide greater flexibility in producing products that can compete in world markets. Twenty foreign trade enterprises whose export assortments were dissimilar to those of any combines (and who could consequently not be subordinated to combines) are now subordinated not only to the Foreign Trade Ministry, but also to some appropriate industrial ministry. Of the 24, 11 operate in about sixty different trading sectors appropriate to the needs of specific combines. Only 10 other such enterprises are subordinated exclusively to the Foreign Trade Ministry (Haendcke-Hoppe, 1984).

The enterprise is a legally independent entity whose director establishes the enterprise's management structure, but this must be done with the approval of the Director General. He works within the framework of the legal structure and the planning coefficients and normatives; he must also function together with the party and the relevant trade union officials. The director's responsibility is to organise the specifics of the production process in such a way as to fulfil the plan while increasing labour productivity and reducing production costs and materials use. Although the combine delivers a set of basic plan indicators (*Kennziffern*) to the enterprise, the latter unit must determine the actual structure of commodity production. The specific use of enterprise funds (social, cultural, bonus and other) is for enterprise decision.

The production process is to incorporate the appropriate techniques that are a part of the scientific-technological revolution. In this process, the detailed production process is to be elaborated and rendered concrete through entering into contracts with other enterprises. The enterprise director hires his own workers and, although general wage schedules are centrally determined, he must determine job classifications and the specifics of wage receipts for individual workers. Finally, the enterprise has a social programme to deliver: education and vocational training must be provided to current and potential workers; medical and housing facilities, and child care facilities are to be provided for the workers.

The description of the responsibilities and the implicit essential interaction between the Director General and the enterprise managers demonstrates that the relationship can be a complex one. However, where enterprises are numerous, production agendas diverse, technologies reasonably complex or varying, and communication less than frequent and detailed, it is clear that 'planning-free zones' (Haffner, 1980) will continue to provide decision manoeuvrability to enterprise managers under *Kombinat* organisation, just as they have previously done. Moreover, as we have seen, the East Germans find it desirable to have combine Directors General intervene little in the functioning of the enterprise.

Problems and challenges of combine formation

It is difficult at this moment to find a specialist on industrial organisation or planning in the GDR who is willing to doubt that combine formation has solved the fundamental problems of planning organisation. Now that the organisational form is in place, the adjustments required to remove remaining inconsistencies, or to respond to the exigencies of technological change, etc., can certainly be made according to perceived need over time. It is clear that some changes will be essential. As Melzer (1986, p. 453) observes, some VVBs were changed into combines simply by an alteration of the name. Some groupings will prove unsatisfactory, and reorganisations will be undertaken except where political disagreements in the planning hierarchy preclude measures regarded as damaging to certain ministries' interest domains.

In this section we wish to consider a number of additional organisational and other related issues that will prove to be substantive problems and challenges over the next few years.

Problems of industrial concentration

For some years analysts have written of East Germany's industrial gargantomania, which is expressed in the growth of GDR production units and combines. There were 10,600 enterprises at the end of 1972; by 1980 only 5,000 remained, and the process of combine formation saw the number sink to around 3,800 (see DIW 1985, pp. 150 ff, for the data and a discussion of GDR industrial concentration). These are joined in extremely large and powerful combines of up to 80,000 workers.

The potential advantages of such organisations of large scale were discussed above. Nevertheless, the process of combine formation was not attended by any soul-searching discussion as to what would represent an optimal degree of concentration for industry.[3] The compelling reason for large production units in the GDR is actually a simple one. It is simply an organisational impossibility to solve communication and co-ordination problems in the planned economy with huge numbers of small units all requiring monitoring, direction and auditing from the centre.

On the other hand, large-scale production presents the difficulty for the centre of managing very large production units. The monopoly power that inheres to a number of combines can dull the incentive to behave competitively with regard to the generation and implementation of product innovation. It may limit the pressure to reduce production costs and to produce efficiently. Several of the beneficial effects of competition may be lost.

Especially damaging would be the combine's monopoly of information needed for planning purposes. Should the Director General come to perceive himself more strictly as an entrepreneur/producer than as a representative of ministerial interests, his incentive to withhold planning information from the centre in pursuit of personal interests would correspond to that of other producers in the combine. Bottesi and Hummel (1984) note that economic legislation alone cannot guarantee a correspondence of combine and general economic interests in society. The responsibility of economic agents alone can assure behaviour that reflects the general interest. Western observers are less sanguine about the likelihood that these agents will be properly motivated and stimulated (in the absence of competitive forces) to generate productive and innovative performance from their industry.

One generally notes that the concentration of economic power generally calls forth an increase of the mechanisms of regulation and control. Such an increase has been observable in the GDR with an increase in personnel and functions for the

State Auditing Office of the Ministry of Finance, Worker-Farmer Supervision, the Office for Standardisation, Measurement and Commodity Inspection, and the National Office for Statistics. Increased monitoring activities have been assigned to the unions, the Free German Youth, and the committees of the National Front (Kinze, Knop and Seifert, 1983). This is seen by some as a substantial growth of the planning bureaucracy adding to the unwieldy nature of the system.

Remaining problems of organisation

The disappearance of the VVB and the advent of the *Kombinat* meant a diminution of enterprise powers in the industrial hierarchy. The enterprises maintain their juridical independence, and the Director General has plenty to do in his own sphere. Nevertheless, the sweeping powers of the combine leadership described above may impinge significantly on those of the enterprise manager. The potential problem is not so much to be understood as the danger of 'petty tutelage' in the inner workings of the enterprise; rather, the parent enterprise may simply appropriate to itself the more advantageous portions of a specialisation arrangement, while delegating less favourable ones. This would be an increase in efficiency at the expense of the subordinated enterprises. Naturally, it would be foolhardy to exaggerate such behaviour, since the manager of the parent enterprise is evaluated in terms of the performance of the whole combine, of which he is also the Director General. But if the subordinated enterprise managers become convinced that any such bias in specialisation assignments or appropriation of advantageous positions is practised (in order to maintain credibility in industrial leadership), the goodwill and co-operation of these leaders would be lost.

The problem of co-operation between and within combines has been cited by Mittag (1985, p. 72) as a remaining significant problem of their organisation. This is not merely a problem of communication, since with the increasing focus of the combine on more strategic planning and the industry's balancing activities, the enterprises are permitted rather freely to make the individual contracts (within and beyond the combine's client firms) their operations require.

One of the basic problems is the supply process within and

between combines. Those enterprises and combines which supply intermediate goods to other production units are too often insufficiently motivated to deliver them with the appropriate 'technical level, quality, durability and reliability' (Bottesi and Hummel, 1984, p. 79). They are still too little exposed to the quality demands of export markets and world competition, and they have been put on warning by the centre that they will be expected to begin to export a share of their output. Likewise, in order to stimulate a far more general concern for quality, it is expected that all enterprises will produce a share of total output (on average around 5 per cent) for sale as final goods. Additionally, the combines producing intermediate goods have been supplied with a goal to replace 30 per cent of its total assortment of goods with new ones annually (Mittag, ibid.).

Internal co-ordination and co-operation are also lacking with regard to research and development. One reads of the complaint that R & D divisions have sometimes developed a component part or a product without paying any attention to whether essential inputs or materials must be imported. Later, there were (easily foreseeable) difficulties getting the needed items. Once again, formal organisational co-ordination does not always suffice.

The reorganisation and new regulations have not solved some very fundamental problems of East German planning. The first of only two which will be mentioned here is the problem of reserves. Combine formation did not address the requirements of flexibility that permit competitive performance in world markets. Production units and enterprises must have the capacity to respond to internal and external economic change, especially changes in final market demands. The plan and planning organisation must leave some room for manoeuvrability in this regard. Taut planning that leaves no reserves with which producers can make spontaneous production changes and shorten order-delivery times cannot meet the challenges presented by world markets.

The second fundamental planning problem, that of price reform, has not yet been solved in the GDR. It has, however, been addressed by the new regulations, and further work has been scheduled for its resolution. Pricing is a key problem in central planning (Melzer, 1983), which has never really been resolved by the centrally planned economies.

It is sufficient for present purposes simply to keep in mind that prices which do not reflect scarcity values cannot convey needed information or motivate agents to make the appropriate substitutions in production and consumption. Particularly debilitating for central planning is the fact that such pricing obscures the real contributions of firms and makes it impossible to reward them for their market performance. Rewards distributed according to the net revenue criterion cannot be just when arbitrarily high (low) prices make it appear that the enterprise has performed well (poorly). The undervaluation of certain kinds of production through non-scarcity prices can result not only in the unjustified loss or gain of profits; it can also lead to a restructuring of production profiles that is not justified.

Decision-making problems

The use of mathematical decision models, once regarded by the GDR as very promising, have proved of little general worth to some kinds of managerial decisions. Certain production, transportation, and other problems are indeed amenable to quantitative analysis, but for many purposes such techniques are viewed as simply too restrictive (too few variables that can enter the analysis, etc.) for practical application.

This is not to say that there is no organised approach to decision-making in the GDR. Organisationally, there is an attempt to permit decision-making at that level of the industrial hierarchy at which the specialised expertise and information exists (the 'specialised knowledge principle', Weidauer and Wetzel, 1981, p. 236). Combines are accordingly to receive assignments that can be performed more rationally and effectively, and enterprises are intended to do the same.

Within the sphere of responsibility of the individual agent, socialist teaching decrees that the decision agent must have knowledge and access to information about the problem, must establish goals or targets, must research the various possible resolutions to the problem, evaluate them, and make the best decision. The quality of the decision will depend on the quality of information, the proper incentives, the clarity of objectives, and so on.

Management decisions are intended to be one-man decisions with collective consultation beforehand. The Director General is to involve the directors of the subordinated enterprises in decision preparation, the party representative, his staff, the specialist directors, and the chairman of the enterprise trade union leadership. But the Director General himself determines the extent to which he considers the collective inputs, and he also establishes the tasks and the composition of the various advisory groups (Schmidt, 1980, p. 11).

With this decision-structure interest groups will often form in the pursuit of the well-being of the relevant sub-groups in the production process (Klein, 1983, pp. 84 ff). The Chief Accountant and other monitoring authorities may represent one such group. Others are the trade union, the Free German Youth, the work brigades, the Chamber of Technology (if represented in the enterprise) and so on. These groups can exert influence of varying intensity on managerial decisions.

Since the most important element of the decision may be the Director General himself, the quality of decision-making in GDR industry may be a rather direct reflection of the quality of the Directors General. The East Germans (unlike the Soviets) are making a concerted effort to provide training for the development of managerial skills on the part of present and future managers (Richter *et al.*, 1981). These individuals are generally highly motivated and accustomed to tight organisation. At the same time, many received their training and developed their professional outlook during the era of extensive development. When growth is demanded, their instinct is to propose more investments of the old types, which can provide no assurance of productivity increases. When planners enquire as to production possibilities they are inclined to favour soft plan targets in the interest of their own enterprise constituencies.[4] They are inclined to avoid introducing new products incorporating risky innovations that might endanger plan-fulfilment, favouring the more certain process improvements that help improve production performance but do not guarantee competitiveness in world markets. They have a proclivity to accept the sluggish socialist work-pace, which reflects the guaranteed security not only of the worker's job, but also of his basic existence, whether or not he is committed to any personal exertion. They show a tendency to reward inadequately risk-taking behaviour on the part of workers in the pursuit of productivity improvement (Weidauer and Wetzel, 1981, p. 274).

Reflections and conclusions

The organisational and regulatory changes of the past four or five years have been extensive and it appears they will be sufficient to overcome some of the most fundamental difficulties of central planning. The present authors do not share a somewhat greater pessimism of some Western observers who see the present institutional changes as a mere continuation of rather ineffective, recurring organisational adjustments. Although we are disinclined to think of even the totality of these changes as genuine economic reform, it is clear that planning has improved substantially. If one considers the combination of all production activities (from R & D, through production, and including domestic and foreign marketing) in one decision-maker, much has been gained. If one considers the *Stammbetrieb* type of combine leadership, in which the Director General is responsible for the parent enterprise as well as for the combine in general, much has been gained.

Certainly, serious problems remain. The changes do not guarantee that socialism will be able to generate the creativity that product innovation requires, or that the endeavour to overcome extensive economic development patterns will in fact result in the 'intensification' desired. It must still be demonstrated that the level of concentration established in East German industry is susceptible to effective management and will not become inimical to the kinds of productive behaviour that more competitive organisation is expected to produce. It is not inevitable that the hierarchical challenges of combine organisation can be mastered; there is no guarantee that communication, co-ordination and co-operation within and between combines will prove sufficiently effective. It appears on the basis of the significant improvements of recent years, however, that the East Germans have solved some substantive problems and are capable of resolving additional challenging ones as well.

NOTES

1. Mr Bryson wishes to thank the International Research and Exchanges Board for a grant making his contribution to this research possible, and the Institute for Socialist Economic Management of the Hochschule für Ökonomie 'Bruno Leuschner' for making his research stay in the GDR pleasant and productive.

2. Apparently unaware of this feature, Keren (1985, p. 124) observes that all these kinds of information are basically inaccessible to planning agents under combine organisation because the combines have less opportunity for direct observation of enterprises than was the case under VVB organisation!

3. The article by Hensel and Kuciak (1984) demonstrates concern with some of the serious questions not too frequently asked in the GDR regarding optimal industrial concentration. Where size for its own sake was once considered worthwhile, it has become quite apparent that different industrial tasks imply varying degrees of appropriate concentration.

4. This tendency in centrally planned economies is not always firmly opposed at the ministerial level. In a major policy speech, Gorbachev (1985) noted the tendency of Soviet ministerial leaders to attempt to achieve extensive investment resources and soft plan targets. If this is the case, there remains no source of pressure to counteract that tendency at the industrial level.

6

The 1981-85 Order of Planning (*Planungsordnung*)

Manfred Tröder

INTRODUCTION

One would have expected that the integration of the combines in the planning process would have been reflected in the planning order. The 'Order of Planning of the National Economy 1981-85' (*Planungsordnung*: henceforth PO) would have been the instrument by which to take into account the organisational innovations and to bring about an improvement in planning (*Anordnung über die Ordnung der Planung der Volkswirtschaft der DDR 1981 bis 1985 vom 28 November 1979, GBL der DDR*, Sonderdruck vom 1 Februar 1980, Nr. 1020, Teile A bis Q). That could have been done, for example, by causing the combines with expert knowledge of production to assist the centre (ministries and the State Planning Commission) in reaching decisions and themselves to include in their planning possibilities for improving performance. This intention, which the planners wished to carry out, was, however, not realised.

(1) The third wave of combine formation 1978-80 had, it is true, largely come to an end when the PO was released, but the time available to take the implications of this into account in the PO was clearly too short. As a result, amendments of the PO were foreseeable for this reason alone.

(2) The problem of the redistribution of the powers of decision-making, rendered necessary by the complete amalgamation of all centrally controlled industrial enterprises into combines, between combine, combine enterprises and ministry was not adequately solved by the 1979 combine decree (*Verordnung über die volkseigenen Kombinate, Kombinatsbetriebe und volkseigenen Betriebe vom 8 November 1979,*

GBL der DDR, Teil I, Nr. 38, p. 355). The ministry retained numerous rights of intervention in the affairs of the combine.

Nevertheless, the essential difference between the 1981-85 PO and the preceding 1976-80 PO is to be found precisely in the fact that the combines — admittedly as yet imperfectly and also, within the period 1981-85, in consequence of numerous alterations, in differing degrees — have been incorporated in the planning process.

CONTENT, PRINCIPLES, FOUNDATIONS AND COURSE OF SOCIALIST ECONOMIC PLANNING

It is possible to subdivide the planning of the national economy into the two component parts of central state planning (planning of the national economy in the narrow sense) and enterprise planning in the broader sense (the planning of the juridically independent economic units — combines, combine enterprises and other enterprises), in addition to regional planning. The powers of decision-making, however, are completely centralised and every economic planning process is based on concrete prescribed goals and directives coming from the central administration.[1] The results of the planning process at the various levels of the hierarchically organised planning system of the GDR are obligatory plans in which, apart from the tasks and goals, the resources to be deployed (funds), the durations and deadlines for the realisation of goals and responsibility for plan fulfilment are laid down with compulsory force.

Central state planning integrates the combines and other economic units into the development of the national economy by prescribing the following: production and performance goals; allocation of resources and quotas (proportions of funds and balances); requirements as regards efficiency; and economic incentives. The targets are prescribed primarily in the form of state plan indicators.

Currently, the obligatory planning time periods for national economic planning are five-year (five-year plan) and single years (annual economic plan). These periods apply equally for all combines: five-year planning, however, applies only to selected enterprises. In this connection the five-year plan is intended to be the chief steering instrument of economic policy, an intention which is to be attained *inter alia* by means of greater assimilation of method and harmonisation of content with the USSR (and other CMEA countries).

On the basis of a comprehensive (minimum) list of obligatory plan indicators for the five-year plan and annual plans, the combines draw up their five-year plan as a long-term plan, their individual annual plan as a medium-term plan and, in addition, so-called 'operational plans' for three-month periods (e.g. quarterly cash plan), months and other short-term planning periods. The ongoing work on (enterprise) plans for these varying timespans is also sometimes called 'the principle of continuous planning'.

In this regard it should be borne in mind that the length of the planning time period is in inverse proportion to the precision attainable in the planning process in consequence of the objectively limited accuracy in predicting future events. More specifically, the precision attained depends not on the timespan of the plan, but on the planning horizon, defined as the time between the drawing up of the plan and the end of the plan period. This, however, presupposes that the plan is available before the start of the plan period. For the drawing up of national economic plans and the co-ordination of central state and enterprise planning so-called 'principles of socialist planning' apply, which are regarded as important organisational principles and political and ideological guidelines and which regulate the organisation and implementation of planning (Authors' Collective, 1982, p. 26).

How many principles of this kind there are cannot be definitely ascertained, although some are repeatedly mentioned in the various sources, for example the principle of the unity of politics and economics. What is meant here is always the primacy of politics over economics and this is reaffirmed in the principle of democratic centralism. Really important decisions on tasks, goals and the deployment of resources are made by the leading authorities of the SED. Other declared principles of socialist planning are that of its scientific nature, that of the continuity of planning and that of the linking of collective and personal interests with overall social needs. In addition, the following principles are especially mentioned: the principle of proportionality; the balancing of plans; the unity of plan, balance and (economic) contract; the principle of the rationality of planning (input of effort into planning); and the principle of the unity and complexity of the plan. The realisation of the principle of the unity of material and financial planning presents particular difficulties.

The already mentioned principle of the scientific nature of planning presupposes a constantly increased regard for (and use of!) economic laws in economic activity associated with the plan. Among these laws of the political economy of socialism particular stress is laid on the requirements of the law of value (of socialist commodity production) and on the law of the planned proportionate development of the national economy. The application of the law of value in this sense requires the valuation of all resources and the fixing of economically 'correct' prices already in planning in order to promote the goals laid down in the plan (e.g. saving of expensive raw materials, production of certain goods, assortments and qualities), as well as to hinder the achievement of others (Melzer, in *DDR Handbuch*, 1985, p. 1032).

This gives rise to the paradox that prices and the monetary values derived from them (costs, profit) on the one hand are themselves the subject of planning, whilst on the other hand 'economically correct' and relatively constant prices represent one of the foundations of medium-term financial planning.

The *foundations of enterprise planning* and of central state planning comprise data about the previous plan and expected fulfilment of the current plan as well as about the probable development of capacities and supply and demand magnitudes. In addition, the data collected in the first place in the enterprise (primary data) on economic activity are recorded, prepared, documented, analysed and passed on in accordance with prescribed guidelines (regulatory methods). Moreover, enterprise planning is based on plan targets and guidance as to content arising from the work of long-term prognostication, which is carried out exclusively by central authorities (the State Planning Commission, ministries). By formulating their own concepts (e.g. for the rationalisation of the production process) the economic units obtain further bases for enterprise planning. Apart from those regarding content there is also the need for organisational and methodological foundations of planning, which are described as regulatory methods.

Regulatory methods (*Ordnungsmittel*) belong among the formal foundations of planning. They are necessary for enterprise planning and above all for central state planning in order to secure a uniform procedure and hence the aggregation of plan drafts and of the plans of economic units by branches, sectors and administrative levels.

The drawing up of enterprise plans (and of the national economic plan) via the various planning stages (plan initiation, plan draft and obligatory plan) is bound up with many harmonisations internal to the enterprise and co-ordinations external to the enterprise, thus calling for an enormous effort of computation. A large number of plan indicators, proportions and variants have to be calculated. In addition, diverse balances need to be drawn up and material input coefficients worked out.

The complexity of the interrelationships between the indicators of the enterprise plan (and its components: plan subdivisions and individual plans) is constantly increasing, especially in the combine. Nowadays it would scarcely be possible to draw up manually an enterprise plan that was free from contradictions and balanced and harmonised in all its parts with sufficient certainty and substantially avoiding planning errors (Authors' Collective, 1977, p. 83). The amount of time available for the drawing up of the enterprise plan would be nowhere near sufficient were the plan to be worked out manually. Even the use of mathematical procedures would in most cases scarcely suffice. Hence the use of electronic processing of data in planning for planning tasks that are capable of being expressed in formulae is regarded as a means of making possible constrained optimisation calculations and also a rationalisation of planning (reduction of effort in time and administration for plan calculations and more rapid amendments). This of course applies to an even greater extent in the case of central state planning which relies upon the primary data of the economic units and their processing effort.

The functioning of national economic planning, computation, statistics and analysis depends in large degree upon uniform regulatory methods (which are also stable in the longer term). Equally, of course, they must be comparable.

To the regulatory methods belong the following:

(1) *Regulations stemming from the methodology of the plan*: the totality of all state ordinances which determine the content of planning and plans, the form and structure of the plan, the content and calculation of plan indicators as well as the timetable relating to the drawing up of the enterprise and national economic plans.

Since 1976 the most important aspect of plan methodology has been the PO, which regulates the planning of the national economy and of its economic units, sectors and regions for both five-year and annual planning. As the tasks and goals of the best possible use of resources and the highest permissible expenditure (quotas, funds) and the efficiency to be achieved within the economic process are (and have to be) laid down in the form of economic indicators of the most varied kind, the PO also contains a comprehensive (minimum) list of the state plan indicators which are to be given to the economic units. To these state plan indicators expressed in temporal, value and physical terms also belong norms, normatives, proportions of balances and quotas for the individual factors of production. These economic plan and information indicators clearly show in their range, structure and relationship to actual economic processes, together with the economic equipping and legal position of the economic units, what rights of participation (in other words, rights of decision-making) are accorded to the economic units in the process of national economic planning. The compulsory list of state plan indicators applies to all economic units (although in lesser degree to small enterprises). The minimum target/obligatory target, differentiated by concrete numerical values and addressed to particular economic units (nowadays the combine), for the drawing up of the plan draft and the final enterprise plan, on the other hand, applies only to that particular enterprise and is intended to be 'tailor made' for it.

The *general guidelines* for the planning of the combines and enterprises in industry and construction set forth in precise detail the methodological and organisational regulations contained in the PO. They lay down uniform modalities for the drawing up of the plan. From these follow, for example, the uniform structure and division of the enterprise plan into what are now ten plan sections, which are subdivided into individual plans and these in turn into standardised forms with indicators. At the same time the running, the internal harmonisation of the plan sections and their external co-ordination with purchasers, suppliers, balancing organs, the bank and the local state (regional) authority are all prescribed.

In addition, the PO and the general guidelines allow of branch-specific planning regulations within certain limits. Various legal ordinances (e.g. Article 29 of the combine decree) also prescribe the drawing up of internal POs for the enterprises of a combine, since great differences (still) exist between combines in regard to the level of organisation.[2]

(2) *Definitions, indicators and concepts* for planning, accounting and statistics, which are issued by the Central State Administration for Statistics (but in general no longer accessible), are intended to make possible the uniform carrying out of calculations and the uniform use of definitions and concepts.

(3) *Forms.*[3]

Among the regulatory methods, finally, particular importance attaches to the following.

(4) *National economic systems of classification and lists*, which serve the uniform recording and grouping of economic transactions in connection with the planning, calculation, analysis and representation of the overall economic process of reproduction. Special mention should be made of: the product and performance list (ELN),[4] with its 100,000 individual entries for all the goods produced in the GDR or imported, which forms the basis particularly of production and sales planning and of balancing; the national economic accounting framework defines the recording in value terms of economic transactions in the form of balances and double-entry book-keeping; the list of balancing organs; the balance register; the enterprise system of classification for assigning enterprises to branches of the economy; the manpower classification system.

These regulatory methods are required to be applied by all state organs, local administrative authorities, combines and enterprises.

BRIEF REVIEW OF THE PO BEFORE THE START OF THE 1980S

Purpose of the PO

In the period 1949 to 1980 only 16 of the 32 economic years were formally covered by (medium-term) perspective plans (Roesler, 1983, p. 178), because plans were repeatedly cancelled (e.g. the second five-year plan in 1958), plan periods altered (a seven-year plan in 1964) or plans only belatedly finalised (e.g. the second five-year plan 1956-60 only in January 1958). Among the reasons given for this were *inter alia* an inadequate mastery of the economic laws of socialism and of economic growth, as well as a lack of ability to react to altered conditions of economic growth.

Continuous alterations, whether in small or larger steps, whether in what was always officially described as 'further perfecting' or *de facto* described as reforms, will probably continue to accompany any centrally administered economy. And yet it ought to be possible, in the view of leading economists and economic jurists, to work out a methodological prescription for planning, accounting and monitoring, which would combine the greatest possible uniformity of planning (despite many peculiarities of production in the branches and sectors of the national economy) and hence a largely computerised processing of data (including aggregation) as well as justifiable planning effort, with longer-term stability of the regulations for those subject to planning. At the same time this compulsory PO should permit a systematic, *ex ante* structuring of the economic process and be flexible enough for adaptations and amendments.

It was with these considerations in mind that a resolution of the Politburo of the SED of May 1972 laid down the 'drawing up of a uniform PO for the national economy and enterprises'. From the spring of 1974 there began in the competent specialist ministries, associations (VVBs) and in selected enterprises and combines consultations on the drafting of the PO.[5] It was the declared aim so to perfect the planning of the national economy that the real (by which was meant realistic) and ambitious plans would secure the unity of long-term planning, five-year planning and annual planning, as well as harmonising not only branch and regional development but also material and financial planning for the securing of the planned proportional development of the national economy in accordance with the requirements of socialist economic integration (Röse, 1974, p. 127).

The PO was designed to enhance the role of the five-year plan as the chief form of state directive for the development of the national economy, its enterprises, combines, organisations and regions. A step in this direction was the regulation subdividing the five-year plan into years (annual slices) and disaggregating the state obligatory plan targets down to the enterprise. At the same time the standing, authority and binding force of central state planning were to be enhanced.

The following improvements were primarily aimed at:

(1) More uniform methods of procedure, easily comprehensible planning methods and clearly defined areas of competence were designed to make enterprise and overall economic planning more readily surveyable and to counter a dangerous tendency towards over-steering.

(2) The problem of a lack of efficiency in the functioning of the economy was to be met by means of 'efficiency planning'.

The 1976-80 PO

This PO (*Anordnung über die Ordnung der Planung der Volkswirtschaft der DDR 1976 bis 1980 — Planungsordnung vom 20 November 1974, GBL der DDR*, 1974, Sonderdruck Nr. 775, Teile a bis c) consisted of three separate parts: *Part I* (500 pages) — provisions for the planning of the national economy's process of reproduction and of its branches and sectors; *Part II* (450 pages) — lists, forms and provisions for their utilisation, and; *Regulations* (of approximately 80 pages), e.g. 'Methodological provisions for enterprises affected by planning on a reduced scale'. These regulations primarily concerned the large number of small and medium-sized enterprises.

With regard to structure, Part I of the PO comprises the introductory section 'Basic Principles' and the section 'General provisions, including lists of state plan indicators and timetables in graphical form', with, in addition, a further 26 sections on the planning of cross-section tasks and on the planning of sectors and branches of the national economy.

The opening section 'Basic Principles' lays down in 57 'prescriptive principles', amongst other things, the chief content of planning, the participation of the workers in the drawing up of the plan, the tasks of the various management levels and the monitoring and accounting of the plans.

Accordingly (Principle 21 of the Basic Principles), the drawing up of the five-year plan and annual plans is carried out in three stages.

(1) The central *plan project* is required to be worked out on the basis of the results of long-term planning and of ongoing analytical and conceptual work. From this the state minimum plan targets are derived and are released for the drawing up of enterprise plan drafts.

(2) The drawing up, co-ordination and defence of the enter-

prise plan drafts, feedback and aggregation up to the level of the State Planning Commission.

(3) The drawing up and confirmation of the national economic plan (generally in the December of the preceding year) and the issuing of the obligatory state plan targets derived therefrom to the enterprises (first quarter of the plan year).

The 'General guidelines for the annual planning of the enterprises and combines in industry and construction' (*Anordnung über die Rahmenrichtlinie für die Jahresplanung der Betriebe und Kombinate der Industrie und des Bauwesens — Rahmenrichtlinie — vom 28 November 1974, GBL der DDR*, 1975, Sonderdruck vom 13 Januar 1975, Nr. 780), released for the first time, is based on the PO and lays down the structure and content and stages of drawing up of the enterprise plan.

The general guidelines require that annual planning regarding enterprises and combines is to be organised as an iterative process. Consequently, the annual planning of enterprises and combines embraces conceptual preparation, the working out of the plan draft and the drawing up of the annual plan.

In between the individual stages of annual planning, decisions and partial results of planning are required to be arrived at and the partial results to be co-ordinated within the enterprise and the combine.[6]

Summary of the innovations and shortcomings of the 1976-80 PO

(1) The State Planning Commission was required to produce, together with the central plan project, a 'directive on socialist rationalisation'. This was to lay down priorities relating to the intensification of social production.

(2) Enterprises and combines (in that order in the PO) were required to work out their own long-term rationalisation and intensification concepts.

(3) In order to ensure co-ordination of development between the sectors and/or branches and the regions, 'complex consultations in the counties' were to be held and regional balances to be worked out.

(4) The enterprises were required to harmonise their plan drafts in terms of content, time and capacity and to co-ordinate

them with regard to the branches and regions.

(5) The enterprises were entitled to such plan targets which were balanced and internally harmonised (Principle 24, Basic Principles).

(6) The plan drafts of the enterprises were to be defended before the respective superior authorities.

(7) Planning in tolerances (by way of exception) was designed to increase the supply of consumer goods to the population which met requirements.

(8) The PO in this form for the first time contained tasks relating to the planning of the following: measures of socialist economic integration in the CMEA; the material and cultural living standards of the population; complex housing construction/housing sector; prices; and the efficiency of social construction.

(9) The planning and calculation of efficiency was intended to make possible the intensification of social production, the priority utilisation of qualitative growth factors. To this end, a system of indicators was prescribed down to the level of the enterprise (complex proof of efficiency), in order to quantify in all its dimensions the relationship between outcome and outlay of economic activity.

Measured in terms of expected improvement the results achieved in practice were rather limited. Through the PO regulations, such as those concerning the drawing up of the five-year plan and annual national economic plans, state budget plans, balances of the credit system and price planning, which had previously been issued separately, were now amalgamated. The long-term planning of the national economy (a plan period of more than five years) was, however, not included in the PO. Tendencies towards over-bureaucratisation increased[7] because improvements achieved via standardisations were again outweighed by innovations.

Although numerous efforts to achieve intensification were made at the various levels of management and several efficiency criteria were introduced into the planning process, it did not prove possible to overcome weaknesses in innovation and a lack of efficiency.

Conclusions

Under the influence of the once again annual corrections of the methodology and, above all, the sudden third wave of combine formation in 1978 (when only 54 centrally directed industrial combines existed), the PO was simply not able to achieve the envisaged stability of the regulations. In a certain sense, the course which in reality the process of combine formation followed in 1978-9, overtook the regulations which had been created. For, with the combines, new organisational forms had been created, to which the PO was in no way geared.

The obligatory state plan targets for the five-year plan 1976-80 (and of the 1977 national economic plan) were only issued under a law dated 7 December 1976.

THE 1981-85 PO

Initial conditions

After the experience of the first PO and in view of the changes which the system of management had undergone as a result of combine formation, the planning regulations should now have been focused on the combines. This, however, as mentioned in the introduction, was not done to a sufficient degree. Why not?

Combine formation in centrally directed industry had been almost completed when on 8 November 1979 the combine decree, to which reference has already been made, was issued. The new legal ordinance, which to some extent was formulated as an afterthought in the light of the new state of affairs, thus came too late to serve as the basis for the process of combine formation. Moreover, it had not provided an adequate solution to the question of the division of decision-making powers between combine, combine enterprises and the ministry, when on 28 November 1979 the 1981-85 PO was issued in the form of a legal ordinance. From this point of view the combine decree was released too soon. The conclusion that can be drawn is that, for whatever reasons, the preliminary work on these two legal ordinances was scarcely synchronised at all. In consequence, it could already be foreseen that fresh alterations would be necessary.

Furthermore, at the start of the 1980s the GDR was faced by

altered conditions of more intensive, rather than extensive, growth. Intensive growth, however, calls for methods of planning and management that are different from those required by primarily extensive growth. The resource-saving type of intensive growth is only to a lesser degree amenable to planning by the central planning authority than is extensive economic growth. The changeover to the new economic strategy took place in 1981, and above all in 1982 and 1983, through a whole range of new legal ordinances, which all also affected the PO (see Chapter 7).

The attempt to comment upon the 1981-85 PO, therefore, encounters considerable difficulties. Which order is to be described? The one which was promulgated in the form of a legal ordinance on 28 November 1979 and whose publication as a special supplement was delayed until 2 February 1980, although it had already been in force since 1 January 1980, or the order which in reality emerged by the end of 1985 as a result of the massive alterations introduced during the course of the five years?

In consequence of the emendations of the PO which started as early as 1980, the 'business foundations' as it were of the five-year plan became invalid, the monitoring of plan-fulfilment rendered extremely difficult and rational economic analysis was made impossible.[8] Nor can the analysis of the so-called 'combine effects' be excluded from this judgement. In 1982 alone two ordinances expressly requiring alterations (the second and the third) in the 1981-85 PO were issued, as well as more than 30 (!) legal ordinances in the form of regulations, decrees, resolutions and also a law — all of which introduced decisive corrections of the content and methodology of planning (see Chapter 7).

Since there simply was no stable PO for the period 1981-85, it is only possible to give a description of how the planning regime operated at a given date. The formal structure of the PO will therefore be described in outline, without recounting all the alterations as to content that were introduced in the various areas of planning in the years from 1980 (these being dealt with in the next chapter). Instead the 'Basic Principles of the PO' contained in the first section will be commented upon. They embody the premises and principles of planning and typify the whole system. After that will be sketched out the basic principles of planning within the combine and, in particular, the actual powers of decision-making of the Director General of the combine. As point of reference, 1985 is chosen, being the last year of the second PO and at the same time the base year of the 1986-90 PO.

The structure of the 1981-85 Order of Planning (PO)

(1) The PO consists of 33 sections, which are arranged under 16 letter-headings.

(2) The 16 letter-headings contain the 26 sections plus the 'Basic Principles' of the first (1976-80) PO, including their designations, albeit in a different order.

(3) Really new are section 17 ('Conceptual preparation of the five-year plan') and what is now the separate section 18, 'Planning of socialist rationalisation'. The planning of vocational training and tasks relating to youth policy was expanded. The balancing of manpower and school-leavers is determined centrally.

(4) The first section contains the 'Basic Principles of the PO' formulated in 51 prescriptive principles. These regulate the following:

(i) The main content of the planning of the national economy.

(ii) The five-year plan and the annual plans (their conceptual preparation; their international co-ordination within Comecon; and the national economic balances and calculations to be drawn up by the State Planning Commission).

(iii) The process of planning. According to this, the drawing up of the five-year plan, annual plans for the national economy, state budget plans and balances of the credit system must take place in the following four stages (see Figure 6.1):

(a) the formulation of the plan project and the announcement of state tasks, as a basis for the drawing up of plan drafts;

(b) the working out of the plan drafts of combines, enterprises, organisations and co-operatives as well as of town and municipal councils, plan discussion, inter-enterprise and regional co-ordination and balancing, harmonisation and defence of plan drafts;

(c) the co-ordination and balancing of the plan drafts of combines, enterprises, organisations and co-operatives as well as of town and municipal councils in the organs managing the economy (ministries), the working out of the plan drafts for the branch of industry (of the ministry) ... and its defence before the relevant superior organ;

(d) the 'overall national economic' (by which is meant national economic or overall economic) co-ordination, balancing and drawing up of state plan documents (as a general rule by the State Planning Commission) and, once they have been decided, the issuing of obligatory state plan targets for the completion and implementation of the plans.

Furthermore, the detailed time-scheduling of the process is separately regulated in other ordinances. The Directors General of combines are given the right to specify further details as to

Figure 6.1: National economic balances and calculations

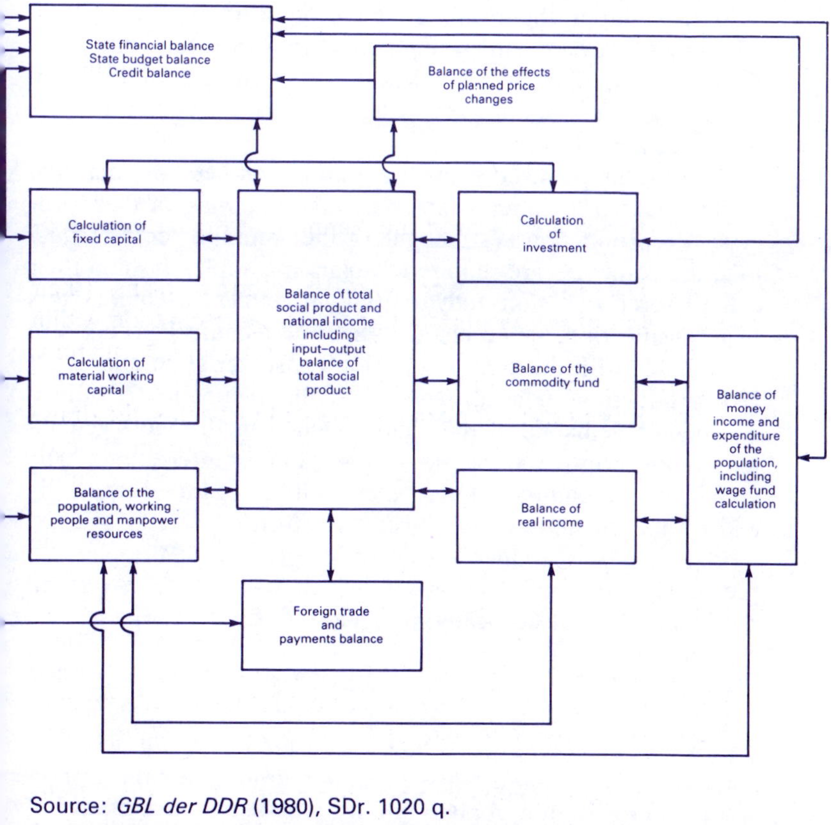

Source: *GBL der DDR* (1980), SDr. 1020 q.

timing for their particular combine. The minimum list of state plan indicators (already amounting to 120) is likewise prescribed. Ministers have the right (within certain limits!) to alter (in other words to extend) the state plan indicators for their particular area of competence.

Even so, the combines have a claim to state plan targets which are balanced and internally harmonised (for the five-year plan disaggregated according to years). Further prescriptive principles lay down in detail how the drawing up, harmonisation and defence of the plan drafts[9] is to be carried out. Complex consultations in the countries (already provided for in the first PO) are designed to ensure that the development of economic branches is harmonised with development in the regions.

The confirmation of plans, the monitoring of plan implementation and the calculation of plan-fulfilment are dealt with in further prescriptive principles.

(iv) Under the heading 'the promotion of the creative initiative of workers and young people in regard to planning', it is stated that they may participate in discussion of the plan drafts and may submit proposals for tapping reserves of performance and efficiency.

(v) This point contains a seemingly endless enumeration of the 'tasks of combines relating to the planning of their process of reproduction'. (Analogue of the combine decree.) *Inter alia,* the combines are required to plan in complex fashion their extended reproduction, fully to bring into effect the chief factors of intensification, to accelerate scientific-technical progress in accordance with the plan, to develop consumer good and ancillary production in accordance with the plan and to fulfil a number of demands of this kind couched in the most general terms. Prescriptive principle No. 48(11) is interesting: 'The guidance and planning of combines shall be organised rationally and with a low input of administrative effort'.

Planning on a reduced scale (principle No. 49) applies, as previously, to small enterprises, which in practice covers all non-centrally (that is locally) directed industrial enterprises and combines.

Finally, the remaining provisions of the 'Basic principles' require that they should be so applied that the strengthening of central state planning is attained *simultaneously* with an increase in the responsibility of economic units for the formulating and realisation of plans and for mobilising the initiative of the collective. The PO, however, leaves open the question of whether and how both components of national economic planning can be *simultaneously* increased in importance.

Shortcomings of the 1981-85 PO

(1) In consequence of the fact that in November 1979 the second PO (1981-85) and the combine decree were issued almost at the same time, the prospects for this five-year plan and its methodological stability appeared to be favourable, even though the 1981-85 five-year plan (more or less a four-year plan) was only given the force of law in December 1981. In terms of structure the second PO differed hardly at all from the first, but, as regards content, it was fundamentally altered by a flood of subsequent alterations.

(2) The allegedly long-term and planned process of combine formation was in full swing at the end of 1979, when the new legal decree on combines was promulgated. The responsibility, tasks, management and foundation of combines are regulated by it. But one looks in vain for the precise duties and juridical rights of combines. Nor, according to Heuer, did it prove possible to translate into reality certain conceptions regarding the placing of the position of the enterprises on a legal footing. This is, moreover, true in particular of the legal side of planning. The procedure for altering the combine plan by means of 'operational interventions' by the ministry in current economic activity is not provided for in the regulations. One looks in vain for a right of appeal on the part of the economc unit *vis-à-vis* its superior authority (introduced in 1967). Hence the legal position of combines is very far from being commensurate with the economic role assigned to them, as was already ascertained in an investigation at the beginning of 1979.[10]

(3) Through the amalgamation of the enterprises of centrally directed industry into 130 ministerially subordinated combines, which had been achieved by 1980, the planning process at the central state level was possibly simplified. Whether this lessens the amount of planning effort is, however, rather doubtful. The PO ought to reduce the administrative effort involved (Basic Principles, prescriptive principle No. 51). The effort involved in plan implementation and in intensified administrative monitoring (of the plan) should, however, in no way be disregarded; consequently, in the final analysis and especially on account of

the innovations, more rather than fewer regulations have come into being.

(4) Planning within the combine and its combine enterprises has not become simpler as a result of combine formation, but the burden on the centre has been lightened. And the combines are able to plan in closer proximity to the production process and, therefore, to reality. The fact must also be noted that, firstly, there exist 'combines' of widely differing kinds as regards size, production profile, regional structure, technological cohesion and the like. Secondly, there are considerable differences, even between combines operating under the same conditions of reproduction, regarding administrative and managerial personnel: in the four combines investigated alone the share of these personnel as a percentage of total employees varies between 14.4 per cent and 21.2 per cent (Gerisch and Wagner, 1982, p. 5).

The combine's room to manoeuvre in the planning process

The combine is managed by a Director General according to the principle of individual management. The development of combines into efficient economic units and similarly of combine enterprises is required to be done through the plan as the chief instrument of guidance: thus states the PO (Basic Principles, principle No. 42). On this matter the combine decree lays down (in Article 9, paragraph 3) 'The Director General secures, by means of the plan and through his own continual, long-term conceptual work, the internal cohesion of the combine's process of reproduction'.

In detail, it is determined that the Director General shall defend the combine's plan draft before the minister, show adherence to and intent to exceed state tasks, and demonstrate the effectiveness of the chief factors of intensification (Article 9, paragraph 6).

It is further provided that the Director General shall fully disaggregate the state plan figures allotted to the combine and pass these down to the combine enterprises (Article 10, paragraph 1 of the combine decree).

Article 11, paragraph 1, lays down that, on the basis of the state plan indicators, the combine shall be responsible for meeting 'demand arising from the requirements of the national economy'.

The Director General of the combine (thus Article 5, paragraph 2 of the combine decree) bears full personal responsibility *vis-à-vis* the SED leadership (and the government and the relevant minister) for the development of the combine and for the carrying out of the combine tasks defined in the resolutions of the Central Committee of the SED and in the legal ordinances.[11]

That the Director General receives instructions only from the minister is, on the other hand, laid down in Article 24, paragraph 1, of the combine decree. The Director General is accorded the right to regulate labour processes within the combine by means of orders (co-operation within the combine, planning etc.). Furthermore, he may decide which tasks shall be carried out centrally within the combine and to what extent financial funds shall be formed in the combine enterprises and centrally in the combine: Article 18, paragraph 2 (i.e. combine effects). These provisions of the combine decree are (albeit not expressly) restricted by the 1982 law on contracts (*GBL*, I, No. 14) and other legal ordinances. Under the heading 'Special management measures', Article 24 of the law on contracts provides that the central state organs may establish 'temporary operational steering for product provisions' obligatory for the economic units. Besides this reinforced binding of the economic units to central directives, with all its consequences for the enterprise plan and the already concluded economic contracts, the law on contracts also establishes priorities for the conclusion of contracts and for the production of the economic units. Economic contracts concerned with making national defence secure in economic terms and with the guaranteeing of internal security must be concluded and carried out in such a way that the needs of the armed forces are to be met *without fail* (Article 25). The economic units must give priority to the concluding and fulfilment of contracts relating to state commissions for science and technology, the export of plant and equipment and also special projects of the Council of Ministers. At the same time sanctions in respect of breaches of state discipline (the economic sanctions to be paid into the state budget, as laid down in Article 109) are made more severe. Delay or refusal in regard to concluding contracts can, according to this article, lead to the payment of an economic fine of up to 500,000 marks. These measures of regimentation and discipline markedly restrict the decision-making power of the Director

General. But this is not all.

State commissions in the field of science and technology are centrally planned and are uniformly directed (by the Ministry for Science and Technology) from research right up to practical application. At the same time there takes place 'product concrete central planning' of the newly developed products of the state plan for science and technology (Authors' Collective, 1985, p. 38). In this way the combines' potential for research and development is deployed by the centre. On the other hand, the combines have administratively prescribed for them an annual renewal rate of production. In addition, *all* industrial combines have to produce consumer goods. Those combines which produce predominantly investment goods, must ensure at least a 5 per cent share (one may well ask why not 2.9 or 13.7 per cent) of consumer goods in industrial commodity production (ibid., p. 66). This production of consumer goods has to be demonstrated via four new plan indicators. In addition 'consumer good head offices' are to be set up in the counties, in order to mobilise and co-ordinate the reserves of the region.

The more stringent provisions concerning the balancing of materials, raw materials and energy are designed to secure the continuous mobilisation of reserves and a flexible adaptation to changes in demand. The fact that since 1985 these balances are being used more as an instrument of *operational* management in the implementation of the plan, is new (ibid., p. 50).

The same purpose is served by the regulation on quarterly and cash planning (*GBL*, I, No. 35, 1984) within the combines and enterprises. Through the central prescription of performance goals, production targets for important balance positions and the recording of excess stocks the operational steering of economic units is achieved. As a final example of the planning powers of the combine, one may mention here the field of investment. Even the Director General of a combine of 30,000 employees for instance and with an annual output of 2,000 million marks, has to report each investment of more than 5 million marks (in the case of certain selected investment projects even without a maximum value) to the 'central office for preparatory planning' within the State Planning Commission (ibid., p. 48). The State Planning Commission also specifies the contractors in the central plan.

In these circumstances the degree to which the combine can independently shape it own process of reproduction is limited.

Problems associated with every PO

The 1979 concept was not able fully to deal with either the integration of combines or increased intensification (perfecting 1983-84). The alterations carried out did not begin to succeed in creating an internally consistent planning concept. It should not be forgotten, however, that external complications from 1982 onwards, and the numerous innovations to which they gave rise, could not have been foreseen.

How is the PO to be evaluated in economic terms? A concept of sufficient clarity cannot be discerned. The perfecting of planning by making provision for long-term planning, by integrating the combines and increasing their autonomy within the planning process and reducing the costs of planning still remains to be achieved.

Apart from the economic aspects, juridically (also as regards the law to be introduced) the following three questions, relating to all the POs, are of interest.

(1) Do we have here a handbook of intended economic actions, which, juridically speaking, is implemented with largely non-binding general provisions, or a true *legal ordinance* concerning the planning process, which contains, besides general non-obligatory task norms, also a sufficiency of those legal norms which regulate the *juridical duties* (and rights) of the central planning authorities and economic units (combines and enterprises), as well as the consequences of derelictions of duty in the planning process?

(2) Does the PO (or the combine decree) enact a right of appeal on the part of the economic units *vis-à-vis* the relevant superior planning authority (usually the industrial ministry; otherwise the county council) in respect of so-called 'operational directives', which amount to periodic interventions in the planned and contractually regulated economic activity? For experience to date, not only in the GDR, reveals a striking contradiction on this point between the economic position of, e.g. the industrial combines under the control of the relevant minister, which are required to shape, independently, a consistent process of reproduction, and the legal character of their rights *vis-à-vis* the superior organ/authority (the ministry).

(3) What is the status of the PO as a normative instrument? Is it in the nature of a law (the equivalent of a GDR planning

law), a decree of the Council of Ministers, or merely a regulation (one of those centrally issued legal ordinances of the lowest order of importance, which every minister is entitled to put into force)? To recapitulate: the inter-enterprise (today inter-combine) supply–purchase relations have, since 1965, been regulated by a full law of the People's Chamber, whereas questions of price calculation and of the use of bonus funds within enterprises have been regulated by a decree issued by the Council of Ministers of the GDR. The third PO, too, was once again merely issued in the form of a regulation by Heinz Klopfer, one of the deputies of the Chairman of the State Planning Commission, in agreement with the Minister of Finance, and not by the Council of Ministers, as the authors incorrectly state in their documentary (ibid., p. 7).

SUMMARY OF THE 1986-90 PO

The 'Order of Planning for the National Economy of the GDR 1986-90' (Planning Order) was declared obligatory as from 1 March 1985, under a decree of 7 December 1984 (*Anordnung über die Ordnung der Planung der Volkswirtschaft der DDR 1986 bis 1990 vom 7.12.84, GBL der DDR*, Sonderdruck vom 1 Februar 1985. Nr. 1190, bestehend aus den Teilen a bis r). This third PO of the GDR covering a five-year period and the corresponding plans must be seen *inter alia* as the outcome of almost forty years of continuous efforts, within the territory of the GDR, to master central state planning (and closely connected with this in terms of both content and methodology the tasks of accounting and control) of the (re)production process at both the enterprise and national economic levels, and to carry it out 'scientifically' and at low cost. By means of planning in conformity with the Soviet model of the centrally administered economy, the intention is to realise in a productive way the 'inherent advantages of socialism'. To this end, the most varied *regulatory methods* of planning (and also accounting, the problems of which will not, however, be gone into here) have been elaborated, tried out, rejected and newly formulated. To date, however, it has not (yet) proved possible to furnish a methodology which remains stable in the longer term, which is both of high normative status *and* which also clearly defines the juridical rights and duties of those involved in the planning process, embodied either in a unified normative document in the form of a law on planning (or at least of a legal decree) or in a series of separate legal regulations which have been synchronised as to content and which are comprehensible in their totality. For the sake of clarity, the main steps along the way to the third PO (which has now been released, but which has only been made available to enterprises and the planning authorities of all levels and sectors through the non-public channel of computer-controlled reference numbers allocated by the State Publishing House of the GDR) are briefly summarised.

In so doing, the demands made of and expectations placed upon the planning system have been traced through the main stages of the economic development of the GDR. Since the interested observer officially only has access to secondary sources, recourse must be had to these to clarify the current position.

In the first official commentary on the 1986-90 PO (Authors' Collective, 1985, *Planungsordnung 1986 bis 1990 ...*), the authors, altogether 18 (!) in number, and all members of the State Planning Commission (SPK) refer to the programme of the SED, which 'establishes' that the workers 'have created in the GDR a stable, efficient, socialist planned economy, which is continually being strengthened and perfected' (ibid., p. 6). Thereupon E. Honecker is quoted to the effect that, in future planning, the primary aim will be 'to bind yet more closely together the plan and economic accounting, and, in this way, to align yet more effectively the economic interests of the combines, enterprises and their collectives with the demands of the state and the national economy' (ibid., p. 7).

No mention is made either of people's needs or of the market and its demands; instead, the demands of the state are given pride of place, thus making clear the role of the individual and the priority accorded to his or her needs, in planning as elsewhere.

In every centralised economy of the Soviet type the production, utilisation and distribution of goods (and services) is steered by means of plans covering periods of varying lengths and with differing degrees of compulsion. The decisions required for this purpose are political in nature and are taken exclusively by the top political leadership, which in the GDR is, in effect, the Central Committee of the SED and, executively, its Secretariat and Politburo.

For this purpose, the political leadership caucuses require a differentiated information system, which is by no means to be equated with official statistics. Sections of such a national economic information system are, for example, the economic (especially that concerned with information for planning purposes), that concerning accounting and statistics (the national economic accounting system, and the information system dealing with science and technology; it is intended to improve their co-ordination by means of databanks (*Anordnung vom 26 Januar 1983 zum koordinierten Aufbau von Datenbanken, GBL der DDR*, Sonderdruck Nr. 1120).

The top political leadership wishes to receive through the information system sufficiently accurate details about the availability of factors of production and, by evaluating these, to be able to take decisions concerning the ranking and order of priority of the possibilities for utilising the goods to be produced. In this connection, the State Planning Commission (Central Ministry of Planning) of the GDR has to calculate the development of proportions and interrelationships of the national economy and to work out variants of national economic development. As a basis for this there are various balances of a material and financial kind — i.e. some in natural and others in monetary terms — that have to be drawn up. Officially, according to the third PO (*Anordnung über die Ordnung der Planung der Volkswirtschaft der DDR 1986 bis 1990*, a.a.O., Sonderdruck Nr. 1190 A, p. 8), the following national economic balances and calculations are to be worked out:

(1) (a) Balance of total social product and national income.
(b) Balance of the origin and use of the real income of the population.
(c) Balance of money income and expenditure of the population.
(d) Aggregate construction balance and use of the output of the construction industry for selected areas by counties.
(e) Balances of the population, working people and manpower resources.
(f) Balances of foreign trade and of international foreign currency relations.
(g) Calculation of the efficiency of social production.
(h) Balances in value terms of the material sectors (this is new).

(i) Material, equipment and consumer goods balances in accordance with the prescribed lists, together with the main indicators for energy, material and stocks.

(j) Calculations of the development and efficiency of fixed capital and investment (this is new)

The Ministry of Finance and the State Bank have *inter alia* to draw up, in co-operation with other central state organs, the following:

(2) (a) A financial balance for the state.

(b) The balance of the revenue and expenditure of the state budget.

(c) A balance of the credit system.

(d) A balance relating to the effects of planned changes in industrial and agricultural prices.

In addition, the Ministry of Transport has recently to work out a transport balance for the GDR. Chief importance, therefore, attaches to the balances for aggregated product groups and material input–output relationships in the national economic production process.

Thus quantities and prices in balances and plans are indispensable elements in the set of instruments of the planning and direction system. 'An economic mechanism of this kind, which seeks a rational combination of central physical and monetary steering and decentralised motivation, contains within itself serious conflicts as regards goals and hence the pressure to introduce reform' (*DIW Handbuch*, 1985, p. 80).

It should be borne in mind that, for the 1986-90 five-year plan, which was only raised to the status of a law in the course of 1986, there exists as yet no juridically regulated planning legislation. Thus the cardinal question in regard to the third PO (whether it is a matter of legal regulations or only of the house rules of the State Planning Commission) seems to be one which is (still) not favourable to universally compulsory and applicable regulations.

SUMMARY

The GDR has had almost forty years' experience in economic planning. In that span of time six-month plans (1948), a two-year plan (1949-50), five-year plans (1951-55), a perspective or seven-year plan and, since 1971, a number of plans, each once again for a five-year period, have been drawn up. For the planning centre and for combines and enterprises the planning process is at the same time also a learning process, which ought, in view of the constant references to 'scientific planning', to be susceptible to scientific evaluation.

The picture changes, however, when it is seen how an economic historian of the GDR assesses the official accounting and the scientific evaluation of medium-term plans, on which he states, *inter alia*:

> Not known, or only insufficiently known, are, on the other hand, the conclusion of the two-year plan, the transition from the second five-year plan to the seven-year plan (in other words, the position of the third five-year plan), the conclusion of the seven-year plan, the formulation of the 'perspective plan to 1970', the modification of this plan in 1968 or 1969, the drawing up of the 1971-75 five-year plan and of the 1976-80 five-year plan etc ... not all relevant archival sources are as yet accessible. (Roesler, 1983, p. 178)

It is to be hoped that this inglorious run of non-evaluated five-year plans will be halted and that the same fate will not befall the plans subsequent to 1980 (and thus the 'etc.' in the above quoted passage).

The imperfect evaluation of the medium-term plans might conceivably furnish *an* explanation for the insufficient stability of the plan, but it is not a very plausible one. A real problem is posed by the central planning authority's predictive accuracy for the five-year period. The timespan neither derives from conditions of the reproduction process, nor is it explicable in scientific terms. It is purely a pragmatic choice. The fact that it is uniformly applied within Comecon facilitates the multifaceted co-ordination of plans between member countries. Apart from this consideration, the five-year period is rather too long. This applies especially to the planning methods (balancing, the prescribing of more than a hundred detailed, compulsory plan indicators per combine) which the planning centre uses in order to combine stability and order in planning with dynamic economic growth and sufficient flexibility when changes become necessary. The external disturbances emanating from the world economy constitute merely one more problem among many.

In addition, however, experience and theory teach that this type of planned economy has inherent difficulties in producing dynamic energies and making better use of factors of production. In consequence, it is not possible for there to be a perfect (and here we are not talking formalistically) PO. The contradiction between the legal norm, the law, which is supposed to bring forth (and secure) the medium-term order, and the necessity for rapid adjustment within the economic process can clearly not be solved by these means.

Heuer, a leading theoretician of GDR economic law, has repeatedly commented upon the problem of plan and law, and on each occasion has set forth the prevailing state of scholarly discussion and knowledge. In a 1982 article he cites Karl Marx, according to whom 'Regularity and order [are] themselves an indispensable factor in any mode of production, if it is to acquire social stability and independence from mere chance or arbitrariness' (Heuer, 1982, p. 387). Heuer then puts forward four reasons, which (according to him), in the opinion of experts on economic law, make it necessary for the planning process in the GDR to be legally regulated, and on the basis of which the jurists 'propose the further development of the juridical regulation of the planning process' (ibid., p. 387).

In order to have some standard of measurement to apply to any development which may have occurred, it should be remembered that in 1979 the same author, looking back over the first 1976-80 PO, said that with it there had been created for the first time a stable, longer-term planning regulation, even though a number of requirements in regard both to the status of the regulation and to its legal counterpart remained unsatisfied, as was also the case in respect of certain ideas as to legal safeguards of the position of the enterprise (Heuer, 1979, p. 183).

To say that the first PO was stable, however, is surely to take too favourable a view. Otherwise, Heuer's views on all other points may be accepted, as far as his criticisms are concerned. In his 1982 contribution Heuer announced a *consistent* legal regulation of planning (Heuer, 1982, p. 388) and in 1984 spoke of undertakings involving a future *all-embracing* legal planning regulation. In 1985 he again described the legal mechanism as indispensable 'if parameters of action and areas of competence are to be laid down, and interests are to be harmonised with one another ...' (Heuer, 1985, p. 83). Once more, in the *Handbook on Economic Law*, published in 1985, the need for a legal regulation of planning and that for subjective rights of combines is emphasised (Authors' Collective, 1985, p. 169). But at the start of the 1986-90 five-year plan there exists neither a consistent nor an all-embracing legal regulation of planning; similarly an unambiguous legal delimitation of the decision-making powers of ministry, combine and combine enterprise is still lacking. That is the reality.

The fate of the first and especially of the second PO makes it appear doubtful whether the GDR can fully succeed in making the five-year plan serve — methodologically, legally and as regards its content — as the chief instrument for steering economic activity. In particular, the question arises as to what part, if any, legal regulations can play in a centrally planned economy. In the sphere of planning the regulations (contrary to official assurances) can hardly be legal in character, since the juridical rights and duties of those involved in the planning process, and responsibility (for example of state organs amongst others) in the case of derelictions of duty, have not been regulated. In general, a dislike on the part of planners and other economists of such legal regulations is discernible; nor have the relevant jurists (Heuer, Pflicke, Hochbaum) succeeded in getting their point of view adopted. Hensel has stated in this connection:

> If such a system is to function, then the only kind of law there can be is what the political leadership declares to be law. Thus central planning does not serve the law, but the law serves the plans of the political leadership. (Hensel, 1978, p. 113)

NOTES

1. 'State planning of the economic process means the centralisation of the whole process of economic decision-making in the political leadership. By introducing an economic system of this kind, the political leadership claims the sole right to decide which goods are to be produced, in what quantities, when and where, and what ends, apart from the economic, the national economic apparatus is to serve. It determines the order of priorities that shall punctuate the course of human existence; it distributes the burdens and rewards deriving from the labour input into economic activity — it alone is active in making decisions throughout the whole of economic life; the working people

are the passive objects of the plans of the political leadership' (Hensel, 1978, p. 112).

2. 'Each of the different kinds of decisions relating to principles must be made in such a way that it is internally consistent and systematic. Where the enterprise plan, with its partial and individual plans is concerned, this task will be made easier by the general guidelines. Nothing comparable exists for the enterprise regulations. Precisely here, however, there exist in numerous enterprises too many regulations, some of which are mutually inconsistent, whilst, on the other hand, basic questions as to management responsibility in the enterprise remain open. Thus, for example, in the VEB Weimar Combine, with its 23 combine enterprises, there are 125 combine and 892 enterprise regulations, whilst the number of enterprise regulations per enterprise varies between zero and 190. An organisational shortfall (and onc that is in part actually illegal) in some combine enterprises contrasts with an organisational excess in others and in the combine as a whole. Investigations have shown that a systematic structuring of regulations would bring about a better implementation of socialist legality, a more effective management and a saving of some 20 per cent in organisational input in the combine' (Hochbaum, 1975, p. 23).

3. Model forms with exactly defined rows and columns count as documents conveying (plan) information with a fixed security classification, like *printed lists* and machine-readable data stores (e.g. defined magnetic tapes).

4. The ELN is supported by a Central Catalogue of Articles (ZAK), which serves as an aid in the exchange of information within and between enterprises (orders, contracts, accounts). (*Anordnung über den zentralen Artikelkatalog vom 20.2.1985, GBL der DDR*, 1, Nr. 87).

5. It was drawn up under the aegis of the State Planning Commission with the assistance of 400 theoretical and empirical experts. The process was based on the GDR's own many years experience and its perceptions, which had been partially tested in practice, by reference to relevant Soviet experience, and also by the effort to achieve the highest possible degree of assimilation to the planning system of the USSR, with which the GDR does 40 per cent of its foreign trade.

In discussions on the draft numerous objections were raised to the numbers and effectiveness of the state plan indicators and also to the details of the administrative regulations.

6. The PO now lists only state plan indicators; the national economic accounting indicators used earlier are now omitted. From 1976 centrally directed industrial enterprises were given some 100 state plan indicators as an obligatory plan target. The enterprises to which planning on a reduced scale applied (about two-thirds of the total number of industrial enterprises) received only a bare 50 state plan indicators.

7. The chief planner of one industrial enterprise said of the enterprise draft for the 1976 annual plan that it ran to 423 sheets, with 491 pages and about 15,300 separate data 'and we were not even able to use machine processing of data because the forms were not designed for this purpose. In view of the effort involved, we ask ourselves to what extent

an economic management (or indeed any) organ could possibly be able to process the information submitted' (Wahl, 1975, p. 11).

8. The PO published in 1980 was amended for the first time by the introduction of new plan indicators (net production etc.). In the ensuing years, further amendments dealt, above all, with the introduction of state commissions for science and technology (priority planning), reinforced centralised balancing, an exceptional extension of the use of norms and normatives for material consumption and stocks (down to the rationing of petrol and diesel oil for vehicles), investment questions, the payment of a wage fund tax by economic units (contribution for social funds), questions of price formation, guidelines for the financing of the national economy, and also the formation of business contracts between economic units (law on contracts).

9. 'Complex economic plan information' is the designation given to the survey of indicators which is required to be worked out in addition to the enterprise plan drafts. It consists of consolidated feedback information and is intended to provide an 'X-ray picture' of the enterprise and thus the basis for uniform calculations of efficiency.

10. The situation in other CMEA countries is the same. 'Investigations in CMEA countries have thus shown that the subjective rights of the large economic organisations *vis-à-vis* the superior organs do not accord with the economic position of the economic organisations. It should be noted that neither the preconditions nor the consequences which arise for the large economic organisations from alterations of plan, have been adequately regulated' (Richter, 1979, p. 47).

11. This passage referring to a legal decree is informative from a number of points of view. In the first place, Directors General, as heads of economic units, are subject to the resolutions of the SED leadership, which is not empowered to legislate. This supposes that all Directors General are members of the SED and means that the political leadership directly steers economic processes. Secondly, state plans are always mentioned before the legal ordinances, which gives the impression that they are not counted among the legal ordinances, whilst being, at the same time, more important than these. And, thirdly, it is evident that the disciplining of Directors General is connected with party and state discipline.

7

The Perfecting of the Planning and Steering Mechanisms

Manfred Melzer

BACKGROUND

The very ambitious targets of the 1981-85 five-year plan (*Gesetz über den Fünfjahrplan für die Entwicklung der Volkswirtschaft der DDR 1981-85* in *GBL. der DDR*, 1981, Part I, pp. 405-16) should be seen as an attempt to solve the most urgent problem facing the GDR at the beginning of the 1980s, namely the foreign trade burden. The GDR economic leadership was forced to react to the worsening situation (growing trade deficits towards the end of the 1970s, sharply deteriorating terms of trade), aggravated by the increases in the world market prices of oil and raw materials (Cornelsen, 1981).

Given, in the first instance, only marginally reducible imports, a high rate of growth of exports was targeted in the five-year plan, in order to be able to bring about a gradual reduction in the level of indebtedness. Bearing in mind the need to motivate the population, it was felt that it was not possible to do without a growth in private consumption. As a result, there developed an extremely strained use side of produced national income, which, even in the case of falling investment, nevertheless demanded a very high rate of growth of production. It was intended to bring this about chiefly by means of an increase in labour productivity accompanied by substantial savings in energy and raw materials.

The economic leadership hoped that combines (see Chapter 5) would give rise to so many impulses for intensification (*Intensivierung*) that not only the foreign trade difficulties, but also some of the still existing serious domestic problems, such as inefficiencies in the use of factors of production (for further details see Melzer, 1980, pp. 361-4) would be overcome (Melzer, 1984a, pp. 281-99).

Actual development in 1981 took place along the lines of the five year plan (Cornelsen, 1982a), although admittedly investment surpassed and private consumption fell short of the planned levels. Despite a drastic increase in exports and a trade surplus in goods, net indebtedness to the West increased to around $11 billion. At the same time the interest–service ratio (annual interest payments as a percentage of exports) increased to a quarter. In general, however, the 1981 performance was quite promising, with the newly formed combines making a positive contribution (see Table 7.1).

In 1982 the position deteriorated (Cornelsen, 1982b and 1983). There were two reasons for this. Firstly, in 1982 oil deliveries from the USSR were reduced by 10 per cent, thereafter amounting to only 17 million tonnes per year instead of the 19 million tonnes previously specified in a long-term trade agreement. Secondly, the attitude of Western banks changed abruptly with regard to the granting of new credits for the conversion of short-term debts. Both factors forced the GDR to react immediately to the new situation. Further economy measures and yet another expansion of the domestic raw material base were essential. Early in 1982 the GDR was also quite unexpectedly obliged to reduce imports drastically and increase exports even more. All this considerably disrupted the functioning of the economy and, in the last analysis, explains the 1982 results, which bore little resemblance to the plan.

The yet again changing conditions forced the GDR economic leadership to take up the challenge which confronted them. They had to realise that combines, as new bodies responsible for certain aspects of economic policy, could not, on their own, provide a strong or rapid enough vehicle for overcoming the pressing and increasingly serious economic problems. Consequently, economic policy had to be amended to stimulate even greater efforts towards export expansion, debt reduction and savings in the consumption of energy and raw materials (Melzer and Stahnke, 1986). At the same time it was necessary to focus indirect steering instruments on the raising of efficiency and domestic performance capacity (Melzer, 1984b). All this is deserving of special notice, because the adaptation processes were required to be carried out quickly and in the context of a socialist planned economy, a system which, in principle, affords but little flexibility.

REFINING THE SYSTEM OF PLANNING AND INDIRECT STEERING

The economic leadership envisaged much greater progress in intensification, introducing, for this purpose, a flood of new planning coefficients, directives and improved management techniques. It was hoped that improvements would flow from greater precision in direct planning and a strengthening in cost-benefit thinking (Cornelsen, Melzer and Scherzinger, 1984). Profitability also was to stimulate intensification and greater cost discipline. The use of credits and improved monitoring mechanisms was directed at the promotion of more efficient production, investment and innovation.

Direct steering

Because the effort to include the combines in the planning process did not achieve the necessary progress in intensification, the *system of plan indicators*, used both for direct guidance and for the monitoring of results, had to be adapted to the new situation. On the one hand, in the drawing up of the detailed combine plan (which involves the competent minister), the Director General now disaggregates the state minimum plan targets into obligatory plan targets for the enterprises (*Anordnung über die Ordnung der Planung der Volkswirtschaft der DDR 1981 bis 1985, Sonderdruck des GBL. der DDR*, 1979, No. 1020; see also *Rahmenrichtlinie für die Planung in den Kombinaten und Betrieben der Industrie und des Bauwesens, Sonderdruck des GBL. der DDR*, 1979, No. 1021). This means that the Director General is accorded a degree of influence which varies from combine to combine. On the other hand, it was necessary to increase the quantity and quality of indicators furthering specific intensification goals, expressing allowable input expenditure and raising efficiency. Since the drawing up of the 1984 plan, the following, introduced in 1983, have been regarded as the main indicators (*Anordnung Nr. 4 über die Ergänzung der Ordnung der Planung der Volkswirtschaft der*

Table 7.1: Indicators of economic development in the GDR (percentage rate of growth)

	1981-5[a] Plan	1981	1982	1983 Actual	1984	1985[b]
Produced national income	5.1	4.8	2.6	4.4	5.5	4.8
Primary energy consumption in the national economy,	—	0.3	−1.8	−0.1	2.7	2
of which: Lignite	—	3.5	2.9	1.6	3.5	—
Industry						
Commodity production[c]	5.1	5.5	3.7	3.9	4.3	4.4
within sphere of industrial ministries						
Commodity production	5.5	5.9	4.3	4.6	4.5	4.5
Net production[c]	—	7.0	5.6	7.1	8.3	9.0
Labour productivity[c]						
(Commodity production)	5.2	4.8	3.4	3.8	3.7	4.2
(Net production)	—	7.0	4.7	5.4	7.6	8.4
Construction						
Construction output (centrally directed)[c,d]	4.2	4	2.9	3.7	2.7	3.9
Finished dwellings,	188.0	185.4	187.1	197.2	207.0	212.2
of which: New construction (in 1000)	120.0	125.7	122.4	122.6	121.7	120.7
Modernisations (in 1000)	68.0	59.6	64.6	74.6	85.4	91.5
Agriculture						
Gross crop production[e,f]	2.1/2.3	1.2	−2.1	0.6	16.7	1.4
of which: Grain (in million tonnes)[g]	10.4	8.9	10.0	10.1	11.5	11.6
Marketed livestock production[f,h]	0.9	2.8	−6.6	2.7	6.7	3.8
Inland transport[i]						
Freight volume,	—	−3.2	−7.3	−2.2	−1.1	−0.7
of which: Rail	—	1.2	2.3	1.0	3.6	3.3
Inland waterways	—	1.9	1.2	3.8	7.0	−13.3
Road	—	−5.1	−12.3	−3.9	−4.0	—
Freight value,	—	−2.1	−6.7	−0.3	1.4	—
of which: Rail	—	−1.1	−3.1	1.6	3.2	—
Inland waterways	—	9.3	−2.9	5.9	9.0	—
Road	—	−5.2	−18.5	−5.3	−5.8	—
Rail electrification	7.2/7.6	6.7	6.7	8.6	10.7	12.7
Retail trade turnover[j]	3.7	2.5	1.0	0.7	4.2	4.2
of which: Foodstuffs and semi-luxuries	3.7	2.9	2.1	1.6	3.3	2.7
Industrial commodities	3.7	2.1	−0.1	−0.1	5.1	5.6
Foreign trade turnover[j,k]	—	10.7	9.2	10.6	8.4	3.5
of which: Imports	—	6.4	4.3	9.0	9.6	3.6
Exports	—	15.4	14.1	12.0	7.3	3.4
Trade balance (in billion VM)	—	−1.1	+5.4	+8.0	+6.9	+7
Net money income of the population	3.7	3.1	2.8	2.3	3.9	4.0
Investment, total[l]	−2.1	2.7	−5.2	−0.0	−4.9	2.2

Notes: a. Average annual rate of growth; b. Provisional data, partly estimated; c. Results for 1981 to 1984 calculated from index numbers; d. 1986-90 whole economy; e. Total crop production; in grain equivalent according to the GDR formula; f. five-year plan figure: average annual rate of growth, taking average of preceding five years in relation to the planned volume in the final year of the new five-year plan period; g. Five-year plan figure: targeted grain harvest in final year; h. Sum of state revenue from slaughtered cattle, milk, eggs and wool; in grain equivalent; i. Excluding sea transport and civil aviation; j. Current prices; k. Including inner-German trade; l. Excluding general repairs; at constant prices. Source: *Statistische Jahrbücher der DDR*; Statistical indicators of short-term economic changes in ECE countries, Geneva; *Planerfüllungsberichte* (the last one: see *Neues Deutschland*, 18-19 January 1986, pp. 1 and 3 ff.).

Source: Cornelsen D., 'Zur Lage der DDR-Wirtschaft am Ende des Fünfjahrplans 1981-85' in *Wochenbericht des DIW*, no. 5 (1986).

DDR 1981 bis 1985, Sonderdruck des GBL. der DDR. 1983, No. 1122): 'net production' (*Nettoproduktion*), 'net profit' (*Nettogewinn*), 'products and services for the population' (*Erzeugnisse und Leistungen für die Bevölkerung*) and 'exports' (*Export*). These replaced two of the basic indicators for performance evaluation introduced in 1980, 'industrial commodity production' (*industrielle Warenproduktion*: a measure of gross output) and 'basic materials costs per 100 marks of commodity production' (*Grundmaterialkosten je 100 Mark Warenproduktion*). The aim here is to avoid the problems of wastage of materials and inflated inter-combine deliveries associated with gross output and to encourage measurement of real value creation. By means of the promotion of net profit (and measurement of labour productivity on the basis of net production), the hope is for an improved relationship between expenditure and result. At present there are around 100 indicators in centrally directed industry.

There is also a multitude of *norms* and *normatives*, designed to reduce the consumption of specific materials. These were reviewed in 1982, tightened in many cases (*Verordnung über die Arbeit mit Normen und Normativen des Materialverbrauchs und der Vorratshaltung, GBL. der DDR*, 1982, Part I, pp. 515 ff.) and the proportion of all inputs covered by them raised (Erdmann, 1982, pp. 401 ff.). In 1982 and 1983, moreover, the *balancing* of raw materials, materials and semi-finished goods was further developed (*Anordnung über die Nomenklatur für die Planung, Bilanzierung und Abrechnung von Material, Ausrüstungen und Konsumgütern zur Ausarbeitung und*

Table 7.2: Indicators of performance evaluation in industrial combines and enterprises

Regulation of June 1980	Regulation of April 1981	Regulation of March 1983
Basic indicators of performance evaluation	*Basic indicators of performance evaluation*	*Basic indicators of performance evaluation*
Industrial commodity production	Industrial commodity production	
Net production[a]	Net production[a]	Net production[a]
Basic materials costs per 100 marks of commodity production[b]	Basic materials costs per 100 marks of commodity production[b]	
		Net profit[c]
		Products and services for the population
		Exports
Further qualitative criteria	*Further qualitative indicators*	*Further important qualitative indicators*
Net profit[c]	Enterprise result	
Increase in labour productivity	Increase in labour productivity	Labour productivity on the basis of net production
Reduction in the cost of production	Reduction in the cost of production	Costs per 100 marks of commodity production
Proportion of products with quality labels	Proportion of products with quality labels	Production of products important in national economic terms, especially newly developed products and products with quality labels
Production meeting contractual obligations for domestic use and exports	Production meeting contractual obligations for domestic use and exports	
	Completion of investment projects/objects on time and meeting quality requirements	Materials costs per 100 marks of commodity production[b]

Notes: a. 'Net production' (simplified) = commodity production *minus* consumption of materials (basic materials, energy, other materials), *minus* consumption of productive services (bought-in services, repairs, transport and warehousing costs, other productive services), *minus* rents and leases, *minus* depreciation; b. In the GDR the concept 'basic materials' (*Grundmaterial*) comprises all the man-made objects which form the material substance of the product. It is thus only part of the wider concept 'materials', which comprises basic materials, energy, water, fuel, lubricants and other materials; c. 'Net profit' (simplified): unitary enterprise result of the enterprise or combine (i.e. including foreign trade profits and losses), *plus* subventions in accordance with statutory provisions, *minus* capital charge, *minus* profits not earned by own economic performance, *minus* profits from exceeding manpower plan, *minus* fines, transferred to state budget.

Source: Scherzinger, A., 'Weiterentwicklung des Wirtschaftsmechanismus in der DDR', in *Wochenbericht des DIW* (1983), No. 41, p. 510.

Durchführung der Jahresvolkswirtschaftspläne — Bilanzverzeichnis, Sonderdruck des GBL. der DDR, 1982, No. 668/13). About 76 per cent of production was then centrally determined in 2,136 balances, whilst a further 2,400 balances (24 per cent of production) were drawn up by the authorised combines (and confirmed by the competent Director General) (see Rost, 1982, pp. 17-18). By 1986 the number of centrally determined balances had fallen to 1,135 (451 state plan balances and 684 drawn up by ministries), whilst the number of combine balances had increased to 3,400. The main intention of the improvements is to align important energy and raw materials more closely with quotas and consumption norms. The equipment balances are to take greater account of export requirements as well as investment priorities and consumer good balances of various groups of goods' prices. Finally, efforts have recently been made to render the relatively rigid balancing processes more flexible, by making it obligatory for the balancing organs to respond to market demands by means of appropriate short-term decisions (*Durchführungsbestimmung zur Verordnung über die Material-, Ausrüstungs- und Konsumgüterbilanzierung, GBL. der DDR*, 1983, Part I, pp. 161 ff.).

In order to be able to adapt inputs of all kinds to changes and improvements in finished products, the *deadlines for ordering and delivery* of semi-finished goods have been reduced by two-thirds (*Verordnung über Bestell- und Lieferbedingungen für Roh- und Werkstoffe sowie Zuliefererzeugnisse- Bestell- und Lieferbedingungen-Verordnung, GBL. der DDR*, 1984, Part I, pp. 9 ff.). Producers were allowed more time to decide on both their final assortments and the necessary inputs. Thus, combines and enterprises have more time to improve goods and change the input mix.

Legislation has also tackled the problem of *high transport costs.* In 1983 the transport sector was subjected to normatives — transport costs, or tonnes per kilometre, both related to the value of goods transported (*Anordnung über die Anwendung von Transportnormativen zur Verbesserung der Planung, Abrechnung und Kontrolle des Transportaufwandes in den transportintensiven Zweigen der Volkswirtschaft — Transportnormativanordnung, GBL. der DDR*, 1983, Part I, pp. 166 ff.) — these normatives being extended to the whole economy in 1984 (*Anordnung über die Anwendung von Transportnormativen zur Verbesserung der Planung, Abrechnung und*

Kontrolle des volkswirtschaftlichen Transportaufwands — Transportnormativanordnung, GBL. der DDR, 1984, Part I, pp. 122 ff.). The aim is to reduce road transport to the benefit of more energy-efficient rail and inland waterways. Since the beginning of 1984, fines have been imposed for exceeding authorised transport coefficients.

Indirect steering

In 1982 the GDR's deteriorating economic situation highlighted the fact that progress in intensification also necessitated an active role for indirect steering. The economic levers, mostly concerned with financial magnitudes, by means of which pressure had previously been exerted to ensure plan-fulfilment, were now, in addition, to be permanently geared to cost-reducing rationalisation on a grand scale (including an increase in exports and import substitution). In 1982 and 1983, to this end, economic accounting was orientated towards the achievement of resource-saving production processes and greater efficiency by cost-reducing efforts. Thus, 'accounting' was added, with an equal ranking, to the classical duo 'management and planning'. The decree on perfecting economic accounting (*Verordnung über die weitere Vervollkommnung der wirtschaftlichen Rechnungsführung auf der Grundlage des Planes, GBL. der DDR*, 1982, Part I, pp. 85 ff.) was almost the first to be issued among the new regulations.

The policy of cost reduction called for a cautious *upgrading of the role of profit*, which until then had only been required to secure the planned financial needs of production units. Profitability became the measurement criterion for rational resource utilisation (*Anordnung über die Finanzierungsrichtlinie für die volkseigene Wirtschaft, GBL. der DDR*, 1983, Part I, pp. 110 ff.). The enterprise, therefore, only retains genuinely earned profit, resulting from cost reductions and increases in production in a situation where the state fixes prices: impermissible profit, stemming from enterprise violations of price or quality regulations, are confiscated. Every year certain reductions in expenditure are to be achieved (especially with respect to energy and warranty/repair work). In addition, in order to achieve further economies, combines have to draw up medium-term cost-reduction programmes, and enterprises are required to submit cost analyses and reports.

If planned profit is achieved, combines and enterprises are able to fulfil their obligations with regard to required production and net profit deductions, and to form their funds according to plan. In the event of a profit shortfall (resulting from non-fulfilment of planned tasks or exceeding of cost norms), however, there not only arise financing difficulties and adverse effects on fund formation, but access to certain funds (the performance and investment funds, for example) can even be denied altogether. If plan targets for profit are exceeded, a higher proportion than in the past can now flow into the enterprise's incentive funds, especially so when this is the result of higher export earnings and export profitability.

The capital charge (*Produktionsfondsabgabe*) is designed to improve capital usage. This 'interest rate' is intended to encourage a more speedy implementation of planned investment projects (*Zweite Verordnung über die Produktionsfondsabgabe*, *GBL. der DDR*, 1982, Part I, p. 126; see also *Verordnung über die Produktionsfondsabgabe*, *GBL. der DDR*, 1983, Part I, pp. 106 ff.). Lower rates are seen as an incentive to complete new projects ahead of schedule, higher ones to deter completion delays. When new plants are put into operation earlier than the planned date, the capital charge has only to be paid from the date of the planned start. Since 1986 the capital charge has been based on the net (as opposed to gross) value of fixed assets to encourage the retention in use of old capital assets (*Verordnung über die Produktionsfondsabgabe*, *GBL. der DDR*, 1985, Part I, pp. 157-8). The capital charge is, therefore, lower on old equipment. The normal charge is no longer a constant 6 per cent, but can be changed according to perceived need in the annual plan.

The planned 'net profit deductions' have to be met in full even when a profit shortfall occurs, whereas previously a part was remitted. Enterprises are thus now compelled to draw on their funds or to turn to credits (although the granting of credit is conditional upon proof of suitable measures being taken towards plan realignment). If the net profit deductions are not realised promptly and in full, the responsible bank is empowered to withdraw the sum due from the relevant accounts of the offending combine or enterprise.

With regard to *fund formation*, the resources of the combine or enterprise, financed from profits and costs, are designated for specific purposes. Their utilisation follows precise, legal regu-

Figure 7.1: Profit utilisation and fund formation in the enterprise

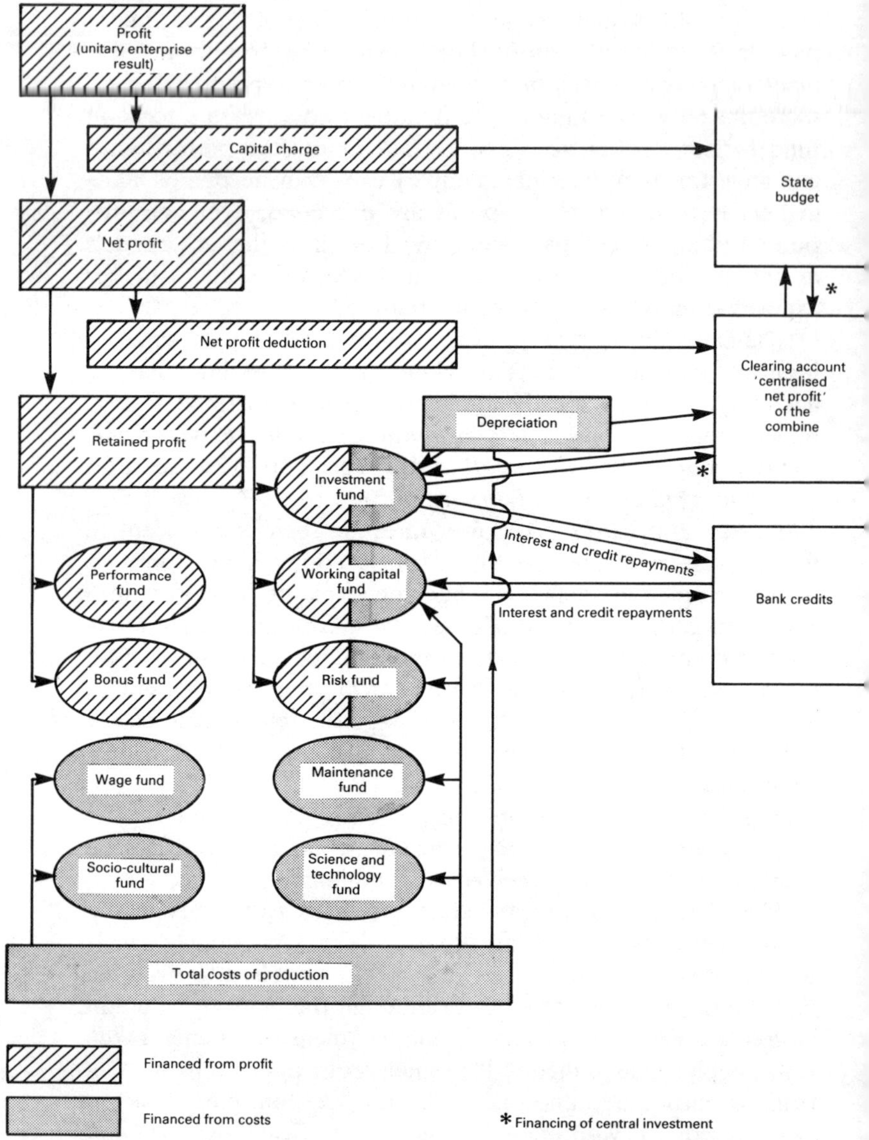

lations and is closely monitored, especially by the banks. The Director General of the combine has centralised profits at his disposal in the form of various funds: a reserve fund (which, among other things, covers the risks involved in innovation and the reorganisation of production processes resulting from the substitution of imports by domestic raw materials); an advertising fund; a fund for science and technology (financed from costs); and a disposal fund of the Director General (*Verfügungsfonds des Generaldirektors*), which rewards special intensification achievements. Important funds, which have to be formed by enterprises (and some also by combines), are: the investment fund (fed from depreciation allowances, profit shares and receipts from the sale of used machinery); the maintenance fund (financed from costs); the risk fund (formed from costs and above-plan profits); the socio-cultural fund (financed out of cost components); the bonus fund; and the performance fund. Some producers of consumer goods have a special fund for fashionable production (financed from specified surcharges). Certain selected enterprises — and now probably all combines — have a foreign currency fund; this is financed from that part of profit resulting from over-fulfilment of export tasks, especially those with high profitability, and used for specific imports (see Authors' Collective, led by Finger and Gertich, 1982, pp. 122-3).

In general, the role of the so-called incentive funds should be emphasised. The *bonus fund* (formed out of shares in profit dependent on the fulfilment of certain indicators) now serves, in particular, the payment of bonuses to the whole workforce for achievements in the sphere of intensification (*Verordnung über die Planung, Bildung und Verwendung des Prämienfonds für volkseigene Betriebe, GBL. der DDR*, 1982, Part I, pp. 595 ff.; see also *Erste Durchführungsbestimmung, GBL. der DDR*, 1982, Part I, pp. 598 ff.). The end of year bonus, in contrast, has, in principle, been frozen at a level of 800 marks per employee. The performance fund (fed from over-plan profits) finances the enterprises' planned production and over-plan, in-house manufacture of machinery and equipment for purposes of rationalisation (*Anordnung über die Planung, Bildung und Verwendung des Leistungsfonds der volkseigenen Betriebe, GBL. der DDR*, 1983, Part I, pp. 121 ff.).

Credit policy in the GDR is employed by state banks to monitor and influence enterprise performance (*Verordnung über die Kreditgewährung und die Bankkontrolle der sozialistischen Wirtschaft – Kreditverordnung, GBL. der DDR*, 1982, Part I, pp. 126 ff.). Low interest rates are intended to stimulate plan over-fulfilment, increases in exports and investment related to intensification (for details see Ehlert, Hunstock and Tannert, 1985, pp. 145 ff.). Enterprises failing to satisfy established efficiency criteria are charged higher rates.

Probably the most important innovation is the 'contribution for social funds' (*Verordnung über den Beitrag für gesellschaftliche Fonds, GBL. der DDR*, 1983, Part I, pp. 105 ff.; see also *Erste Durchführungsbestimmung, GBL. der DDR*, 1983, Part I, p. 106), which was introduced in industry at the beginning of 1984 and in construction, foodstuffs and water supply at the beginning of 1985. Since 1986 transport and forestry have also had to pay the contribution. This is a sort of payroll tax of 70 per cent of the wage fund. It is not so much a financial compensation for state services relating to education, old age, health etc., but, far more, a way to encourage a more rational use of labour by raising its cost. For new products this contribution is included in the determination of prices, but for goods already in production before 1984 the previous prices continue to apply until they are adjusted in a centrally administered price revision. GDR planners are now awaiting achievable economies in manpower. In the meantime a revenue supplement is allowed (*Anordnung über die Planung und Zuführung des Staatlichen Erlöszuschlags, GBL. der DDR*, 1983, Part I, pp. 164 ff.), but this only covers a part of the levy in order to retain a stimulus for a more efficient use of labour.

Recent regulations have also modified GDR *pricing* practices. Price calculation rules currently require a more careful accounting of cost elements than in the past. Since 1976 there have been annual, staged price revisions, reflecting the price increases for energy and materials. The pricing of new products in accordance with the price-performance relationship is no longer practised, due to the lack of any objective criteria for measuring use-value and, above all, the frequent overstating of improvements by enterprises (for more details see Melzer, 1977, pp. 59-62). At present, the prices of new products are determined on the basis of calculable costs (including the contribution for social funds) (*Anordnung über die zentrale staatliche Kalkulationsrichtlinie zur Bildung von Industriepreisen — Kalkulationsrichtlinie*, GBL. der DDR, 1983, Part I, pp. 344 ff.), taking account of a price limit already set in the development phase (*Anordnung Nr. Pr. 475 über Kosten- und Preisobergrenzen, GBL. der DDR*, 1983, Part I, pp. 131 ff.) and the prevailing material input norms. At first extra profits were permitted for a period of three years (only for two years since 1986), according to the efficiency criteria attained (e.g. the level of export profitability). The producer now has to cede to the user a share of the cost reductions realised during the first two years (*Anordnung Nr. 2 über die zentrale staatliche Kalkulationsrichtlinie zur Bildung von Industriepreisen, GBL. der DDR*, 1985, Part I, pp. 377 ff.). After that period of time prices must not exceed an expenditure level (including normal profit) fixed by the state organs (*Anordnung Nr. Pr. 475/1 über Kosten- und Preisobergrenzen, GBL. der DDR*, 1985, Part I, pp. 383 ff.). For commodities already in production prices are still kept constant for a number of years, during which cost reductions (by means of reduced materials usage, for example) and, consequently, increases in profit could be achieved. Goods with quality labels are allowed a 2 per cent mark-up. For '*exquisit*' and '*delikat*' goods much higher profit supplements are allowed (*Anordnung Nr. Pr. 441 über die Preisbildung für Exquisiterzeugnisse, GBL. der DDR*, 1984, Part I, pp. 106 ff.): these are sold in special shops at higher prices. Spare parts are also permitted higher profit supplements. On the other hand, planners penalise through price reductions those older commodities which are below quality norms and certain given standards.

Monitoring

The central organs in the GDR have to be in a position to monitor and assess the subordinate units in the hierarchy. Plan-fulfilment, the behaviour of production units and the workings of economic levers all have to be monitored. Monitoring is scarcely to be distinguished from direct and indirect steering since these instruments contain (or ought to contain) such elements.

There have, of course, always been monitoring organs, but, since the beginning of the 1980s, they have had to be focused more on making intensification an important goal (von Grumbkow, 1984). New bodies (such as the State Balancing Inspectorate and the Inspectorate for Quality) had, therefore, to be created and the powers of existing bodies extended (e.g. the authority of the Chief Accountant and of the banks) in order to monitor the actual results relating to greater efficiency in the use of scarce resources.

The role of the monitoring authorities also extends to the submission of proposals for improvement. Banks, therefore, are not only important state organs for monitoring efficiency and its adherence to the plan, but also, for example, make suggestions as to what could (or has) to be done to improve the preparation of investment projects. In general, the mechanisms were strengthened in order to counter the increased powers of combines and to prevent departures of production from state goals.

EFFECTS AND LIMITATIONS OF THE NEW ECONOMIC EXPERIMENT

There is now an incentive system in operation that leads to greater profits for combines and enterprises (stemming from a reduction in the consumption of energy and materials, a more efficient use of capital or some savings in other costs), although the contribution for social funds, in the absence of drastic economies in the use of manpower, draws off a large part of these. With the given set of instruments greater progress in intensification can be made, and it seems to be substantially more suited to carrying out the strategy of the 1980s than the set of instruments used in the 1970s. This is certainly a definite step forward.

It must be clearly said, however, that these new measures are far less extensive than, for instance, the NES reforms of the 1960s. The bundle of measures which has been changed during the period 1982 to 1984 is not as consistent as that of the NES and there is no underlying new theoretical model. Instead, in a short period of time all the regulations in force have been reviewed and amended in the light of the emergency situation; only a few completely new instruments have been added. There is, nevertheless, a unifying concept, namely that of the 'drive for intensification'. The instruments can be said to be refined to a significant extent, especially when due consideration is given to the relatively short term the authorities had to come up with adequate solutions to the urgent problems.

The present economic mechanism has had clear successes. The specific consumption of energy and materials could be decreased considerably and a more efficient use of labour and capital attained. Above all, a deficit in trade with the West has been turned into a surplus, which, in turn, has reduced the GDR's indebtedness (to between $5 billion and $6 billion in

1985 *vis-à-vis* Western banks). This has considerably eased the foreign trade burden compared to the early 1980s. A glance at Table 7.1 shows that the GDR performed well as regards growth rates after the troublesome year of 1982. In 1983 the growth rate of produced national income was 4.4 per cent (Cornelsen, 1984), in 1984 5.5 per cent and in 1985 4.8 per cent (Cornelsen, 1985 and 1986). It should be mentioned here that in 1984 and 1985 the very good performance of agriculture had a positive effect on overall growth rates. Although total growth over the 1981-85 five-year plan period was below target, the GDR's growth displayed dynamism, despite the increasing external and internal economic problems.

It must be noted that private consumption was well below plan, especially in 1982, the year of serious disruptions. Consumer good shortages persisted in 1983. Retail trade turnover in nominal terms increased by scarcely 1 per cent in both years. With prices for new consumer goods rising, living standards declined a little over the period. 1984 and 1985, however, were years of consolidation, with retail trade turnover in nominal terms increasing by a good 4 per cent in both years and the situation relating to consumer goods returning to normal. The blame for the mid-term decline lies decidedly more with the disruptions of 1982, which forced import reductions and certain production slow-downs, than with a further lower ranking of consumption in the hierarchy of goals (that indeed was hardly the real intention of the economic leadership).

Even with this good overall performance and the consolidated position with respect to private consumption, it cannot be denied that there are weak spots in the new mechanisms. This is especially the case for the continued shortcomings with respect to innovation, motivation and efficiency. Despite the improvements made, the system of indirect steering lays most stress on negative incentives, with positive incentives seemingly undervalued or not very great. Above all, the possibilities open to combines and enterprises to use part of their profits for purposes of interest to them are still very restricted. Net profit is still a very limited yardstick for measuring performance, due to its high 'sensitivity' to changes in other data, e.g. product mix (Hoss, 1984, p. 192). Thus, a firm with many intensification successes, but not many innovations, could possibly have a much higher profit than another with many new products and technological improvements, if the latter experiences many unforeseen development costs which (not counting as calculable costs) exceed the amount of extra profit calculated in the prices. Another negative feature involves producers trying to increase production of those lines giving rise to relatively good profits at the fixed prices instead of those satisfying urgent demands. The system of wages and bonuses also seems to be insufficiently differentiated to induce the workforce to greater effort.

An important hindrance in operation during the first half of the 1980s was the restrictive investment policy (the price of the export strategy). It unquestionably hampered the necessary structural changes and technological innovations, since investment allocations could not be adequately made available. The new investment policy (*Neues Deutschland*, 10-11 November 1979, p. 3 and *Neues Deutschland*, 8 July 1980, pp. 3-4) envisaged the modernisation and rationalisation of the existing capital stock (Ebert and Opel, 1982, pp. 424 ff.), as well as the focusing of new projects on important sectors and high technologies. Modernisation is supposed to bring about efficiency by the combining of old and new equipment (Haberland and Rosenkranz, 1984, pp. 627 ff.). But, with total investment falling, the production by enterprises of in-house machinery and equipment for rationalisation purposes affords only limited relief here. Moreover, the delay in scrapping obsolete plant (the retirement of old capital stock has been reduced by an average of 30 per cent) (*Anordnung zur Überprüfung und Überarbeitung der normativen Nutzungsdauer und der Abschreibungssätze für Grundmittel, GBL. der DDR*, 1983, Part I, pp. 236 ff.; see also *Anordnung Nr. 2 zur Überprüfung und Überarbeitung der normativen Nutzungsdauer und der Abschreibungssätze für Grundmittel, GBL. der DDR*, 1984, Part I, pp. 187 ff.) will bring about increases in repair costs and act as a brake on innovation.

Above, all, however, the still distorted price relationships make it difficult to arrive at a rational measurement of efficiency (Melzer, 1983, pp. 51 ff.) and hence the choice of the most rational production solutions from among the large number of possible changes in output, even amongst those consistent with the set plan tasks.

Combine formation and the intensification policy itself have created new problems (Melzer, 1986). While there have been improvements on the information side (such as the creation of shortened channels) the position of the Director General has been strengthened at the expense of the enterprises (Erdmann and Melzer, 1980). In the case of the combine with a parent enterprise there is the danger that the latter will appropriate advantageous portions of a programme and/or allocate disadvantageous portions to other enterprises. There are the criticisms in the GDR itself that too many short-term directives still have to be given (Ladensack, 1980, pp. 164-5), that the functions of those specialist managers who are members of the combine board are not always clearly delimited (Authors' Collective, led by Friedrich and Koziolek, 1981, pp. 174 ff.) and that the responsibilities of the individual enterprise are not laid down with sufficient precision. Multi-level accounting within the combine may lead to contradictions (as in the case of when restructuring of production or the undervaluation of certain production lines, due to distorted prices, can cause an individual enterprise to incur unjustified losses, while the overall performance of the combine improves). Last, but not least, the monopoly position of the combine can have negative effects on production and changes in production (Melzer, 1981, pp. 95 ff.). The minister, therefore, may have difficulty comparing the performance of different combines, with an individual Director General explaining away a poor performance on the grounds of unique circumstances. Repeated efforts to compare profits and efficiency of different combines and enterprises (Salecker, 1984, pp. 355 ff.) are doomed in a situation where prices are distorted. The minister also has to be careful that certain actions may disrupt production in a combine which is the sole supplier in the GDR for special products.

Nevertheless, it is important to note that, given the ruling out of greater decentralisation (for reasons suggested earlier) by the economic leadership, combines, together with the perfecting of the set of instruments, seem to provide a second-best way of tackling the problems faced by the GDR in the prevailing circumstances. With their specialised knowledge and experience, the combines can aid decision-making by the central authorities, even where prices are distorted. With the GDR interested in new production structures and technologies, the combines can contribute their specialised expertise in production, provided, of course, that controls and a kind of international competition work, at least to some extent, against monopolistic attitudes that are too strong.

CONCLUSIONS

The new policy cannot be regarded as a solution for long. The GDR economic leadership is aware of the persisting limitations and has started on an interesting series of economic measures designed to bring about improvements, a series which will have to be continued (Melzer, 1984c, pp. 53 ff.). The second half of the 1980s has seen the launch of this campaign and three aspects are of considerable importance:

1. The start of a new stage in the intensification strategy, its goal being 'the complex, consistent and optimum use and effect of all intensive growth factors' (Wenzel, 1985, p. 17). The idea is, on the one hand, to economise on many resources and, on the other hand, to convert them immediately into completely new production lines (Heinrichs, 1984, pp. 971-2). In industry new products as a percentage of total production (both in value terms) is planned to reach 30 per cent in 1986, having been 17 to 20 per cent in recent years (Schmidt, 1985, p. 627). To carry this out 'concepts of highly refined production' have been developed (Jurk *et al.*, 1985, pp. 59 ff.), which will have a positive effect on innovation (see Chapter 8 for details).

2. An improved 'efficiency planning' has been introduced. Although the true level of efficiency cannot really be determined in the presence of price distortions, increases in efficiency are hoped for in the joint use of a number of indicators (for example, materials cost intensity, economising on inputs, cost reductions, productivity, and capital and export profitability). In addition, production units have to meet certain conditions (Authors' Collective, led by Rost, 1985, p. 30): the increase in labour productivity must be greater than that of capital per employee and of wages; exports of new commodities should increase faster than expenditure on R&D; new products should represent a higher proportion of exports to the West than the proportion of total exports taken by exports to the West. Combines and enterprises have to prove the real effects of planned intensification measures, especially those of R&D (ibid., pp. 31-4). The various efficiency calculations are to be made during the period of plan preparation (Ritzschke, 1985, pp. 87-8) and, in order to attain a higher standard, combines and enterprises have to draw careful comparisons of these calculations with other production units (Müller, 1985, pp. 92 ff.). Quite a number of limited improvements may result from all

this, but not many really significant ones in the absence of a solution to the problem of prices.

3. 1985 saw the revaluation of all fixed capital assets on the basis of the prices of capital goods operational from 1986 onwards (*Anordnung über die Umbewertung der Grundmittel, GBL. der DDR*, 1984, Part I, pp. 450 ff.). The new values are designed to provide an improved measure of profitability and capital productivity. Previously, the capital stock was not evaluated on the basis of a consistent set of prices (for example, homogeneous capital goods produced in different years had very different values). The hope now is that combines and enterprises will be encouraged to use machinery and equipment more efficiently. The higher values will also affect depreciation rates and this, in turn, may affect prices (see Chapter 9 for details).

All this will lead to certain positive effects on innovation and efficiency, although these would be even greater if the problems associated with combine and enterprise motivation could be lessened. It should be mentioned here, however, that the new Order of Planning gives the Director General of the combine the right to demand quarterly planning from his enterprises (*Anordnung über die Quartals- und Monatsplanung sowie über die Freisetzung und effektive Verwendung materieller Fonds, GBL. der DDR*, 1984, Part I, pp. 417 ff.; *Anordnung über die Ordnung der Planung der Volkswirtschaft der DDR 1986 bis 1990, GBL. der DDR, Sonderdruck Nr. 1190a, 1985*, Part A, pp. 5 ff., especially pp. 14-17; see also *Verordnung über die volkseigenen Kombinate, Kombinatsbetriebe und volkseigenen Betriebe, GBL. der DDR*, 1979, Part I, p. 356). Since the Director General has the power to decide upon important specific production targets, changes in the enterprise's production profile could, if necessary, be brought about every three months, provided state plan targets for the whole year are guaranteed. This creates much more flexibility in planning, especially when difficulties arise, and if the Director General allows enterprise managers to engage fully in discussions about basic decisions this might give rise to a 'touch of decentralisation' in certain circumstances.

Günter Mittag recently announced a number of new measures linking the investment fund even more closely to modernisation and rationalisation (Mittag, 1986, pp. 3 ff.). Probably a higher proportion of (extra) profits might flow into the investment fund, for use in rationalisation projects (e.g. high technologies, bio-technology) which are efficient and which take a short time to be realised. Even though the details are not known, this announcement illustrates that future changes can be expected in the attempt to overcome at least some of the existing weaknesses. This clearly allows perfecting to be seen in quite a promising light.

8

Product and Process Renewal in GDR Economic Strategy: Goals, Problems and Prospects

Manfred Melzer and Arthur A. Stahnke

INTRODUCTION

When the 11th Socialist Unity Party (SED) Congress convened in East Berlin on 17-21 April 1986, the conditions facing East German planners were quite different from those they had confronted just five years before.[1] As preparations for the earlier Congress took place, performance indicators showed lagging growth rates over the previous five years; in 1986, however, the comparable figures registered modest, but clearly upward, trends. In 1981, the economy was burdened by a heavy foreign debt, unfavourable price movements on the international market and persistent trade imbalances. By 1986, the debt in favour of the West had been substantially reduced, trade balances were much more positive and the volatility of prices on the international markets had essentially passed. At the beginning of the present decade, the objective of sustaining growth by 'intensive' means was little more than a goal; by 1986, solid evidence of intensive growth was on hand, seemingly vindicating the 'strategy of the 1980s'. And finally, while in 1981 the really quite comprehensive modifications of the economic system itself were barely underway, by 1986, in the short run, only refinements were seen as still needed, a nut tightened here, a new light bulb there — figuratively speaking of course.

And so, perhaps, it was both understandable and with considerable justification that General Secretary Honecker reported to the Congress in 1986 that 'The German Democratic Republic possesses a smoothly functioning socialist planned economic system. That system has demonstrated itself to be dynamic, flexible, and capable of high performance'

Table 8.1: Indicators of the GDR's economic performance and planned growth (annual average rate of growth in per cent)

	1971-5	1976-80		1981-5		1986-90
	Actual	Plan	Actual	Directive	Plan	Directive
Produced national income	5.5	5.0	4.1	5.1-5.4	5.1	4.4-4.7
Industry						
Industrial commodity production, of which:	6.5[a]	6.0	5.0	5.1-5.4	5.1	3.7-4.1
Sphere of industrial ministries	6.6	—	5.5	5.5-5.9	5.5	4.1-4.4
Labour productivity	5.2[b]	5.4[c]	4.7[b]	5.1-5.4	5.2[c]	8.3-8.6
Construction						
Construction output	5.7[d]	5.0[e]	4.5[d,f]	3.4-3.7[e]	3.4[e]	3.0-3.4
Output within the sphere of the Ministry of Construction	6.7[a]	6.5[g]	5.3[f]	4.2-4.6[g]	—	3.4-3.7
Completed dwellings[h] of which:	122	150	163	186-190	188	212.8
New construction	80	110	112	120	120	118.6
Modernisation	42	40	51	66-70	68	94.2
Agriculture[i]						
Gross crop production[j]	2.3	3.6-4.5	0.4	2.0-2.2	2.1-2.3	2.0-2.8
Crop yields: Grain	7.8	1.8-3.9	1.4	2.0	2.0	11.8-12.0
Potatoes	−4.2	—	−2.9	3.0-3.9	—	
Sugar beet	0.9	—	2.2	2.4-3.7	—	
Marketed livestock production,[k] of which:	6.2	2.8	3.8	0.9-1.0	0.9	1.4-1.8
Slaughtered cattle	7.6	3.0	4.4	1.2-1.3	—	
Milk	4.2	2.6	2.4	0.4-0.5	—	
Eggs	7.6	1.9	4.7	1.0	—	
Transport						

Domestic trade						
Retail trade turnover,[m]	5.0	4.0	4.1	3.7-4.1	3.7	4.0
of which:						
Foodstuffs and semi-luxuries	3.5	2.5-3.0[n]	3.5	(< average growth)	(< average)	2.7
Industrial goods	6.9	4.5-5.0[n]	4.8	(> average growth)	(> average)	5.3
Foreign trade		13.4	—	10.2	6.3	—
Turnover,[o] of which:						
Imports	14.1	—	10.3	—		
Exports	12.8	8.4[p]	10.2	8.4[p]	8.4[p]	
Investment,[q]						
of which:	4.1	5.2[r]	4.8	1.8-2.3	−2.1[s]	3.3
in industry	4.7	—	6.4	—	—	
Net money income of the population	4.8	4.0	3.8	3.7-4.1	3.7	3.9-4.1

Notes: a. Calculated from index numbers; b. Gross production per worker and employee; c. In sphere of the industrial ministries (basis commodity production); d. Construction sectors of the economy; e. In the national economy; f. Estimated: g. Construction output; h. Average annual output in 1000 dwellings; i. Actual data: average annual changes with regard to all annual values of relevant time period compared to the annual average of the preceding five-year period. Plan data: annual average change from annual average of the preceding five-year period with respect to the planned volume of the final year 1980 or 1985; j. Total crop production per unit of area: in grain equivalent according to the GDR formula; k. Sum of state revenue from slaughtered cattle, milk, eggs and wool in grain equivalent; l. Taking into account fluctuations during the period under consideration; m. current prices; n. Commodity supply; o. Current prices, including inner-German trade; p. Exports to socialist countries; constant prices.
q. Excluding general repairs and foreign participation; 1975 prices; with regard to total volume carried out in relevant time period; r. Planned volume of 234 billion marks 1976 to 1980, related to investment in 1975; respectively 1967 prices; s. With respect to a planned total volume of 256 billion marks.

Source: *Statistische Jahrbücher der DDR*; *Statistische Praxis*; *Economic Commission for Europe, Geneva*; *Entwurf der Direktive des IX. Parteitages der SED zur Entwicklung der Volkswirtschaft der DDR 1976-80* (ND from 15 January 1976); *Fünfjahrplan 1976-80 (GBL der DDR*, 1976, Part 1, No. 46); *Direktive des X. Parteitages der SED zum Fünfjahrplan für die Entwicklung der Volkswirtschaft der DDR in den Jahren 1981 bis 1985* (ND from 18-19 April 1981); Plan fulfilment reports, calculations and estimates of the DIW; *Fünfjahrplan 1981 bis 1985 (GBL der DDR*, 1981, Part 1, pp. 416 ff.)

Source: *Wochenberichte des DIW* (1981), no. 31 and (1983) no. 5; *Direktive zum Fünfjahrplan* 1986-90: see *Tribüne*, 22 and 23 April 1986, pp. 9-16 and 5-6.

(*Bericht XI*, p. 44). This confidence, even if not entirely warranted[2], was echoed by Günter Mittag in his presentation of the draft five-year plan to the same Congress: 'The GDR possesses a smoothly functioning socialist planned economy through which the Party's clear concept for the system's further development can be executed, based on the foundations already laid.' (*Direktive XI*, p. 8).

Though the point is tangential to our major objective in this chapter, it is worth noting that the confidence and self-satisfaction expressed repeatedly by Honecker, Mittag and others at the 11th SED Congress was in sharp contrast with the assessments of the Soviet economy presented to the 27th Congress of the Communist Party of the Soviet Union in Moscow just two months earlier.[3] The important fact, however, is that the GDR achievement has been all the more impressive in that it was not brought about in an environment of universal success within the socialist community.

One should not lightly dispute the view of the GDR leadership that the economy it directs has delivered a rather notable success and that its short- and middle-term prospects are excellent. The GDR is governed by sober men who have demonstrated realism in their actions, and the economy by any reasonable measure is functioning well. However, it is our view that the GDR is still some distance from success in its efforts to improve and transform its full range of products to bring them up to world market standards, and that the strategy the GDR planners are presently pursuing to that end has serious built-in limitations. To the extent our position should prove correct, the GDR will remain a great step or more behind the most advanced industrialised economies even if, as seems likely, the economy continues to make measured progress towards more optimal efficiencies and higher productivity.

This, then, is the topic we will ultimately consider. The GDR planners call this '*Höhere Veredlung*', which can be translated as 'greater refinement and transformation' of both products and processes. It is likely that it was precisely these difficult tasks which explain why the targets laid down in the *Direktive* for the second half of the Eighties are not so very much orientated to the ambitious plan targets of the preceding five-year plan period (see Table 8.1). Rather, the GDR economic leadership is seeking to stabilise present actual development (Cornelsen, 1986b), admittedly in the context of a greater drive for innovation and increased use of key technologies. Greater attention than before is now paid to private consumption and investment, while exports are still given priority.

THE INTENSIFICATION STRATEGY AND INVESTMENT POLICY

Before we examine the objectives and specifics of *Höhere Veredlung*, it will be well to review briefly the recent development and evolution of current GDR economic strategy. In its most general sense, this strategy has called for continued economic growth through 'intensive' means. In ordinary Western terminology, this translates into growth through productivity gains and increased efficiencies. While in the past GDR economic growth had been achieved by expanding plant capacity and to some extent by mobilising more fully the potential labour force, growth was now to be accomplished while capital, labour and material inputs were simultaneously to be sharply constrained. In fact, these constraints were unavoidable, given the circumstances the GDR faced, and this was the only possible means of sustaining economic growth.

This general objective of growth through intensification was made rather precise by Günter Mittag at a 1983 conference of GDR economists when he said:

> We are dealing here with qualitatively new steps. These include, among others, the imperatives that the specific consumption of materials and energy per unit output must

Table 8.2: Annual average rates of growth: actual 1981-85 and target ranges 1986-90

	Actual 1981-85	Directive 1986-90
	Annual average rate of growth (%)	
Produced national income	4.4	4.4-4.7
Industrial commodity production:		
Economy as a whole	4.4	3.7-4.1
Within sphere of ministries	4.7	4.1-4.4
Construction output	3.4	3.4-3.7
Retail trade turnover	2.5	3.9-4.1

> decrease more rapidly than the rate of increase in production, that the increase in labour productivity [output in value per worker or per hour of labour] must be greater than the increase in produced value, and that labour productivity must increase faster than capital intensity [value of plant and equipment per worker]. ('Theoretische Verallgemeinerung der Erfahrungen der Entwicklung der Kombinate für die Leistungssteigerung in der Volkswirtschaft, insbesondere bei der Nutzung der qualitativen Faktoren des Wachstums', *Ökonomische Strategie der Partei — klares Konzept für weiteres Wachstum* (Dietz Verlag, East Berlin, 1983), p. 16.)

The basic, qualitative nature of the changes foreseen is projected in Figures 8.1 and 8.2 below.

This intensification-orientated strategy in a period of great pressure on the GDR economy pretty well dictated its investment policy for the 1980s. Indeed, unlike previous five-year plan periods, when investments increased roughly parallel to national income growth, the 1981-85 Plan directed an annual

Figure 8.1: Development of produced national income and of productive consumption (1975 = 100)

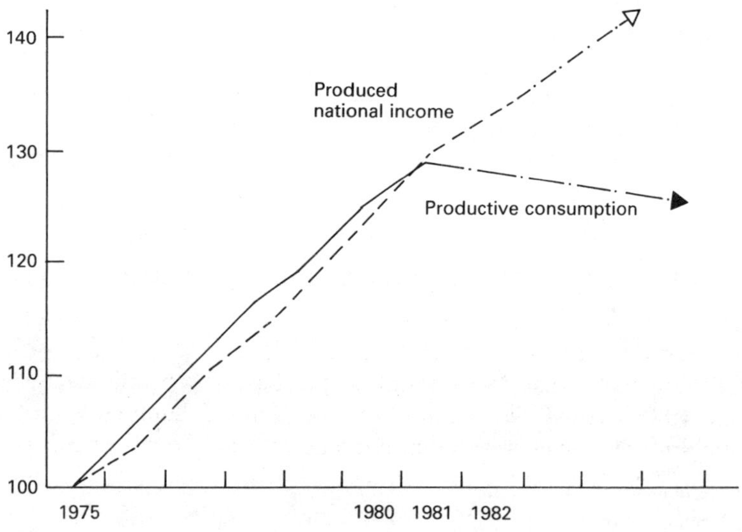

Source: *Ökonomische Strategie der Partei*, pp. 20-1.

Figure 8.2: Development of industrial commodity production and of consumption of economically important energy inputs, raw materials and materials within the sphere of the industrial ministries (1975 = 100)

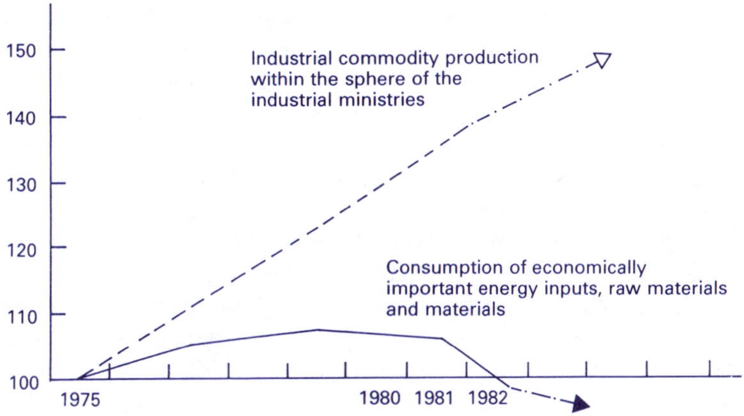

Source: *Ökonomische Strategie der Partei*, pp. 20-1.

decrease of approximately 2.1 per cent. Although this investment target was exceeded in fact, and (in 1980 prices) investment for both the 1976-80 and the 1981-85 years was roughly constant at approximately 264 billion marks in 1980 prices, this was still a far cry from the 3.7 per cent average annual increase for the earlier period (i.e. 1976-80).

The Draft Plan for 1986-90 calls for investment to total 346 billion marks, but in 1985 prices. This is about 27 billion marks more than that expended during 1981-85, in 1985 prices (*Milestones in the Development of an Advanced Socialist Society in the GDR: Facts and Figures.* Hereafter: *Facts and Figures.* Compiled by the Departments of the Central Committee of the SED and the Central Statistical Office of the GDR, April 1986, p. 44). Taking the actual 1985 result as the base (62.6 billion marks at 1985 prices), in relation to the planned cumulative total volume this gives an annual average rate of growth of 3.3 per cent. The snap on the investment purse has been opened somewhat, but the coming five years will still be a more parsimonious period than the heady days when investment levels totalled some 30 per cent of national income. This restrictive investment policy was not and is not supposed to lead to a slow-down in economic growth. Indeed, one GDR economist went so far as to argue:

> There is no historical evidence to prove that in the development of socialist planned economics the limitation of resources will necessarily result in negative consequences for economic growth. Much more to the point is the effort directed in the strategy to increase labour productivity, as well as to the tasks of planning and management. Our economic strategy for the 1980s, therefore, calls for a significant growth in labour productivity, and a comprehensive improvement in our overall efficiency and quality of output. Indeed, so long as productivity levels in CMEA economies lay significantly behind those found in leading capitalist countries, enormous reserves might well remain even as our labour productivity increases. (Steeger, 1982, p. 12)

In addition to the relative cut-back in investment outlays as a percentage of value produced, the GDR planners have also faced other severe constraints as they devised the specifics of their investment policy. For one thing, given its still precarious foreign trade position, the GDR has been forced to restrict its raw materials imports, although it is not a country rich in natural resources, and to make do with its domestic assets to the greatest extent possible. This has meant in practice that the extraction and refinement of lignite quality coal and potassium salts has had to be expanded, even though that has entailed even greater ratios of investment per unit value of output. Although GDR statistics in satisfactorily disaggregated form are difficult to obtain, it can still be said that an increasing percentage of all industrial investment has been committed to energy and fuels production: in 1975, the figure was 24 per cent; in 1980, it was 34 per cent; and, in 1985, a good 40 per cent.

Second, a significant slice of all investment (approximately 10-13 per cent) has been directed for the past ten years to the housing construction programme. (See Table 8.3. This percentage will be much higher when the necessary investment in building materials, water supply and long distance heating systems is included.) Since this programme will be completed only in 1990, since it has been heralded endlessly as the

Table 8.3: Investment in the GDR (excluding general repairs) by economic sector, 1961-85

Sectors of the economy	Five-year average										Structure			
	1961-65	1966-70	1971-75	1976-80	1980	1981	1982	1983	1984	1985	1960	1975	1980	1985
	Billion marks (1980 prices)										%			
Industry[a]	9.87	14.73	21.12	26.93	29.34	30.28	29.83	31.02	28.65	29.34	47.6	48.5	53.8	56.1
Construction	0.38	0.94	1.16	1.72	1.39	1.23	1.00	0.65	0.71	0.59	2.6	3.5	2.5	1.1
Agriculture and forestry	2.58	4.14	5.05	5.51	5.31	5.47	5.05	4.58	4.09	3.86	11.9	11.8	9.7	7.4
Transport, post and telecommunications	2.13	2.70	3.74	4.67	4.60	4.83	3.90	3.80	4.01	4.67	10.5	10.4	8.4	8.9
Domestic trade	0.66	1.54	1.44	1.91	1.65	1.49	1.30	1.23	1.33	1.47	2.8	3.6	3.0	2.8
Other producing sectors[b]	0.09	0.26	0.39	0.49	0.33	0.31	0.33	0.35	0.43	0.43	0.5	1.0	0.6	0.8
Non-producing sectors,	4.06	5.77	8.54	11.60	11.89	12.40	11.70	11.47	11.25	11.97	24.1	21.2	21.8	22.9
of which:														
New housing construction	2.31	2.30	3.51	5.21	5.79	6.15	5.87	6.21	6.28	6.76	13.6	9.0	10.6	12.9
Other non-producing sectors[c]	1.75	3.47	5.03	6.39	6.10	6.25	5.83	5.26	4.97	5.21	10.5	12.2	11.2	10.0
Total investment[d]	19.77	30.08	41.44	52.83	54.51	56.01	53.11	53.10	50.47	52.33	100.0	100.0	100.0	100.0

Notes: a. Including productive handicrafts (excluding building handicrafts); b. Organs of economic management and institutes of all producing sectors, projecting and computing enterprises, publishing houses, domestic repair combines, textile cleaners; c. Education, culture and the arts, health and social security, sport and tourism, services sector, state administration and state organs as well as social organisations; d. Discrepancies in the totals because of rounding of numbers.

Sources: *Statistische Jahrbücher der DDR; Statistisches Taschenbuch der DDR* (1986).

cornerstone of GDR social policy, and since it obviously has great popular appeal, this investment commitment is as good as set in stone, to the detriment of other possible investment options.

Third, a significant portion of the remaining investment capacity has been directed to the further modernisation of the transportation and communications network. For example, the current five-year plan calls for the electrification of a further 1,500 kilometres of the country's railway network, an increase of over 50 per cent above the 925 kilometres that were added during the years 1981-85.

Finally, investment has been directed preferentially to key technologies and processes such as computer manufacture, bio-technologies, and micro-technology. The 1986-90 plan, for example, calls for a five-fold increase in semi-conductor production, a 3.5-fold increase in 'computer power', and a three-fold increase in the production of bio-technological substances. (For authoritative information and discussion of GDR investment policy and its implications see: *Neues Deutschland*, 10-11 November 1979, p. 3; *Verordnung über die Duchführung von Investitionen, GBL der DDR*, 1980, Part 1, pp. 107 ff.; *Zweite Verordnung . . ., GBL der DDR*, 1980, Part 1, pp. 15-16; *Dritte Verordnung . . ., GBL der DDR*, 1981, Part 1, pp. 375 ff.; Ebert, E. and Opel, G. in *Einheit*, April 1982, pp. 424 ff.)

When one takes all these factors into account, the investment resources left over are meagre, and the strategy for those sectors of the economy not favoured by special status is essentially the following set of elements: existing capacity is to be utilised better and more efficiently; investment is to be concentrated on modernisation of existing plant, rather than on new construction; producing units are to cut back on the retirement of obsolete or obsolescent equipment, to repair, modernise and/or renovate existing machinery and to use it more intensively through greater reliance on shift work; and investment for expansionary purposes, where absolutely essential, is to be concentrated on relatively few projects so that added capacity can be brought into production with maximum speed.

In the face of these guidelines, and given the paucity of resources, rationalisation of existing plant by a variety of means has been seen as the only option available (Melzer, 1978, pp. 29-48). By remodelling or reconstructing existing plant, savings of the order of 40 to 50 per cent have been foreseen, at least in the most ideal of cases, as against the costs of new construction.

Particularly great emphasis has been placed on intra-enterprise and *Kombinat* rationalisation (Haker, 1983, pp. 18-19; Rind, 1985, pp. 11 ff. and 21 ff.). That is, more efficient means of production are to be conceived at the production level itself, spurred where possible by the introduction of ultra-modern technologies in key places, but while also using mostly the equipment on hand, or at most by adding a new machine only where necessary (Gerisch, Rosenkranz and Siefert, 1983, pp. 823 ff.). The advantages thus achieved are also to be compounded by stretching production time to a second and/or third shift of work. Of course, a part of this strategy has been the effort to improve the repair and maintenance facilities and practices, and so to reduce the 'down time' within the enterprise.

The intended transformation of existing plant is to take place in three stages or at three levels: the modernisation of individual machines; the linking together of modernised machinery through the installation of automised sub-processes at strategic points in the larger production cycle (working place automisation); and the joining together of modernised machinery into automised processes (process automisation) (Hinkel and Langendorf, 1985, p. 630).

Initially, the use of robots was the most publicised means of making these linkages. Each robot was to replace two or three workers on the average, and the 1981-85 plan called for the building and installation of some 40-45,000 of them. In fact, the plan was over-fulfilled, but it is also well to remember that in GDR usage the term 'robot' implies much less in the way of performance capabilities than in the West, and that of the 50,000 or so said to be presently in use, perhaps only 3,000-4,500 would measure up to the more stringent criteria of the non-socialist world. Also, since most of the robots are produced where they subsequently are used, it seems almost certain that they are typically rather simple in design and capacity. Even so, they continue to be seen as key to further rationalisation, and the current five-year plan calls for the building and introduction of an additional 70-80,000 of them.

More recently, computer-aided design and manufacture (CAD/CAM) has taken on great importance in GDR calculations. As of April 1986, some 11,200 CAD/CAM stations were said to be in place, twice the number in operation 'just a few months before'. By 1990, 85-90,000 are to be embedded in the production process (*Facts and Figures*, p. 34).

When comprehensive internally designed rationalisations are the order of the day, the matter of capacity to execute the task becomes immediately apparent. Fundamental to the strategy in the minds of GDR planners is the fact that some *Kombinate* are very large units (50-75,000 employees), with great resources that can be concentrated or dispersed at will, especially when aided by the research and development capabilities of the research specialists affiliated with the Academy of Sciences and GDR universities and *Hochschule.* Such units (i.e. the *Kombinate*) are thought to be large enough to create special units or even entire factories to which the tasks of devising and executing rationalisations can be assigned. Smaller projects have also been encouraged, to be executed by individual producing units themselves.

When one looks for successful results with rationalisations and more generally with intensification as a whole, one is struck by the extent to which they have been achieved through the elimination of waste and/or the reduction of factor inputs per unit output. Data on basic raw materials and energy usage, for example, show that these inputs per unit output have declined at an average annual rate of 5.3 per cent since 1981, and in absolute terms their usage has increased by only 9.6 per cent over that same time frame. Figure 8.3 below displays these trends.

Beyond these comparatively reliable figures, evidence of successful intensification is not so readily at hand. To be sure, according to official sources, only 40 per cent of the 1981-85 national income growth is to be attributed to savings in consumption of factor inputs, leaving 60 per cent to other causes. Some truth must rest with this assertion, for there have clearly been technological breakthroughs (e.g. the development of improved crude oil cracking processes). Moreover, the introduction of robots, computers and the thousands of new (and presumably better) products must also have been salutory, at least to a degree.

Nevertheless, pricing, quality determination and the designation of products as 'new' are all administrative decisions, and in such circumstances both technical difficulties and parochial interests have doubtless promoted some mischief in the sense of exaggerating accomplishments. Both common sense and a good bit of available evidence suggest that such has been the case, and the proper conclusion is most probably that the dynamic

Figure 8.3: National income and productive consumption (1975 = 100)

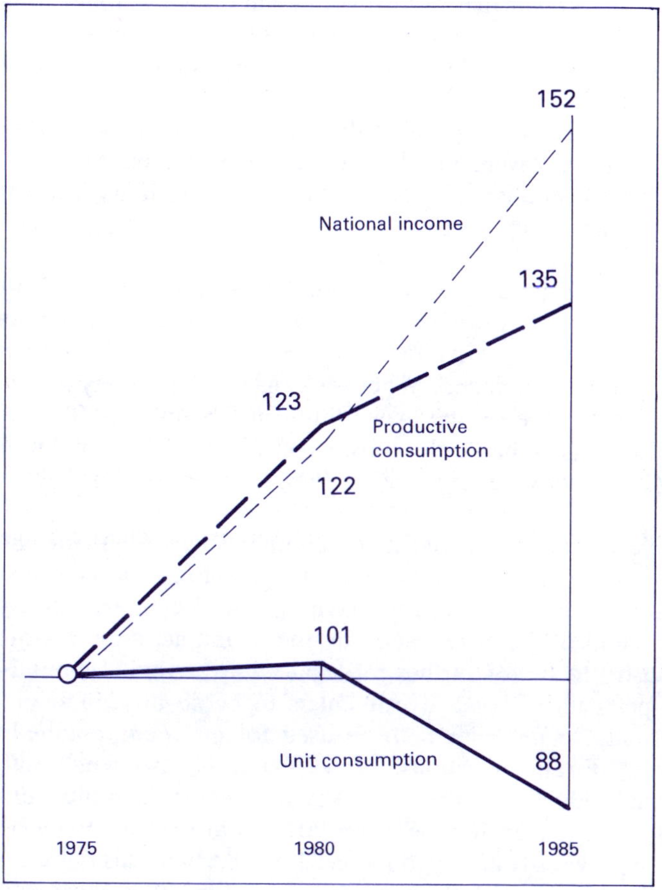

Source: *Facts and Figures*, p. 40.

elements of intensification have lagged behind the passive ones.

A simple way of putting this is that intensification has resulted more from shortening skirts, reducing wall thicknesses and/or thinning brandy, than from the more efficient production of newer and better fabrics, bricks or spirits. In addition, the very concept of rationalisation itself implies real limits as to the degree of transformation that can be achieved. As one GDR expert puts it: 'It is hardly possible to construct a nuclear power plant by means of reconstructing a power plant driven by coal energy' (Langendorf, 1983, p. 768). The same limits are obviously also present in the rationalisation of the GDR auto plant that produces Trabants. The 'Trabbie', despite a new tail-light or horn, and despite the greater speed with which it is now produced, remains a remarkably primitive automobile.[4]

There can be no question that the GDR planners understand this point very well, and that they are seeking means to solve the problem it implies. Politburo member Mittag himself has been very direct on the matter:

> It makes little sense to utilise the time [and/or resources] saved through rationalisations to produce already outmoded products in greater quantities, products for which there is little or no demand. Whoever is interested merely in finding ways to save on the expenditure of labour or to free superfluous jobs has only considered the first half of his task. (*Ökonomische Strategie der Partei*, note 6, p. 82)

Nevertheless, rationalisation continues to be a major part of the intensification strategy, even if it is no longer its centrepiece. The plan for 1986-90, for example, calls for approximately 80 per cent of all investment in the manufacturing sectors of industry to be for further rationalisations; overall, about 50 to 55 per cent of total investment is to be so used, and of that amount, 25 per cent is to be used for internally planned and executed rationalisations. However, it is also true that the annual reductions in fuel and key raw materials inputs per unit output projected for the 1986-90 plan are substantially below those previously achieved for 1981-85. Perhaps this is partly due to the fact that GDR planners understand that skirts can be shortened only so much, walls can be made only so thin and brandy only so weak before further 'savings' become plainly dysfunctional. Hence the need for '*Höhere Veredlung*', to which we now turn.

HÖHERE VEREDLUNG: STRATEGY AND METHOD

Höhere Veredlung has rather consistently been identified as the key to success in the present phase of the GDR's strategy for comprehensive intensification. For example, a recent authoritative GDR publication on the topic begins its didactic presentation as follows:

> We have begun a new phase in the realisation of our economic strategy in which we have set our goal as sustained, long-term, comprehensive intensification. As was made clear at the 9th Plenum of the Central Committee, we must now take a qualitatively new step towards the greater refinement and transformation of products and production in the years immediately ahead. (Jurk *et. al.*, 1985, p. 8)

When one examines the full range of the discussion on this topic, it becomes clear that much that is being said is but a repackaging of previous themes, the most simplistic of which was the slogan of several years ago: 'From less, produce more!'[5] In fact, this should not be surprising, for the objective has always been higher productivity in all its forms and manifestations.

However, *Höhere Veredlung* does have unique elements, and new measures, norms and procedures have been established to direct the economy along this path of development. The just-cited brochure provides a rather precise definition of the term:

> *Höhere Veredlung* means the production of goods having better or higher quality, and thereby the achievement of additional new value. Products so manufactured are in demand. They are purchased with satisfaction in the GDR itself, and/or are sold for favourable prices on the international market. *Höhere Veredlung* should achieve an increasing economic effect in two ways: first, through a significant improvement in the utility of a given type of product; and second, through a reduction of the previously used materials and energy for the old product, as measured through the entire production process, beginning with the recovery of raw materials. (*Höhere Veredlung*, p. 8)

The goal of *Höhere Veredlung* is to be achieved by a series of somewhat more specific tasks: the securing of a high rate of product and production renewal; a much increased production of new, high-value, durable consumer goods, above all from production by the metal processing industry; an over-achievement of the targets for export, brought about mostly by a higher percentage of new products; the securing of a thoroughgoing, high product quality; a reduction of consumption of factor inputs in the production process; savings in crucial raw materials, energy and other material inputs; and an increasing pace in the installation and use of key technologies such as micro-electronics and robots, thus to increase labour productivity decisively, and to achieve the more effective use of capital goods and investment (ibid., p. 27).

Given the high expectations or even demands implied by this thrust towards product and process renewal, and given the restricted investment resources available, GDR planners decided that the methods and procedures for reaching investment decisions (which had already been sharpened in 1981) were once more to be substantially revised. The results were put into place in September 1985.

The new regulations were to ensure that investments would result in greater efficiencies through the introduction of the newest possible technologies, as well as reductions in labour inputs and the timespan during which investment projects were to be completed (within two years). Serious attention was to be directed towards the question whether the purposes of the project might not be met more cheaply and quickly through rationalisation and modernisation of existing capacity. In addition, a proper ratio between the outlays for construction and equipment was to be achieved, while, simultaneously, it was also imperative that the projected costs should not be overrun. To that end, state controls (e.g. through the Central Inspectorate for Investment) were strengthened. In particular, each project was to be worked out in all its details and parameters, and when finally executed (after proper approvals of course) those elements were to be strictly observed. Before a project could be started, however, it required specific prior central approval. Only then would it be incorporated into the planning process (*Verordnung über die Vorbereitung von Investitionen, GBL. der DDR*, 1985, Part 1, pp. 197 ff.; *Zweite Durchführungsbestimmung zur Verordnung . . ., GBL. der DDR*, 1985, Part 1, pp. 205 ff.).

The current five-year plan includes many norms and/or targets that are intended to bring about *Höhere Veredlung*, some of which have already been noted. But in addition to the targets for such new technologies as robots and computers, for such basic processes as crude oil refinement or coal gasification, for productivity gains, or for reductions in factor inputs per unit output, or even outlays for science and technology, two additional stipulations in the plan are of special interest here.

1. The annual 'renewal (or innovation) rate of production' is to be 'over 30 per cent by value' by 1990; in the consumer goods sector, it is to be 30 to 40 per cent, and in the special area of young people's fashions, it is to reach the astonishing level of 70 per cent. At first glance, this mandated annual renewal rate of production seems extremely high, and perhaps unrealistic; one might even infer that over three to five years the entire range of GDR products is to be renewed. In fact, however, nothing so grandiose is foreseen, for the operationalisation of this term has made the 30 per cent figure quite achievable, even if the economy performs about as it has in the recent past. It is worth noting that the renewal rate for 1985 was already 27.5 per cent according to official reports. For one thing, both the value produced by new processes and the value of new products are to 'count' towards the 30 per cent. Moreover, although our evidence here is from interviews rather than published sources, products and processes may be considered 'new' for up to 24 months after their first appearance or use, a practice that is justified with the consideration that peak production typically cannot be reached until a period of time has elapsed. Finally, new products and processes are weighted advantageously by assigning them higher prices than those previously in effect for the replaced items.

2. In addition to the annual renewal rate, the current five-year plan stipulates that 15-16,000 new products are to be in production by 1990, of which at least 60 per cent are to match the best comparable products on the world market. We have no easy means of determining the significance of the figure (e.g. its size as a percentage of all products produced in the GDR) though we can probably safely assume that some 'new' products will be only slight modifications of the goods they replace, a point to which we will return below.

Beside the plan based norms we have already considered, *Kombinate* are also now required to develop a comprehensive strategy for the refinement and transformation of their respective product profiles, and to incorporate this strategy for *Höhere Veredlung* into their planning mechanisms. Such plans are to include the following information: the basis and goal of the *Kombinat*'s refinement programme; the usage of science and technology to raise effectiveness; the ways key technologies will be used to speed up labour productivity advances; the implementation of new technologies foreseen to reduce energy and material consumption, including reductions in the production of semi-finished products; modifications expected in production and export structure to ensure steady product renewal, qualitative improvement, and increased profitability; projected development of durable consumer goods production for both domestic sales and for export; planned plant and equipment modernisation and improved investment effectiveness; increased utilisation of the qualitative factors of social (public) wealth; planned territorial distribution of production and its rationalisation, planned reductions in transport costs; and planned reductions in the share of gross domestic product taken up by costs of production, expected cost reductions and improvements in factor input to value output ratios (*Höhere Veredlung*, pp. 43-4). It seems obvious that the directorates of the GDR producing units will be forced by these norms and obligations to take *Höhere Veredlung* seriously.[6] Whether their responses will be to innovate or to give the mere appearance of innovating is less certain.

Höhere veredlung evaluated

We noted earlier that in our view the *Höhere Veredlung* programme is not likely to bring about a breakthrough towards a comprehensive upgrading and transformation of GDR technology,[7] manufacturing processes and products, though GDR planners have correctly identified this objective as critical to long-term successful economic performance. On the other hand, some success is very likely, at least to the extent that the GDR, technologically speaking, will remain in step with worldwide developments, but some distance behind the most advanced Western economies. We conclude with the reasons for this assessment.

First and most obviously, the investment resources available are simply not great enough for the task ahead. To be sure, in gross terms investment is planned to equal almost 25 per cent of GDR national income for the next five years, a still relatively high figure compared with Western industrialised states, even if it is well below the 30+ per cent levels of the 1970s. The problem lies with the level of need for investment. On the one hand, investment needs for securing the stable supply of energy and key domestic raw materials are growing markedly, as we noted earlier. But on the other hand, most or all technologies and products are admittedly obsolete or outmoded to some degree, and hence are seen (no doubt often correctly) as susceptible to real improvement through rationalisation. That is the irony of the rationalisation strategy: it is in fact an admission that nearly every process could be more efficient. To the extent that this proposition is true, and everyday experience in the GDR suggests repeatedly that in the main it is, GDR investment needs are enormously greater as a ratio to its productive capacity than those, for example, needed in the Federal Republic or the US. Thus, even assuming that GDR investment is now effectively and efficiently undertaken, one cannot conclude from the fact that its investment levels are as high as those in the West that GDR activity here is similarly adequate to its needs.

The second point follows from the first: because investment resources are so limited, GDR planners have opted for an investment strategy based heavily on the reorganisation and modernisation of existing plant, to a considerable extent by internally executed rationalisations. This rationalisation orientated strategy implies far-reaching consequences for the evolving characteristics of GDR capital assets. Expansion of new capital will be slow and the retirement of old equipment from production will be retarded.[8] It is indisputable that such plant and equipment is and will be relatively inefficient, susceptible to more frequent breakdowns and higher maintenance costs, and less capable of producing precision products.

Thus, it seems most unlikely that seeking *Höhere Veredlung* while retarding the growth of new capital will succeed over a period of time. The GDR economy needs both new plant and equipment, as well as more rational and efficient principles for organisation and operation. Only where old plant has been grossly misused is it likely to be significantly improvable, even with a robot here and a CAD/CAM station there.

The GDR apologist would here urge the importance of the 'scientific and technological revolution' and the efforts now being made in this area to harness that revolution for fruitful ends in both social and economic terms. There is considerable merit to this argument, for the GDR expends an amount equalling about 4 per cent of its national income on science and technology. Its research and development work force includes nearly 200,000 people, or 6 to 7 per cent of its labour force, and it has recently reorganised the research community so as to link it more directly with the production process.

On the other hand, there are some very significant negative implications built into the GDR's strategy to exploit the marvels of science and technology. For one thing, the entire environment in which *Kombinat* leadership must operate (and one suspects the same is true for researchers at the Academy of Sciences and in the universities) is one of great pressure from the centre, applied through the administrative directive. In addition, the achievements mandated are to be accomplished despite very short supplies of resources, and relatively little flexibility in their allocation and/or use. That is, the Directors General of combines are greatly limited in the range of their possible decisions to invest, to hire or release employees, or to use a different mix of material inputs.

These two factors, i.e. the predominance of centrally imposed administrative levers as the means of obtaining desired goals, and the almost exclusive use of the stick at the expense of the carrot, are likely to induce undesirable responses at the production level, first because real achievements have been made so difficult to realise, and second, because administratively measured successes can be recorded at the operational level by administrative means, even if the economic benefits are negligible.

To illustrate, the thrust of the entire GDR economic strategy is to induce change and/or innovation, but to do so without taking risks. Producing units are required to achieve results with limited rations, and their leaders can hardly take chances on schemes that might turn sour or end up failures. The combines *must* fulfil their annual plans, and their control over R&D efforts will necessarily be exercised to meet that first imperative.

Of course, GDR authorities speak of 'willingness to take risks' in a most laudatory fashion, and an occasional expert will even go so far as to argue that failures in R&D work can sometimes be more useful in the ongoing process of scientific progress than successes with only short-term impact.[9] Nevertheless, the reality seems still to be quite different: develop new technologies and products, but only when enough is known from prior achievements in the West, to make certain that the risk is minimal!

As to the matter of 'administrative' plan-fulfilment, it is clear that the results with *Höhere Veredlung* will turn significantly on the specific (administrative) decisions that 'newness' has been achieved, and on the determination of how broadly that newness can be spread over affected but existing production systems. To take an extreme case, if a new process is developed to produce a windscreen wiper, should the value of the entire auto be booked as 'new?' Or, if glass rather than plastic is fed into an existing process to make a 'new' tail-light, are we again to count the entire auto as 'new?' In these cases, the answer would certainly be a resounding: 'No!' Nevertheless, seeking generous definitions of newness and inclusive methods of allocating affected value will almost certainly be the typical strategies of producing units as they strive to fulfil their plans as effortlessly as possible. And such strategies will sometimes succeed, for the producers have the superior fund of relevant knowledge about the 'new' product or process.

This may seem to be a rather gloomy assessment, and it may well be appropriate to stress in closing that predicting GDR success in this regard depends significantly on the criteria used in measuring it. For example, we noted earlier in a negative context that producing more Trabants is hardly an indication of successful progress towards product and process renewal. On the other hand, a GDR citizen waiting for his/her name to arrive at the top of the list of those who have ordered a Trabbie might well see the situation differently; at least the car will be his or hers several months sooner.

Putting this point more generally, the production of more and sometimes better products, even if they often remain below world market levels, will doubtless help relieve the high demand pressures of GDR consumers. That, in turn, will play a positive role in further securing the political stability and support of the citizenry, and it will also fulfil the pledge of the party leaders to improve the well-being of their people. It would be difficult not to see that as success of a sort.

NOTES

1. The key documents for the two congresses are as follows: For the 10th, *Bericht des Zentralkomitees der Sozialistischen Einheitspartei Deutschlands an den X. Parteitag der SED* (Dietz Verlag, East Berlin, 1981); *Direktive des Parteitages der SED für die Entwicklung der*

Volkswirtschaft der DDR in den Jahren 1981 bis 1985 (Dietz Verlag, East Berlin, 1981). For the 11th, *Bericht des Zentralkomitees der Sozialistischen Einheitspartei Deutschlands an den XI. Parteitag der SED* (Dietz Verlag, East Berlin, 1986); *Direktive des Parteitages der SED zum Fünfjahrplan für die Entwicklung der Volkswirtschaft der DDR in den Jahren 1986 bis 1990* (Dietz Verlag, East Berlin, 1986). When cited hereafter, they will be called: *Bericht X. or XI.*, and/or *Direktive X.* or *XI.*

2. The claim that the economy is 'flexible' seems particularly dubious, though, as noted, Honecker's general satisfaction was not without a basis in performance.

3. See, for example, General Secretary Gorbachev's comment: 'Today, the prime task of the [Soviet] Party and the entire people is to reverse resolutely the unfavourable tendencies in the development of the economy, to impart to it the due dynamism and to give scope to the initiative and creativity of the masses, to truly revolutionary change' (*Political Report of the CPSU Central Committee to the 27th Party Congress* (Novosti Press Agency Publishing House, Moscow, 1986), p. 31).

4. Despite the fact the *IFA-Kombinat Personenkraftwagen, Karl-Marx Stadt* produces and continues to produce the obsolete and inefficient 'Trabbie', it was cited by Günter Mittag at the 1986 Seminar of *Kombinat* Directors General in Leipzig as one of those *Kombinate* that over-fulfilled their obligations for the achievement of additional internally constructed rationalisations. See: *Mit qualitativ neuen Schritten zu höchsten Leistungen: Seminar des Zentralkomitees der SED mit den Generaldirektoren der Kombinate und den Parteiorganisatoren des ZK am 13. und 14. März 1986 in Leipzig* (Dietz Verlag, East Berlin, 1986) p. 25.

5. The reader need not think that he or she is the first to carry this slogan to its extreme: 'From nothing, produce everything!' East Germans also have a sense of irony.

6. Thus, they have to express their efforts relating to product and process renewal in the form of 40 plan indicators, which are to be checked twice a year. As these efforts cannot be planned with great accuracy, however, combines are allowed to make changes within their concepts when this is necessary.

7. For a cogent and balanced consideration of GDR technological progress and prospects for the immediate future see: Krakat, K., in *FS-Analysen* (1986), no. 2, pp. 39-54.

8. It should be noted that the growth of total fixed assets was not much lower in the first half of the 1980s than in the second half of the 1970s, in spite of retarded investment. The reasons are obvious: less retirement of old capacities and reduction in the amount of 'unfinished investment' by speeding up the completion of projects.

9. See, for example, the interview in the GDR weekly *Wochenpost*, 2 August 1985, given by the then GDR economist Harry Maier. In 'Wissen und Zeit gewinnen', pp. 16-17.

9

The Pricing System of the GDR: Principles and Problems

Manfred Melzer

In recent years the pricing system of the GDR has, for a number of reasons, become more and more of a problem. The mid-1970s saw sharp increases in the cost of energy and raw materials within Comecon. This forced the economic leadership to amend domestic prices, a restructuring necessary in order to provide adequate stimuli to economise on these inputs. Increases in current prices at different production stages were implemented, but these changes, on an almost annual basis, were not able to eliminate the distortions in price relationships.

As far as planning and plan accounting are concerned, constant value relations over a number of years are needed to enable comparisons to be made between plan targets and actual achievements. On the other hand, price distortions deny a meaningful measurement of efficiency for different outputs. It would seem to be important, therefore, to ask the question as to whether or not there are signs of an improved pricing policy.

THE FUNCTIONS OF PRICES

In market economies the price system equates supply and demand, provided there is effective competition. This co-ordinating mechanism provides the economic units (firms and private households) with information about profitable output and beneficial goods supply. In a planned economy the central plan replaces the price system as the output co-ordinating principle. Since, of course, planning cannot be all-embracing, central goals must also be implemented by means of indirect steering instruments (economic levers, such as prices, taxes, credits, interest rates and bonuses). In this connection, prices assume an important role, making possible, for example, both the expression of certain plan magnitudes and the comparison of different performances in value terms. But prices also play an important incentive role. In conjunction with other economic levers (such as net profit and its use) they are employed to promote certain goals (for example, price increases to encourage the economical utilisation of materials, and differentiated, temporary profit supplements to stimulate the development of new products). Prices are, in principle, both the *subject* of planning (i.e. they help to determine the size of plan tasks, so that, in general, they must be fixed by state authorities) and the *instrument* for the implementation of plan goals (in this respect, however, the degree to which it is possible to harmonise prices with plan goals is problematical).

In theory, a centrally planned economy would produce a set of optimal prices, provided that, for the plan period, they reflected the relative scarcity of the goods conforming with plan goals. The 'model of optimal planning' developed by Novozhilov and Kantorovich attempts to derive 'shadow prices', by means of appropriate matrix operations, from the alignment of state plan goals (as demand) with the given production conditions and resources. In reality it has not, however, proved possible to determine, even approximately, shadow prices which are able to equate supply and demand. It seemed expedient, therefore, as a second best and practical way as it were, to fix prices on the basis of 'economically necessary expenditure' (*volkswirtschaftlich erforderlicher Aufwand*). In this connection, the question of how certain attribution problems (such as those of determining the necessary expenditure, imputing profit, or reducing individual enterprise to socially necessary costs) are solved is not of prime importance, since there remains, in any case, the decisive advantage of a *rational measuring function of prices.* For micro- and macro-economic decisions, the costs arising can, in each case, be used as an orientational yardstick.

The problem is that the socialist state does not want to gauge the costs of its (in part politically determined) goals by this yardstick alone, whilst in a number of cases it debars the calculation of expenditure-equalising prices altogether. But, in consequence, the state finds itself in the dilemma of having to sacrifice to state objectives the primacy of seeking in principle to achieve expenditure-equal prices.

An important example of prices not being equal in expenditure terms is the price differentiation of consumer goods on social grounds. For years the prices of a range of basic foodstuffs (e.g. bread, potatoes, fish, meat and bakery products), children's clothing and certain services (such as housing, public transport, laundry and hairdressing) have been deliberately sold below production costs. These highly subsidised goods and services contrast with luxuries such as television sets, cars, washing machines, refrigerators and cameras, which are burdened with high, product-related levies. Prices here exercise a certain *distribution* function, the aim being that of redistributing income, in some degree, to low-income groups.

Insofar as the *stimulation* function of prices is concerned, which has already been touched upon, from the mid-1970s to the end of 1983 it was considered expedient to orientate price formation for new and further developed products towards the improvement of use values (price–performance relationship). This, however, amounted to the abandonment of purely cost-related price formation.

Finally, it should be pointed out that the attempts to ensure that domestic prices reflected the worldwide increases in raw material and energy costs, in order to secure savings, brought disadvantages for planning. For, as a consequence, the prices used in plan calculation became fictitious, in the sense that real value relationships were clearly at variance with the *function of prices as an instrument of planning and calculation.* Thus, neither the plan prices of 1975 (for the period 1976-80) nor the plan prices of 1980 (for the period 1981-85) were able to take into account the changes in price relationships which had occurred within these plan periods. In the present (1986-90) five-year plan, too, it is proving possible only to a limited degree to compare attained performances with plan values. In plan calculation, various price bases have to be compared and these can often only be linked together by means of crude conversion keys: this again seriously impairs the clarity of planning.

As long as the prices of individual goods can be seen neither as a measuring rod of necessary economic expenditure nor as expressing the urgency of demand as reflected in the plan, a planning directed towards anything approaching optimal efficiency is simply not possible, lacking as it does a yardstick for the degree of economic efficiency of the various sorts of output.

Figure 9.1 illustrates the types of prices in use today, differing according to the number of elements they contain and the functions they perform. Unlike the wholesale and retail selling prices for consumer goods, industrial transactions are made at what are known as industry prices. These are the 'enterprise price' (*Betriebspreis*, which comprises calculable costs plus the planned profit allowable under the prevailing calculation regulations) and the 'industry price' (*Industrieabgabepreis*: enterprise price plus product-related levy minus product-related subsidy). Since no product-related levy is generally payable on capital goods, the enterprise and industry price are the same for them.

HISTORICAL REVIEW

An important element in the reforming endeavours of the NES was the re-setting, in the period 1964-67, of all industrial prices on the basis of the estimated costs of 1967. With the creation of 'cost correct' prices, and thus of economically justifiable measuring rods of value, a significant portion of the substantial price distortions was intended to be eliminated. The old prices[1] were mostly still based on 1944 prices, thus promoting the wasteful use of low-priced (heavily subsidised) raw materials, encouraging one-sided assortment structures, and hindering technical progress (since, given the price distortions, it was not possible to determine the efficiency expected from new goods and technologies).

The reforms began with the revaluation of the gross fixed capital stock of industry in mid-1963 at 1962 replacement prices. In 1964 the previously low depreciation rates were raised, on the basis of the revalued capital stock. The new depreciation rates were incorporated in the new values of the price reform.

The industrial price reform took place in three stages: first raw materials and materials, then semi-manufactures and, finally, finished products. The first two stages affected a production volume of 50 billion marks, the average price increases being 70 per cent and 40 per cent respectively. The third stage involved a volume of 100 billion marks, the average price increase amounting to 4 per cent. Rises in the prices of consumer goods were ruled out.

Figure 9.1: The price structure of capital and consumer goods

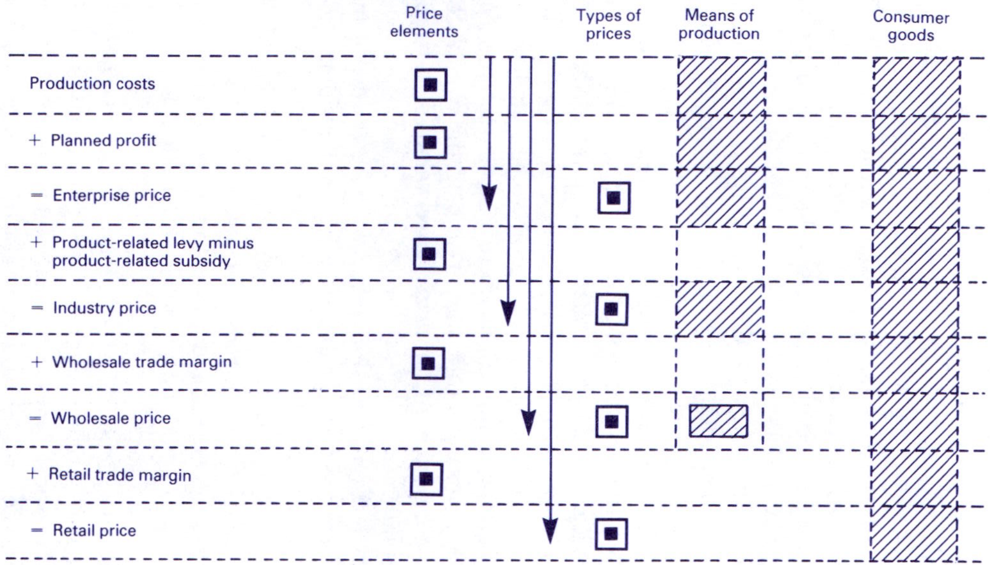

Source: **Lexikon der Wirtschaft–Preise** (East Berlin, 1979), p. 175.

Although the industrial price reform noticeably improved price relationships and markedly reduced state subsidies, the new prices still exhibited considerable deficiencies. These included estimation errors resulting from the taking of estimated average values of manufacturing costs in 1967 and the use of conversion coefficients for raw material groups, and insufficient allowance for capital costs (since interest rates were not considered at all and depreciation rates were once again incorrectly set so that, by 1967, the 1962 value yardsticks employed in the revaluation of the capital stock were already out of date). Moreover, the prices created by the industrial price reform took account of neither the given scarcity relationships in the GDR nor the urgency of demand.

In the last few years of the NES period, 1968-70, three interesting pricing policy measures were taken to overcome some of the price deficiencies already mentioned:

(1) The introduction of the 'capital-related price type' (*fondsbezogener Preistyp*), which was meant to take account of the 'economically necessary capital expenditure' in the price, as measured in terms of the capital utilisation of the most efficient enterprise in a product group. The profit to be calculated in the price was fixed at a maximum of 18 per cent of this capital expenditure; from this profit was to be paid the capital charge (6 per cent per annum of the *actual* gross value of all fixed and working capital).[2]

(2) The creation of *price dynamisation measures*, by means of which price falls were meant to be triggered automatically as cost reductions occurred in the course of time.[3] For new and further developed products a price degression was established,[4] which was designed to bring about increased profit at first, then continual price and profit reductions to the manufacturer of the particular product, and, finally, when the product became technically obsolete, losses.[5]

(3) The introduction of *differentiated price forms* in order to achieve greater flexibility in price formation. In addition to the former fixed prices which obtained almost universally, maximum and agreed prices were now also introduced. Maximum prices, which could be undercut, were, above all, for consumer goods and for products subject to rapid technical development. Agreed prices are those which are allowed to be freely agreed between producers and purchasers without confirmation by price organs (especially for special and one-off products, special

machines and research services).

Until the recentralisation of the economic system at the end of 1970, a third of production had already been converted to capital-related prices; with the remaining (mostly capital-intensive) output price increases would have been necessary. Hoped-for price reductions via price dynamisation measures did not occur; instead there were price increases. Efficient enterprises were amongst those that preferred, even in the case of savings, a cost calculation at the previous level, so as to finance investment inconspicuously. With regard to price degression, the enterprises cited rising prices of raw materials, materials and of semi-finished products, carrying out product alterations before they found themselves in the area of price degression at all.

With the dismantling of the NES at the end of 1970, the price dynamisation measures were scrapped, the conversion to further capital-related prices was interrupted and a general price freeze introduced. For new and further developed products a very complex and bureaucratic price formation procedure was established, which conferred important rights upon leading central organs (e.g. the Council of Ministers and the Office for Prices). At the same time, all consumer goods prices were 'frozen' and a generally applicable calculation guideline introduced.

The price defects, reduced through the industrial price reform, increased markedly once again. While prices were nominally constant, shifts in the value relationships between goods caused by continuous cost changes remained hidden. Price increases via product alterations (when cheaper goods disappeared from assortments and were replaced by more expensive, new, altered products) likewise remained concealed. Thus, prices from the industrial price reform stood side by side with capital-related and newly calculated prices.[6]

NOTES

1. Before 1964 the prices of important raw materials were well below production costs, which necessitated substantial state subsidies. Thus, for example, the prices of products such as coal, gas, electricity, timber, iron, building stone and roofing tiles only covered 45 to 60 per cent of the effective production costs. In contrast, some consumer goods bore heavy taxes in the form of product-related levies.

2. Since the price only took into consideration the 'optimal' capital input and the 'most favourable' level of stocks, while the capital charge was imposed on the *actual* capital expenditure, the enterprise could maximise net profit, with given manufacturing costs, only by improving its utilisation of capital.

3. In this case enterprises were allowed to deduct in full from the net profit deduction to be paid to the state the profit losses arising from the price reductions.

4. The price degression was aligned with the period of the 'economic life' of the product (i.e. the probable period of saleability).

5. Theoretically it can be argued against both methods that they perpetuate price distortions and incorrect price relationships in so far as these had arisen through the valuation of the fixed capital assets data (as a reference point for the calculation of permissible profit) at 1962 prices (which still applied before the industrial price reform).

6. Due to a serious illness, Manfred Melzer was unable to complete the final section of this chapter in time for publication. Interested readers are welcome to apply to Dr Melzer for the final section.

10

The GDR Financial System

Hannsjörg F. Buck

In the centrally planned economy of the GDR the financial system acts as an agent for the implementation of state policies, which have priority over the interests of private households and enterprise management and workforces. The 'unitary state financial system' (*einheitliches staatliches Finanzsystem*) embraces considerably more fields of activity relating to financial policy than that, for example, of the 'public financial system' (*öffentliches Finanzsystem*) of the Federal Republic. In consequence of the rapid expansion of the state sector of the economy at the end of the 1940s and during the 1950s, a private financial sector of the economy of any significance could not develop. All the existing institutions concerned with finance, money and credit (for example, banks, savings banks and insurance companies) became components of the state sector. Accordingly, the 'enterprise finances' (*Betriebsfinanzen*) of the state-owned producer organisations also belong to the public financial sector of the economy, reinforced by their close links with the state budget. Budgetary revenue and expenditure, the enterprise finances of socialist economic organisations and the financial transactions of banks and state insurance institutions have been merged into one 'unitary socialist financial system'. This is illustrated in Figure 10.1.

The GDR financial system is divided into two sectors: centralised state finances and the decentralised finances of socialist enterprises and combines.

The sector of centralised state finances comprises the components listed below:

(1) The budgets of the central state (republic) and territorial administrations at the county (*Bezirk*), district (*Kreis*) and

Figure 10.1: Basic functions of financial policy and the financial system in the GDR

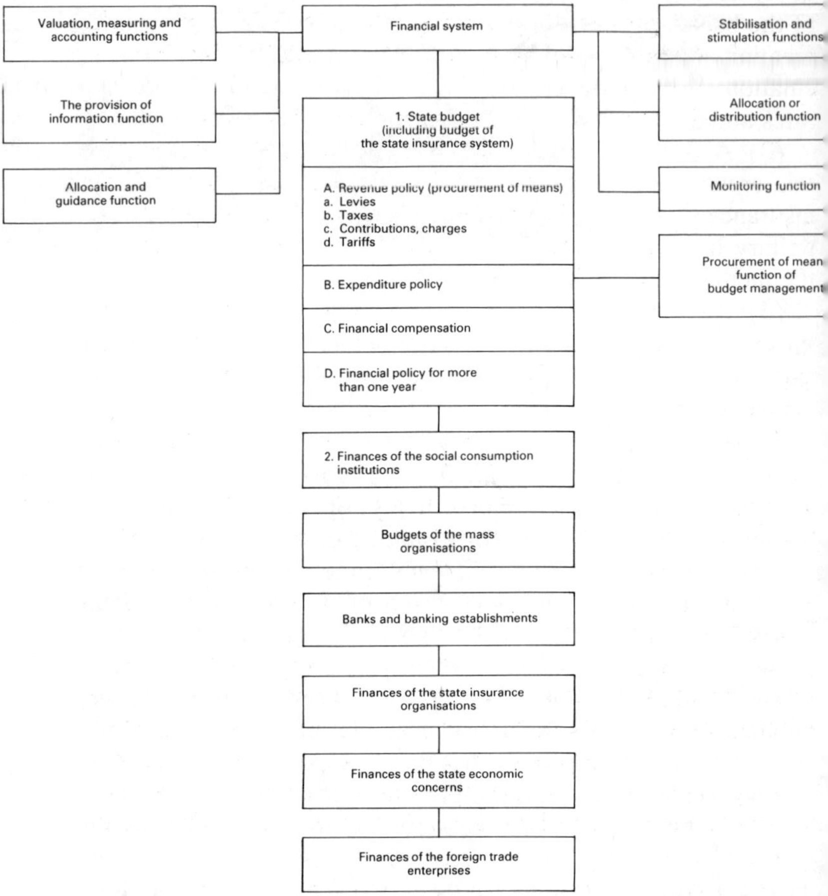

Source: Buck, H.F., 'Finanzsystem' in *DDR Handbuch* (1979), p. 387; *DDR Handbuch* (1985), p. 404.

municipality (*Gemeinde*) level, which are merged into a public consolidated budget. Also included in this sector is the social insurance budget.

(2) The State Bank (*Staatsbank*), the commercial banks (*Geschäftsbanken*) and the savings banks (*Sparkassen*). The banks are included in the state financial sector in order to make them recipients of state directives. In this connection they receive, above all, the functions of allocation, financing the cen-

trally determined plan tasks and supervising the fulfilment of these tasks by the customer enterprises in their charge. The government controls the most important commercial activities of the banks, putting at the service of state economic policy the creation and destruction of money, the regulation of cash in circulation, the overall granting of credit, the setting of interest rates and the handling of the payments and clearing system.

(3) All insurance institutions are also owned by the state. To this area of the state financial system also belongs the social insurance system (which has been developed into a national or unitary insurance system) for workers and employees and for the members of producer co-operatives.

(4) An especially important component of the financial system is the state-created 'currency system' (*Währungsordnung*) and 'currency policy' (*Währungspolitik*) shaped by the state leadership (see Figure 10.2).

As far as the sector of decentralised state finances is concerned, the funds which are held in bank accounts and in the accounts of socialist enterprises (and which are not centrally administered by the government and its executive authorities, but whose utilisation, to a limited extent, is decided upon at a lower level) are part of the financial resources of the state. These funds are intended to be utilised by the managements of producer organisations on their own responsibility for the financing of plan tasks. The financial resources necessary for enterprises to fulfil their enterprise and plan tasks must, in principle, be earned on their own account. If, however, their earning capacity is insufficient for this, they then receive the shortfall (under defined conditions) in the form of bank credits or budgetary grants.

The sector of decentralised (public) financial management embraces the finances of two groups of socialist organisations (which differ from one another, among other things, in their forms of ownership): the nationally owned enterprises and combines, and the producer co-operatives (*Produktionsgenossenschaften*), for example the agricultural producer co-operative (*Landwirtschaftliche Produktionsgenossenschaft*).

Thus the public financial system of the GDR includes all the monetary resources established and administered by government authorities, territorial administrations and socialist production units (cash holdings and bank deposits), the financial flows circulating between these economic units and the keeping

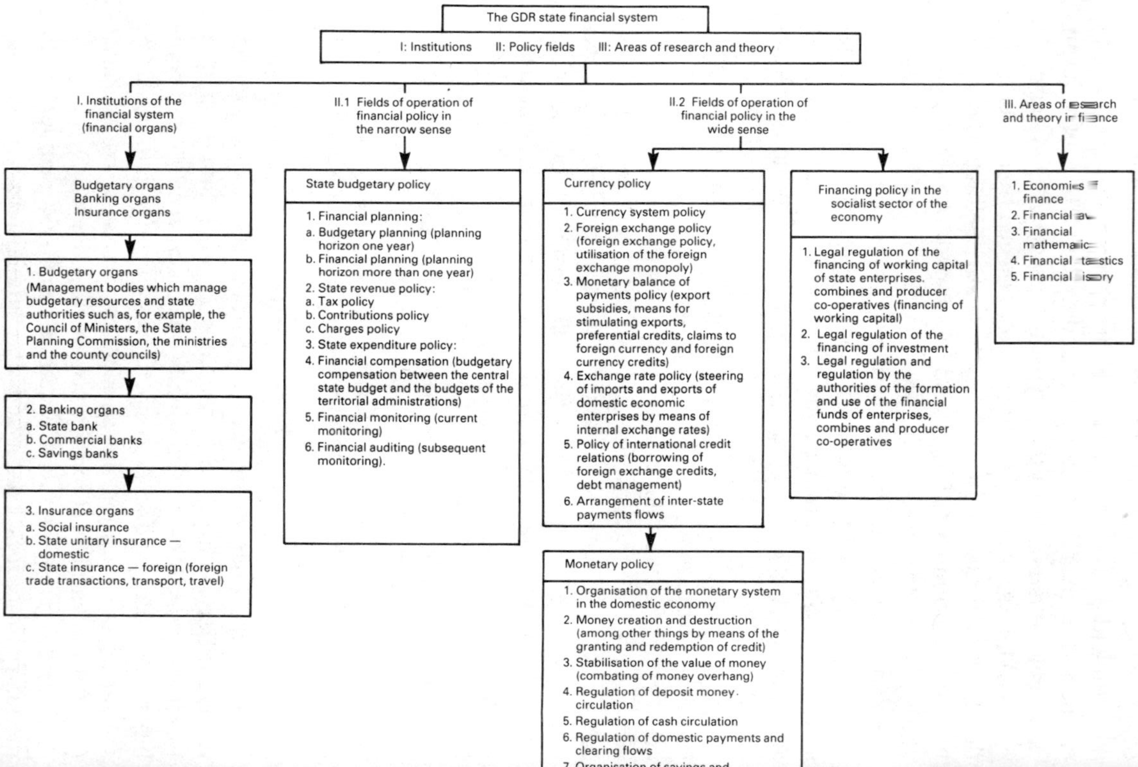

Figure 10.2: The state financial system of the GDR

of accounts on the utilisation of state funds (see Figures 10.1 and 10.2).

Outside of this comprehensive 'socialist financial system' there remain only three areas: the financial assets and financial management of handicraftsmen and the rest of the private business sector; church finances; and the income and expenditure of private households, together with the savings of individuals and associations.

FUNCTIONS OF THE FINANCIAL SYSTEM AND THE TASKS OF FINANCIAL POLICY

The GDR is a developed industrial country in which the services of money are used in many different ways. The main function of the financial system and financial policy is to realise state economic goals. Specifically, the financial system has seven roles to fulfil: measuring and accounting; provision of information; guidance (allocation); procurement of resources (procurement of state revenue for the financing of public tasks); stimulation and stabilisation; distribution; and monitoring (see Figure 10.1).

(1) The accounting function. On the basis of state-determined prices for goods and services, money and the financial system serve the state authorities and economic enterprises as an instrument for the rendering of accounts about the results of state policy measures and enterprise activities (i.e. measuring function of finances, among other things in the form of cost accounting, profit and loss determination and budgetary accounting).

(2) Economic guidance by means of financial policy. The GDR economic leadership uses a whole array of different financial policy instruments to align the economic activities of the state-owned economic concerns with performance targets in conformity with the plan, and to prevent a utilisation of factors of production in contravention of the plan and serving the particular interests of the individual enterprise. These include taxes, tax reliefs, subsidies, performance bonuses, money fines, credits granted on state-prescribed conditions and centrally fixed deposit and credit rates of interest. In addition, these 'monetary regulators' are used by the economic leadership to encourage

the willingness to perform of workers and enterprise employees, to steer consumer demand in directions approved by the state, and to encourage saving. At the centre of the financial policy steering of the behaviour of workers and consumers lies the adaptation of the supply of to the demand for labour, and the matching of the effective demand of the population to the supply of goods and services provided by the consumer goods industry, handicrafts and other economic sectors. The attainment of these goals is served, among other things, by the appropriate taxation of earned income (wage taxation), the levying of turnover and excise taxes (differentiated according to various sorts of consumer goods) and the selective use of subsidies and budgetary expenditures. At the same time these 'economic levers' are used to determine which proportion of the annual volume of goods and services produced is to go to private households, and which to the state and state enterprises (in order to be able to fulfil their particular public tasks).

(3) Procurement of resources function. In order to be able to supply public goods and services (for example, education, health care, social services and culture), and to be able to enlarge and modernise the capacity of state enterprises, the state also needs revenue. To this end the government, with the help of taxes, contributions and charges, concentrates a considerable proportion of national income in the state budget.

If one delimits the expenditure volume of the 'consolidated state budget' of the GDR to make it comparable with that of the public overall budget of the Federal Republic (i.e. the sum of the expenditure volumes of the federal government, the states and the municipalities; excluding the welfare benefits and pension payments paid for out of the contributory revenue of social insurance), the state in the GDR in the period 1975 to 1984 claimed between 65 per cent and 85 per cent of national income for its own purposes (i.e. the state's share of produced national income calculated at 1980 prices). In the Federal Republic, by contrast, the state does not claim even two-thirds of that share of national income appropriated by the state in the GDR.

(4) Stimulation and stabilisation tasks of financial policy. In the centrally planned economy of the GDR the directives given to the management and employees of state enterprises and producer co-operatives are supposed to guarantee a stable

economic environment, to provide full employment, and ensure a constant and high rate of economic growth. In practice, however, the Soviet-socialist economies, to a greater or lesser extent, experience fluctuations in economic activity, and even cyclical ups and downs in economic development. But, as a rule, the growth slow-downs and economic crises, which occur periodically, do not lead to substantial *open* unemployment, a massive decrease of capacity utilisation in enterprises, or the closure of economic concerns. The programming of desired economic development (intended and used as the motor of the economy via the planning authorities) is, however, in no way sufficient to achieve the result that the overall functioning of the economy in reality runs along the lines laid down by the economic leadership, and that the executors of plan fulfilment (enterprises, workers) perform in the manner required in the plan targets. The economic leadership is, therefore, additionally obliged to ensure that state plan targets are achieved by means of financial and budgetary methods of steering and promotion, monetary incentives (e.g. bonuses and tax reliefs) and monetary sanctions (punitive taxes, interest surcharges, interest on arrears). A further indispensable method of applying discipline is the threat of differentiated penalties for those enterprises and workers who do not meet their plan obligations and behave in a manner contrary to plan.

As regards stabilisation, monetary and financial policy has, above all, to help achieve two tasks. Firstly, there is the need to avoid the costly alternating under- and over-utilisation of productive capacity in enterprises and combines associated with economic fluctuations. Secondly, monetary steering must be used to prevent disturbances in the economic process caused by disproportionate increases in the supplies of money and goods. In a centrally planned economy the aggregate economic instabilities associated with such disproportionate growth cannot be eliminated through the free play of prices for producer and consumer goods, and through the flexible adaptive reactions of enterprises to price impulses. The prices of goods and services are fixed by the state, and often remain the same for years. Thus, in the centrally planned economy of the GDR, the task of balancing and stabilisation falls, to a considerable degree, to state financial planning and policy. Among the possible monetary and financial policy measures that may be taken, taxes and subsidies, credit and interest rates are the most important steering instruments, promoting the willingness to perform of enterprise management, workers and employees, and stabilising and harmonising in relation to one another the economic processes programmed in advance in the economic plans. Although wage levels and wage structure are determined by the state in the GDR, the stimulation of performance by means of wage policy does not belong to the field of financial policy.

Together with the programming of economic development by means of plan dictates and economic commands, these instruments of financial policy are used, above all, in order to achieve three economic policy goals:

(a) A satisfactory rate of economic growth (thus raising general prosperity).

(b) The mobilisation of as yet undiscovered reserves of performance.

The utilisation of financial policy primarily for stimulating economic growth is justified, above all, in terms of ideology. In so doing, the political leadership of the GDR pursues the goal of outdoing the Western market economies by means of a higher performance capacity and better economic results, in order, in this way, in the competition between the two systems, to be able to give proof of the alleged superiority of Soviet socialism.

(c) Elimination of blocked purchasing power and the combating of the negative results in aggregate economic terms of suppressed inflation (excess balance inflation: *Kassenhaltungsinflation*).

In order to realise the first two of the above mentioned aims in the field of growth policy, the state leadership of the GDR is concerned to promote the willingness to perform of the workers by means of selective tax reliefs and through differentiated reductions of the burden of levies when taxing wages, and so bring about new growth impulses in the economy. Thus, the fiscal authorities in the GDR have, for example, entirely given up taxing overtime bonuses and the special increments for work performed at night, on Sundays and on holidays. Also tax-free are the end-of-year bonuses, which are paid out from the enterprise bonus fund to management and enterprise collectives after the end of the economic year, in cases where enterprise plans are fulfilled and over-fulfilled. In order to stimulate innovation, moreover, remunerations of less than 10,000 marks, which are paid to innovators and inventors for the utilisation of innovator suggestions and patents, are not liable to taxation.

(5) Distribution tasks of financial policy. In contrast to the Western industrial states with their market economies, the Soviet-socialist states do not really have to depend on making use of the taxation of wages and income and the redistribution of the tax revenue, accrued with its aid, via the state budget, in order to attain a greater degree of fairness in the distribution of the national income that has been earned. In the GDR the government possesses the almost complete power of disposal over the productive potential of the national economy and over the product achieved thereof. For this reason it is, in principle, possible for the government to distribute the earned product of the aggregate economic labour process (net rewards for labour, profits, consumer and investment goods) directly to the state, the economic enterprises and the population (workers, pensioners and so on).

As the economic history of the Soviet-socialist states has shown, however, a satisfactory fine-tuning and distribution policy cannot be achieved only by means of a direct distribution of income for working people which is no longer corrected by taxation. In order to spur on the industriousness of working people and to steer manpower into branches and regions — in which there exists a greatly unsatisfied demand for labour — highly differentiated performance-related wages are one of the most effective means of inducement and incentive. If the economic leaderships of the Soviet-socialist states are to make use of this mobilisatory wages policy for reasons of growth policy, then the fiscal authorities subsequently have to intervene with corrective measures for redistribution in the thus created primary distribution of nominal income. Otherwise there will arise, after a certain period of time, considerable differences in the distribution of income and wealth within the population, which will lead to social conflicts and which, moreover, are not reconcilable with the official propaganda about the social convergence of classes and strata in a socialist state. Hence, in the GDR, too, direct taxes on income, turnover and excise taxes differentiated by categories of consumer goods (necessities, luxuries) and the state budget itself have to undertake distribution policy tasks. These redistribution instruments of financial policy must, in addition, see to it that the transfer incomes awarded to pensioners, the handicapped, those injured in accidents, the sick, those in need and those on grants can also be financed.

(6) The financial system as an instrument of economic control. In contrast to the market economies of the West, the economic leadership in the centrally planned economy of the GDR has assigned to the 'public' financial system numerous monitoring tasks in the field of economic policy. Without the monitoring exercised by the financial system, the ongoing supervision by the authorities over plan-fulfilment in the economic enterprises would remain very incomplete. The result would be that during the economic year plan deviations would not be recognised in good time, the causes of contra-plan developments could not be discovered and the economic leadership would not know where they should intervene most effectively in order to remove disproportions in plan-fulfilment. For those reasons, the state leadership of the GDR has, for example, so constructed the combined turnover and excise taxes, with which the consumption expenditure of consumers on industrial goods and semi-luxuries are burdened, and so organised the form of their collection that the economic and financial authorities are able to monitor, by means of levies which come in at fixed taxation dates, whether the enterprises in the consumer goods industry are fulfilling their production and sales plans (see Figure 10.1).

THE STATE BUDGET OF THE GDR (STATE BUDGETARY SYSTEM, STATE REVENUE AND EXPENDITURE POLICY)

The budgets of the central state (republic) and of the territorial administrations (counties, districts and municipalities) are combined into one 'consolidated budget' (*Einheitshaushalt*). In the GDR the budgets of the territorial administrations have been given the collective designation 'budgets of local state organs' (*Haushalte der örtlichen Staatsorgane*).

All basic questions of revenue and expenditure policy in the state as a whole are decided exclusively by the party leadership of the SED (Politburo of the Central Committee of the SED) and the central state government (Council of Ministers of the GDR). The consolidated budget, administered under the

This representation of the consolidated state budget and the county and district budgets is based on the interlocking box principle.

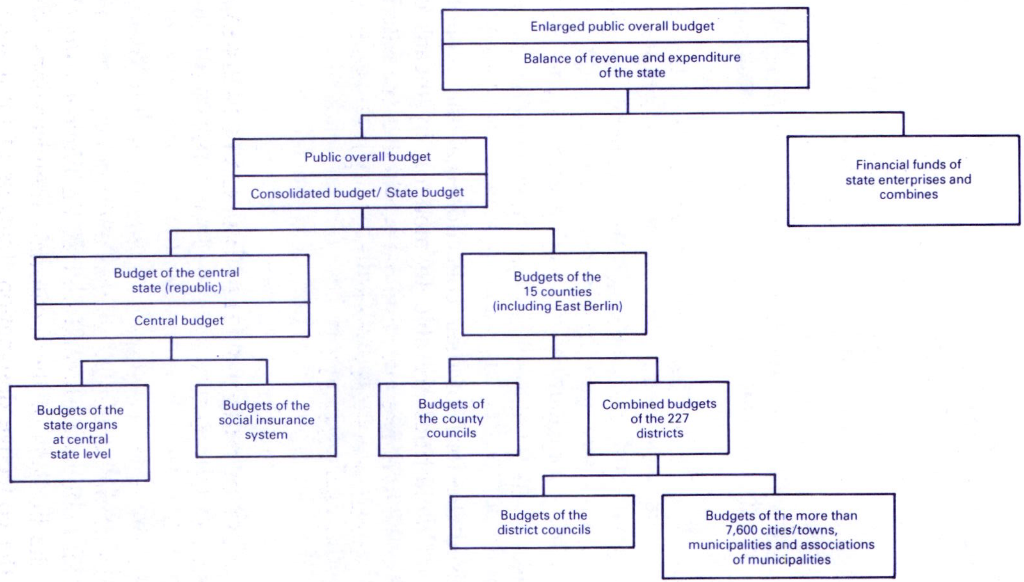

Source: Buck, H.F., *Steuerpolitik im Ost-West-Systemvergleich* (Berlin Verlag, East Berlin, 1982), p. 24; *Statistisches Jahrbuch der DDR* (1986), p. 1

supreme command of the Council of Ministers, is subdivided into four groups of individual budgets.

(1) The individual budgets of the supreme organs of state at the level of the central state. To these budgets belong, above all, the budget of the Council of Ministers and the budgets of the specialist and branch ministries, as well as the state offices. The totality of these subdivisions makes up the budget of the central state.

(2) The budget of the social insurance system for workers and employees and that for the members of producer co-operatives.

(3) The budgets of the counties and districts.

(4) The budgets of the municipalities and municipal associations.

Thus, the 'state budget of the GDR' (i.e. public overall budget) embraces, on the revenue side, all the money receipts (taxes, contributions, charges, revenue from public undertakings) which flow into the central and local budgets, and the revenue from contributions to social insurance. On the expenditure side of the budget, all the money sums which are spent by the state authorities are allocated in order to realise the domestic and external policy goals of the ruling monopoly party (and of the government appointed by it), and in order to finance public goods.

In the GDR, in conformity with the unitary form of the state and with the intention of the political leadership to shape financial policy from a position of command, the central state has exclusive authority over finances and revenue in relation to taxes, contributions, tariffs and most charges. Even the municipalities have once again been deprived of those few powers which were accorded to them during the early years after the war and which tended towards a limited degree of authority over their finances and revenue: these were taken away again only four years after the foundation of the state (in October 1949) by the law on the organisation of the state budget of 17 February 1954.

The 'local representative bodies of the people' at the county, district and municipality level are not allowed to create new kinds of taxes in order to obtain revenue and in order to finance local community tasks. The government has only allotted to the regional executive authorities a limited 'administrative sovereignty' in the sphere of levies. According to Article 9, para-

Table 10.1: Planned revenue and expenditure of the consolidated budget of the GDR 1980-86

Sub-budgets	1980 Revenue billion marks	%	1980 Expenditure billion marks	%	1982 Revenue billion marks	%	1982 Expenditure billion marks	%	1984 Revenue billion marks	%	1984 Expenditure billion marks	%	1986 Revenue billion marks	%	1986 Expenditure billion marks	%
Budget plan of the republic (central state)	105,710.6	68.0	92,400.7	59.4	126,237.5	71.0	112,357.7	63.1	152,773.5	72.9	139,299.6	66.4	174,496.2	71.8	159,245.9	65.6
Budget plans of the counties, districts and municipalities	34,575.7	22.2	34,575.7	22.3	36,327.1	20.4	36,327.1	20.4	40,250.3	19.2	40,250.3	19.2	51,137.5	21.1	51,137.5	21.1
Budget plan of the social insurance system	15,118.2	9.8	28,363.1	18.3	15,348.1	8.6	29,152.9	16.4	16,591.3	7.9	29,945.2	14.3	17,246.1	7.1	32,336.4	13.3
Surplus			65.0	—			75.0	0.1			120.0	0.1			160.0	
Revenue and expenditure of the state budget	155,404.5	100.0	155,404.5	100.0	177,912.7	100.0	177,912.7	100.0	209,615.1	100.0	209,615.1	100.0	242,879.8	100.0	242,879.8	100.0

Source: Laws relating to the GDR state budget plan; author's own calculations.

graph 4, of the GDR constitution of 1968, levies and taxes may only be raised on the basis of laws. Accordingly, in the GDR the only two state authorities which possess the power to promulgate laws and are empowered to pass tax laws, are the government (Council of Ministers) and the 'supreme body of representatives of the people' (i.e. the People's Chamber).

In the GDR the SED leadership has only entrusted to the central government certain rights, as below:

(1) To submit and also, to some extent, to promulgate organisational laws, under which the budget management of all territorial administrations is organised and regulated in its operation.

(2) Only the Council of Ministers has been empowered to plan the main outlines of the state procurement of means and to decide about all important questions of expenditure policy. From this centralisation of powers of decision-making in financial policy at the highest level of the state, it follows that all the revenue which the fiscal authorities receive from taxes, other levies, charges and contributions, belong to the central state. The 'local organs of state' (i.e. territorial administrations) obtain their budgetary resources, necessary to finance the public tasks

Notes: a. Revenue received by the GDR state budget, excluding receipts from charges, contributions and fines. To the latter receipts belong penalty interest rates payable by combines when they exceed credit durations, and also the money fines levied upon these production organisations in cases of excessive, non-norm-compatible utilisation of energy, and when prescribed quotas of materials and manpower allocations are exceeded and so on. Not included are the varieties of taxation of the rather small number of market gardening producer co-operatives (*Gärtnerische Produktionsgenossenschaften*), producer co-operatives of freshwater fisheries (*Produktionsgenossenschaften der Binnenfischerei*) and the breeders of fur-bearing animals (*Produktionsgenossenschaften der Werktätigen Pelztierzüchter*) and the dairy co-operatives (*Molkereigenossenschaften*) in so far as they belong to the Association for Farmers' Mutual Assistance (*Vereinigung der gegenseitigen Bauernhilfe*).

b. Like the counties and districts in the GDR, the municipalities and associations of municipalities possess no financial sovereignty of their own. Admittedly, the state leadership has entrusted to the municipalities the gathering of certain taxes on grounds of expediency. The revenue derived from the levies flows into the municipal budgets. It is expended for purposes of fulfilling the public tasks entrusted to the municipalities by the central state. In accordance with the centralisation of decision-making customary in centrally planned economies, the municipal authorities (municipal councils and municipal assemblies) have to obtain approval for the budget plans drawn up by them from the state organs to which they are subordinate.

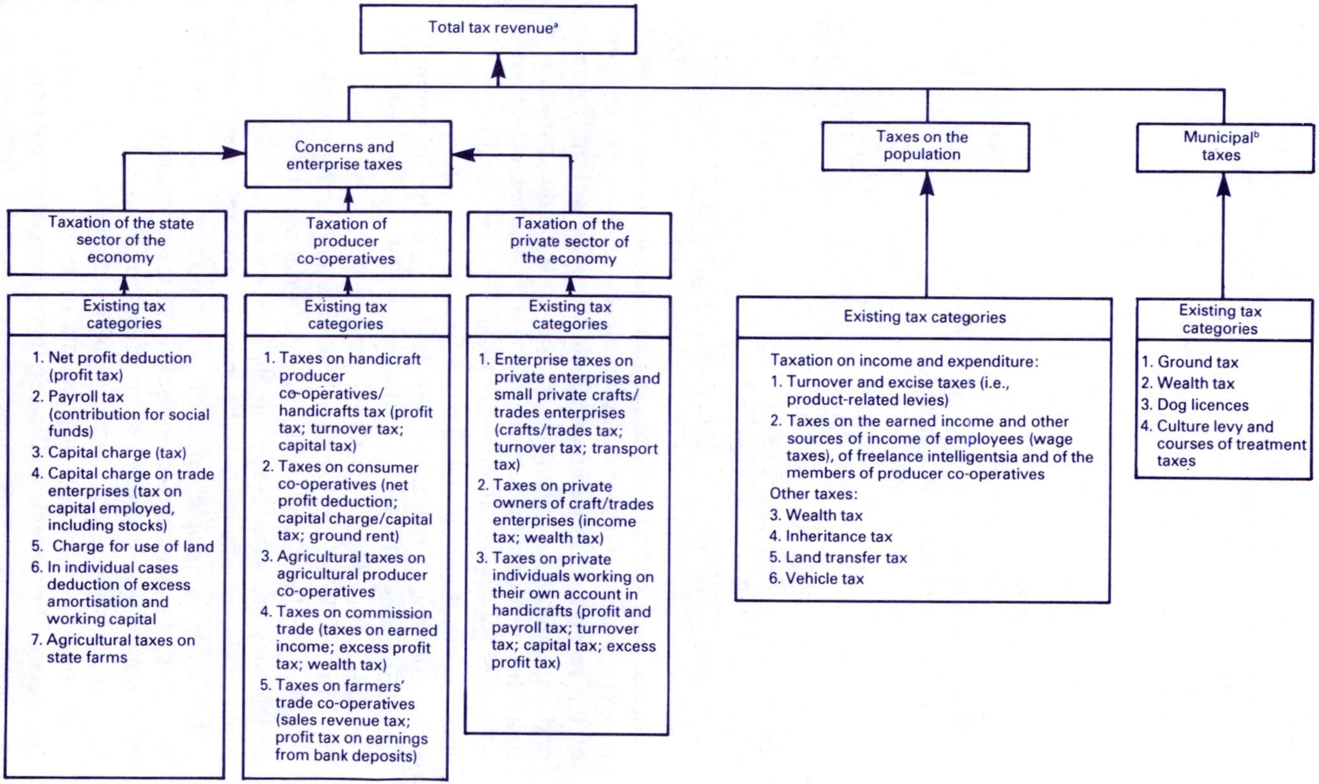

Source: Buck, H.F., *Steuerpolitik im Ost-West Systemvergleich* (Berlin Verlag, East Berlin, 1982), pp. 76-7

entrusted to them, predominantly in the form of grants (i.e. transfers) allocated to them from the account of the central state. In the budgetary year 1982 the tasks assigned to the counties, districts and municipalities in the national economic plan and in the organisation laws were financed to the tune of over 54 per cent with the aid of allocations of financial resources made available from the central budget. In 1984 around 52 per cent and in 1985 around 41 per cent of the financial requirements of the territorial state organs was covered from the central budget. The remaining revenue obtained by the territorial administrations arises out of income sources which the central state has made over to them. They are permitted to draw upon these resources on their own responsibility within the framework of the limits prescribed to them by the central authorities for particular tax-payers. Into the local budgets flow, above all, the levies paid by the economic enterprises directed at the county and local levels, and municipal taxes (tax on land and buildings, dog licences and other levies) (see Figure 10.4).

In the GDR the budgets of the individual municipalities, cities/towns, districts and counties are integrated successively into the consolidated budget. Apart from the municipal budgets, each budget — beginning with the district budgets and going right up to the overall state budget — includes the budgets of the respective subordinate territorial units with all revenue and expenditures. Starting from the bottom, the pyramid of individual budgets (in accordance with the interlocking boxes principle) embraces, at the four levels of state administration, the budgets of around 7,600 municipalities, the budgets of 227 town and country districts, the budgets of the 15 counties (including East Berlin) and the budget of the central state (republic). (See Figure 10.3.)

In the GDR the smaller territorial units must comply with the budgetary policy directives of the territorial administrations, to which they are subordinate, in their revenue and expenditure policy. The obedience on the part of the regional 'representatives of the people' and their administrations (i.e. councils) in their budgetary conduct to the will of the respective superior state authorities, is enforced by means of a large number of ways of exerting power, guidance and discipline.

Among the monetary instruments of steering employed by the state and economic leadership in the domestic economy (to which belong budgetary, monetary, banking and credit policy), the greatest importance attaches to budgetary policy. This predominant place enjoyed by budgetary policy stems, above all, from two causes. In the first place the state budget is by far the greatest catchment area for capital (*Kapitalsammelbecken*) in the national economy. Between two-thirds and four-fifths of the produced national income of the GDR is annually concentrated in the consolidated budget, and then expended for purposes of realising economic and social policy goals mostly chosen by the centre. This powerful potential for financing gives budgetary policy a dominant influence among financial and monetary steering systems employed by the economic leadership. For the state leadership of the GDR the state budget is the 'main financial plan of the national economy'. In the second place, in comparison with the other means of monetary steering, budgetary policy possesses a comparatively much larger (and more rigorous) applicability for the economic steering carried out by the state.

In consequence of the high concentration of national economic capital in the state account in the GDR, many more tasks of production and investment in the field of the economy are financed out of the state budget than are in the market economy of the Federal Republic. Hence, the state budget of the GDR extensively embraces financing processes which, in market economies, with a preponderance of private ownership of the means of production, fall into the area of the financial management of autonomous concerns and which are there recorded in the cost accounting, the enterprise balances and in the profit and loss accounting. In the centrally planned economies of the Soviet type the task of the state budget does not thus confine itself merely to financing a certain provision of traditional public services (popular education and enlightenment, health care, precautions against epidemics, care of the aged, fire precautions, road building, promotion of science and the arts and so on) and, in addition, to making possible financially the production of a selected number of meritorious goods and services (e.g. entrusting waste removal to state enterprises). In the economic system of the GDR the state account and budgetary policy has to undertake an almost unlimited amount of financing, stimulation, stabilisation and redistribution tasks, because here almost all goods produced in the national economy are converted into 'public goods'. In the Soviet-socialist systems there is scarcely any longer any space that is not controlled by the state in the economic, social and cultural fields.

Listed below are the chief financing tasks of the GDR state budget typical of the system in the economic field:

(1) The payment for the initial endowment of newly established enterprises in industry, construction, transport and communications and foreign trade with the fixed and working capital required by the enterprise.

(2) The joint financing of complete, new works divisions in existing state enterprises (i.e. earmarked financial grants).

(3) The taking over of the losses sustained by state-owned enterprises, in cases where the State Bank is no longer prepared to make available further support and bridging credits.

(4) The aiding of state enterprises adversely affected by major price increases in the prices and costs of imported raw materials and semi-finished products (i.e. the cushioning of price shocks occurring in world markets by granting product-related price support subsidies).

(5) The taking over of a part of the production costs of those *Kombinate*, individual enterprises and public utilities, which are obliged to sell below cost to private households particular foodstuffs, industrial goods and public services (drinking water, long-distance heating, power) on the orders of the state (price decree). These compensation payments, met from the state account, are made available in the GDR, in the form of 'product-related price supports', to the state enterprises and producer co-operatives.

(6) The financing of most land improvements in agriculture and all investments in the area of water supply and management (with the exception of enterprises' own water facilities in industry).

(7) The financing of the whole of geological research, as well as a significantly large share of all research and development activities carried out in the national economy.

The state leadership of the GDR is convinced that this massive, centralised allocation of capital, via the state budget, is the best way of executing a 'highly effective structural and expansion policy in the national economy' and one that is orientated towards state priorities.

Revenue of the GDR state budget

(1) Tax revenue accruing from the state sector of the economy. By far the highest yielding source of taxation are those taxes paid by the state sector of the economy (enterprises, combines, state farms). In the seven years from 1979 to 1985 inclusive, on average 47 per cent of the total revenue of the GDR budget (not counting accruals in the form of contributions for social insurance) derived from that sector of the economy owned by the state (see Table 10.2).

Ranged in order of their fiscal yield to date, there have flowed since 1984 four categories of taxes from the state sector of the economy into the state account (see Figure 10.2):

(a) Profit tax (i.e. net profit deduction).

(b) The production fund levy on production and trade (*Produktions- und Handelsfondsabgabe*), i.e. capital charge on the fixed capital and stocks employed in production and trade enterprises.

(c) The payroll tax imposed with effect from 1 January 1984, which in the GDR has been given the title 'contribution for social funds' (*Beitrag für die gesellschaftlichen Fonds*). The payroll tax was initially only levied upon industrial enterprises. From 1985, however, construction enterprises have also had to pay this tax.

(d) The rental charge made for the use of land.

From 1980 until 1983 the net profit deduction paid by state enterprises was the single highest yielding tax in the GDR. During this period it surpassed in yield for the first time the differentiated turnover and excise taxes, which are paid by the population. Price surcharges on semi-luxuries and on luxury industrial goods imposed in the form of 'product-related levies' brought the highest accrual of tax revenue in the years 1956-7 to 1979. Since the introduction of the new payroll tax in 1984, profit tax has once again brought in less revenue to the state budget than turnover and excise taxes. Among the taxes on concerns, however, it remains the highest yielding source of tax revenue.

In terms of capacity to yield, the capital charge has so far been the second most important tax on enterprises. The capital charge on production and trade enterprises provided the government in East Berlin in the years from 1976 to 1985 on average with 13 to 14 per cent of its entire budgetary revenue (see Table 10.2).

Table 10.2: Structure of the revenue side of the state budget of the GDR 1976-85 (contribution made by the individual tax categories and particular groups of tax-payers to the total revenue of the GDR state budget)

	1976	1978	1980	1982	1983	1984	1985
				%			
1. Direct and indirect taxes levied upon private households:							
a. Revenue deriving from the taxation of private consumption expenditures (turnover and excise taxes; product-related levies)	32.1	29.9	27.0	23.1	22.3	25.6	21.1
b. Wage tax and income tax of self-employed individuals (i.e. freelance intelligentsia)	5.2	5.2	4.8	4.6	4.5	4.1	3.9
2. Tax revenue from the state sector: (taxes on concerns; deductions from nationally owned enterprises, combines and VVBs):							
a. Profit tax (net profit deduction)	21.5	22.0	27.5	32.1	31.7	20.5	18.6
b. Payroll tax (contribution for social funds)	—	—	—	—	—	10.2	12.2
c. Capital tax (capital charge, including that on trade enterprises) and rental charge for the use of land	13.6	13.8	12.7	13.0	13.1	12.9	13.3
d. Deductions from state banks	3.6	4.2	4.1	4.5	4.1	3.9	3.9
3. Levies on enterprises and institutions in agriculture (excluding state farms); revenue derived from charges on enterprises in water supply and management	1.1	1.7	1.4	1.2	1.6	3.5	4.2
4. Taxes on handicrafts and levies on other co-operatives[a]							
a. Taxes on handicraft producer co-operatives and other trade co-operatives[a]	2.4	2.3	2.1	2.2	2.3	1.9	1.9
b. Taxes on private handicrafts and trades	2.2	2.1	2.1	2.2	2.2	2.0	2.0

5. Revenue from the services of research institutions of the Academy of Sciences and institutes of higher education	—	0.3	0.2	0.3	0.3	0.3	0.3
6. Deductions from the income of state institutions in education, health, social welfare, culture, care of youth and sport	5.9	6.1	5.5	5.3	5.2	4.9	4.6
7. Revenue from state service institutions and fees received by the state administration, and by radio and television	—	0.9	0.7	0.8	0.8	0.7	0.6
8. Municipal taxes	0.5	0.5	0.4	0.3	0.3	0.3	0.2
9. Non-attributable revenue, balances carried over and budget surpluses	11.9	11.0	11.5	10.4	11.6	9.2	13.2
Total revenue of the state budget (excluding revenue in the form of contributions to social insurance)	100.0	100.0	100.0	100.0	100.0	100.0	100.0

Note: a. To the other co-operatives belong, among others, consumer co-operatives and farmers' trade co-operatives.
Source: Official budget accounts of the Council of Ministers for the People's Chamber of the GDR; author's own calculations.

In 1983 48.9 per cent of the revenue of the public overall budget of the GDR derived from taxes levied on the state sector of the economy. This contribution to state revenue was once again made up of 64.7 per cent in the form of profit tax receipts and 26.6 per cent in the form of revenue raised by taxation of the capital employed in the state sector of the economy. Deductions from banks contributed 8.5 per cent to the tax revenue from the state sector of the economy. The levying of rental charges for the use of land contributed only the modest proportion of 0.2 per cent to the deductions from this sector of the economy. The introduction of the new payroll tax in 1984 brought about a considerable change in the structure of the tax revenue contributed by state economic enterprises. In 1985 revenue from taxes on concerns was broken down as follows: profit tax 38.8 per cent; payroll tax 25.5 per cent; capital charge 27.5 per cent; levies on banks 8.1 per cent and rental charges for the use of land 0.1 per cent.

Figure 10.5: The 'three-channel deduction system' of taxation of concerns in the state sector of the ec…omy of the GDR from 1 January 1984

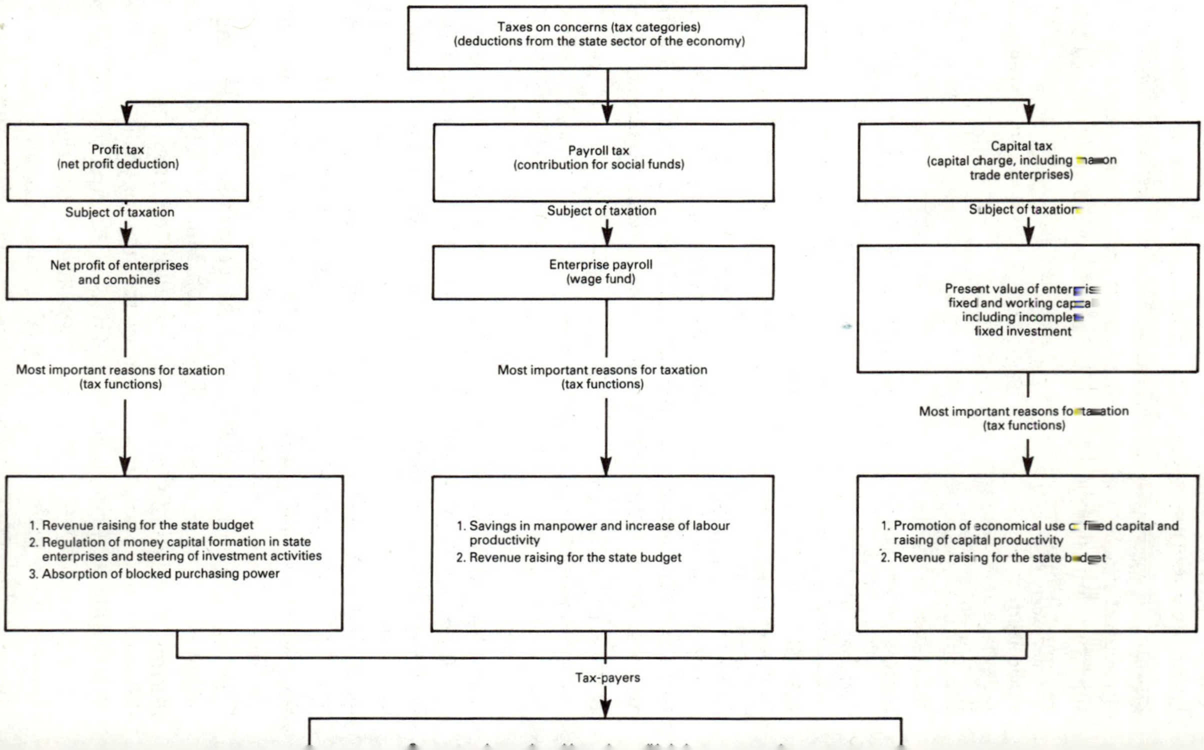

(2) Indirect and direct taxation of private households in the GDR. After taxes on concerns, the taxes paid by the population (working people and consumers) provide the largest amount of revenue (see Figure 10.4). In 1983 the population, through the taxes that it paid, contributed 47.16 billion marks to the state account and in 1985 53.54 billion marks. With this revenue in 1983 around a quarter of the state tasks decided upon by the government were financed. In so far as the taxation levied upon private households is not directly connected with the running of a private handicraft, trade or trades enterprise, the taxes paid by the population flow into the state account almost entirely from three sources of revenue:

(a) Turnover and excise taxes, which are differentiated according to individual industrial consumer goods and semi-luxuries (i.e. product-related levies).

(b) Taxation of the wages and salaries of workers and employees.

(c) The income tax, lower than normal, which is demanded from selected groups of the self-employed (inventors, doctors, writers, artists); i.e. burden of levies on the freelance intelligentsia who enjoy taxation privileges.

In contrast to the Federal Republic, in the GDR the emphasis of the taxation of private households (working people, consumers) lies not on direct, but on invisible, indirect taxation. Therefore, this contrast also explains, for example, the fact that in 1983 only 4.5 per cent and in 1985 only 3.9 per cent of total budgetary revenue was accounted for by the taxation of earned income (see Table 10.2). On the other hand, taxes levied on private consumption expenditures contributed revenues to a total of 22.3 per cent of all budget receipts in 1983 and 21.1 per cent in 1985. For the citizens of the GDR there derived from this the following tax burden: in 1985, on average, when purchasing industrial consumer goods and semi-luxuries to the value of 100 marks, he was obliged to pay 59.4 marks worth of turnover and excise taxes.

(3) Other budgetary revenue. The state budget receives further revenue in the form of tax payments by the collectivised agricultural enterprises (i.e. agrarian taxes), from levies on the output of private and co-operative handicraft enterprises, from the charges levied by state institutions in the area of social consumption (for example, health care, institutes of higher edu-

cation, academies, cultural centres) and from municipal taxes. Of significance here, in particular, is the taxation capacity of the private handicraft enterprises. In the period 1976-83, they annually contributed considerably more in tax to the state budget than the whole of the fully collectivised sector of agriculture was able to in agrarian taxes (in 1983 budgetary revenue from taxes on private handicrafts and trades amounting to 3,795 million marks, with agrarian tax payments from agriculture only coming to 1,424 million marks). Revenue from agrarian taxes has exceeded that from the taxation of private handicraft enterprises only since the earning capacity of socialist agricultural enterprises has substantially increased through the comprehensive raising of producer prices for agricultural products in 1984-85.

Expenditure of the GDR state budget

To the characteristics inherent in a centrally steered national economy on the Soviet-socialist model belongs the fact that the government transmutes the budget into the largest catchment area for the capital of the national economy. In addition, budgetary financing is used to realise the objectives of the state's growth and structural policies in the economy (i.e. steering of the economy by means of the central allocation of money capital).

In contrast to the Federal Republic, where expenditure for the purpose of the social security of the citizens takes first place in the order of priority of the various expenditures of the public overall budget, in the GDR expenditure for the promotion of the economy forms the most important category of use for budgetary resources. Accordingly, budgetary expenditure for the financial support, reconstruction, rationalisation and modernisation and for the expansion of state and co-operative production enterprises also occupies a predominant place amongst the expenditure categories. In 1983 the state leadership of the GDR spent on *direct* promotion of the economy and the financing of industrial and enterprise research in the area of the socialist sector of the economy 17.1 per cent of all the budget funds expended (the standard of comparison for this percentage figure is provided by total expenditure less the social services financed from the contributions in respect of social insurance). In total the government of the GDR made available in 1983 for the *direct* promotion of the economy and for enterprise research in industry, agriculture and forestry 30.02 billion marks (total expenditure of the consolidated budget, excluding the contributions for social insurance, in 1983 amounted to 175.86 billion marks). In the budget year 1985, budgetary allocations to state enterprises and producer co-operatives amounted to 31.31 billion marks (14.3 per cent of total expenditure).

If, to the budget expenditure which is used for the *direct* promotion of the economy and for the support of enterprise research, is further added that budget expenditure which, in the form of price-support subsidies, serves *indirectly* to secure the economic efficiency of socialist economic enterprises and the promotion of their growth, the government in East Berlin in 1983 spent around a third of all budget funds (29.6 per cent) for the purposes of financial support and for the development of the socialist production organisations (enterprises, combines, agricultural producer co-operatives and so on), and in 1985 they accounted for 32.9 per cent. A comparison with preceding years also shows how privileged a position the socialist economic enterprises in the GDR enjoy as recipients of taxation monies. In the years 1981 and 1982 the East Berlin state leadership expended 30.4 per cent and 29.9 per cent of all budget funds for the purposes of their economic safeguarding and strengthening.

After expenditure for the direct and indirect promotion of the economy (see Table 10.3: expenditure under headings 1, 4, 6 and 12), 'expenditure in respect of social security' (pension and welfare payments to pensioners, the sick, the handicapped and the needy) forms the second most important expenditure priority of the GDR state budget. In 1983, 80 per cent of state expenditure for social purposes consisted of grants to social insurance, and in 1985 83 per cent. In the GDR social insurance is charged with the task of a comprehensive national insurance for the maintenance and care of citizens (the insured and surviving relatives) in old age, in illness, in handicap, after accidents at work and during maternity. Social insurance combines the obligatory and optional additional insurance undertaken by citizens. Those insured, under the latter, can increase their old age pensions by paying higher contributions. As the contributions of the insured to the compulsory national

Table 10.3: Ranking of state expenditures of the GDR according to expenditure categories[a] (per capita budgetary expenditure)

	1978	1980	1982 marks	1984	1985	Average increase in expenditure 1979-85 %
1. Direct support and promotion of state enterprises in industry, construction, trade and agriculture	1,214	1,343	1,701	2,284	1,768	+5.5
2. Expenditure on social welfare and grants for social insurance[b]	924	1,039	1,047	1,023	1,101	+2.6
3. Overtly allocated expenditure for the armed forces, border troops, border installations and the arming of the factory militia[c]	641	727	883	934	1,010	+6.7
4. Indirect support and promotion of agriculture and subsidising the low prices of basic foodstuffs	461	469	724	1,237	1,656	+20.0
5. Expenditure on education, vocational training and adult education[b]	442	467	522	558	581	+4.0
6. Indirect support and promotion of industry, water supply (drinking water), passenger transport and the repair trade by means of financial support for a dual pricing system for the producer prices and retail prices of selected industrial goods, and welfare and other services (price support subsidies)	396	538	594	679	792	+10.5
7. Expenditure on health care[b]	343	380	456	520	556	+7.2
8. Expenditure on new housing and the modernisation and repair of dwellings, and expenditure for the						

repayment of interest on and principal of credit taken up by state construction enterprises for new dwellings	240	282	361	438	506	+11.2
9. Expenditure on state administration[b]	215	222	222	229	244	+1.8
10. Expenditure on the maintenance and modernisation of the means of transport and transport facilities and for the deployment of rolling stock (excluding investment for expansion)	198	176	193	221	285	+5.3
11. Expenditure on the arts, culture, the media, news services and on agitation and propaganda[b]	131	137	152	163	177	+4.4
12. Expenditure on basic and commissioned research[d]	130	154	175	172	203	+6.6
13. Expenditure for the maintenance of universities, institutes of higher education and technical schools and on grants[b]	115	128	144	151	162	+5.0
14. Expenditure on energy and heat supply to dwellings, provision of open spaces, refuse disposal, administration of state housing, official management and allocation of housing, and the subsidisation of rents	83	96	140	181	213	+14.4
15. Expenditure on state security, public order, the police, justice and the penal system[b]	49	55	67	71	76	+6.5
16. Expenditure on *new* institutions for the education, welfare and care of the population in residential areas (including kindergartens, young people's homes, schools, hospitals, old people's and nursing homes, sports centres, public meeting places and official state buildings)	37	43	57	84	125	+19.0

17. Expenditure for the maintenance of sports facilities, the holding of sporting events and the promotion of competitive sport[b]	19	22	25	28	31	+7.2
18. Other budgetary expenditure (including non-attributable state expenditure)	1,212	2,203	2,776	2,420	3,158	+14.6
Expenditure per capita in total[e]	6,850	8,481	10,239	11,393	12,644	+9.2

Notes: a. The basis for the determination of the ranking of state expenditures is the 1978 *per capita* expenditures for the various categories. Thus, the table shows the changes which have taken place over the period 1978-85 in state policy and expenditure priorities.

b. The expenditure figures only take current expenditures into account (for maintenance, repairs and replacement investment) and not investment outlays for expansion purposes (expenditure on *new* defence installations, e.g. for new barracks, rocket-launching pads, runways on military airfields and quays for naval bases; budgetary grants for the expansion and modernisation of armaments enterprises; a considerable part of the outlays for arming the working-class factory militia with light and medium weapons — the militia numbering 400,000 men. These military costs have to be borne by state enterprises).

c. The *overtly allocated* expenditures for the armed forces and armaments (National People's Army, border troops and factory militia) do not include many outlays for military purposes, with the consequence that actual expenditure for the military (army, navy and airforce), for training and for the equipping of the army and its auxiliary forces is, in reality, considerably higher than that shown in the table. The officially given 'expenditure for national defence' does not include the following outlays for military purposes: research on defence, and the higher training of the officer corps of the National People's Army and of special units. In addition the military budget does not take account of expenditures on civil defence and on the paramilitary training of the members of state youth organisations (Young Pioneers and the Free German Youth) and of schoolchildren.

d. Covered in this budgetary category are grants for industrial research and for enterprise research in agriculture and forestry. This source also finances the R&D activities of state academies (including the Academy of Sciences), institutes of higher education and the independent research institutes. The promotion of industrial research and enterprise research in agriculture and forestry accounted for over 55 per cent and about 56 per cent of state expenditure on basic and commissioned research in 1983 and 1985 respectively.

e. Total expenditure, excluding social insurance outlays financed by contributions, balances carried over from the previous year and frozen budget surpluses.

Source: Budget accounts of the GDR Council of Ministers for the People's Chamber; author's own calculations.

insurance have long since been frozen, the contributions of the insured and enterprises to social insurance have since 1982 not sufficed to cover even half of the expenditure of social insurance. From 1981 until 1985 the state has been obliged to make itself responsible on average for 46 per cent of social expenditure on social insurance and to finance it by transfers of taxation funds.

In the Federal Republic expenditure on education and the institutes of higher education occupies second position in the ranking of services financed from public funds. In contrast to this, the state leadership of the GDR has allotted to expenditure in respect of education and institutes of higher education only the fourth place in the ranking of state priorities for expenditure; indeed, it stands below expenditure on the military and measures for securing the borders (see Figure 10.6).

Both in the Federal Republic and the GDR expenditure on armaments and defence represents the third most important category of expenditure in the public overall budget. Admittedly, a considerable part of the budget funds used in the GDR for military purposes is concealed under other headings and is not shown under the budget heading 'expenditure in respect of national defence'. To these belongs, amongst other things, the expenditure on military construction projects, defence research and pre-military training of the young. For this reason it is necessary to increase by a considerable amount the *per capita* amount calculated for the GDR over and above the 'overtly shown expenditure in respect of the military and measures for securing the borders', if one wishes to record and show the actual military burden in marks (East) per GDR citizen (see Table 10.3). This adjustment would not, however, make any change in the ranking of the expenditure priorities.

What is conspicuous is that transport and communications occupies only a relatively low position in the ranking of categories of expenditure in the GDR (see item 10 in Table 10.3). Concerning the exact volume of expenditure in respect of investment for purposes of expanding the transport and communications sector of the economy (e.g. investment in new roads and the construction of new railway stations), the East Berlin state leadership is admittedly silent. Nevertheless, all available information on this matter confirms that, even if this expenditure were to be taken into account, this would, at most, raise the ranking of transport and communications as a recipient

Figure 10.6: Ranking of the most important expenditure groups in the public overall budget of the FRG and the GDR (percentage, 1980)[a]

FRG		Ranking		GDR
Social security (including expenditure by the social security institutions)	45.7	1	25.0	Expenditure for the support and promotion of the economy
Expenditure on education and higher education (primary and secondary, vocational training, higher and technical education, other)	9.8	2	20.7	Social security (including expenditure by the social security institutions)
Defence	5.5	3	7.7	Overtly allocated military expenditure (including border troops etc.)
Health, sport and recreation	4.4	4	6.3	Expenditure on education and higher education (primary and secondary, vocational training, higher and technical education, other)
Transport and communications and news service	4.2	5	5.0	Housing, environmental planning, new community institutions and communal services (including waste disposal)
Housing, environmental planning and communal social services	4.2	6	4.7	Health, sport and recreation
Support and promotion of the economy	3.9	7	1.9	Transport and communications and news service
Public security and order, maintenance of the law (the judiciary)	3.0	8	1.6	Science, R&D (promotion of research outside higher education institutions)
Science, R&D (promotion of research outside higher education institutions)	1.4	9	1.0	The arts, culture and cultural work among the masses (cultural affairs)
The arts and culture (cultural affairs)	0.7	10	0.6	Public security and order, maintenance of the law (the judiciary)
	17.2	other expenditure categories	25.5	

of budget funds by a single place.

In contrast to the Federal Republic, in the GDR almost the entire transport and communications network is in state ownership (aviation, the railways, inland and sea-going shipping, road haulage) and is, therefore, financed at the expense of the state. In consequence, it might really have been expected that the expenditure on transport and communications would have occupied one of the foremost places in the order of ranking of the expenditure categories. While, however, in the Federal Republic expenditure on transport and communications occupies fourth place in the ranking, in the GDR transport and communications (including expenditure on investment for expansion) has to be content with seventh place in the hierarchy of state expenditure.

Note: a. As a result of the different economic systems, a comparison of the categories of budgetary expenditure in the two German states is only possible through the juxtaposition of highly global expenditure categories. Figure 10.6, based on the percentages accounted for by the respective expenditures in the overall public budget, shows the importance of the individual expenditure categories in the two German states. Admittedly, such measurements lead to certain distortions where the outlays contain a high proportion of labour costs, for example, in expenditure on the armed forces, state administration and internal state security (the police, security services, the judiciary and the penal system). The wages and salaries paid out in these areas in the GDR are, on average, about a half those of the FRG for comparable work and profession. Because of this gap in wage and salary levels, the percentages for those expenditure categories which include relatively high labour costs are lowered, so that at first sight it appears as if the state in the GDR spends little on the armed forces, the administration of the state and the economy, the police, state security, the judiciary and the penal system.

It must, in addition, be noted that a lower percentage share accounted for by 'expenditure on the arts and culture' in the FRG than in the GDR does not mean that less is spent in the former for these purposes than in the latter. In contrast to the GDR, the arts and cultural life in the FRG are in large part promoted through the initiative and financial contributions of private persons and institutions (foundations, firms etc.), whereas culture and the arts in the GDR are almost exclusively guided, financed and monitored by the state.

In the category 'other' and 'non-attributable' state expenditures are, among other things, outlays on the Foreign Service, the support of communist parties in the Third World, the maintenance of the SED party apparatus, of the parties of the bloc and of the mass organisations, financing propaganda activities, and selected outgoings on the armed forces and armaments.

Source: Buck, H., in *Zahlenspiegel Bundesrepublik Deutschland/DDR — ein Vergleich* (Bundesministerium für innerdeutsche Beziehungen, Bonn, 3rd edn, 1985), p. 57.

The cause of this neglect is that transport and communications (with the exception of the three international ports of Rostock, Wismar and Stralsund) still belong to those sectors of the economy which are disadvantaged when the economic leadership allocates capital. As a result of the chronic shortage of capital in the GDR and the privileged position accorded over three decades to industrial investment, the expansion of capacity in enterprises producing capital goods and the demand for investment goods from the armed forces, the border troops and state security organs, there remained until fairly recently only insufficient residual amounts of investment capital for the modernisation and the expansion of the capacity of transport and communications and for urgently needed investment in water supply and management, in domestic trade, in the enterprises supplying communal services and in handicrafts.

After the explosive increase in oil prices on the world market, and subsequently on the Comecon market, from 1973-74 on, however, the GDR was forced radically to alter its transport and communications policy in order to substitute the then extremely expensive oil with other forms of energy. To this end, great efforts were made to switch transport from the roads (lorry freight) to the railways and inland waterways as quickly as possible. At the same time, rail traffic had to be converted to electric traction and away from the previously predominant diesel locomotives. From 1980 onwards, the increasingly forced tempo of electrification of the two lines from the Saxonian industrial area in the south of the GDR (Dresden, Leipzig, Halle and Cottbus) via East Berlin and Magdeburg to the international port of Rostock served this purpose. This expensive programme for modernisation of the GDR railway network led, especially from 1982, to a sharp rise in budgetary outlays on transport and communications.

Despite this unusual increase in outlays, industry and con-

Table 10.4: State expenditure per capita in the GDR on transport and communications 1978-85

Year	1978	1979	1980	1981	1982	1983	1984	1985
Expenditure *per capita* in marks	198	181	176	188	187	193	221	285

Source: Budget accounts of the Council of Ministers.

struction, defence, internal security of the SED regime and housing remained the expenditure priorities of GDR budgetary policy.

Up to 1971-72, the building of dwellings, too, counted among the continuously neglected sectors when it came to the allocation of investment funds. In order substantially to improve the housing conditions of around ten million citizens of the GDR, to halt the deterioration of the older housing stock and to make a start on restoration and in order to solve the housing question as a social problem by 1990, it was resolved to adopt a massive programme of building and modernising dwellings. Since then the new building and modernisation of dwellings has stood at the centre of state social policy. This also manifests itself in the fact that (apart from categories 4 and 16 in Table 10.3) expenditure on housing has increased the most in the period 1979 to 1985 (see expenditure headings 8 and 14 in Table 10.3).

THE FUNCTIONS OF MONEY IN THE SOVIET-SOCIALIST ECONOMIC SYSTEM OF THE GDR

Marx and Engels predicted that, in a socialist/communist economic system, money would no longer have any justification and would disappear. Once communist relations of production had been established people would be able to do without the services of money, because, under the new relations of production, there would no longer be 'commodity production' (*Warenproduktion*) for mostly anonymous consumers. Its place would be taken by a planned production for needs and consumers known in advance. Since, in such a method of production, all individual labour would always at the same time be socially useful labour, its social recognition would no longer (as in the capitalist commodity economy) first have to be sought by a valuation in money and through an act of exchange in the market. In addition, the new communist method of production, in which the pleasure in work would no longer be suppressed by capitalistic methods of exploitation, would guarantee such a high level of productivity that all the needs of all consumers could be assured. A mobilisation of the willingness to perform of the workers and enterprises by tempting rewards in money would, therefore, be dispensable.

None of these prophecies made by Marx and Engels has been fulfilled. The economic systems of socialism, as actually practised in the East, are money economies. As in all economic systems based on the division of labour, specialisation and exchange, money is also in the industrial economy of the GDR an indispensable component of the centrally planned economy of the Soviet-type, which has been introduced there. As a standard of evaluation and a measuring rod for prices, money forms the basis of individual and aggregate economic calculations and measurements of efficiency. Most of the demands for performance which are made by the state economic leadership of the executors of the plan (combines, enterprises, work brigades), are expressed in money units (i.e. plan targets in value terms). By means of promises in money (payment by result, piece-work bonuses, money premia), the willingness to perform of individual workers and enterprise personnel is stimulated. With the aid of money enterprise managements and the economic authorities control, in each case, performances in respect of production and sales, producers are rewarded and the distribution of produced national income is effected in accordance with priorities determined by the state. Almost the whole exchange of output between the economic units (production enterprises, private households, state authorities) is carried out with the assistance of money (purchase and sale; payments and clearing). All economic units put aside a portion of the reserves they have created as disposable working capital in monetary assets (cash hoards, cash resources, savings deposits).

As commodity production, exchange, reward in accordance with performance and valuation are likewise fundamental components of any Soviet-socialist economic system, it is not surprising that the basic functions of money, which it performs in market economies, resemble those functions which have been allotted to it in the centrally steered state economies. In the view of those who represent official monetary theory in the GDR, this similarity is only present admittedly on a superficial level, for the social content of the functions of money within socialism is, according to them, fundamentally different from that obtaining in a capitalist market economy.

As in market economies, money performs the following tasks in the Soviet-socialist centrally planned economies:

(1) standard of value and measuring rod for prices (unit of valuation for goods and services, unit of account and means of expressing prices);

(2) medium of exchange;

(3) means of payment;

(4) means of accumulation (formation of financial reserves for the state and for the state economic concerns) and means of saving for the population.

In contrast to the currencies of the states organised on market lines, the national currencies of the Soviet-socialist economies are not meant to and cannot serve as an international means of exchange (i.e. world money). The type of currency created by the governments of these states represents a medium of exchange which can only be used within the domestic economy (i.e. internal currency). 'World money' is only produced by the socialist states when they mine gold inside their own country (as, for example, the USSR) and use this internationally accepted means of payment to settle import obligations or to carry out international financial transactions. As a result of the picture given so far of the functions of money in the GDR, it can be stated that money is indispensable, even where in a national economy private ownership of the means of production has been abolished and the rate of growth of production and the expansion of the capacity of enterprises are not determined by market impulses, but, in the first place, are guided by an all-embracing, fully binding state plan.

There are, however, differences in the use of money in alternative economic systems. In the market economy of the Federal Republic the function of money as a medium of exchange is of the greatest importance. On the other hand, for the economic administration of the GDR money is of greatest use as a unit of account. For this economic system money provides the indispensable measuring rod of value, with whose aid economic calculations can be made, economic successes and failures can be ascertained and the economic activities of state enterprises can be monitored. The basis of economic planning and accounting are prices. Since in the GDR these are overwhelmingly dictated by the economic authorities, the economic quality of prices as an instrument for providing information and guidance for the efficient valuation of resources depends on whether the fixed prices decreed by the state accurately reflect the existing scarcity relationships of goods and services. If they do not satisfy these informational demands then distorted plan prices and the calculations of costs and results built up upon them, will mislead performance interests and the economic activities of the plan authorities and economic concerns.

In order to make the economic accounts of all economic units within the national economy comparable, the state leaderships in the socialist economic systems have to lay down a certain quantity of the money stock as a *basic unit* (*Grundeinheit*). This basic quantity is declared by law to be the national money or currency unit. The currency unit of the GDR is the 'mark'.

In contrast to the market economies, in the centrally planned economies the function of money as a medium of exchange has, in many ways, been restricted by the state direction of the economy. Restrictions of this kind are decreed by reason of objectives and principles, which are partly of an organisational policy (ideological) and partly of an economic policy (guidance system-related) nature. Thus, for example, private households in the GDR are not permitted to purchase means of production with their savings, in order, let us say, to found an industrial enterprise, to set up a freight business, or to open a copying centre. Similarly, it is not possible for them to exchange domestic currency for the convertible currencies of other states. The state enterprises are forbidden to spend the money revenues they have earned, or reserves of financial capital they have saved, for unplanned purposes.

Of the total stock of money in the GDR which is in the possession of entities other than banks (i.e. enterprises, authorities, the population), only the cash holdings of private households and their sight deposits in banks and savings-book deposits can be described, to some extent, as freely disposable money. For if the purchasing interests of GDR citizens are not directed towards the means of production, foreign currency or other forbidden goods, but towards consumer goods and services, then, under the freedom of consumer choice allowed them, they are permitted to spend their money in accordance with their individual preferences and are not regimented by legal and official restrictions on use.

In the Soviet-socialist centrally planned economies, too, money, in its role as a unit of account and as a measuring rod for value, becomes devalued or even unusable if its purchasing power does not remain stable. Such losses in purchasing power are, as a rule, caused by a rapid increase in the price level. If price increases are the cause of a decline in purchasing power, then, in a centrally planned economy, the state pricing authorities are responsible. As a rule, only these authorities — and not the production and trade enterprises — have the right to fix

Figure 10.7: Instruments of monetary policy in the GDR

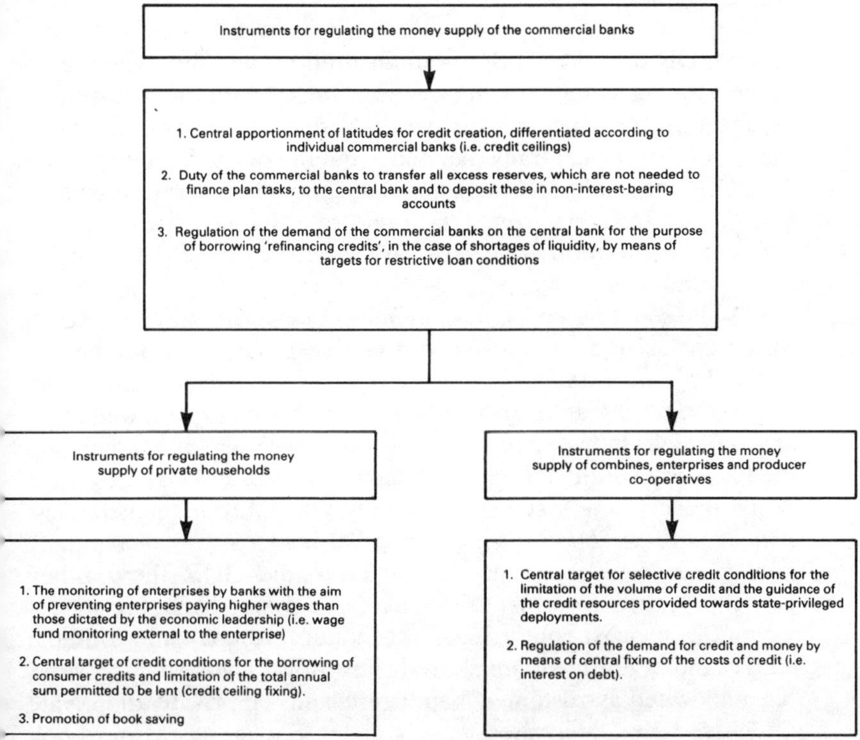

prices. The real value of money as a medium of exchange also declines if, with a virtually constant price level, increasingly numerous and ever-greater deficiencies in the supply of goods or supplies arise (i.e. formation of a cash and deposit money overhang). Above all, through the appearance of these disproportions between purchasing power demand and the supply of goods, the functions of money as a store of value and as a liquidity reserve are affected. In order to preserve and secure confidence in the value of the currency, so that money can fulfil its tasks to the greatest possible extent, in the GDR, too, the government and the State Bank must orientate their economic and monetary policies towards restricting the money stock in circulation, stabilising the purchasing power of money and strengthening its usefulness as a medium of exchange, in order that the formation of a money overhang may be avoided and the emergence of black markets be prevented.

Organisation and tasks of banks and savings banks in the GDR

In the GDR the tasks of the credit institutions and the structure of the banking system are, in essence, stamped with the methods of directing the economy, to which, within the organisational framework of the centrally planned economy of the Soviet type, the SED leadership and the state economic administration give preference. Deriving from this frame of reference, two principles of organisation are decisive for the structure of the banking system:

(1) the setting up of '*universal banks of a particular kind*', to whose exclusive care is assigned a certain group of customers, selected by the state;

(2) the setting up of *special banks*, which are only allowed to deal with selected commercial bank tasks (such as, for example, the financing and handling of foreign trade transactions).

To the banking system belong the State Bank of the GDR (*Staatsbank der DDR*), the commercial banks and the savings banks. As regards commercial banks, in the GDR there are active only two foreign trade banks, one major bank for servicing the socialist enterprises in agriculture, forestry and foodstuffs, and a group of small credit institutions, to which have been allocated as customers handicrafts and the private and co-operative trade enterprises.

In contrast to the market economy of the Federal Republic, where private banking business and territorial and other bodies have set up a large number of different types of banks, in the GDR the state leadership has founded but few credit institutions. All money, credit and banking business, necessary for the functioning of a Soviet-socialist centrally planned economy, has been concentrated in them. The banking system is, in consequence, characterised by a massive concentration of concerns.

In the market economy of the Federal Republic the predominant type of commercial bank is the 'universal bank'. It offers bank customers almost all the usual banking services and lines of business (deposit business, granting credit, issue of securities and other securities business, dealings in foreign notes and coins). In order to transform the banks in the GDR, under strict governmental supervision, into agents for the implementation of state economic policy, the economic leadership of the GDR has abandoned the 'universal bank principle' in the market economy sense in the setting up of the state banking system. In consequence, in the GDR even the commercial banks entrusted with a wide range of tasks (i.e. universal banks of a particular kind), such as the Bank for Agriculture and Foodstuffs, are not permitted to offer all the usual banking services and to transact business with all interested private persons and enterprises embodying all forms of ownership. In the GDR the banks and savings banks can only undertake those banking tasks which have been assigned to them by the legislature with respect to a likewise legally delimited group of customers. It follows from this, on the other hand, that the enterprises and citizens of the GDR do not have the right to choose for themselves a bank in which they have confidence. They have to accept that credit institution which the state has decided shall be responsible for them. While private individuals still have the possibility of choosing between a number of branches of savings banks, the enterprises and combines in industry and construction, for example, are officially assigned to the branches of the State Bank competent to deal with them. Given so high a level of concentration and such an allocation of business areas, competition among the banking institutions is neither possible nor desired. The setting up of branches of foreign credit institutions in the GDR is not permitted.

In the GDR the business activity of all banks is stamped with the particular features peculiar to the system of centrally planned economic management:

(1) The granting of credits to individual enterprises and amalgamations of enterprises in all branches is permitted to state and co-operative banks alone. Through the conferral of a *monopoly in the granting of credit* upon the state administered banking organisation, a private money and capital market in the GDR has been deprived of any basis.

(2) It is strictly forbidden for state, co-operative and also the remaining private economic enterprises to either grant credits to their customer enterprises (payment objectives) or themselves receive credits (i.e. ban on supplier credits).

(3) All credits granted by banks have to be for *specific purposes* only and must serve the fulfilment of state plan goals.

(4) What deposit, credit, delay and penal interest rates may be charged by the banks is not decided by them themselves; instead the obligatory interest rate tables relevant in each individual case are decided upon by the Council of Ministers and

Table 10.5: Overview of state-determined interest rates in the GDR (position in 1986)

I. Target interest rates on credits to nationally owned production organisations (enterprises, combines and VVBs) in industry and construction among others for the financing of investment and the provision of working capital (excluding production units in agriculture and foodstuffs).

<u>Credits for fixed and working capital.</u>

a.	Credits in the framework of the specified credit ceiling (*planned* credits). Basic rate of interest	5.0%
b.	Credits for the fulfilment of plan tasks in cases where the credit receiver has not been able to achieve the contractually agreed performance and efficiency improvements: surcharges up to a maximum interest rate of	8.0%
c.	Credits with an enhanced risk for state banks: interest surcharges up to a maximum interest rate of	8.0%
d.	Credits for the financing of R&D projects and for rationalisation and modernisation measures (introduction of new key technologies); interest discounts to	3.8%
	or even	1.8%
e.	Above-plan credits for enterprise economic activities welcomed by the state (i.e. credits for economic activities in the state interest); basic interest rate	5.0%
f.	Above-plan credits to overcome self-incurred liquidity bottlenecks and to cover payments obligations in the case of credits falling due (i.e. credits contrary to plan); interest surcharges of	1.0%
	up to	3.0%
	maximum penal interest rate (especially in the case of credits restoring solvency)	12.0%

II. Target interest rates for credits to nationally owned production units (enterprises, state farms) and to producer co-operatives in agriculture and foodstuffs.

(1)	Interest rates for investment credits:	
a.	Credits to finance measures to raise soil fertility; interest rate	2.0%
b.	Credits to finance the fixed capital needed to convert agricultural production to industrial-type production technologies; interest rate	2.0%
c.	Credits for the construction of rational animal housing and greenhouses; interest rate	2.0%
d.	Credits for the purchase of new machines and other investment; interest rate	5.0%
(2)	Interest rates for working capital credits:	
a.	Credits in the framework of the specified credit ceiling (i.e. planned credits); basic interest rate	5.0%
b.	Credits for selected rationalisation measures deemed particularly important by the state for the mechanisation of the labour process and for the conversion of animal and crop production to industrial-type production processes;[a] interest discounts of	1.0%
	up to	3.0%
	Minimum interest rate	2.0%
c.	Credit repayment delays and above-plan credits to overcome self-incurred liquidity bottlenecks; interest surcharges on the basic	

	rate from	1.0%
	up to	3.0%
	Maximum penal rate	8.0%

III. Target interest rates for credits to handicraft producer co-operatives (PGHs).

a.	Credits in the framework of the specified credit ceiling (*planned* credits); basic interest rate	5.0%
b.	Credits for the support of newly founded PGHs during their first two years; interest rate	2.0%

IV. Target interest rates for credits to improve housing conditions.

a.	Credits to state and enterprise home-building units and to home-building co-operatives; interest rate	4.0%
b.	Credits to state and co-operative home-building units in agriculture, forestry and foodstuffs.[b]	4.0%
c.	Credits to the private owners of rented dwellings; interest rate[c]	4.5%
d.	Credits to the selected families of industrial and agricultural workers with many children for the construction of their own homes:	
	credits for the purchase of construction materials; interest rate	0.0%
	credits for carrying out the construction work; interest rate	4.0%

V. Target interest rates for credits to private households.

a.	Consumer credits (installment credits for the purchase of certain consumer durables selected by the state); interest rate	6.0%
b.	Consumer credits to families with many children;[d] interest rate	3.0%
c.	Credits to young married couples (family foundation loans); interest rate	0.0%

Notes: a. Details as to the purposes for which the reduced interest credits can be obtained and the obligatory credit conditions imposed on the credit receiver are laid down in the instructions issued by the Minister for Agriculture, Forestry and Foodstuffs; b. It is possible to obtain interest concessions. Such reduced interest credits for home building, however, are only granted up to the level of the conceded normative construction costs less than the value of the construction by agrarian enterprises themselves required by the authorities; c. The interest rate set may, in special cases, be reduced or delayed; d. In special cases, the banks may waive interest altogether on social grounds.

Source: *Verordnung ... vom 22.12.1971, GBL. der DDR* (1972), Part II, p. 41 ff.; in the version published on 15.5.1974, *GBL. der DDR*, Part I, p. 235; *Anordnung ... vom 15.2.1977, GBL. der DDR*, Part I, p. 45 ff.; *Kreditverordnung vom 28.1.1982, GBL. der DDR*, Part I, p. 126 ff.; also the first and second implementing regulations of this decree, *ibid.*, p. 133 ff.; Ehlert, W.; Hunstock, D.; Tannert, K. (eds), *Geldzirkulation und Kredit in der sozialistischen Planwirtschaft* (Verlag Die Wirtschaft, East Berlin, 1976), pp. 142-52 and 202-29; Tannert, K. 'Funktionen und Prinzipien des sozialistischen Kredits und ihre Rolle bei der Stimulierung der Effektivität', in Authors' Collective *Geld und Finanzen in der sozialistischen Reproduktion* (Verlag Die Wirtschaft, East Berlin, 1977), pp. 203-19; Authors' Collective led by König, E., *Das sozialistische Finanzwesen der DDR* (Verlag Die Wirtschaft, East Berlin, 1978), p. 128; Ehlert, W.; Hunstock, D.; Tannert, K., *Geld und Kredit in der DDR* (Verlag Die Wirtschaft, East Berlin, 1985), pp. 130-1 and p. 140.

the management of the State Bank.

(5) In order to force slow debtors who are in arrears to keep to the contractual agreements entered into and impel them to fulfil their repayment obligations, these enterprises have *punitive interest rates* imposed upon them by the banks. While credits which serve to realise plan tasks (i.e. planned credits) normally bear an interest rate of 5 per cent per annum (i.e. the basic rate of interest), the banks are permitted to demand of borrowers who do not repay their debts in time (i.e. extra-plan overdue credits) penalty interest rates of up to 12 per cent per annum.

(6) All enterprises, combines and producer co-operatives have to keep, with the 'house banks' assigned to them, a system of giro accounts, specified according to the tasks of concerns (finance fund accounts), so that the banks and economic authorities are enabled to supervise, on a continuing basis, plan adherence and the profitability of production organisations.

(7) All inter-enterprise payments have basically to be transacted via the giro network of the banking organisation without the use of cash, in order in this way, too, to ensure the most airtight state control possible over the quality of performance of the economic enterprises. Cash payments between enterprises have been restricted by legislation to trifling transactions. Moreover, the payments and clearing processes to be employed are laid down by law and the allowable repayment times are officially fixed.

The State Bank of the GDR

At the apex of the banking organisation stands the 'State Bank of the GDR' (see Figure 10.8). Until 1967 it operated under the name of the 'German Central Bank' (*Deutsche Notenbank*). In accordance with Section I of the law on the State Bank it is 'the central organ of the Council of Ministers for the realisation of the totality of the monetary and credit policies decided upon by the party and government' (*GBL der DDR*, Teil I, 62/1974, p. 580). From this it follows that the State Bank of the GDR is bound by the directives of the government and, in contrast to the German Federal Bank, possesses no autonomy *vis-à-vis* the state leadership as regards currency and monetary policy. In order to make sure of the desired interlinking of state economic policy and currency and monetary policy as regards personnel,

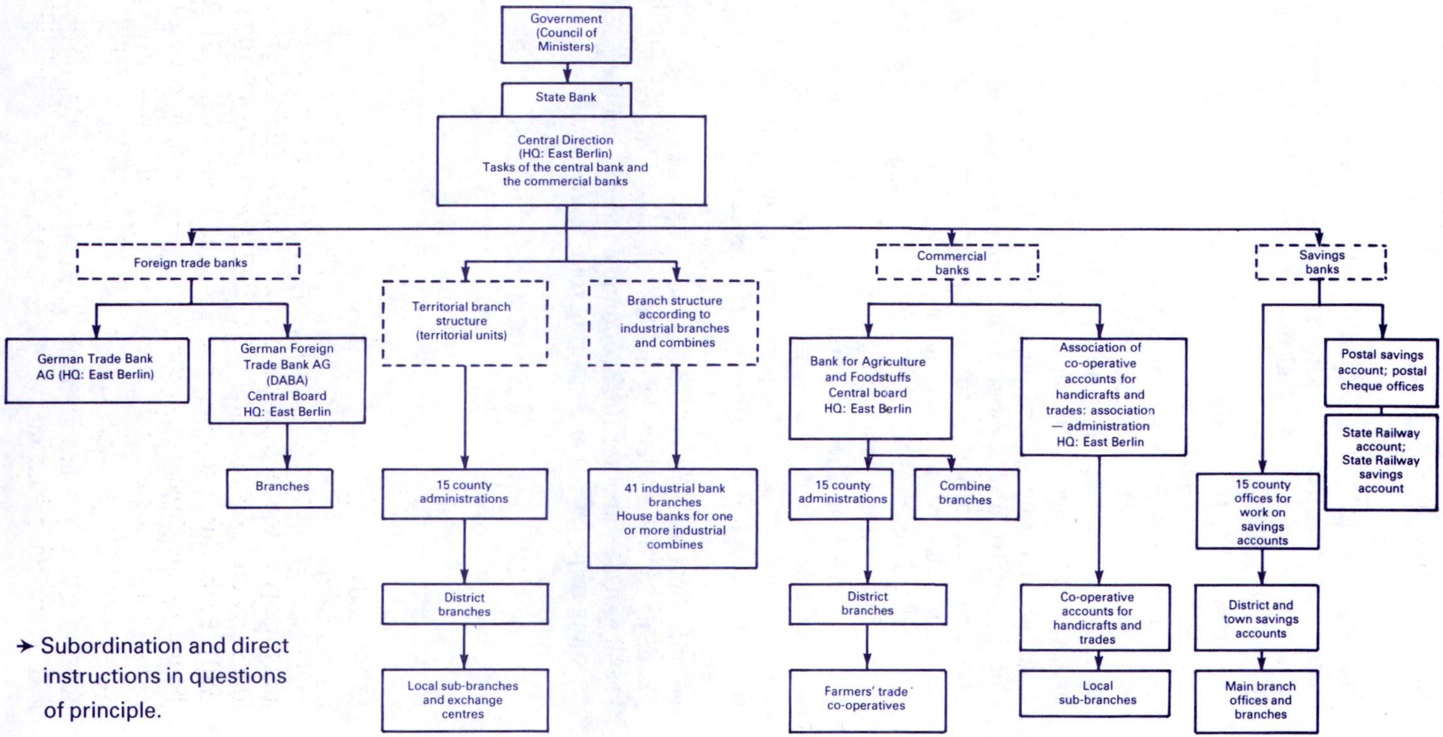
Government (Council of Ministers)
State Bank
Central Direction (HQ: East Berlin) Tasks of the central bank and the commercial banks
Foreign trade banks
German Trade Bank AG (HQ: East Berlin)
German Foreign Trade Bank AG (DABA) Central Board HQ: East Berlin
Branches
Territorial branch structure (territorial units)
15 county administrations
District branches
Local sub-branches and exchange centres
Branch structure according to industrial branches and combines
41 industrial bank branches House banks for one or more industrial combines
Commercial banks
Bank for Agriculture and Foodstuffs Central board HQ: East Berlin
15 county administrations
Combine branches
District branches
Farmers' trade co-operatives
Association of co-operative accounts for handicrafts and trades: association — administration HQ: East Berlin
Co-operative accounts for handicrafts and trades
Local sub-branches
Savings banks
Postal savings account; postal cheque offices
State Railway account; State Railway savings account
15 county offices for work on savings accounts
District and town savings accounts
Main branch offices and branches
➔ Subordination and direct instructions in questions of principle.

too, the President of the State Bank has been appointed a member of the Council of Ministers. His appointment and dismissal is, in practice, decided upon by the party leadership of the SED (Politburo).

In contrast to the German Federal Bank, the State Bank has been assigned a double task. In its role as a central bank it has to fulfil all the tasks of a central bank. To these belong, in the first place, the issue of notes, the control of the circulation of cash, the administration of the liquid reserves of the commercial banks and savings banks and the regulation of the latitude which the banking system possesses for the granting of loans (see Figure 10.7). The State Bank alone has the right to produce and issue currency units (banknotes, coins). In addition, it has been charged with all the monetary transactions of the financial administration (i.e. executive financial organ and accounting centre for the state budget).

With regard to the enterprises and combines of the most important sectors of the economy (industry, excluding foodstuffs, construction, transport and communications, state domestic trade), it is, furthermore, responsible for fulfilling all the tasks of a commercial bank. These mainly comprise the granting of short-term credits (financing of working capital), the financing of investment by means of long-term credits, the keeping of accounts for the economic concerns and the general handling of payments and clearing transactions for its customer enterprises.

In the GDR the central board of the State Bank administers the state foreign exchange account (*state foreign exchange monopoly*; foreign exchange management). It is, furthermore, responsible for the fixing of the rates of exchange in respect of both commercial and non-commercial payments transactions. In its hands lies the sale to the population of narrowly restricted quotas of foreign currencies with, of course, only the foreign currencies of those states where GDR citizens are allowed to travel being sold (sale of travel allowances). On behalf of the government, the State Bank concludes with the central banks of other states and with the two community banks of the socialist economic alliance Comecon (these being the International Bank for Economic Co-operation and the International Investment Bank) framework agreements concerning the technical procedures for handling cross-border payments and clearing flows and, in addition, concludes credit agreements.

The President of the State Bank can issue directives to the managements of commercial banks and savings banks. He watches to see whether these institutions obey government decrees and whether they make efficient use of their credit and interest rate policies as instruments for the fulfilment of the state's economic plans. At the county, district and city/town level the State Bank maintains branches which are, at the same time, the accounting centres for the other banking institutions.

Commercial banks

In 1985 the circle of customers of the Bank for Agriculture and Foodstuffs (*Bank für Landwirtschaft und Nahrungsgüterwirtschaft*: BLN) included *inter alia* 465 state farms, 3,905 agricultural producer co-operatives (*Landwirtschaftliche Produktionsgenossenschaften*: LPGs), 205 market gardening producer co-operatives (*Gärtnerische Produktionsgenossenschaften*) and 211 inter-enterprise factory farming plants (*zwischenbetriebliche Grossmastanlagen*). Just as in the case of the State Bank, in so far as this deals with commercial bank tasks, the BLN has been assigned the following responsibilities: in each individual case it is to encourage the willingness to perform of agricultural enterprises by means of an appropriate fixing of the amount of credit, interest payable, due dates for repayment and other credit conditions and to strengthen their discipline with regard to plan-fulfilment. The commercial banks have thus been entrusted by the state with the task of not only passively registering plan violations by and efficiency shortcomings in enterprise managements, but also of actively exerting influence on these same managements by word and deed, so that causes of loss-making are eliminated, performance reserves are mobilised and labour productivity is raised (i.e. stimulation function).

The farmers' trade co-operatives (*Bäuerliche Handelsgenossenschaften*: BHGs; rural trade and credit co-operatives), which are subordinate to the BLN, are obliged to look after the banking needs of the rural population in purely agricultural areas, in which there is no dense network of branches of the savings banks. They are responsible for the collection of the savings of the co-operative farmers, of the workers and employees of the state farms, and of the rural and forestry

Table 10.6: Liabilities and assets of the GDR with respect to the banks of the Western industrialised countries (OECD countries)[a] 1977-86 (position as of 31 December)

	1977	1978	1979	1980	1981	1982	1983	1984	1985	1986
					in million US dollars					
Liabilities (credits taken up)[b]	5,197	6,572	8,130	9,967	10,523	8,855	8,482	8,347	10,292	12,091
Assets[b]	933	1,255	1,979	2,130	2,245	1,964	3,489	4,549	6,549	7,469
Net indebtedness with respect to Western banks	4,264	5,317	6,151	7,837	8,278	6,891	4,993	3,798	3,[illegible]61	4,622
					in million US dollars					
Note: Supplier credits from Western export firms[c]	—	—	1,800	2,000	2,200	2,100	2,300	2,300	2,[illegible]00	2,400
					in million DM					
Cumulative GDR deficit in bilateral trade balance with the FRG[d]	2,970	3,680	3,910	3,870	3,650	3,800	4,100	3,100	3,500	4,100

Notes: a. OECD countries excluding the FRG. Hence, the data on the liabilities and assets of the GDR with respect to Western banks do not include the liabilities *vis-à-vis* West German banks and the assets held by these banks.

Also not considered in this table, of course, are bank liabilities and assets with respect to credit institutions in the Third World (the non-OECD area).

The annual changes in bank debts and assets are varyingly influenced by changes in the value of the dollar according to the size of such fluctuations, since about 45-50 per cent of the GDR's hard currency credits are denominated in dollars. A similarly high percentage of total GDR assets in Western banks is in dollars.

b. To the figures for liabilities and assets given by the Bank for International Settlements (Basle) was added the share of the 'residual' falling to the GDR (i.e. the residue of the bank debts or assets of the CMEA with respect to Western banks *in toto* not apportioned to individual member states of Comecon).

c. Gross indebtedness stemming from supplier credits extended by Western export firms in the OECD countries (excluding supplier credits from the FRG). The figures are based, in part, on estimates by international economic organisations (OECD etc.).

d. Deficit of the GDR *vis-à-vis* the FRG in respect of inner-German trade (supplier debts/payments obligations). The financial balance from trade in goods and in services has been taken into account. This trade is settled almost exclusively in 'clearing units' by means of a clearing procedure between the two central banks. A clearing unit of account (*Verrechnungseinheit*: VE) has the purchasing power of a DM. In exceptional cases, relating to especially urgent purchases by the GDR in the FRG, payment in DMs is also allowed. These payments are transacted by means of the special 'S' account in the Bundesbank of the FRG. So far, the GDR has made little use of this means of payment for goods and services. Trade which was carried out in part with the aid of cash payments is also included in the financial balance shown.

Source: Quarterly reports of the Bank for International Settlements (Basle); *Statistisches Bundesamt der Bundesrepublik Deutschland: Spezialstatistik zum Warenverkehr mit der DDR und mit Berlin (Ost)*, Fachserie 6, Reihe 6.

workers; they also handle the cashless payments and clearing flows for these population groups. The BHGs are a component part of the rural mass organisation, which has been given the name 'Association for Farmers' Mutual Assistance', and which was set up by the government to enable it to exert political influence on and to mobilise, in the economic sense, co-operative farmers and agricultural workers.

The German Foreign Trade Bank (*Deutsche Aussenhandelsbank* AG: DABA) and the German Trade Bank (*Deutsche Handelsbank* AG) are concerned exclusively with the financial aspect of foreign trade transactions (exchange of goods, licence trade, transfers of services) and with the entering into and handling of international financial transactions (taking up of foreign currency credits, fulfilment of debt servicing obligations, foreign currency dealings in hard currencies). In order to confer on these two state foreign trade banks the label of a reputable firm in their business relations with the West, the Government in East Berlin has clothed the two banks in the legal garb of a joint-stock company (*Aktiengesellschaft*: AG). This is intended to facilitate the setting up of export and import transactions with Western trading partners and to emphasise the creditworthiness of GDR banks *vis-à-vis* Western lenders of capital. Notwithstanding this 'capitalistic' legal form, both institutions are in reality banking authorities which are owned by the state and obliged to obey instructions.

While the German Trade Bank AG only handles banking transactions with Western business partners, the area of competence of DABA comprises the financial aspects of the cross-border exchange of goods and services both with Western and Third World states, and it is also responsible for ensuring an efficient settlement and the rapid exchange of documents relating to all transfers of goods and services with the partner banks in the states of the socialist camp. Internally, the Foreign Trade Banks operate as middlemen and financial switch points between the state foreign trade enterprises (i.e. institutions of the state foreign trade monopoly) on the one hand and the export and import enterprises (production enterprises) on the other. The DABA, with its branches, finances and monitors 44 foreign trade enterprises, six foreign trade corporations, four consultancy firms for capital investment planning abroad, and a number of institutions charged with specialised foreign trade tasks. It grants them credits in both marks and hard currencies, in so far as the state's hard currency earnings allow. One hundred permanent correspondent banks count among its foreign business partners. It maintains a number of bank representatives of its own in Paris, London, Rome and Belgrade.

A special position is occupied in the GDR by the co-operative banks for handicrafts and trades (*Genossenschaftskassen für Handwerk und Gewerbe*), in which category there were around 150 institutions at the end of the 1970s. They are the successor institutions of the earlier people's banks in central Germany. The owner of these banks is, in each case, a co-operative. Their members are exclusively private handicraftsmen, retail traders, proprietors of restaurants and private tradesmen. The capital resources of these banks are formed from shares in the respective co-operatives. In addition, they also receive capital grants from the State Bank, as far as handicraft producer co-operatives (PGHs) are counted among their credit customers. As well as the collection of savings, the management of the business accounts for their customers and the handling of their cashless payments flows, the co-operative banks grant credits to registered members and also to PGHs. In the conduct of their business, the co-operative banks are bound to abide by the directives they receive from the Ministry of Finance and from the State Bank.

Savings banks

For the citizens of the GDR who seek advice on money matters and require banking services, the savings banks are the most important money and credit institutions. As is the case in the Federal Republic, the savings banks in the GDR, too, are institutions of the town and country districts. Different to the situation in the former country, however, is the fact that in the GDR the system of savings banks is controlled centrally by the State Bank central board and the district offices of the central bank. Moreover, the district councils (district administrations) also have the right to issue directives. The district and town savings banks of the GDR have main branches, branches and agencies in department stores and enterprises in their local business areas. At the end of 1980 the network of savings banks branches comprised 3,451 main branches and branches. In the last five years, many branches have been closed because of personnel shortages and in order to reduce enterprise costs. In mid-

Table 10.7: Development of the accumulation of financial assets of the population of the GDR 1950-85[a] (position as at 31 December)

Year	Total savings	Cash hoards	Savings in bank accounts (savings deposits)	Proportion of cash hoards to total savings
		billion marks		%
1950	4.64	3.36	1.28	72
1955	9.06	4.12	4.94	45
1960	22.04	4.54	17.50	21
1965	36.44	5.16	31.28	14
1970	59.56	7.41	52.15	12
1971	63.40	7.68	55.72	12
1972	68.75	8.78	55.97	13
1973	74.30	9.18	65.12	12
1974	79.50	9.58	70.22	12
1975	85.45	10.14	75.31	12
1976	90.70	10.49	80.21	11
1977	97.93	11.31	86.08	12
1978	103.96	11.91	92.05	11
1979	109.43	12.37	96.96	11
1980	111.98	12.25	99.73	11
1981	115.28	12.32	102.96	11
1982	120.10	12.53	107.57	10
1983	126.22	13.03	113.19	10
1984	132.01	13.35	118.66	10
1985	138.23	13.65	124.58	10

Note: a. Since the economic leadership of the GDR has abolished savings in the form of *building society accounts* and *stocks and shares*, this table illustrates the development of almost all private wealth formation since 1950. The only items not accounted for are the private hoards of foreign exchange in DMs, dollars or other hard currencies, and the holdings of private individuals in savings-linked personal insurance schemes (insurance savings).

Source: *Statistische Jahrbücher der DDR*.

1986, the savings banks organisation consisted of only 2,400 main branches and branches and 800 sideline agencies. At the same time, the savings banks employed around 20,000 people, of whom over 80 per cent were women. To the customers of the savings banks belong wage and salary earners, self-employed professionals, retail traders, private handicraftsmen and tradesmen, as well as a proportion of the producer co-operatives.

Deposit business (*Passivgeschäfte*)

The focus of the business of savings banks is on deposits

(depositing, payments and clearing flows). At the centre of the work of the savings banks, therefore, lies the promotion of the willingness to save of private households and the collection and administration of savings. At present the citizens of the GDR keep around 17.6 million giro savings and savings-book accounts with the town and district savings banks. In them, at the end of 1985, some 100 billion marks in savings were deposited. Over 80 per cent of the total savings deposits of the GDR population are concentrated in the savings banks. In mid-1986, the GDR savings banks administered more giro savings and savings-book accounts than there were residents (17.6 million accounts, population 16.6 million). The remaining just under 20 per cent of savings deposits, which are not held in the accounts of the town and district savings banks, are distributed among the following public banks and institutions: the co-operative banks for handicrafts and trades (BHGs); State Railways savings and loans banks, post office savings banks and postal cheque offices.

Altogether, around 22 million private giro savings and savings-book accounts are at present administered by the people's banks. It follows from this that, on average, every GDR citizen possesses one or two savings accounts. At the end of 1985 private households in the GDR had saved around 7,480 marks *per capita* in savings accounts. These savings comprise both voluntary and forced savings. The latter arise when the supply of consumer goods is too small and patchy and, moreover, does not correspond to consumer demand as regards range. If citizens with purchasing power are unable to find a rational use for a part of their incomes, then this represents forced savings. In consequence of the inadequate supply of attractive and qualitatively satisfactory consumer goods on the domestic market, for example, the supply of goods and retail trade turnover in the GDR increased by only 77 per cent in the period 1970-85, while the savings of the population (in the form of bank accounts and cash hoards) increased by 132 per cent.

While savers in the Federal Republic are able to choose from among a whole array of forms of savings those most appropriate to their needs, citizens of the GDR are offered only two forms of savings in total, that of giro savings and that of the savings book. Incentives through the differentiation of interest rates according to the fixed term of the deposit, by means of which true savers could be rewarded and efforts could be made to attract free financial capital into bank accounts and to tie it down there for longer terms, do not exist in the GDR. The holdings in giro savings accounts and deposits in savings-book accounts yield a *uniform* rate of interest of 3.25 per cent per annum.

It is certainly surprising for the observer who is not familiar with conditions in the GDR to find that the citizens of the second German state, in addition to forming sight deposits and savings accounts, constantly keep a considerable part of their surplus monetary resources in cash hoards (in 'savings stockings'), although this form of savings yields no interest. In 1985 every three-person household kept in the house, on average, more than two months' salary (2,460 marks) as a liquid reserve (see Table 10.7).

The cashless payments flows, organised by the savings banks, are mainly handled by the giro savings accounts (giro transfers, standing orders, direct debiting etc.). At present around 70 per cent of working people, students and pensioners receive their wages, salaries, grants and pensions in cashless form.

Loan Business (*Aktivgeschäfte*)

In the GDR all banks serving the population are forbidden to give overdrafts. Citizens who repeatedly overdraw their account are penalised. The loan business of savings banks is given below.

(1) The one-off granting of interest-free credits on preferential social grounds to young married couples (maximum age 30) is designed to make it easier for them to furnish and fit out their houses or to purchase their own dwellings in a co-operative venture. Until the 11th Party Congress of the SED (17-21 April 1986), there was an upper limit of 5,000 marks on this type of credit. Since then, however, young people can borrow up to 7,000 marks, while the maximum credit term has been extended from five to eleven years. The granting of these new preferential credit conditions was long overdue, to compensate young people for the steep rise in state-determined prices for furnishings and fittings, especially in the last five years.

A portion of the sum owed is written off for each child born to the marriage (1,000 marks for the first child, 1,500 marks for the second and 2,500 marks for every subsequent child). These credit aids are, moreover, meant to check the decline in the birth rate, to stop the fall in total population, and to encourage population growth (i.e. consumer credit in the service of state population policy). At the end of 1985, 73,359 young couples had taken up marriage-foundation loans and had borrowed 483 million marks from the people's banks on the exceedingly favourable terms that apply. The losses of revenue from interest sustained by the savings banks through the granting of these interest-free loans are made good by the state. Similarly, the state has to step in when the banks serving the population are obliged to write off a portion of the credit debt of young married couples, since they are fulfilling legal requirements. In 1985, by reason of registering births, young couples were let off a portion of their liabilities in 126,834 cases, which cost the state budget a total of 162.5 million marks.

(2) Consumer and hire purchase credits, which every citizen in the GDR can take up. These loans are not burdened with contributions to the fulfilment of social and population policies and usually have to carry a rate of interest of 6 per cent. In the case both of the foundation-of-marriage loans and of normal consumer credits, however, no cash is paid out to the borrowers, but a 'letter of credit' (*Kreditkaufbrief*) is issued to them in the amount of the loan. With this letter they are not able to acquire all the consumer durables on offer in retail trade, but they must be content to purchase those consumer goods selected and listed by the Ministry for Trade and Consumer Supply for this purpose. The lists of these goods can be seen on request by interested parties in every branch of the savings banks (i.e. consumer credit as a means of guiding sales).

(3) In so far as private households are allowed to build their own homes (e.g. families of rural workers with many children), the savings banks grant, in case of need, long-term loans to the individuals wishing to build; the interest rates on these credits are around 4 per cent as a rule. If the individual builder keeps below the state expenditure norm in the construction of the home, such thrift is rewarded with a reduction in interest.

(4) Finally, the savings banks make available credits for working and fixed capital purposes to those private enterprises providing services and private handicraft enterprises which come within their sphere of business. These loans bear a rate of interest of 5 per cent per annum.

11

Agriculture

Konrad Merkel

THE AGRARIAN SYSTEM

A country's agrarian system, seen as part of the overall economic and social system, is determined, in general, by the ideas and principles according to which the social and economic relations of the people engaged in agriculture both among themselves and with the means of production are shaped. In concrete terms, these organisational principles express themselves, in a given social framework, in agriculture and the countryside as well as in the legal relations of economic life in the agrarian sector, especially in the realised forms of ownership, of agricultural concerns or enterprises and of agrarian markets. Accordingly, the adoption of a particular agrarian system involves a far-reaching political decision and not merely the choice of particular forms of agricultural enterprises.

Phases of development

The policy choices which moulded the present agrarian system in the GDR were made at the end of the Second World War, when the system of government in Germany collapsed, the Soviet army moved into its German zone of occupation and the Soviet military administration assumed authority in this part of Germany. In order to combat the chaotic economic and especially the food situation, as it existed in the whole of Germany at the time, it was essential to reorganise economic life. It did not, however, prove possible to arrive at a uniform solution of this problem in all four zones of Germany, because of the divergent political positions of the Soviet and the three Western economic powers. In the Soviet zone of occupation the creation of socialist ownership of the means of production had already been initiated immediately after the end of the war with the expropriation, without compensation, of landholdings over 100 hectares, of almost all of the larger industrial firms and of all existing credit institutions and private insurance companies. In addition, the existing central planning and steering of economic processes was retained, and the establishment of a new, centrally run administration of the economy in the Soviet zone of occupation was systematically pursued and concentrated on the political leadership. Since then, the real centre of decision-making has been the leadership group of the SED represented by the Politburo and the Central Committee and its Secretariat, whilst the state apparatus is primarily responsible for carrying out the decisions taken by these leading organs of the party.

With the centralisation of political power in the SED leadership and bureaucracy, the decisive political precondition was created for transferring the economic and social system developed in the Soviet Union itself, with its essential political, state and economic institutions and practices, its forms of production and organisation, legal principles and ideological doctrines, to this portion of Germany and incorporating it in the constitution following the foundation of the GDR as a state. Communism, which the policy of the Soviets aimed from the outset to spread to the whole of mankind, means the planned predetermination, guidance and securing of the path of development prescribed by organisational policy for the 'building of socialism' in agriculture and in the countryside, as elsewhere. The system of central planning, management and steering of the economy and society, which was set up in the Soviet occupation zone of Germany by the occupying power in conformity with the Soviet model and which in the course of time was further developed in the GDR, has exercised a decisive influence upon overall developments in the state polity and thus also upon the shaping of the agrarian structure. There is, indeed, scarcely another area of life in the GDR in which since 1945 changes so profound have made themselves felt as in the social structure of agriculture. These changes were brought about by agrarian policy measures which, determined by communist doctrine in its Soviet version, primarily aimed at a 'revolutionary transformation' of the existing agrarian system, characterised by the preponderance of peasant family farms. Even if the direction, range, intensity and form of direct steering interventions in agriculture and the agrarian structure have undergone a number of changes over time, nevertheless GDR agrarian policy has the long term aim of fully subjecting agriculture to the concept of a centrally guided planned economy without private ownership of the means of production and of putting into practice the model of a socialist agriculture inherent in Marxist-Leninist theory.

The system of agriculture which was the GDR's historic legacy and which largely consisted of peasant family farms, has developed, in the course of time and in several successive stages, into today's socialist-collectivist agrarian system. As with the present agrarian systems in the other countries of east-central and south-eastern Europe which came under Soviet control after the end of the Second World War, this was not the result of any democratic decision by the people concerned. The question of whether and how far the people currently employed in agriculture concur with the agrarian system obtaining there as being the socially most desirable, must remain open, since it cannot as yet be answered scientifically.

The process of the socialisation of agriculture, implemented in stages, is characterised by two radical changes: at the beginning a land reform in favour of small farmers, whilst retaining a number of the nationalised, formerly private large landed estates as well as the demesnes and other public enterprises in the form of state farms (*volkseigene Güter*, VEG: 1945-46); thereafter collectivisation (1952-60), using three types of agricultural producer co-operatives (*landwirtschaftliche Produktionsgenossenschaften*: LPGs), differing according to the degree of socialisation. Type III, as the highest form (the others being gradually transformed into this type), largely corresponded to the form of producer co-operative realised in the Soviet *kolkhoz*. The ensuing third stage of development is characterised by the centrally guided co-operative formation of large-scale socialist agriculture, which has led since 1967 to special, industrial-style production enterprises in agriculture.

The transition to industrial production methods means the step-by-step assimilation of agriculture to the conditions prevailing in industry as regards management, organisation and production technologies as well as the working methods and lifestyles of the rural population, in order thus to eliminate the economic and social differences between industry and agriculture, between town and country and between worker and farmer. The industrialisation concept for agriculture in the GDR is not primarily economic but socio-political in character, even though its social and economic goals are closely connected. First place goes to the postulate of 'bringing the class of co-operative farmers closer to the working class'. In the co-operation economy are systematically created the preconditions for a 'socialist community of people'. Here work is done together and problems solved communally. Co-operation is thus the most important means by which the political leadership of the GDR seeks to realise socio-political goals in close connection with economic in agriculture. At the same time, it is supposed to become possible, along the path which has been marked out, to transform co-operative-socialist ownership (*genossenschaftlich-sozialistisches Eigentum*: members' collective ownership, into which private ownership of the means of production had first been transformed through collectivisation) into the higher socialisation category of co-operative-socialist ownership (*kooperativ-sozialistisches Eigentum*: enterprises' collective ownership). This form of ownership is intended to form a transitory stage in future development towards the intended highest form of ownership, namely people's ownership.

From the economic point of view, the transition to industrial production methods in agriculture means a gradual departure from traditional production methods, characterised by the all-round agricultural enterprise producing both crops and livestock; in the 1960s this was still embodied in the traditional agricultural co-operatives and state farms. The specialisation of production connected with the industrialisation of agriculture implies a basic division of labour between crop and livestock production, i.e. the systematic dissolution of the union within the enterprise of crop and livestock production and the establishment of independent, specialised enterprises engaging in crop production on the one hand and animal husbandry on the other. The separating out of the individual branches of agricultural production (and, within these, even of individual production sections) from enterprises previously engaged in combined production and the amalgamation of these branches into independent production units, however, requires that this agrarian structure, involving a high degree of specialisation and division of labour, should in turn be furnished with an interlocking framework. This takes the form of institutionalised co-operation, i.e. inter-enterprise (instead of intra-enterprise as hitherto) product exchanges on the basis of contractual agreements both among the specialised agricultural enterprises and also between these and the service enterprises. The latter have likewise, in consequence of the labour division industrialisation of agriculture, been established as independent special enterprises for the support of the specialised crop and livestock production enterprises. For example, the agro-chemical centres (*Agrochemische Zentren*: ACZs), which deal with fertilisers, plant pest control and the necessary transport, and the district enterprises for rural technology (*Kreisbetriebe für Landtechnik*: KfL) for the maintenance and repair of agricultural machinery.

From these interventions in the organisational system linking primary crop and secondary livestock production enterprises in the GDR (undertaken in the socio-political interest of industrialisation and specialisation in agriculture) have arisen a number of serious problems for the economic efficiency and profitability of its agricultural production, which came to public knowledge at the beginning of the 1980s under the pressure of worldwide changes in overall economic conditions, and which caused 'improvement of the relationship between expenditure and result' being from then on ranked as a chief task in agriculture. Even though cost saving and economic thinking have recently been placed more in the foreground (several measures of administrative reorganisation have been taken to this end), to ensure an economically rational agrarian production would require, above all, fundamental alterations in the organisation of agrarian production. So far, these have not occurred and are, indeed, not to be expected.

Enterprise structure

The concentration and specialisation of agrarian production is expressed in a continuously falling number of agricultural enterprises, whose average acreage is, at the same time, increasing (see Tables 11.1 and 11.2).

In 1985, after the organisational separation of crop and livestock production had taken place, the socialist agriculture of the GDR consisted of only 4,797 production enterprises. These

Table 11.1: Socialist agricultural enterprises in the GDR

Enterprise category	Number of enterprises				Percentage share of enterprises in the LN of socialist agriculture as a whole.			
	1960	1970	1980	1985	1960	1970	1980	1985
State farms: total,	669	511	469	465	6.7	7.5	6.9	7.5
of which:								
Crop production	—	—	66	77	—	—	6.1	6.6
Animal husbandry	—	—	319	314	—	—	—	—
Specialised crop production	—	—	84	74	—	—	0.8	0.9
Agricultural producer co-operatives: Total,	19,313	9,009	3,946	3,905	91.7	91.7	85.0	90.9
of which:								
Crop production	—	—	1,047	1,144	—	—	84.1	89.6
Animal husbandry	—	—	2,899	2,761	—	—	—	—
KAP[a] and ZBE[b] crop production	—	—	87	11	—	—	7.5	0.9
Market gardening producer co-operatives	298	346	213	205	0.2	0.4	0.3	0.3
ZBE[b] livestock production	—	—	299	211	—	—	—	—
Other[c]	—	—	—	—	1.4	0.4	0.3	0.4
Total number of socialist enterprises	20,280	9,866	5,014	4,797	100.0	100.0	100.0	100.0

Notes: a. KAP: co-operative divisions for crop production; b. ZBE: inter-enterprise organisations; c. Not classified in detail.

Source: *Statistisches Jahrbuch der DDR* (1986 and preceding).

Table 11.2: Average sizes of socialist agricultural enterprises in the GDR (in hectares of land used for agricultural purposes)

Enterprise category	Average sizes of enterprises in hectares of LN			
	1960	1970	1980	1985
State farms: total	591	866	870	945
crop production	—	—	5,454	5,057
Agricultural producer co-operatives:				
total	280	599	1,276	1,369
crop production	—	—	4,755	4,608
KAP and ZBE: crop production	—	—	5,075	4,607
Market gardening producer co-operatives	46	60	79	79

Source: *Statistisches Jahrbuch der DDR* (1986 and preceding).

comprised: 1,232 crop-producing enterprises with an average land area of 4,636 hectares of LN (*landwirtschaftliche Nutzfläche*: land used for agricultural purposes) per enterprise; 3,286 livestock-producing enterprises, with an average livestock of 1,576 GV (*Grossvieheinheit*, large livestock equivalent: 1 GV = 500 kilogrammes live weight) per unit; 74 specialised crop-producing enterprises (ornamental plants, tree nurseries etc.); and 205 market gardening producer co-operatives (*Gärtnerische Produktionsgenossenschaften*: GPDs).

In addition there were 264 ACZs, servicing the production enterprises, which were jointly formed by the crop-producing enterprises as inter-enterprise organisations (*Zwischenbetriebliche Einrichtungen*: ZBEs), 158 Kfls, various special inter-co-operative organisations (*Zwischengenossenschaftliche Einrichtungen*: ZGEs), such as those in agriculture, forestry and construction, also land improvement co-operatives, and, furthermore, nationally owned enterprises for the manufacture of organic fertilisers, for drying and pelletisation, and mixed feed works.

THE IMPORTANCE OF AGRICULTURE FOR THE ECONOMY

Economic considerations

The supply role of agriculture is rated highly in the GDR. The point that Honecker made in his report to the eighth Party Congress in 1971, still applies; namely that it is more advantageous for the GDR to supply socialist agriculture with more and improved means of production than to import foodstuffs which one could produce oneself. As regards supplying the population with foodstuffs, the GDR's agrarian policy, just like that of every member of Comecon, is strongly autarkic. The task assigned to agriculture — that of continually improving the supply of foodstuffs to the population and of raw materials to the food processing industry from domestic production — also explains why increasing agricultural output whilst at the same time raising productivity is still one of the most important economic goals for agriculture. This is so even given the great problems encountered in reducing production costs and raising profitability in agriculture.

In 1985 agriculture and forestry accounted for around 11 per cent of the total employed labour force in the GDR, compared to the FRG's approximate 5 per cent. In the period 1935-38, before the start of the Second World War, the territory of what are now the GDR and the FRG accounted for about 22 and 27 per cent respectively. Thus the percentage share has fallen by twice as much for the FRG compared with the GDR since then. This relatively high employment ratio in the GDR is the result not only of low capital investment, but also of factors such as the special forms of collective labour organisation in the GDR, as well as differing criteria of definition.

The position of agriculture in the economy of the GDR is also clear from its share of national economic expenditure and the contribution it makes to national product. In 1985, agriculture accounted for 14.2 per cent of the total fixed capital stock (*Grundmittel*: production capital minus land and livestock) and 7.4 per cent of total gross investment in the GDR. In 1960 these shares were 14.4 and 11.9 per cent, in 1970 15.5 and 13.0 per cent, and in 1980 14.6 and 9.7 per cent respectively. In contrast, in 1985 agriculture accounted for 8.1 per cent of net product (in 1960 16.9, in 1970 12.0 and in 1980 8.4 per cent: see Tables 11.3 and 11.4).

A falling number of agricultural employees, replaced by capital goods, and a declining contribution by agriculture to national product, which are typical for highly industrialised economies, are thus also characteristic of conditions in the GDR. It must be pointed out, however, that, contrary to this

Table 11.3: Indicators for the position of agriculture in the economy of the GDR

Indicator	Unit	1960	1970	1980	1985
Employees in agrarian sector[a]	in 1000	1,304	997	878	922
Capital stock[b] of agriculture	in million marks	31,353	57,403	93,790	110,500[d]
Investment[b,c] in agriculture	in million marks	2,125	4,721	5,313	3,865
Contribution of agriculture to net product[b]	in million marks	13,510	14,954	16,619	19,995[d]
	Percentage of national economy				
Employees in agrarian sector[a]		17.0	12.8	10.7	10.8
Capital stock[b] of agriculture		14.4	15.5	14.6	14.2[d]
Investment[b,c] in agriculture		11.9	13.0	9.7	7.4
Contribution of agriculture to net product		16.9	12.0	8.4	8.1[d]

Notes: a. Agriculture and forestry, employees excluding apprentices, position as of 30 September; b. Price basis 1980; c. Excluding investment participation (in other countries); d. Provisional.

Source: *Statistisches Jahrbuch der DDR* (1986).

trend, the manpower figures only decreased up to 1977, but thereafter gradually increased. In 1985 socialist agriculture (excluding the ACZs) was already employing some 48,000 more persons than in 1977. This development, which is promoted by the economic leadership of the GDR, is due to the fact that in several areas of agrarian production the reduction in manpower proceeded more rapidly than the mechanisation of certain labour processes, thus causing a manpower deficiency. In order to secure the economically necessary volume of output in agricultural foodstuffs and raw materials, it was therefore 'necessary not to permit a further reduction in manpower' (Report of the Central Committee given to the 10th Party Congress of the SED, 11-16 April 1981, by Erich Honecker). This was required, above all, in the interest of cutting overtime, which, in crop production at harvest time and in animal husbandry generally throughout the year, represented a heavy burden, especially in agricultural producer co-operatives with limited manpower. The disproportions between the supply of and the demand for labour still existing in many places would have an extremely negative impact on the meeting of agrotechnically favourable deadlines and on ensuring that the requisite intensity of care was given to animals. This is one

Table 11.4: Agricultural capital stock and investment per employee and per unit of area

Year	Capital stock[a]	Investment[a]	Capital stock[a]	Investment[a]
	Per employee[b]		Per hectare of LN[c]	
		in marks		
1960	23,441	1,630	4,882	331
1970	55,657	4,735	9,129	751
1980	104,649	6,048	14,956	847
1985	125,500[d]	4,192	18,711[d]	621
		1960 = 100		
1970	237	290	187	227
1980	446	371	306	256
1985	535	257	383	188

Notes: a. Price basis 1980; b. In agriculture and forestry, excluding apprentices; c. land used for agricultural purposes; d. Provisional.

Source: *Statistisches Jahrbuch der DDR* (1986).

reason why it was important to counteract the reduction of manpower potential in agriculture resulting especially from the age structure and no longer, as was done in 1960s and 1970s, to release manpower in favour of other sectors of the economy.

Agriculture is relatively more important in the GDR than in the FRG, measured in relation both to its contribution to the national product and to total employment. It follows from this that, although the contribution which agriculture makes to national product is relatively greater in the GDR than in the FRG and other Western countries, yet the contribution which the agrarian sector has so far made to aggregate economic growth by releasing manpower to the other sectors of the economy has been less than in most of the industrial countries of Western Europe. It is in this context that the relatively high capital investment which has flowed into agriculture and forestry until recently should be seen. The forced direction of capital investment into agriculture in the 1960s and 1970s inevitably retarded both the development of typical growth industries and also improvement of the infrastructure needed for the creation of non-agricultural jobs, and thus took place at the expense of higher aggregate growth rates. From the point of view of the economy as a whole, it seems doubtful whether, given the relatively large share of total investment going to agriculture, one can speak of a primacy of industrial over agricultural productivity in the GDR, given its ranking as an industrial state; it may, rather, be the case that, precisely through the attempt to aim at both goals at once, national economic production potential has thus far been impaired and overextended.

In order to develop, both administratively and organisationally, the forward and backward linkages of agriculture with other branches of the economy and the linkages with trade and to make it into a component part of the overall system, the subsystem agriculture and food processing was first formed with the aim of further developing it into an agro-industrial complex (*Agrar-Industrie-Komplex*: AIK).

Ecological considerations

As well as the overall economic appraisal of agriculture, its ecological evaluation has gradually increased in importance in the GDR too. As a result of the high degree of specialisation and concentration of agriculture in large-scale enterprises, above all in mass livestock rearing in factory farms, a whole range of serious environmental problems has arisen. These concern, above all, the utilisation of animal excrement. The chief environmental problems have proved to be liquid manure, production effluents and silo oozing in factory farms. Limited storage capacity for liquid manure, an insufficiency of drainage channels for silos and long transport distances force a year-round continuous disposal of liquid manure and prevent its planned use at suitable times and in appropriate crop production. According to weather conditions, this leads to more or less severe damage to the soil structure and hence to a considerable reduction in soil fertility. Moreover, the release of large quantities of liquid manure in the environs of factory farms, especially those involved in pigs and poultry, and the practice in some cases of releasing wastes containing nitrogen and phosphates into streams and other ground water, are responsible for the relative atrophying of part of the GDR's waters.

Apart from soil and ground water, the air, too, is being considerably more heavily polluted by factory farming (at least in the vicinity of agricultural units) than by the traditional rearing of livestock in buildings of more modest size. That the gases given off by mass livestock rearing are not only foul smelling, but also, because of the high content of germs and dust, are harmful to animals and the humans in charge of them, and, furthermore, to the environment, is shown by the fact that in proximity to such units forests show signs of dying.

FOUNDATIONS OF CROP AND LIVESTOCK PRODUCTION

Use of soil

In 1985 land used for agricultural purposes (LN) in the GDR amounted to 6.23 million hectares, just 58 per cent of the whole area of the economy. As is characteristic of other industrial countries, in the GDR, too, the non-agricultural use of land suitable for agricultural purposes is reducing the area available for cultivation. Between 1960 and 1985 the loss of cultivable land amounted to 195,926 hectares in all. In 1985, relative to the population, the ratio was 267 people per 100 hectares of LN, or 0.37 hectares of LN *per capita.* The amount of available agricultural land *per capita* in the GDR is almost twice that in the FRG, but in comparison with the socialist countries it is relatively small (Czechoslovakia 0.45; Poland 0.53; Hungary 0.62; Romania 0.67; Bulgaria 0.70 and the USSR 2.15 hectares of LN *per capita*).

As Table 11.5 shows, about three-quarters of the LN in the GDR is accounted for by arable land and one-fifth by meadowland. The arable/meadowland ratio has shown a naturally determined inertia over time. In contrast, the cultivation ratio (arable land ratio), i.e. the percentage share of arable land taken up by individual crops or groups of crops per year, is much more subject to change. All the same, this crop ratio does show a certain constancy, since the main crop groupings of grain, root crops and fodder, taken together, regularly account for some 90 per cent of the arable area, while only some 10 per cent is used for all other arable crops (pulses, vegetables and garden plants, oil seeds, tobacco and other commercial crops). Shifts in cultivation over time have so far been confined to changes in the amount of land used for the three main crop groupings mentioned as well as changes within each grouping.

In the period 1960 to 1985 developments in cultivation are characterised by a trend towards expansion of grain and field fodder crops and a concomitant reduction of root crops. While

Table 11.5: Use of agricultural land in the GDR

Type of cultivation or crop	1960 1000 hectares	1960 %	1970 1000 hectares	1970 %	1980 1000 hectares	1980 %	1985 1000 hectares	1985 %
	Land used for agricultural purposes and types of cultivation							
Arable land	4,848	75.5	4,618	73.4	4,760	75.9	4,717	75.8
Meadowland,	1,362	81.2	1,469	23.4	1,235	19.7	1,252	20.1
of which:								
Meadows[a]	(823)	(12.8)	(725)	(11.5)	(608)	(9.7)	(531)	(8.5)
Pasturage[b]	(440)	(6.9)	(662)	(10.5)	(532)	(8.5)	(633)	(10.2)
Other land[c]	212	3.3	202	3.2	276	4.4	257	4.1
Land used for agricultural purposes	6,422	100.0	6,289	100.0	6,271	100.0	6,226	100.0
	Arable land according to main types of cultivation[e]							
Grain,	2,319	47.8	2,287	49.5	2,526	53.1	2,519	53.4
of which:								
Bread grain	(1,364)	(28.1)	(1,279)	(27.7)	(1,385)	(29.1)	(1,434)	(30.4)
Fodder and industrial grain	(955)	(19.7)	(1,008)	(21.8)	(1,141)	(24.0)	(1,085)	(23.0)
Root crops,	1,201	24.8	1,017	22.0	797	16.8	765	16.2
of which:								
Potatoes	(770)	(15.9)	(667)	(14.4)	(513)	(10.8)	(475)	(10.1)
Sugar beet	(240)	(5.0)	(192)	(4.2)	(250)	(5.3)	(233)	(4.9)
Root crops used for fodder	(191)	(3.9)	(158)	(3.4)	(34)	(0.7)	(57)	(1.2)

Field fodder crops,	852	17.6	923	20.0	968	20.3	960	20.4
of which:								
Clover and lucerne	(175)	(3.6)	(356)	(7.7)	(277)	(5.8)	(321)	(6.8)
Green and silo maize	(439)	(9.1)	(337)	(7.3)	(365)	(7.7)	(360)	(7.6)
Pulses	91	1.9	53	1.2	49	1.0	55	1.2
Oil and fibre plants	170	3.5	116	2.5	134	2.8	158	3.3
Remainder of land[d]	215	4.4	222	4.8	286	6.0	260	5.5
Arable land	4,848	100.0	4,618	100.0	4,760	100.0	4,717	100.0

Notes: a. Excluding open land; b. Excluding common grazing land; c. Gardens, orchards, vineyards, tree nurseries and osier beds; d. Outdoor vegetables, seed grounds, crops for ploughing under, other cultivation and fallow; e. Harvest land.

Source: *Statistisches Jahrbuch der DDR* (1986).

in 1960 the share of arable land devoted to grain of around 48 per cent had reached what was probably the lowest limit capable of meeting the requirements of human consumption and of fodder and straw for the livestock, it rose steadily in subsequent years and has remained at about 53 per cent since 1975. The proportion of land devoted to arable fodder production, which was around 18 per cent in 1960, has since increased to about 20 per cent. In contrast, the share of root crops in arable land fell from around 25 per cent in 1960 to some 16 per cent in 1985, this reduction being due to a marked decrease in fodder root crops and potatoes, whilst sugar beet has taken a roughly constant 5 per cent of arable land.

As a result of the lower proportion of meadowland in LN hectarage, fodder production in the GDR is relatively strongly dependent on purpose-grown fodder for supplying a planned high cattle stock and thus to a significant extent (14.8 per cent of arable area in 1985) falls back on less productive intercropping with its uncertain yields.

Livestock

The realisation of the plan goals set for livestock production is dependent on the size of the stock of animals and also the output of individual animals, for which, in turn, a well co-ordinated continuous supply of fodder in both quantitative and qualitative terms is essential. Table 11.6 shows individual livestock numbers between 1960 and 1985.

Leaving aside year-to-year fluctuations, the GDR's livestock total has steadily increased in size over time. In 1985 the GDR recorded its highest livestock total up to then, with 5,887,000 'large livestock equivalent' (*Grossvieheinheit*: GV). Livestock density (livestock per unit of area) was likewise at a previously unequalled level with around 95 GV per hectare of LN (compared to about 80 GV in 1970).

While the overall livestock total in 1985 was about 17 per cent higher than in 1970, looked at under separate categories the figure for cattle shows an increase of 12 per cent, pigs 34 per cent, poultry 18 per cent and sheep no less than 60 per cent. At the same time the stock of horses and goats was rapidly reduced. The number of sheep, which had been falling until 1970, has since increased steadily and in 1985 reached the

Table 11.6: Livestock in the GDR

Animals	1960	1970	1980	1985
	Livestock in thousands (position as of end of year)			
Horses	447	127	70	105
Cattle,	4,675	5,190	5,723	5,827
of which: Cows	2,175	2,163	2,138	2,064
Sheep	2,015	1,598	2,038	2,587
Goats	439	135	24	22
Pigs	8,316	9,684	12,871	12,946
Poultry,	36,910	43,034	51,611	50,680
of which: Laying hens[b]	28,121	25,470	26,844	25,161
	Livestock in 1000 'large livestock equivalent'[a]			
Horses	470	132	71	96
Cattle	3,454	3,603	3,937	4,054
Sheep	178	146	185	230
Goats	35	11	2	2
Raw fodder feeders	4,137	3,892	4,195	4,382
Pigs	839	970	1,316	1,302
Poultry	148	172	206	203
Total livestock	5,124	5,034	5,717	5,887

Notes: a. Calculated according to the 'large livestock equivalent' used in the FRG; see Statistical Yearbook for Food, Agriculture and Forestry (1983), p. 118; b. Over six months old.

Source: *Statistisches Jahrbuch der DDR* (1986).

unprecedented figure of 2.59 million. The number of horses, which was at its lowest in 1977 with 66,000 animals, has, however, continuously increased since then, reaching 105,000 animals once again in 1985.

Within the cattle and poultry stocks, which in 1984 and 1981 reached their respective record levels with 5.85 million and 54.31 million animals, the number of cows and laying hens respectively has remained fairly steady over time, but with a slight tendency to fall.

FACTORS OF PRODUCTION IN AGRICULTURE

The production potential of agriculture is directly linked with its factor inputs; that is, labour and capital (including land). Since the share of agriculture in total labour and capital and the agricultural use of land have already been dealt with, what is required here is to give a differentiated account of agricultural manpower and its equipping with yield-raising mechanical-technical production and labour aids.

Manpower

Number according to size of enterprise

The socialist transformation of the structure of agricultural enterprises has necessitated a fundamental alteration of the structure of rural society. A characteristic of the large-scale collective special enterprise, which has become the dominant type of enterprise in GDR agriculture, is its rich endowment of manpower. In comparison with other highly industrial countries, manpower input in GDR agriculture, with around 12 AK (*Vollarbeitskräfte*: 'full-time manpower'; see Table 11.7) per 100 hectares of LN at present, seems disproportionately high. In FRG agriculture with its predominantly family farms, the corresponding figures are an average of about 8 AK per 100 hectares of LN for all enterprise sizes taken together, and only 3 AK for enterprises of 50 hectares and over. This not only epitomises the differing levels of economic development in the two German states, but also in itself provides an index of variations in agricultural labour productivity, giving cause for doubts as to the economic efficiency of GDR enterprise organisation and demonstrating that the large-scale, manpower-intensive form of organisation in agriculture there was adopted for political and not economic purposes. In no other highly developed industrial economy, be it the USA, the UK, Sweden, Belgium, France or Japan, has the large-scale agricultural enterprise richly endowed with manpower become the predominant type of enterprise.

Numbers according to forms of ownership

In 1985 there were 885,813 members of agricultural and 28,083 members of market gardening producer co-operatives respectively in the GDR. Of the permanent employees in agriculture (excluding forestry, the veterinary service, pest control and the agro-chemical centres), about three-quarters were permanently employed members of agricultural producer co-operatives (see Table 11.7).

The dominant position of co-operative farmers in agriculture relates not only to the prominent place they occupy in agricultural employment, but also to the fact that they farm about 87

Table 11.7: Agricultural manpower in the GDR

Manpower category	1965	1970	1975	1980	1985
Employees (excluding apprentices) in agriculture and forestry in 1000s	1,179	997	895	878	922
Employees (excluding apprentices) in agriculture (including agro-chemical centres) in 1000s	1,122	946	841	823	860
Permanent employees (excluding apprentices) in agriculture (excluding agro-chemical centres) in 1000s	1,042	908	808	794	836
'Full-time manpower' (AK)[a] in 1000 (AK)	938	817	728	715	753
per 100 hectares of LN	14.7	13.0	11.6	11.4	12.1
Members of agricultural producer co-operatives in 1000s, total in 1000s	1,004	938	877	827	886
of which: permanent in 1000s	874	755	637	591	693

Note: a. 'Full-time manpower' (*Vollarbeitskräfte*: AK): permanent agricultural employees multiplied by the constant factor 0.9.

Source: *Statistisches Jahrbuch der DDR* (1982 and 1986).

per cent of the LN in the GDR, own about 89 per cent of the livestock and dispose of over 80 per cent of the capital stock in agriculture. In the socio-political consciousness of the SED, the special class role of co-operative farmers in socialist society derives from their position as socialist owners of the means of production and from the ability which is ascribed to them to combine modern large-scale agricultural production with time-honoured peasant traditions and experience, to practise co-operative democracy and to apply the performance principle as well as pursuing their interests in accordance with the demands of co-operative work.

Educational qualifications and social structure

Training for a career in agriculture enjoys a high priority in the GDR. In 1985 the percentage of permanent employees in socialised agriculture in the GDR with completed vocational training totalled 90.5 per cent (2.5 per cent having been to university; 6.3 per cent to technical colleges; 6.6 per cent certificated master craftsmen; and 75.1 per cent qualified as skilled workmen). Categorised by their positions in the enterprise, in 1985, of the total of 922,014 working people and 41,108 apprentices in agriculture and forestry, 28.9 per cent were workers and employees, 66.2 per cent were members of producer co-operatives, 0.6 per cent self-employed and assistants within the family, and 4.3 per cent apprentices.

The total proportion of full-time female employees in agriculture fell from 45.1 per cent in 1970 to 40.5 per cent in 1985, while that of young people (below the age of 25) increased from 7.2 to 13.5 per cent between 1970 and 1980.

Labour income

GDR agrarian statistics only give figures for average monthly earned income for full-time workers and employees in state farms and for the production workers employed full time there. In 1985 these came to 1,074 marks and 1,068 marks respectively. The average income of co-operative farmers, which, besides the sums paid out of the wage fund for labour units earned, bonuses, marriage supplements, state child support and social grants, also includes revenue earned in the personal domestic economy and, where relevant, compensation for land shares, cannot be quantified here. According to the relevant GDR literature, although at the beginning of the 1960s there was still a clear social differentiation in earned income levels between co-operative farmers and agricultural workers and between them and industrial workers, these have meanwhile been overcome to an extent where for all practical purposes these differences no longer exist (Groschoff, 1979, p. 55). Even if income parity has now been brought about between agriculture and industry, it must not be forgotten that this has been achieved at a relatively high cost in terms of the labour time of those employed in agriculture.

Means of production

Chemical fertilisers and plant pest control

In the GDR great efforts are made to utilise technical progress in agriculture in the form of means of production which increase yields, minimise losses, improve quality, save labour and reduce labour effort. Of the means of production deriving from the industrial sector of the economy, it is the use of chemical fertilisers and plant pest control agents in crop cultivation and of concentrated fodder in animal production which is the real precondition for the increase of yields in crop and livestock production. As regards chemical fertilisers the GDR has, for the past two decades, attained a volume of available key fertilisers which in international terms puts it among the group of fertiliser-intensive countries in the world.

While chemical fertilisers directly serve to increase yields, measures of plan pest control taken to secure yields do so indirectly. The input of plant treatment agents has steadily increased up to 1980 and has maintained this position since then. About two-thirds of supplies comprise herbicides, the remaining one-third is made up of fungicides and insecticides (see Table 11.9).

Feedstuffs

In contrast to the equipping of crop production with yield-raising means of production, the supply of concentrated fodder, necessary to develop livestock output fully, has remained relatively deficient. The main reason for this is that imported concentrates require large outlays of hard currencies, because high-protein fodder in particular is in the main only obtainable in the Western world market. This also explains the recently more emphatically voiced political requirement that domestic production should increasingly fill fodder demand by tapping all possible fodder reserves, and that imports of fodder grains and other feedstuffs should be drastically reduced. This orientation towards domestic production of fodder, which mainly involves increasing the output of grain, potatoes, sugar beet and meadowland, confronts fodder production with an extremely difficult problem, whose solution is of central economic

Table 11.8: Supply of chemical fertilisers to GDR agriculture in kilogrammes of pure fertiliser per hectare of LN

Economic year	Nitrogen (N)	Phosphate (P_2O_5)	Potash (K_2O)	Lime (CaO)
	Kilogrammes of pure fertiliser per LN			
1960-1	38.5	35.1	82.3	117.1
1970-1	83.7	64.3	99.1	197.7
1980-1	119.3	64.4	86.7	189.6
1984-5	118.6	51.3	87.4	218.6

Source: *Statistisches Jahrbuch der DDR* (1986 and preceding).

Table 11.9: Supply of plant pest control agents to GDR agriculture

Item	1965	1970	1975	1980	1985
Plant pest control agents:					
Total in tonnes (undiluted)	8,219	18,567	22,480	27,009	26,731
Kilogrammes per LN	1.3	3.0	3.6	4.3	4.3
of which:					
Herbicides in tonnes (undiluted)	6,197	13,758	15,004	18,067	18,179
Kilogrammes per LN	1.0	2.2	2.4	2.9	2.9

Source: *Statistisches Jahrbuch der DDR* (1986).

importance to the total output of agriculture. The attempt is being made to ease the shortage of concentrates primarily through the manufacture of industrially prepared mixed fodder (see Table 11.10).

Between 1970 and 1982 production of mixed feed per 'large livestock equivalent' almost doubled. Compared to the FRG, where in the financial year 1981-82 about 1,267 kilogrammes of mixed fodder per GV was produced, the GDR figure was 1,053, about 83 per cent of the FRG level. If, however, not only mixed fodder, but also concentrates are included in the GDR figure and then compared to those in the FRG, the quantitative and also the qualitative differences in supply, and hence the lag, become more clearly apparent.

Technical equipping

The factor input in agriculture is characterised not least by the number, volumes and types of available agricultural machinery. In the GDR the mechanisation of agriculture has been strongly promoted. This is shown in the increase in the stock of machinery (see Table 11.11).

The raising of the technical level is apparent from the fact, among others, that, despite the, in some cases, falling number of agricultural machines, the available machine performance per unit of area has been raised. Thus, between 1970 and 1985 as regards tractors alone the average performance capacity increased from 43.4 horsepower to 68.3 hp or around 58 per cent and the average engine performance per 100 hectares of LN from 102.4 hp to 173.3 hp or around 69 per cent. Similar progress can be seen with regard to other important key

Table 11.10: Production of mixed fodder in the GDR

Year	Total output (1,000 tonnes)	Percentage share of pellets	Percentage share of various animals in total output				Output per 'large livestock equivalent'[a] (kilogrammes)
			Cattle, sheep and horses	Pigs	Poultry	Other	
1955	127	—	—	—	—	—	25.4
1960	704	—	—	—	—	—	136.4
1965	1,665	4.0	17.3	55.1	24.0	3.6	347.5
1970	2,909	20.0	21.5	48.6	26.8	3.1	582.4
1975	4,439	30.0	25.0	49.6	23.4	2.0	812.3
1980	5,811	31.6	25.1	52.9	20.7	1.3	1,042.7
1982	6,075	27.8	23.2	57.3	18.7	0.8	1,063.2

Note: a. Calculated according to the 'large livestock equivalent' used in the FRG.

Source: Lüdtke, H. in *Getreidewirtschaft*, vol. 8 (1983); *Statistisches Jahrbuch der DDR* (1983).

Table 11.11: Stock of selected machines in the socialised agriculture of the GDR

Machines	Unit	1960	1970	1975	1980	1985
Tractors (number)	1,000 (standard)	70.6	148.9	140.0	144.5	158.0
(horsepower)	1,000 hp	2,283	6,440	7,585	9,288	10,790
Performance: hp per tractor	hp	32.4	43.3	54.2	64.3	68.3
Tractor: hp per 1000 hectares LN	hp	35.5	102.4	120.4	148.1	173.3
Lorries	1,000 (standard)	9.3	27.2	42.5	51.6	54.6
Trailers	1,000 (standard)	80.0	232.6	233.5	257.5	287.0
Combine harvesters	1,000 (standard)	6.4	17.9	11.2	13.6	16.9
Potato lifters	1,000 (standard)	6.4	12.0	9.2	7.9	8.1
Beet toppers	1,000 (standard)	—	5.9	6.3	4.2	2.9
Beet lifters	1,000 (standard)	3.7	5.3	4.9	2.9	2.5

Source: *Statistisches Jahrbuch der DDR* (1986); CMEA statistical yearbook (1983).

machinery (i.e. the main machines of a technological chain process) — for example with self-propelled harvesting machines and transport vehicles — through which the capacity of the 'mobile energetic basis' has been increased.

The statistics for the stock of machines alone admittedly do not say much about their actual input effectiveness. This is frequently reduced by deficiencies in the supply of spare parts and by bottlenecks in regard to repairs. Even though the extent of these limitations is not known in detail, the indications of lack of care in the employment and conservation of machinery and equipment as well as the lack of weatherproof garaging sites permit of the conclusion that there is a relatively large need for repairs and thus a considerably reduced efficiency in the use of the existing technology.

Whilst in crop production machine capacity makes possible fully mechanised harvesting of grain, potatoes and sugar beet as laid down in the plan, the work in animal husbandry is far less mechanised, though it is admittedly less amenable to mechanisation. The present technological and technical level of animal husbandry is very diverse and is variously characterised by highly mechanised, modern plant, semi-stationary/mobile processes and manual processes.

In 1981 the proportion of manual work in fodder distribution and mucking out in livestock units was respectively as follows: milking cows 26 and 15 per cent; cattle in factory farms 44 and 30 per cent; and pigs in factory farms 45 and 40 per cent. Since machinery and equipment have the purpose of raising the productivity of human labour by means of labour saving, labour easing and improvement in quality, the heavy investment which has led to the existing equipping with technology, in combination with the high employment ratio in agriculture, clearly shows that the substitution of labour by capital required to raise labour productivity in GDR agriculture could only be carried through to a relatively limited extent.

AGRICULTURAL PERFORMANCE

Output and productivity

GDR statistical publications regularly give figures in physical terms for important individual products and/or groupings of crop and animal products and for livestock. Aggregate production data, which could provide a basis for assessing the performance of agriculture as a whole, are, however, not published. An orientation exclusively towards selected individual products (for example, per hectare yield of grain or milk yield per cow), which is used to generalise about overall agricultural performance, can easily lead to unwarranted conclusions, especially since the total volume of agrarian production depends on the weather, which can affect individual branches of production in a widely varying manner from year to year. Because, therefore, only figures for the total output of agriculture will provide a secure basis for judgement, the following analysis will furnish, in addition to GDR production figures for individual commodities, also the results of aggregate calculations for the various sectors of agriculture computed with the aid of a 'grain equivalent key' (*Getreideeinheitenschlüssel*). Such carefully coordinated calculations, tested by decades of experience, are taken for granted in the FRG in statistical reporting on its agricultural performance in quantitative terms. Methodologically consistent calculation procedures also make possible output and productivity comparisons between the two German agricultures, which is helpful if only because there exist no absolute yardsticks of agricultural performance.

The quantitative performance of GDR agriculture, leaving aside the setbacks of individual years, has developed positively with respect both to increasing the volume of production and to raising yields per hectare and output per standard animal. The volume of foodstuffs production (which embraces all foodstuffs and raw materials supplied by both crop and livestock production for commercial purposes) increased from around 18.85 million to 25.52 million tonnes of grain equivalent over the 15-year period from 1970 to 1985, an increase of about 6.67 million tonnes of grain equivalent or 35 per cent (see Table 11.12).

By far the largest part of the increase in the production of foodstuffs is accounted for by animal products. The structure of foodstuffs production (i.e. composition according to crop and animal products and their subdivisions) is thus dominated by livestock production (see Table 11.13).

In the 1980s, as in the FRG, nearly 80 per cent of foodstuffs was accounted for by animal products and just over 20 per cent

Table 11.12: Output, yields and labour productivity in GDR agriculture

Item	1957-61	1962-66	1967-71	1972-76	1977-81	1985[c]
Gross crop production						
Million tonnes grain equivalent	18.23	18.74	20.79	22.30	23.76	28.35
Per hectare LN in decitonnes grain equivalent	28.3	29.4	33.0	35.4	37.8	45.5
FRG[a]	32.2	34.0	39.7	42.8	48.8	—
GDR as percentage of FRG (= 100)	87.9	86.5	83.1	82.7	77.5	—
Foodstuffs production						
Million tonnes grain equivalent, of which:	16.37	16.53	19.02	22.05	23.44	25.52
Crop	4.03	4.07	4.23	4.73	4.82	5.14
Livestock	12.34	12.46	14.79	17.32	18.62	20.38
Per AK[b] in decitonnes grain equivalent	—	—	224.4	298.1	329.0	338.9
FRG	—	—	368.5	509.8	670.5	—
GDR as percentage of FRG (= 100)	—	—	60.9	58.5	49.1	—
Livestock production less imported feedstuffs						
Million tonnes grain equivalent	2.09	1.97	2.52	4.06	3.83	3.02
Percentage of total output of foodstuffs	13	12	13	18	16	12
Percentage of livestock foodstuffs production	17	16	17	23	21	15
Net output of foodstuffs						
Million tonnes grain equivalent	14.28	14.56	16.50	17.99	19.61	22.50
Per hectare LN in decitonnes grain equivalent	22.2	22.8	26.2	28.6	31.2	36.1
FRG	29.7	31.4	35.0	38.1	43.7	—
GDR as percentage of FRG (= 100)	74.7	72.6	74.9	75.1	71.4	—

Notes: a. As a result of changes in the criteria of the land survey of the FRG, hectare yields after 1979 are not fully comparable with those up to 1978; b. Permanent employees (excluding apprentices) in agriculture (excluding forestry, veterinary service and plant protection as well as agro-chemical centres), corrected by a factor of 0.9 — data from 1964 only; c. Provisional.

Source: Author's own calculations, based on data from the statistical yearbook of the GDR for 1986 and preceding years, and usng the FRG's grain equivalent key — *Statistisches Jahrbuch über Ernährung, Landwirtschaft und Forsten* (1983), p. 124.

Table 11.13: Output structure of foodstuffs in the GDR

Product	1967-71 1000 tonnes grain equivalent	%	FRG %	1983-4 1000 tonnes grain equivalent	%	FRG %
Crops:	4,234	22.3	19.6	4,580	19.4	19.3
Grain	2,103	11.1	9.3	2,467	10.5	9.6
Pulses	15	0.1	—	17	0.1	—
Oil seeds	238	1.3	0.3	289	1.2	0.9
Potatoes	539	2.8	2.1	332	1.4	1.1
Sugar beet	970	5.1	4.5	1,020	4.3	4.2
Vegetables	137	0.7	0.4	164	0.7	0.3
Fruit	157	0.8	1.5	261	1.1	0.8
Other	75	0.4	1.5	30	0.1	2.2
Animal products:	14,792	77.7	80.4	18,986	80.6	80.7
Slaughtered livestock:						
Cattle	2,862	15.0	19.7	3,295	14.0	19.6
Calves	111	0.6	1.3	50	0.2	0.9
Sheep	155	0.8	0.2	137	0.6	0.3
Pigs	4,511	23.7	23.6	6,442	27.3	23.6
Poultry	416	2.3	2.0	705	3.0	2.5
Goats	15	0.1	—	—	—	—
Rabbits	(64)	0.3	—	199	0.9	0.2
Cow's milk	5,163	27.1	27.1	5,947	25.2	28.2
Goat's milk	62	0.3	—	9	—	—
Eggs	963	5.1	6.0	1,331	5.7	4.3
Wool	307	1.6	0.2	484	2.1	0.2
Livestock changes	+163	0.8	0.3	+387	1.6	0.9
Total output of foodstuffs	19,026	100.0	100.0	23,566	100.0	100.0

Source: Author's own calculations, based on data from the statistical yearbook of the GDR for 1986 and preceding years, and using the FRG's grain equivalent key — *Statistisches Jahrbuch über Ernährung, Landwirtschaft und Forsten* (1983), p. 124.

by crop products. It should be stressed here that, despite the differing agrarian systems, the structures of foodstuffs production in the two Germanies display certain similarities in essentials. Out of total primary crop production, expressed as gross crop production (*Brutto-Bodenproduktion*), in the GDR about two-thirds is fed to livestock. On top of this come various types of imported fodder, which are substantially involved in increasing the volume of foodstuffs derived from animals. Larger quantities of feedstuffs were imported or obtained via inner-German trade only from 1970 onwards, following setbacks in agriculture partly caused by the weather. In line with the resolutions of the

Table 11.14: Yields in physical terms in crop and livestock production in the GDR

Product	1957-61	1962-66	1967-71	1972-76	1977-81	1985
	Crop yields in decitonnes per hectare					
Grain total, of which:	24.4	26.7	31.3	35.9	36.5	46.2
Wheat	31.0	32.2	38.0	39.9	43.3	52.9
Rye	20.7	21.8	24.7	27.5	27.7	36.3
Barley	27.9	30.8	33.5	40.2	37.9	49.5
Oats	25.0	27.2	31.6	34.2	35.4	42.0
Maize	21.6	20.3[a]	26.3	32.4	43.9	39.3
Potatoes	161.2	177.2	176.4	165.6	193.7	259.9
Sugar beet	261.6	262.6	298.6	265.9	292.6	318.0
Turnips	469.7	522.2	605.1	615.7	597.0	565.4
Clover and lucerne (hay equivalent)	58.9	61.3	68.5[b]	78.2[c]	97.9	112.3
Meadows (hay equivalent)	43.7	40.3	46.9	56.8	69.7	80.6
	Products per animal					
Cattle:						
Milk yield[d] per cow in kilogrammes	2,627	2,778	3,304	3,701	3,847	4,370
Meat per animal[e] in kilogrammes live weight	80	92	112	125	121	121
Live weight per slaughtered animal (excluding calves)	332	337	384	417	408	403
Calves	62	68	97	100	91	75
Pigs:						
Meat per animal[e] in kilogrammes live weight	104	101	113	121	124	131
Live weight per slaughtered pig in kilogrammes	121	118	116	121	119	120
Slaughterings in percent[f]	85	86	98	100	104	109
Hens:						
Eggs per hen[e]	132	137	164	189	202	216

Notes: a. Average for the years 1962, 1963 and 1966 only: data for 1964 and 1965 missing; b. From 1969 including clover grass; c. From 1976 including mixed cultivation of lucerne and grass; d. On basis of 3.5 per cent fat content; e. Based on average; f. Slaughterings as percentage of average pig stock.

Source: *Statistisches Jahrbuch der DDR* (1986 and preceding).

10th Party Congress of the SED, these imports were to be gradually reduced to zero and replaced by increasing domestic production of grain and feedstuffs (mainly by increasing yields). In the period 1970 to 1984 about 22 per cent on average of animal foodstuffs production was dependent on imported feedstuffs: in 1985 this was still 15 per cent. The order to end imports of feedstuffs posed major problems for agriculture production, which are not immediately apparent from the rising physical yields of individual crop and animal products per unit of area and per livestock unit (see Table 11.14).

In the GDR, potatoes and sugar beet, as the most intensive arable crops, make heavy demands in terms of the state of cultivation, structure and humus content of soil, crop rotation and the organisational care devoted to all cultivation and harvesting procedures. The fact that production of precisely these two crops has consistently represented a relatively modest proportion of total output (potatoes), or even shown a negative average annual growth rate of about one per cent between 1967 and 1982 (sugar beet), clearly indicates that there are serious constraints upon the growth of total crop output, which must be seen primarily as a result of reduced soil fertility. If one seeks the complex causes for this, they are to be found chiefly in the system-conditioned organisation of production and labour and also in production and working technologies. Speaking only of the large-scale mechanised techniques involved in soil cultivation, tilling, applying fertilisers, tending and harvesting, among the many factors affecting yields, the unsatisfactory growth rate of crop production (recognised as such in the GDR itself) is mainly attributable to the fact that there is still lacking a precise organisational co-ordination of the labour input of these techniques to the most favourable timing in terms of the seasons and the weather, if full efficiency is to be achieved. The causes of such deficiencies lie in the agrarian system of the GDR with its collective labour regime and its huge, highly specialised production units. The ill-timed carrying out of tasks in crop production inevitably has an adverse effect upon soil structure. Moreover, specialisation in certain main crops has led to problems of rotation, whilst enlargement of fields, to in some cases more than 100 hectares, has produced symptoms of erosion. Both these features, coupled with the use of heavy machinery and further in combination with the almost continuous outflow of liquid manure (due to inadequate storage capacity), have contributed to soil-structure damage and, consequently, to output losses.

Light is thrown on the difficulties in the way of a further increase in total crop output by data contained in the specialist literature of the GDR, according to which 30 to 40 per cent of the 4.73 million hectares in total of arable land is deficient in humus and 3.5 million hectares are affected by compression damage (of which 50 per cent is topsoil damage). If the achieved increase in crop production has, even as matters stand at present, been unable to meet the increased demand for feedstuffs in order that animal output potential may be realised to the full, then the planned elimination of imports of feedstuffs (which also helped to compensate for output fluctuations caused by the weather) will in future yet further exacerbate the problems involved in seeking to raise agricultural output and productivity.

If one compares the average quantitative agricultural performances achieved in the period 1980-84 by the GDR and the FRG, it is possible to draw a number of conclusions. As an approximate percentage of FRG levels, the GDR figures are as follows: gross crop production per unit of area 76 per cent; output per 'large livestock equivalent' 82 per cent; and total net production of foodstuffs per unit of domestic area (i.e. excluding imported feedstuffs) 65 per cent.

The greatest differences arise in labour productivity. Between 1970 and 1984 labour productivity in agriculture (production of foodstuffs per AK) in the GDR increased by 45 per cent, but in the FRG by 98 per cent. As an approximate percentage of the FRG's level, the figures for the GDR were 58 per cent in 1970-74, 53 per cent in 1975-79 and 44 per cent in 1980-84. Consequently, the GDR growth rate of labour productivity in agriculture in the period of 1970-74 to 1984 of 1.1 per cent ways only about a fifth that of the FRG (5 per cent). Thus, despite a steadily improving performance, the GDR's labour productivity in 1985 reached a level already attained by the FRG in 1968.

These differences in agricultural performance also explain why, despite the fact that the amount of agricultural land *per capita* is greater in the GDR than in the FRG and despite the latter's higher nutritional standards, the level of national self-sufficiency in foodstuffs and feedstuffs is virtually identical in the two German states. Admittedly, it must be noted as regards the respective levels of self-sufficiency that the GDR is a centrally administered economy in which plans decide what and how much is to be produced, imported or exported and thus, ultimately, put at the disposal of the population. Hence, the level of self-sufficiency should not be measured by the production and consumption quantities resulting from the free play of market forces, but only by the quantities made available to the population. In the GDR the level of self-sufficiency in 'agricultural primary products' is given as 91 per cent for 1980

(Rembel, 1983, p. 40). The available data do not, however, show whether livestock production based on imported feedstuffs is included in this calculation, which seems probable.

ECONOMIC EFFICIENCY

The shortcomings in economic development that are connected with the industrialisation of agriculture are apparent not only from the unsatisfactory growth and at times stagnation of physical yields per hectare or per standard animal (as is admitted in the GDR), but also, above all, from the steep rise in production costs and an increasingly inefficient use of available resources. Although there is no official reporting of revenue/expenditure ratios in agriculture, the available data nevertheless provide a sufficiently reliable basis for an estimate of the economic efficiency of GDR agriculture.

If the transition to industrial production methods in agriculture was primarily motivated by the economic consideration that the effects of concentration and specialisation in raising productivity and profitability levels in agriculture would be comparable to those in industry, then this expectation has proved to be mistaken. The enlargement of fields and the separation of crop and livestock production has resulted in sharp increases in intra- and inter-enterprise distances and hence in idle time. Thus, for example, the formation of specialised large-scale enterprises in crop production is largely to blame for the doubling of transport distances for feedstuffs, liquid manure and stable dung, and, in turn, for an input of diesel fuel of between 160 and 170 litres per hectare of LN in crop production in co-operative and state farms alone, which is nearly 40 per cent more than the quantity used on average in FRG agriculture (which, moreover, includes animal husbandry and in any case has a much higher level of output). Furthermore, in most branches of production specialisation hinders the spread of labour over the economic year and thus reduces the productive utilisation of manpower to the detriment of labour productivity.

The explosive rise in the early 1980s in the world price of oil and hence of fuels, fertilisers and plant pest control agents, resulted in great pressure being exerted on agriculture to make more efficient use of all inputs. How urgent these economies are is evident from the fact that, despite administratively set prices for agricultural products and means of production, with a largely stagnating net agricultural product, the productive consumption necessary for its achievement has clearly increased. Despite the subsidies for fertilisers and plant pest control products, fuels, machines, spare parts and other means of production (which increased more than seven-fold between 1975 and 1982), agricultural production costs have continuously risen. One indicator for this is the decline in net product per 1,000 marks of capital stock in the agrarian sector, which fell from 227 marks in 1975 to 172 marks in 1985. Correspondingly, a unit of foodstuffs production was produced for around 116 marks in 1975 and around 134 marks in 1985 (see Table 11.15).

Specialist authors in the GDR, indeed, admit that the rising costs in agricultural production have led to 'a falling trend in essential indicators of efficiency' (Tillack, 1983, pp. 13-16). Thus, a comparison of the results of 1980 and of 1973-75 shows

Table 11.15: Indicators of economic efficiency in GDR agriculture 1975-85

	Net output of agriculture and forestry[a]			Production consumed[b]	
Year	Total	Per 1,000 marks of capital stock	Per employee	Per unit of net output	Per decitonne of grain equivalent of foodstuffs production
	million marks			marks	
1975	16,522	227	18,471	1.61	115.7
1976	14,669	190	16,704	1.87	123.0
1977	16,378	201	18,750	1.76	126.5
1978	15,856	185	18,082	1.92	130.8
1979	16,673	187	19.029	1.86	134.9
1980	16,619	177	18,918	1.90	131.8
1981	17,083	174	19,314	1.91	135.1
1982	16,715	162	18,804	—	—
1983	17,540	162	19,467	1.80	133.7
1984	19,210	171	21,013	1.71	131.6
1985	19,995[c]	172	21,687	1.71	133.9

Notes: a. Price basis 1980; b. Consumption of raw materials, materials and semi-finished products, depreciation and rents, leases and rentals (excluding subsidies); 1975 price basis until 1980, from 1983 price basis of 1980; no data for 1982; c. Provisional.

Source: *Statistisches Jahrbuch der DDR* (1986 and preceding); author's own calculations.

that in crop production the capital stock grew by 42 per cent and that, per unit of area, production costs (21 per cent) rose more quickly than gross product (14 per cent), while gross income (−1 per cent), gross profit (−24 per cent) and accumulation (−47 per cent) fell. With an increase of the capital stock in animal husbandry of 15.4 per cent, production costs here increased by 12.9 per cent and gross product by 10.2 per cent, while gross income (−0.3 per cent), accumulation (−14.6 per cent) and gross profit (−14.6 per cent) fell. Personal income per full-time worker equivalent (*Vollbeschäftigteneinheit*: VBE) in crop and livestock production, with figures of 17 per cent and 6.3 per cent respectively, increased more markedly than net product per unit, with 13 per cent and 3.1 per cent. This shows that the oft-repeated economic propaganda principle of 'only that which is first earned can be consumed' has, at least temporarily, been shelved for socio-political reasons. If, in addition, we take into account the increasing burden imposed on the state budget by subsidies (between 1975 and 1982 price supports for agricultural means of production increased from 0.95 billion marks to 6.91 billion marks, and for stabilising the prices of foodstuffs in the shops from 7.18 billion marks to 11.67 billion marks), it becomes clear that the result aimed at with the industrialisation of agriculture has indeed been obtained in terms of the set socio-political goals, but that the failure to materialise of the expected economic achievements of GDR agriculture, however, continues to pose serious problems of reform. As with the other countries where socialism is currently being put into practice, the situation in the GDR raises the central question: how far must and how far may structural changes in agriculture go in order to remain acceptable to the ruling party — that is, without shaking the foundations of the communist exercise of power?

12

The Foreign Trade and Payments of the GDR in a Changing World Economy[1]

Hanns-Dieter Jacobsen

OVERCOMING THE LIQUIDITY CRISIS

At the beginning of the 1980s the GDR was burdened with foreign trade and payments difficulties more severe than ever before in its history. The economic turbulences culminated in increased economic pressure from both the West and the East. For one thing the GDR got caught in the wake of the international debt crisis, which derived from the inability of Poland and Romania to repay; for another, the GDR had to suffer a cut-back in Soviet crude oil deliveries of more than 10 per cent and, simultaneously, an abrupt increase in the price of Soviet oil of nearly 50 per cent.

The two events had a cumulative effect, since the GDR was now not only forced to obtain a part of its energy requirements from the West and to provide additional hard currency for this purpose, but also, much more importantly, was obliged for the sake of its reputation as a reliable economic partner and borrower, to reduce its indebtedness to the West by the timely repayment of the mainly short-term credits.

The GDR economic planners' formula for dealing with the crisis was to increase exports, above all to the West, and, simultaneously, to reduce drastically imports from the West, in order to achieve large surpluses. At the same time, the GDR made extensive use of its opportunities in inner-German economic relations to moderate the foreign trade and payments burden, in that it shifted a part of its trade with the West to inner-German trade (*innerdeutscher Handel*: also variously translated as inter-German or intra-German trade) and, in addition, by means of a number of humanitarian concessions, made possible two government-supported one-billion credits from the Federal Republic. Admittedly, these measures were not sufficient to prevent the population of the GDR suffering from shortages of consumer goods, or to stop long-term damage being done to the GDR's potential for capital accumulation.

Nevertheless, at the start of the second half of the 1980s, it can be confirmed that the GDR, in comparison to its Comecon partners, has been able to overcome the turbulences and now appears to be in a position to move on from the surmounting of its economic problems by means of short-term crisis management to the meeting of 'normal' challenges.

STRUCTURAL, REGIONAL AND INSTITUTIONAL CHANGES IN THE GDR'S FOREIGN TRADE AND PAYMENTS AT THE BEGINNING OF THE 1980s

Data

It has for several years been somewhat difficult to obtain a comprehensive quantitative overview of the foreign trade and payments activities of the GDR, because the official GDR statistics do not even furnish data on exports and imports, but only on turnover (and then only in valuta marks). But even their informative value is limited, because the relationship of the VM to the domestic currency is not known. For this reason a quantitative analysis of the GDR's external economic relations must, for the most part, enlist the help of 'mirror statistics', i.e. the data of the GDR's partners, or the CMEA Statistical Yearbook which is published in Moscow. The conversions which are thus necessitated naturally produce imprecision, for example, in the case of exchange rate fluctuations, which lessen the exactness of the available data (see Haendcke-Hoppe, 1978).

External economic relations of the GDR[2]

As a country endowed with few natural resources, the GDR has to rely on extensive foreign trade. The share of exports or imports in the produced national income of the GDR is probably about 17 or 18 per cent; precise figures are not possible because of the above-mentioned statistical inexactitudes.

The main trading partners of the GDR are the CMEA countries (in 1985, 63 per cent of exports and 64 per cent of imports) and, among them, the USSR accounted for about 38 per cent of the GDR's foreign trade between 1981 and 1983. From the start of the 1960s, when the USSR accounted for almost half of the GDR's foreign trade, the GDR clearly strove to lower the high proportion taken by the USSR by means of a regional diversification of intra-bloc trade, and considerable progress was made in this respect; by 1974 this proportion had fallen to less than a third. At the beginning of the 1980s the importance of the USSR, it is true, increased once again. Restrictions in the world economy after 1979 led once more to an enhanced interdependence of the two countries. Here bilateral trade is characterised by a marked complementarity: the Soviet Union supplies, above all, industrial raw materials, semi-finished products and energy (more than 80 per cent of the GDR's crude oil requirements are met by the Soviet Union; this amounts to almost a quarter of total imports), whilst the GDR exports mainly finished products (more than a half of GDR exports are investment goods; more than 10 per cent industrial consumer goods).

The GDR transacts about a quarter of its total foreign trade with the other CMEA partners, Czechoslovakia taking second place among the socialist trading partners with close to 8 per cent. Trade with Czechoslovakia, Poland and Hungary has much more of a substitute character, whereby machines and equipment, as well as other investment goods, are very important. In trade with the other CMEA countries, on the other hand, that complementary structure predominates which also characterises trade between the GDR and the USSR, with the GDR receiving industrial raw materials and agricultural products.

The external economic shocks of the early 1980s led to a certain reorientation of the GDR's foreign trade towards Comecon. In this way the GDR could use the general advantages of its integration within Comecon, in that, in contrast to trade with the West, there exist assured markets and a fundamentally stable raw material supply, while finally, too strong a sensitivity to external economic disturbances caused by the industrial countries can be avoided.

There are, however, a number of hindrances. The industrially highly developed GDR is linked in the CMEA with partners whose economic and technological level of development is, in part, considerably below that of the GDR, so that decisive impulses for the GDR's own economic growth cannot be reckoned with. The ambitious goals of the 1971 Complex Programme could only be realised in part: a trade-promoting convertibility of CMEA currencies was not attained and plan co-ordination is still largely limited to co-ordination of foreign trade plans. Besides this, the GDR has, since the beginning of the 1980s, had to tolerate additional burdens imposed by the economic difficulties in Poland (non-deliveries, credits), which narrow its room to manoeuvre with regard to foreign trade and payments.

The Western industrial countries (including the Federal Republic of Germany) accounted for less than 20 per cent of the GDR's foreign trade at the start of the 1960s, with inner-German trade at times accounting for more than a half of that.

As détente developed, the share of GDR foreign trade accounted for by the West did, it is true, noticeably increase, but the GDR's policy of regional diversification in Western trade, which was supposed, for political reasons, to lead to a relative decline in the importance of inner-German trade, stressed, above all, other countries of Western Europe such as Austria, Sweden, France and Great Britain (see Table 12.1). At the start of the 1980s inner-German trade no longer even accounted for as much as a third of the GDR's trade with the Western industrial countries.

The commodity structure of the GDR's trade with the West, it is true to say, differs considerably from that of CMEA intra-bloc trade (see Tables 12.2 and 12.3). In recent years the GDR has more and more imported investment goods and, in contrast, has exported basic materials and producer goods. It was thus not in a position to develop sales of investment goods in Western markets; in trade with the West the GDR's foreign trade structure suggests a relatively low level of development.

Not least for this reason, it is not surprising that during the 1970s the GDR's trade with the OECD countries (excluding the Federal Republic) was basically in deficit — a direct result of its borrowing from the West. When the liquidity crisis hit in 1981 and 1982 (the net debt of the GDR reached a high point of $10.19 billion at the end of 1981), the GDR reduced its imports from OECD countries by a drastic 25 per cent and increased its exports

Table 12.1: Trade with OECD countries[a] (DM billion)

Country	1970	1976	1980	1981	1982	1983
			OECD imports from the GDR			
OECD, total	1,506	2,715	3,818	4,954	5,794	6,208
Belgium, Luxembourg	118	237	263	369	331	330
France	155	472	500	594	689	705
Italy	129	236	337	458	392	302
Netherlands	167	220	359	545	521	592
Great Britain	141	272	368	425	569	643
Sweden	171	389	593	694	1,028	1,065
Denmark	80	134	268	322	388	453
Austria	102	188	300	367	422	307
Switzerland	49	52	74	92	98	112
Japan	142	34	72	101	89	79
USA	34	34	88	118	143	163
Finland	62	90	160	197	194	203
Spain	17	69	80	223	234	202
Greece	26	89	142	118	95	118
Norway	29	88	101	181	446	504
Turkey	42	49	32	41	52	69
Other OECD countries	41	60	81	108	104	120
			OECD exports to the GDR			
OECD, total	1,658	3,287	4,522	5,527	4,142	5,040
Belgium, Luxembourg	58	191	235	193	124	274
France	218	535	578	1,052	623	666
Italy	97	207	255	372	303	219
Netherlands	143	335	371	454	246	260
Great Britain	149	202	391	362	267	234
Sweden	284	417	286	329	191	160
Denmark	32	85	177	104	72	99
Austria	96	250	416	476	511	900
Switzerland	93	214	239	270	266	184
Japan	54	123	252	336	468	833
USA	119	163	867	668	541	355
Finland	69	160	161	213	160	161
Spain	29	53	48	505	141	105
Greece	49	71	91	62	39	47
Australia	62	24	34	39	41	64
Canada	1	118	15	8	42	420
Other OECD countries	74	137	105	84	106	59
			Percentage share of the GDR in total OECD foreign trade			
Imports	0.18	0.16	0.15	0.17	0.19	0.20
Exports	0.20	0.21	0.20	0.20	0.15	0.17

Note: a. Excluding inner-German trade.
Source: *Bundesamt für Gewerbliche Wirtschaft; Statistics of Foreign Trade (OECD);* DIW calculations.

Table 12.2: Commodity structure of the foreign trade of the GDR with OECD countries[a]

Product groups[b]	1971-75[c]	1976-80[c]	1981	1982	1983
	GDR imports (DM million)				
Total[d]	2,247	3,599	5,537	4,142	5,040
	Percentage shares				
Products of the basic materials and producer goods industries,[e] of which:	37.8	33.4	25.2	24.6	26.4
Iron and steel[f]	8.2	6.1	3.4	4.9	7.8
Chemical products[g]	17.5	16.3	14.3	12.4	12.3
Industrial investment goods, of which:	31.6	29.7	32.9	37.0	36.4
Steel construction products	6.3	6.6	8.4	7.1	4.2
Mechanical engineering products	16.7	14.4	14.4	20.3	20.5
Electro-technical products	3.6	4.0	5.1	5.6	7.6
Industrial consumer goods, of which:	10.7	9.7	8.9	9.5	7.4
Textiles and clothing	7.7	7.3	6.9	7.4	5.5
Agriculture and foodstuffs industries[i]	19.1	26.6	32.5	28.4	29.4
	GDR exports (DM million)				
Total[d]	1,987	3,008	4,954	5,794	6,208
	Percentage shares				
Products of the basic materials and producer goods industries,[e] of which:	33.9	40.8	55.3	61.6	66.0
Mineral oil products	3.4	9.0	20.4	28.7	30.3
Iron and steel	6.3	7.1	6.2	6.1	6.7
Chemical products[g]	18.5	17.6	21.9	18.4	18.3
Industrial investment goods, of which:	29.3	27.5	19.0	18.3	15.9
Mechanical enginineering products	9.4	8.7	7.5	7.5	5.6
Vehicles[h]	6.1	5.5 1.5	1.2	1.6	
Electro-technical products	7.0	7.3	5.6	5.3	5.0
Industrial consumer goods, of which:	20.3	21.5	17.1	15.2	14.2
Musical instruments, toys and jewellery	4.5	4.2	3.4	2.9	2.6
Textiles and clothing	5.9	5.5	4.0	3.6	3.4
Agriculture and foodstuffs industries[i]	15.4	9.4	8.0	4.3	3.2

Notes: a. Excluding inner-German trade; b. West German industrial classification; c. Five-year average; d. Including unspecified products (share less than 1 per cent); e. Including products made from synthetic materials and mining products; f. Including foundry products and products of wire-making, cold-rolling mills and steel reduction; g. Including products made from synthetic materials and rubber products; h. Road vehicles, water craft and aircraft; i. Including horticultural products and forestry, hunting, fishery and tobacco products.
Source: *Bundesamt für Gewerbliche Wirtschaft*; *Statistische Jahrbücher der DDR*; *OECD Monthly Statistics of Foreign Trade*, Series A; DIW calculations.

by 17 per cent, which made it possible to achieve a surplus of over $600 million.

Finally, however, this restructuring process in OECD trade was only feasible because the GDR had at its disposal in inner-German trade an array of instruments, isolated from it in settlement and currency terms, which it used extensively for purposes of crisis management (see Tables 12.4 and 12.5). From the middle of 1981, whilst its imports from the West as a whole fell only slightly, the GDR shifted a part of its demand for Western goods from the OECD countries to inner-German trade (see Figure 12.1, p. 251).

In doing this, the GDR made substantial use of its financial elbow-room, as is apparent, for example, in the attainment of a record cumulative surplus in mid-1983 of 4.5 billion VE (*Verrechnungseinheit*: clearing unit of account). Thereafter, inner-German trade returned to normal; at the end of 1983 the cumulative balance amounted to only 4.1 billion VE, with the trend downwards (see Table 12.6). In 1984 the GDR increased its exports to the Federal Republic (at more than 1.3 billion VE the surplus was higher than ever before) and was thus able to normalise the liquidity position (see Table 12.7).

Inner-German trade thus turned out to be a stabilising factor in the surmounting of the GDR's economic problems. Furthermore, the GDR's earnings in convertible currencies proved to have a stabilising effect. The Federal Republic's payments to the GDR for Berlin's transport and communications (and its contributions to the associated investment costs), together with the revenue earned by *Intertank, Intershop* and *Genex-Geschenkdienst,* came, in total, to DM2.0 to 2.5 billion per year (Volze, 1983, p. 188 ff.). These revenues contributed to the reduction of the GDR's convertible currency debt. From the end of 1981 to the end of 1984 the GDR halved its net debt in convertible currencies, and did so not only through the repayment of credits, but also by means of a large build-up of assets in Western banks. The Federal Republic played no small part in this reduction of the debt and the restoration of the international creditworthiness of the GDR, in that in the summers of 1983 and of 1984 it provided guarantees for two untied credits of DM1 billion and DM950 million respectively. All in all, the GDR has thus managed to consolidate its foreign trade and payments position and to create relatively favourable preconditions for the new 1986-90 five-year plan.

Table 12.3: Commodity structure of foreign trade

Product groups[a]	1970	1976	1980	1981	1982	1983	1984
			Million valuta marks				
Imports, total	20,357	45,920	62,970	67,000	69,678	76,197	83,501
Machinery, equipment, means of transport	6,962	14,465	19,395	21,440	22,571	22,763	21,710
Fuels, mineral raw materials, metals	5,619	13,271	23,110	24,656	27,881	30,174	34,736
Other raw materials[b] and foodstuffs	5,720	11,434	11,901	11,926	11,390	13,563	14,780
Industrial consumer goods	916	2,204	3,149	3,283	2,865	3,353	4,760
Chemical products,[c] building materials and other products	1,140	4,546	5,415	5,695	5,171	6,324	7,515
Exports, total	19,240	39,540	57,131	65,927	75,231	84,227	90,402
Machinery, equipment, means of transport	9,947	20,244	29,308	32,238	36,467	40,261	42,398
Fuels, mineral raw materials, metals	1,943	4,468	8,455	11,076	13,918	14,908	15,820
Other raw materials[b] and foodstuffs	1,424	4,112	3,656	4,945	5,191	6,654	7,503
Industrial consumer goods	3,887	5,694	8,455	9,296	10,683	11,876	13,651
Chemical products,[c] building materials and other products	2,039	5,022	7,256	8,373	8,952	10,528	11,029
Balance,[d] all products	−1,117	−6,380	−5,840	−1,073	5,353	8,030	6,901
Machinery, equipment, means of transport	2,985	5,780	9,913	10,798	13,916	17,478	20,688
Fuels, mineral raw materials, metals	−3,675	−8,803	−14,655	−13,580	−13,964	−15,266	−18,916
Other raw materials[b] and foodstuffs	−4,297	−7,322	−8,245	−6,981	−6,199	−6,909	−7,276
Industrial consumer goods	2,970	3,490	5,307	6,013	7,818	8,523	8,891
Chemical products,[c] building materials and other products	899	476	1,840	2,678	3,781	4,204	3,514

				Percentage shares			
Imports, total	100	100	100	100	100	100	100
Machinery, equipment, means of transport	34.2	31.5	30.6	32.0	32.3	29.9	26.0
Fuels, mineral raw materials, metals	27.6	28.9	36.7	36.8	39.9	39.6	41.6
Other raw materials[b] and foodstuffs	28.1	24.9	18.9	17.8	16.3	17.8	17.7
Industrial consumer goods	4.5	4.8	5.0	4.9	4.1	4.4	5.7
Chemical products,[c] building materials and other products	5.6	9.9	8.6	8.5	7.4	8.3	9.0
Exports, total	100	100	100	100	100	100	100
Machinery, equipment, means of transport	51.7	51.2	51.3	49.9	49.5	47.8	46.9
Fuels, mineral raw materials, metals	10.1	11.3	14.8	16.8	18.5	17.7	17.5
Other raw materials[b] and foodstuffs	7.4	10.4	6.4	7.5	6.9	7.9	8.3
Industrial consumer goods	20.2	14.4	14.8	14.1	14.2	14.1	15.1
Chemical products,[c] building materials and other products	10.6	12.7	12.7	12.7	11.9	12.5	12.2

Notes: a. CMEA classification; b. Including semi-finished products for industrial purposes; c. Including fertilisers and rubber; d. Exports minus imports.

Source: *Statistische Jahrbücher der DDR*; *Statistisches Taschenbuch der DDR* (1985); DIW calculations.

Table 12.4: Deliveries by the Federal Republic[a] in inner-German trade

Products or product groups	1971-75[b]	1976-80[b]	1981	1982	1983	1984	1985
				DM million			
Total	3,203	4,653	5,576	6,382	6,947	6,403	7,903
				Percentage shares			
Products of the basic materials and producer good industries,[c]	53.8	52.4	55.7	56.9	57.6	59.8	58.3
of which:							
Crude oil	2.5	8.0	12.4	10.9	9.7	10.3	8.9
Iron and steel[d]	12.8	9.8	7.1	10.9	15.9	12.8	11.8
Chemical products[e]	23.2	20.4	19.7	21.7	20.1	22.4	19.6
Inorganic and organic basic materials and chemicals	7.4	9.0	10.0	11.5	10.9	12.4	11.0
Products of the investment good industries	23.8	28.3	25.5	20.0	18.2	16.0	18.7
of which:							
Mechanical engineering products	17.3	19.5	17.4	13.9	11.1	9.9	8.8
Products of the consumer good industries,	9.5	7.5	7.5	7.4	6.8	7.5	8.8
of which:							
Textiles and clothing	6.1	3.9	4.1	4.2	4.0	4.2	3.8
Products of agriculture[f] and of the foodstuff and semi-luxury industries,	11.7	10.6	10.0	14.5	16.3	15.5	13.3
of which:							
Feedstuffs (oilcakes and meal)	5.1	2.9	3.6	4.9	6.7	7.1	5.1
All products[g]	100	100	100	100	100	100	100

Notes: a. Including Berlin (West); b. Five year average; c. Including mining products; d.Including foundry products and products of wire-making, cold-rolling mills and steel reduction; e. Including products made from synthetic materials and rubber products; f. Including hunting, forestry and fisheries; g. Including non-classified products.

Source: *Statistisches Bundesamt*: *Warenverkehr mit der Deutschen Demokratischen Republik und Berlin (Ost)*, *Fachserie 6, Reihe E (Jahreshefte)*; *Bundesanzeiger*; DIW calculations

Table 12.5: Purchases by the Federal Republic[a] in inner-German trade

Product or product groups	1971-75[b]	1976-80[b]	1981	1982	1983	1984	1985
				DM million			
Total	2,791	4,381	6,051	6,639	6,878	7,732	7,636
				Percentage shares			
Products of the basic materials and producer good industries,[c]	38.5	47.3	57.1	55.8	54.7	55.7	55.3
of which:							
Mineral oil products[d]	9.8	19.9	26.9	25.7	22.9	22.7	20.3
Iron and steel[e]	7.7	6.5	5.2	4.9	6.1	6.4	7.4
Chemical products[f]	8.9	10.7	12.9	13.3	13.3	13.6	13.2
Products of the investment good industries,	10.7	10.6	9.6	10.0	10.5	10.8	11.1
of which:							
Mechanical engineering products	3.5	3.1	2.6	2.8	2.7	2.5	2.9
Electro-technical products	3.5	3.9	3.2	3.4	3.9	4.4	4.2
Products of the consumer good industries,	30.6	27.1	21.4	23.0	23.4	23.4	23.7
of which:							
Furniture	4.1	3.5	3.7	3.7	3.7	3.8	3.4
Textiles[g]	10.5	9.2	6.4	6.8	6.6	6.7	7.2
Clothing[h]	8.8	7.6	5.0	6.1	6.4	6.5	6.5
Products of agriculture[i] and of the foodstuff and semi-luxury industries,	19.5	14.3	11.2	10.6	11.0	9.6	9.5
of which: Slaughtered livestock[j]	—	—	4.4	4.2	4.1	3.3	3.4
All products[k]	100	100	100	100	100	100	100

Notes: a. Including Berlin (West); b. Five-year average; c. Including mining products; d. Petrol, diesel, heating oil etc.; e. Including foundry products and products of wire-making, cold-rolling mills and steel reduction; f. Including products made from synthetic materials and rubber products; g. Mainly domestic and furnishing textiles, hosiery and knitwear; h. Mainly outergarments; i. Including hunting, forestry and fisheries; j. Including fresh pigmeat; k. Including non-classified products.

Source: *Statistisches Bundesamt*: *Warenverkehr mit der Deutschen Demokratischen Republik und Berlin (Ost), Fachserie* 6, *Reihe* 6 (*Jahreshefte*); Bundesanzeiger; DIW calculations.

Cost of consolidation and the adaptability of the system

The process of adaptation to international economic challenges has, however, led to structural changes which may hinder growth in the longer term and thus threaten the realisation of ambitious economic and social policy postulates. The problems indicated above explain why the GDR leadership adopted an extremely restrictive economic policy at the start of the 1980s, with the growth of money income and consumer supply being reduced. After some time, the resultant consumer good shortages eased and left behind no deep imprints. But investment, too, was reduced. In 1982, 1983 and 1984, for the first time in the history of the GDR, investment fell.

The attainment of external economic consolidation by means of a reduction in investment in total and/or by increasing investment in sectors which did not primarily serve productivity growth, but rather the development of a domestic basic materials basis and thus the economic security of the GDR, was and still is linked with economic risks. It was this policy that adversely affected the growth goals striven for in the 1981-85 five-year plan and threatened to damage the basis of the new five-year plan.

The fact that the negative economic effects following the external economic consolidation nevertheless did not infringe especially seriously on domestic economic development is undoubtedly due, in part, to a reduction of 'waste potential'. Another factor was the effectiveness of the economic reforms which were introduced with the combine reform of 1979 and continued with the 'perfecting' of the economic mechanism. In this way the GDR demonstrated a certain adaptability.

The aim of the combine formation decreed in November 1979, was to increase industrial efficiency; almost the whole of industry was tightly amalgamated into 132 centrally directed and 93 county-directed combines (Thalheim, 1984, p. 17 ff.). Subsequent years saw the introduction of a number of additional legal and administrative measures whose aim was to raise the level of productivity in the national economy, to reduce, by limiting energy and material consumption, the losses sustained, and, by a better flow of information between party and state planning and guidance authorities on the one hand and the enterprises on the other, to improve communications. Within the framework of these provisions, a relatively high level of suc-

Table 12.6: Statistics relating to inner-German trade

	Cumulative surplus[a]	Agreed swing	Utilised swing[b]	Payments by GDR via special account 'S'	Relative debt position[c]	Swing financing share[d]	Swing-purchases ratio[e]
	DM bill	DM mill	DM mill	DM mill	%	%	%
1970	1.35	380/440[f]	387	46	68	29	19
1971	1.20	440	413	110	52	34	18
1972	1.75	585	539	24	74	31	23
1973	1.75	620	592	317	66	34	22
1974	1.71	660	559	251	59	29	17
1975	2.39	790	711	161	72	30	21
1976	2.53	850	786	370	67	30	20
1977	2.97	850	748	187	75	25	19
1978	3.68	850	677	71	94	18	17
1979	3.91	850	748	34	85	19	16
1980	3.87	850	745	12	69	19	13
1981	3.65	850	676	19	60	19	11
1982	3.80	850	582	66	57	15	9
1983	4.10	770	543	73	60	13	8
1984	3.10	690	215	70	40	7	3
1985	3.50	600	170	50	46	5	2

Notes: a. Surplus of the Federal Republic of Germany, financing balance from merchandise trade, services and the cash account (special account 'S'); b. Swing actually utilised by the GDR, yearly average; c. Ratio of cumulative surplus to purchases of goods from the GDR; d. Ratio of utilised swing to cumulative surplus; e. Ratio of utilised swing to purchases of goods from the GDR per year; f. To 9 May: 380; from 10 May: 440.

Source: *Statistisches Bundesamt*: *Warenverkehr mit der DDR und Berlin (Ost), Fachserie* 6, Reihe 6 (*Jahreshefte*); data of the Bundesministerium für Wirtschaft and of the Bundesministerium für Innerdeutsche Beziehungen; DIW calculations.

cess was achieved with regard to intensification, which continued to be accompanied by changes in the organisation of foreign trade and payments.[3] At the beginning of the new five-year plan period 1986-90 the foreign trade organisation of the GDR comprised 64 foreign trade enterprises, which have the authority to conduct foreign trade transactions on an operational basis. These can be divided into five groupings (Haendcke-Hoppe, 1985, p. 8). The largest involves 23 foreign trade enterprises directly subordinate to the combines (hence, they are called combine foreign trade enterprises). Another twelve foreign trade enterprises are subordinate to various ministries. Yet another grouping of twelve is also subordinate to industrial ministries, but these enterprises have been reorganised into 61 foreign trade units, which are supposed to co-operate with the combines. These units do not have legal rights of their own. This is not the case with the fourth grouping,

Table 12.7: Development of inner-German trade since 1970

	Merchandise trade				Increase in merchandise trade over previous year					
					Current prices			Constant prices[b]		
	Purchases[a]	Deliveries[a]	Turnover	Balance	Purchases	Deliveries	Turnover	Purchases	Deliveries	Turnover
	DM million				Percentage					
1970	1,996	2,415	4,411	420	27.5	6.3	15.0	—	—	—
1971	2,319	2,499	4,817	180	16.2	3.4	9.2	15.1	3.0	8.5
1972	2,381	2,927	5,308	547	2.7	17.2	10.2	1.6	15.3	8.7
1973	2,660	2,998	5,658	339	11.7	2.4	6.6	−3.5	−6.1	−4.9
1974	3,252	3,671	6,923	418	22.3	22.4	22.4	−3.6	1.3	−0.8
1975	3,342	3,922	7,264	579	2.8	6.8	4.9	4.9	5.3	5.3
1976	3,877	4,269	8,145	392	16.0	8.9	12.1	6.6	3.3	5.1
1977	3,961	4,409	8,370	448	2.2	3.3	2.8	1.8	3.[illegible]	2.5
1978	3,900	4,575	8,475	675	−1.5	3.8	1.2	1.1	3.5	2.4
1979	4,589	4,720	9,309	131	17.7	3.2	9.8	−9.1	−3.7	−6.0
1980	5,580	5,293	10,873	−286	21.6	12.2	16.8	5.6	2.8	4.0
1981	6,051	5,575	11,626	−476	8.4	5.3	6.9	−1.4	−2.6	−2.1
1982	6,639	6,382	13,022	−257	2.7	14.5	12.0	10.3	12.3	11.4
1983	6,878	6,947	13,825	69	3.6	8.8	6.2	6.0	7.7	7.0
1984	7,732	6,403	14,135	−1,329	12.4	−7.8	2.2	7.2	−11.7	−3.7
1985[c]	7,640	7,900	15,540	270	−1.3	23.4	10.9			

Notes: a. By the Federal Republic of Germany, including Berlin (West); b. With regard to price development calculated by the DIW; c. Provisional figures.

Source: Federal Statistical Office: *Warenverkehr mit der Deutschen Demokratischen Republik und Berlin (Ost)*, *Fachserie* 6, *Reihe* 6 (*Jahreshefte*); DIW calculations.

which consists of seven enterprises and combines. These have direct foreign trade responsibilities and are, thus, able to conduct their own foreign trade transactions. The final grouping covers ten foreign trade enterprises, mainly providing foreign trade services, which are still subject to the direct authority of the Ministry of Foreign Trade. It must be noted, however, that all the foreign trade enterprises still come under the supervision of the Ministry of Foreign Trade (see Figure 12.2). Nevertheless, it is clear that the strict separation of production and foreign trade, which has characterised previous periods, is being eroded to a certain extent. Although the reform process is going on, and it is not yet possible to draw final conclusions, the modifications already made have the following effects: the Ministry of Foreign Trade has been ousted from its role as the sole guardian of the monopoly of foreign trade; the obligation to fulfil foreign trade plans has been transferred to the level of the combine and enterprise; through the partial integration of foreign trade processes, new rights of decision-making have been conferred upon the combine; combines and enterprises have, for the first time, been given a voice in the conclusion of foreign trade contracts.

By splitting up the once rigidly centralised foreign trade organisations into specialised foreign trade enterprises, the GDR leadership has succeeded in carrying out more rapidly the adaptation processes which had become inevitable and to react better and more flexibly to internal and external pressures.

ECONOMIC AND POLITICAL CHALLENGES AT THE START OF THE 1986-90 FIVE-YEAR PLAN

At the start of the 1980s the GDR thus got into serious economic difficulties, the outstanding features of which were a high level of indebtedness to Western banks, a sharp reduction of imports (especially from OECD countries) accompanied by an increase in exports, and finally, consumer good shortages in the GDR. The attempts of the GDR leadership to overcome the foreign trade and payments problems by means of economic policy and administrative measures have shown that the GDR has available to it certain (albeit limited) economic and political margins of latitude for improving its external economic position within the framework of the five-year plan which started in 1986.

What will certainly not change in the new five-year plan is the idea of intensive growth, a concept already characteristic of the 1981-85 five-year plan. As regards domestic economic goals, the improvement of the standard of living of the population has priority, now as before. Consequently, further improvements in the supply of goods, together with the conclusion of the housing programme by 1990, will absorb the major part of existing capacity, so that there will still not be much room to manoeuvre as regards an expansive investment policy. Nevertheless, emphases can be discerned in the micro-electronics sector and in the basic materials industries, which are intended to grow more than proportionately.

External economic relations, too, probably enjoy a high priority in the new five-year plan. The experiences of recent years have demonstrated that the competitiveness of manufacturing industry is too limited to be able to continue to realise surpluses in trade with the West. For this reason structural changes are necessary precisely in the sphere of foreign trade and of the export-orientated industries, in order not to be exposed once again to externally determined pressures.

The complexity of the pattern of GDR interests*

The realisation of the goals as they have been reflected in the five-year plan will, however, also not in any way be problem-free, even under the now more favourable external conditions. For, even if it is one of the commonplaces of any analysis of the GDR's external economic relations, it must always be stressed that the GDR is a country poorly endowed with raw materials and is, moreover, forced to develop foreign markets in order to earn the foreign exchange which will make it possible for the GDR to obtain the imports essential for economic growth. Its strong dependence on foreign trade has, since its foundation, constantly forced the GDR, in forming its external economic relations, not only to obey the laws governing its own planned economy and to take account of domestic economic bottlenecks, but also to allow for economic and political factors which arise in the international political and economic system. Through its economic interlinking with Eastern Europe and the

*For greater detail on this see Jacobsen, 1984, pp. 144-68.

USSR, the GDR's room for manoeuvre is strongly affected by developments within the member states of Comecon; events such as those in Poland at the start of the 1980s have correspondingly also given substantial shocks to the course of the GDR's economy. But the economic links with Western markets, too, exert a considerable influence on development in the

Figure 12.1: GDR imports from OECD countries and from the Federal Republic 1981-84 ($ billion)

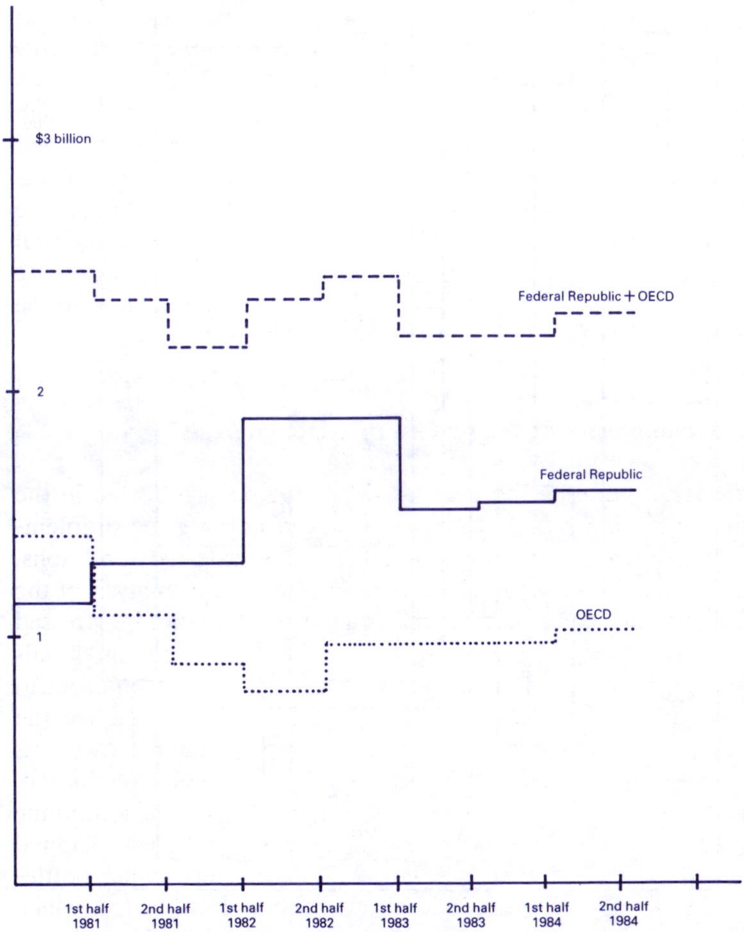

Source: Rösch, F., *Innerdeutsche Wirtschaftsbeziehungen*, 11 Symposium der Forschungsstelle für gesamtdeutsche wirtschaftliche und soziale Fragen, Berlin, 21-2 November 1985, p. 4.

Figure 12.2: System of management and organisation relating to the GDR's foreign trade

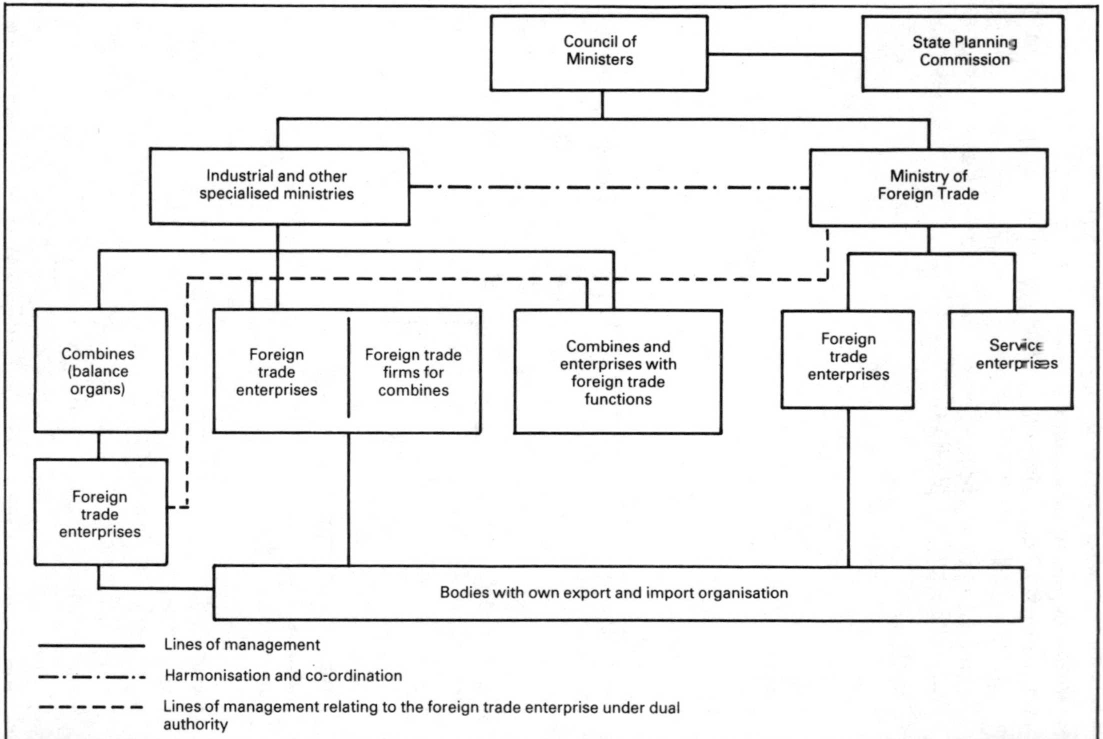

GDR: recessions and inflation in Western countries, as well as increasing protectionism in the world economy, do significant harm to the developmental prospects of the GDR.

In the above-mentioned areas, the position of the GDR is not fundamentally different from that of the other countries of Eastern Europe. There are, however, a number of factors which are 'GDR-specific'. An essential goal of the GDR leadership is the guaranteeing of a relatively high level of economic development, because it contributes substantially to political stability within the GDR and confers a certain legitimacy upon the rule of the GDR leadership. The quantitative and qualitative improvement in the standard of living plays, if anything, an even more important role with regard to political stability in the GDR than in the other communist states of Eastern Europe, because the GDR's political leadership is not to the same degree able, as are the leaderships in, say, Hungary, Poland or Romania (especially in the case of externally caused crises or of Western sanctions), to call forth a feeling of national solidarity and to make use of this by way of compensation. In the GDR a certain pride is undoubtedly felt in its economic achievements and, accordingly, a sort of 'national consciousness', but there is a lack of historical traditions peculiar to the GDR which has only marginally been made good by the more recent efforts of the GDR leadership to claim certain pre-socialist developments as precursors of its own model of society. The partition of Germany is still felt very deeply in the GDR and, accordingly, there is still a strong fixation on the Federal Republic. This, in turn, exerts great pressure on the GDR leadership to guarantee at least the material well-being of the population in order, as far as possible, to nip any dissatisfaction in the bud.

Relatively small and, at the same time, raw-material-poor countries such as the GDR, are, as a rule, forced to spread their dependence, i.e. to reduce the danger of economic and political shocks from other countries to their own economies. This goal is very difficult for the GDR to achieve because it has, above all in the USSR, but also in the Federal Republic, two major economic partners which are especially able to exert influence on the external economic and political behaviour of the GDR.

THE ROLE OF THE USSR AND OF OTHER CMEA COUNTRIES

Since the early 1960s the share of the USSR in the GDR's foreign trade has shrunk to a little over 30 per cent. Even so, the economic dependence of the GDR on the Soviet Union is still considerable: the GDR obtains by far the major part of its vital raw materials from the USSR and, at the same time, supplies the USSR with a large part of its industrial goods. This economic linkage, which is by no means purely disadvantageous to the GDR (since, especially in the 1970s and early 1980s, the GDR obtained raw materials and energy at prices lower than those which it would have had to pay on the world market), is of central importance to the GDR and is set to continue for the foreseeable future.

For some time there have been indications that the USSR is trying to reduce its subsidisation of the economies of the East European countries. The Comecon summit, held from 12 to 14 June 1984 in Moscow, quite clearly put an end in practice to the comprehensive efforts at integration of the 1970s, and once again formally accorded to bilateral relations between CMEA countries that importance which they had in any case long possessed. In the context of these relations the USSR expects its East European partners (including, of course, the GDR) 'to supply foodstuffs and industrial consumer goods, several kinds of construction materials, machines and equipment of high quality and technically of world standard' (cf. Declaration on the main directions of the further development and deepening of economic and scientific-technical co-operation between member countries of Comecon, Moscow, 14 June 1984), if it is to continue to meet East European needs as regards raw materials and energy.

These expectations on the part of the USSR create further pressure on the economy of the GDR. In particular, the demand for increased exports of consumer goods to the USSR reduces the possibility for the GDR of expanding its hard currency sales to the West. Like other East European countries, the GDR is still suffering from the effects of the recession at the beginning of the 1980s, which was worsened in the period 1981 to 1983 by the West's reluctance to grant credits and by the deterioration of the terms of trade *vis-à-vis* the USSR (see Table 12.8). For reasons of domestic policy, it is essential pre-

Table 12.8: Terms of trade of the GDR

	Price index for socialist countries		Terms of trade[a]	Price index for non-socialist countries		Terms of trade[a]			Terms of trade[a]	
	Exports	Imports		Exports	Imports		Export price index	Import price index		
1960	100.00	100.00	100	100.00	100.00	100	100.00	100.00	100.00	1960
1961	100.50	100.01	100	100.40	94.88	106	100.47	98.70	101.79	1961
1962	100.68	100.29	100	96.38	92.10	105	99.73	98.48	101.27	1962
1963	101.07	97.10	104	96.39	90.54	106	100.05	95.57	104.69	1963
1964	100.92	98.13	103	96.13	91.16	105	99.80	96.29	103.65	1964
1965	101.83	98.28	104	96.63	93.64	103	100.47	96.98	103.60	1965
1966	98.74	93.14	106	94.00	93.06	101	97.05	93.12	104.68	1966
1967	96.46	89.89	107	96.56	89.02	108	96.49	89.65	107.63	1967
1968	96.55	89.78	108	93.40	87.40	107	95.79	89.18	107.41	1968
1969	96.83	90.87	107	97.66	89.47	109	97.05	90.48	107.26	1969
1970	98.01	92.76	106	104.90	94.04	112	99.72	93.15	107.05	1970
1971	97.40	94.19	103	105.65	96.23	110	99.38	94.82	104.81	1971
1972	97.62	96.33	101	105.29	98.85	107	99.40	97.16	102.31	1972
1973	98.53	97.94	101	119.59	106.69	112	103.41	100.88	102.51	1973
1974	101.80	106.78	95	153.82	126.14	122	113.96	113.72	100.21	1974
1975	112.36	134.58	83	154.06	131.26	117	121.16	133.45	90.79	1975
1976	107.95	129.15	84	166.06	137.20	121	119.97	131.99	90.89	1976
1977	110.68	136.72	81	161.40	139.08	116	120.24	137.45	87.48	1977
1978	110.71	137.70	80	156.05	139.97	111	119.56	138.38	86.40	1978
1979	112.64	142.31	79	180.51	148.05	122	125.10	144.30	86.69	1979
1980	107.87	136.63	79	210.67	159.67	132	126.71	144.20	87.87	1980
1981	112.21	148.40	76	242.63	173.90	140	137.13	155.94	87.94	1981
1982	115.03	153.52	75	238.96	177.30	135	141.59	160.29	88.33	1982

Note: a. Index of export prices as percentage of the index of import prices.
Source: DIW calculations.

cisely for the GDR to increase the internal supply of consumer goods and, at least for the long term, to raise the standard of living. The explicit demand of the USSR for deliveries of these goods, however, adversely affects domestic supplies or, alternatively, their use as hard currency-earning exports to the West.

Above all, however, the demand for equipment of 'world technical standards', in other words for advanced technology, confronts the GDR economic planners with great difficulties. First of all, improvement of this kind cannot be achieved without additional imports of Western capital goods, licences and know-how as well as of advanced technology. In respect of the latter, further difficulties have been created for the East by the recently tightened COCOM controls and the continual opposition of influential sections of the US administration to increased technology transfer. But even if this problem could be overcome (e.g. by increasing high-tech imports from non-COCOM countries), there would still be the question of how the efficiency of the GDR economy could be so raised as to correspond with Soviet wishes. Even if the GDR has been able to improve economic efficiency and to achieve some success in reducing its hard currency debt (not least by means of a number of changes in its economic organisation, e.g. combine formation), it is difficult to imagine that it will be able to make substantial progress in this area without further economic reforms. There are admittedly indications that the GDR will try to place one of its priorities in the 1986-90 five-year plan in the field of advanced technology, in order to be able, from a more independent position, to prevent the technology gap with the West from getting any wider (Krakat, 1984, pp. 63-106).

The present stance of the USSR seems to be conditioned by the intention not to increase deliveries of energy and especially of raw materials to the East European countries, including the GDR, which could force the GDR into additional investment in energy conservation and in the development of alternative energy sources, or else into the spending of hard currency in order to satisfy its growing energy needs from third countries.

Economic relations with the other East European CMEA members do not under these circumstances seem to be very promising either, not only because a comprehensive development of economic relations with Poland and Romania is scarcely possible, and would, indeed, not be very rewarding, but also because the attempts which were formerly made to multilateralise the economic processes within the CMEA (e.g. by mans of plan co-ordination, the setting up of international economic organisations) are today not realisable. It is, admittedly, quite possible to imagine that the GDR will develop its bilateral relations with Comecon members such as Czechoslovakia and Hungary in order at least to prevent the fixation of its economy within the CMEA on the USSR from becoming any stronger.

The role of the Federal Republic of Germany and of other Western industrial countries

The other major trading partner of the GDR is the Federal Republic. Even though the share of GDR trade with the Federal Republic is substantially lower than that with the USSR (the former, however, according to GDR figures, has never fallen below 8 per cent), the Federal Republic is the GDR's second most important trading partner and ranks first among the Western countries. The organisation of this commodity exchange, which is not seen as foreign trade by the Federal Republic (see Lambrecht, 1982, pp. 3-17; Jacobsen, 1984, pp. 136-43), displays a number of special features, which are advantageous above all to the GDR and which the GDR has so far not wished to forego, despite repeated affirmations of national sovereignty. These special features of inner-German trade enable the GDR to enlarge its sales opportunities in the Federal Republic through being exempt from tariffs and levies and enjoying value-added tax concessions. In the 1970s, as indeed in the preceding period, the GDR certainly made use of these opportunities, but did so moderately, because it has always been anxious not to be too dependent on the economic exchange with the Federal Republic, possibly laying itself open to political blackmail if it did so.

In times of economic difficulties, however, inner-German trade becomes more attractive to the GDR, e.g. when unforeseeable difficulties arise on account of certain economic bottlenecks in the GDR or of shortages of foreign currency. This was especially the case in the years 1982 to 1983, when the GDR activated its economic links with the Federal Republic by partially substituting, as already mentioned, inner-German trade for OECD trade and using the opportunity to take up two large credits. Thus the Federal Government and the *Bundesbank* helped stabilise the international ability to pay of the GDR and to moderate external pressure.

The data from 1983 onwards show that the GDR, as before the crisis, is once again trying to diversify regionally its trade with the West, and to expand trade with countries such as France, Japan and also Canada (especially grain). The neutral countries of Europe (particularly Austria and Sweden, but also Finland and Switzerland) are likewise attractive as alternative trading partners for the GDR. Their potential importance is, however, lessened by the fact that these countries' room to manoeuvre politically and economically with regard to the East could be reduced by measures taken by the Western allies within the framework of COCOM or by unilateral measures in the field of export controls taken by the USA (in that these countries would be uncoupled from technological innovations in the leading Western countries). All in all, there can be no doubt that economic relations between the GDR and the Federal Republic are of special importance and have contributed substantially to increasing the external economic elbow-room of the GDR.

THE GDR'S MARGINS OF LATITUDE FOR ACTION

In recent years the GDR has gained in international standing. In this respect the GDR's external economic relations and opportunities have played a considerable role, especially in the solution of its economic problems. It was, after all, primarily foreign trade and payments pressures, in a period of increased East-West confrontation, which led to adverse effects on growth in the GDR and which at the end of the 1970s began more and more noticeably to hamper the development of the GDR. The raising of new material prices and especially of oil after 1973-4, and above all after 1979, had increasingly noticeable effects on the GDR. The deterioration of the terms of trade, especially with the USSR, coupled with excessive imports from the West, created an increasing trade deficit which could not be closed by increasing exports to the West, where, in consequence of the recession, demand was in any case falling. Rather, it had to be financed by borrowing, especially from the West. The GDR finally succeeded in dealing with these difficulties and in restoring its reputation as a relatively smooth-running planned economy, partly by means of its own efforts in the sphere of economic policy, and by modification of the system, but also through the comprehensive utilisation of the advantages to be found in the inner-German relationship. From this it became apparent that, attempting to overcome external economic problems, the GDR has available to it certain, albeit limited, margins of latitude.

Thus, it has become clear in recent years that, for example, the importance of the GDR as an ally of the USSR has increased rather than decreased. Processes of political and social erosion in Eastern Europe (as in Poland) or a greater degree of independence (as in Hungary) have conferred a relatively greater importance on the GDR for economic, political and military reasons. The increasingly important part being played by technically complicated machines and equipment and by advanced technology has made the GDR (which already for some considerable time has been devoting increased attention to these sectors) more attractive. The USSR's expectation of gaining access to technologically more advanced products, especially via the GDR, as expressed, for example, at the June 1984 Comecon Summit, affords a clear indication of this trend. In the attempt to meet this challenge and, at the same time, to attain a high rate of economic growth, the GDR can point to the necessity of making extensive use of the economic opportunities which it finds in the West and especially in the relationship with the Federal Republic. In this line of argument a special role is played by the already mentioned pressure to improve material prosperity, which guarantees political stability in the GDR.

Nevertheless, this economic elbow-room of the GDR has clear political limits. Too strong an integration of the GDR in the Western world's economy and too great a dependence in the sphere of advanced technology, which, as far as the Soviet Union and the Eastern alliance are concerned, would be fraught with political risks which, at times of increased tension between East and West, would represent a potential for disturbance. Admittedly, there clearly exists in the GDR a readiness to exploit, in the longer term yet more than previously, the advantages of the international division of labour in Western trade also, but this comes second to ensuring the security of the system. In the final analysis, it has, so far, always been the case that a heightening of the East-West conflict has impaired the economic and political room to manoeuvre of the smaller East

European countries (and that applies also to the GDR). Only to the degree in which steps towards détente become possible and the East-West atmosphere becomes less tense, will the GDR, too, be in a position to strengthen its external economic relations.

NOTES

1. This contribution derives from a research project promoted by the *Deutsche Forschungsgemeinschaft* on the theme of 'Margins of latitude enjoyed by the GDR in the field of foreign trade and payments'.

2. The data upon which this chapter is based were made available by the DIW.

3. Cf. authors' collective under the leadership of E. Faude, G. Grote and C. Luft, *Sozialistische Aussenwirtschaft* (East Berlin, 1984), pp. 16 ff. and 301 ff. The differences become especially noticeable if a comparison is made between this volume and the relevant passages in the preceding version of this textbook. Cf. Authors' Collective under the leadership of E. Faude, G. Grote and C. Luft, *Sozialistische Aussenwirtschaft* (East Berlin, 1976), pp. 169 ff. and 269 ff.

13

The Role of the GDR in Comecon: Some Economic Aspects

Werner Klein

INTRODUCTION

The Council for Mutual Economic Assistance (Comecon or CMEA) forms the institutional basis of the many and varied attempts at and manifestations of the integration of the economies of the countries belonging to this organisation. The economic systems of most of these countries are characteristic of the type of centrally administered economy for which the Soviet system is the model. The only exceptions are Poland, in particular, and Hungary, where radical reforms have taken place. These reforms, it is true, scarcely affect economic relations between these two countries and the other member states as far as the methods of the integration policy itself are concerned. On the contrary, the focus of integrative efforts within Comecon is the organisation of the external economic relations of all these countries strictly according to the principles of state planning and management, despite all differences in detail.

In order to understand the significance of the GDR within Comecon it is, first of all, necessary to discuss the basic organisational and institutional conception of the foreign trade and payments system of the GDR. The next section will then deal with the institutional structure of Comecon and the methods and principles of its integration policy, based on the programmes agreed within Comecon. In the final section some selected examples will be used to illustrate the economic position of the GDR within Comecon and the resulting consequences for the economy of the GDR.

INSTITUTIONAL AND CONCEPTUAL ASPECTS OF THE FOREIGN TRADE AND PAYMENTS OF THE GDR

An essential feature of the GDR's foreign trade and payments is the so-called 'state foreign trade and payments monopoly' (*staatliches Aussenwirtschaftsmonopol*), which embraces not only a monopoly on foreign trade, but also monopolies on foreign exchange and transport. Under the foreign trade monopoly, which is, indeed, laid down in Article 9 Section 5 of the GDR's 1974 Constitution, the management and planning of foreign trade is to be carried out solely by means of the 'socialist state power' (Authors' Collective, 1985, p. 19). Like the other sectors of the economy, the foreign trade and payments of the GDR are subject to central state management and planning (see Figure 13.1)

The highest state authority responsible for decision-making in this area is the Council of Ministers of the GDR, which is furnished with all-embracing powers and to which is subordinated the State Planning Commission as the body directly responsible for planning and plan co-ordination, including foreign economic relations. Answerable to the Council of Ministers are the industrial ministries and the Ministry of Foreign Trade in their capacity as organs of central state management. Until foreign trade was reorganised in connection with the combine reform from 1978 onwards, the Ministry of Foreign Trade possessed wide-ranging powers in regard to the GDR's foreign trade and payments (drawing up the foreign trade plan, planning the regional structure of exports and imports, planning foreign exchange revenue and so on). Subordinate to the Ministry of Foreign Trade are the foreign trade enterprises, whose task it is to carry out the foreign trade plans. In principle, these enterprises alone are allowed to enter into foreign trade transactions.

The present organisation of the state foreign trade and payments monopoly in the GDR is the result of the far-reaching combine reform mentioned above (see Haendcke-Hoppe, 1985, pp. 5 ff.). Until the end of the 1970s, the GDR's foreign trade was handled by 30 to 35 juridically independent, centralised foreign trade enterprises, each of them equipped with a broad export palette and most of them directly subordinate to the Ministry of Foreign Trade. This rather inflexible organisational structure was broken up in consequence of the above reform.

Figure 13.1: The management and planning of socialist external economic relations

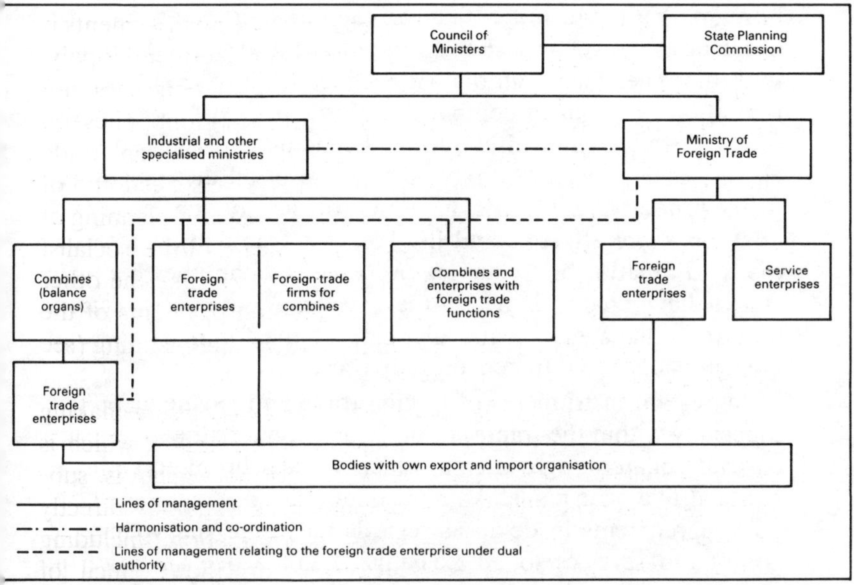

Source: Authors' Collective, *Sozialistische Aussenwirtschaft (Lehrbuch)* (East Berlin, 1985), p. 305.

At present 64 foreign trade organisations in total, mostly in the form of foreign trade enterprises, are entrusted with the conduct of foreign trade transactions. According to their respective subordination, it is possible to distinguish various types of such organisations. Thus today, for example, 23 foreign trade enterprises function as combine foreign trade enterprises (*Kombinats-Aussenhandelsbetriebe*) directly subordinate to combines; seven enterprises and combines have the authority to engage directly in foreign trade. Only ten foreign trade enterprises remain directly subordinate to the Ministry of Foreign Trade. As Figure 13.1 shows, the combine foreign trade enterprises, which are especially important today, are subordinate to the combine itself, as well as to the Ministry of Foreign Trade (dual subordination). The intention is that in this way the combine shall, on the one hand, be directly in touch with its own foreign economic relations, while, on the other hand, the state monopoly of foreign trade and payments is not eliminated by the new organisational structure.

The foreign trade monopoly in the GDR has, however, undergone modifications in consequence of the fact that its functions are no longer concentrated solely in the Ministry of Foreign Trade, but rather that, on the one hand, co-ordination procedures between the Foreign Trade Ministry and the industrial ministries (see Authors' Collective, 1985, p. 39), and, on the other, the right of combines to participate via the combine foreign trade enterprises, have been institutionalised (see Haendcke-Hoppe, 1985, p. 17). The aim of all these measures is to render the GDR's handling of its foreign economic relations more effective and flexible. It is true that, as a result, the co-ordination and planning procedures within the economic system have changed, yet, in the new organisational structure, too, *state* management and planning of the foreign trade and payments of the GDR remain fully preserved.

Important instruments of foreign trade and payments policy, especially within the framework of Comecon, are the long-term, basically bilateral agreements, which are synchronised with the national five-year plans. Annual commodity protocols spell out these agreements in detail as regards the value and volume of goods and services to be exchanged. Value determination in Comecon trade is based upon so-called contract prices. Because the 'mark of the GDR' and the domestic currencies of the other Comecon countries are not convertible, there is a strict separation of domestic and foreign trade prices. GDR imports are, therefore, valued in valuta marks (foreign currency marks: VM) and are credited to the importing and exporting economic units at unrevealed internal rates of exchange. Since 1975, as a consequence of the price turbulences on the world markets (oil price shocks), the basis for the annual fixing of contract prices within Comecon has been the average of world market prices for comparable products over the previous five years (the Moscow price formula). In the absence of an intra-bloc price system capable of functioning efficiently, the attempt is made, by this means, to adapt prices to developments in world markets with time lags and on a sliding scale. The rate of exchange of the VM against the transferable rouble, which is the unit of account used within Comecon, is, because of the inconvertibility of Comecon domestic currencies and of the transferable rouble, state-determined and not made known officially. For this reason, the published foreign trade statistics, expressed in VMs or transferable roubles, scarcely permit conclusions to be drawn about the real export profitability of a country.

INSTITUTIONAL FOUNDATIONS, PRINCIPLES AND METHODS OF INTEGRATION POLICY WITHIN COMECON

Historical background

Comecon was founded on 18 January 1949 by the Soviet Union, Bulgaria, Poland, Romania, Czechoslovakia and Hungary (see Uschakow, 1983, pp. 219 ff.). Albania became a member in February of the same year and the GDR did so on 27 September 1950. Mongolia followed in 1962, Cuba in 1972 and Vietnam in 1978. Given the effective resignation of Albania in 1962, Comecon now has ten full members. Co-operation agreements exist between Comecon on the one hand, and Finland, Iraq and Mexico on the other. Other socialist countries (Afghanistan, Angola, Ethiopia, the People's Republic of China, Laos, Mozambique, North Korea, South Yemen and Nicaragua) have observer status at sessions of the Council and in other Comecon organs. Yugoslavia has partial associate status.

The establishment of Comecon, on the initiative of the Soviet Union under the leadership of Stalin, can be attributed in essence to political rather than, in the first place, to economic reasons. For one thing, in 1948, after a political dispute between Tito and Stalin, Yugoslavia left a Cominform which was under the ideological leadership of the CPSU (see Seiffert, 1982, pp. 25 ff.), thus providing an example which could have had imitators. For another, European countries in the Soviet sphere of control (Poland, Czechoslovakia and Hungary) were invited to participate in the USA's European Recovery Programme (the Marshall Plan). From this point of view, Comecon was from the start an institution for the establishment of political links between the member states under the leadership of the USSR. At first, the economic importance of Comecon as a whole and for its member countries remained rather limited (see Thalheim, 1980, p. 121). Admittedly, this changed in the Sixties, when, from 1960 onwards, the institutional development of Comecon was significantly promoted in consequence of a Statute passed by the member states. This again furnished the precondition for the intensification of economic activity, especially between Comecon countries, on the basis of various programmes agreed at Comecon level.

Organisational structures

In contrast to the European Community, which possesses the character of a supranational institution in areas of foreign economic relations laid down by treaty, Comecon is merely an international organisation. The emphasis on national sovereignty as a basic principle in the co-operation between Comecon countries, is duly reflected in the powers of Council bodies and in the associated procedures for the formulation of decisions. The institutional structure of Comecon is divided into chief organs and advisory sub-organs (see Seiffert, 1982, pp. 25 ff.).

The following belong to the chief organs:

(i) The Council session. This is the highest Comecon authority, consisting of representatives of the member countries under the chairmanship of the prime minister of the host country; it meets annually, the venue rotating between the various capitals of the member states. The meetings of party chiefs, which on the whole do not take place on a regular basis, may, though they are not provided for in the statutes of the CMEA, also be seen as specific procedures for the formulation of decisions within Comecon.

(ii) The executive committee. This is the chief executive organ of the Council and comprises the deputy prime ministers.

(iii) The committees. These deal with the areas of co-operation relating to planning, material-technical supply, scientific-technical co-operation and in machine building. The committees comprise the relevant national departmental heads, their tasks being self-explanatory.

(iv) The standing commissions. These take the form of nineteen branch and four functionally delimited commissions whose task it is to promote the development of co-operation between the CMEA states in their respective areas. The commissions

comprise national departmental ministers and are in each case located in the capital of the minister who serves as chairman. East Berlin is the location for three standing commissions, namely for the chemical industry, for construction and for standardisation.

(v) The Secretariat. This is the only Council institution which is permanent and not made up of special representatives of the members, with the Secretary, as the highest full-time functionary, at its head. The duties of the Secretariat, whose headquarters are in Moscow, are in essence confined to the carrying out of all the necessary administrative work for the chief and sub-organs.

So-called standing conferences of specialist ministers, special working groups and three institutes with general tasks (standardisation, socialist world system and management of industry) act as secondary or ancillary organs.

Six industrial branch organisations function as special Council organisations, including 'Interchim' which has its headquarters in Halle (GDR), three transport and two post and telecommunications organisations, as well as three organisations with scientific tasks. In this connection, mention should be made of two Comecon banks, the International Investment Bank and the International Bank for Economic Co-operation. The role of the International Investment Bank is, primarily, to finance joint investment projects of member countries; to this end it also figures in international money and capital markets in the role of borrower. The task of the International Bank for Economic Co-operation is, above all, to deal with the technical side of the payments flows resulting from the trade relations between member countries.

In this regard, each member maintains a clearing account with the Bank. Clearing takes place on the basis of the transferable rouble, an artificial currency unit, which, although nominally having a gold backing equivalent to that of the valuta rouble of the USSR, can, nevertheless, not be converted either into the valuta rouble or the domestic rouble of the USSR, nor, indeed, into any other foreign or domestic currency of the member countries of the CMEA. Officially, however, a rate of exchange of the transferable rouble against the US dollar is given, which is calculated according to a basket of important Western currencies and is from time to time adjusted in line with value changes within the basket (1980 transferable rouble = $1.53; 1985 transferable rouble = $1.25). Even today members' positive or negative payments balances with one another cannot be cleared multilaterally (except against Western hard currencies), but can only be settled on the basis of the relevant bilateral trade agreements.

The fundamental principles of co-operation within Comecon, as laid down in the Council Statute and other documents, are based upon the respecting of state sovereignty, independence, national interests and the equality of rights of member states. From this ensues, firstly, the principle of unanimity in all decisions of Council bodies, which since 1967 has been applied in a modified form (in that unanimity is required in the case of resolutions of member countries 'interested' in particular projects). Secondly, the CMEA is expressly not a supranational organisation, so that its organs can only make recommendations, which can always only be carried out by national decisions. Khrushchev's attempt in 1962 to turn Comecon into a supranational planning organisation failed in the face of Romanian resistance.

Concepts, methods and areas of co-operation

Since the end of the Sixties co-operation within the CMEA has taken on a new dimension, which goes far beyond the relations which, up till then, had in the main only consisted in foreign trade. In the Complex (Comprehensive) Programme, resolved upon in 1971 at the 25th session of the Council (see *Grunddokumente des RGW*, East Berlin, 1978, pp. 44 ff.), 'socialist economic integration' was formulated as the leading idea of Comecon co-operation. Similarly, in the GDR 1974 Constitution (Article 9, Section 1), the 'purposeful realisation of socialist economic integration' was demanded. In the 1971 Complex Programme, integration is defined in general terms as a conscious and planned process of the international, socialist division of labour, of the assimilation of national economic development levels, and of enlargement of the internal market of the CMEA countries. The process of integration itself is to be based upon many and various forms of co-operation and co-ordination of the economic activities between members.

The 1971 Complex Programme contains a whole gamut of

different measures corresponding to the manner and methods of integration policy within the CMEA. The catalogue of economic and non-economic goals which are to be attained with the help of this programme is extensive. Mentioned in the first place are: maximum growth of the national economies; structural improvements; meeting the members' requirements for fuels, energy and raw materials; assimilation of the respective economic levels of development; expansion and stabilisation of the 'socialist world market'; strengthening of the defence capacity of the member countries.

The latest example of the attempts that are being made to promote integration within Comecon is the December 1985 'Complex Programme 2000' (Novosti Press Agency, Moscow, 1985) resolved upon at the 41st session of the Council in Moscow. It confirms the guidelines and methods of integration policy within Comecon, as laid down in the CMEA Statute and in the 1971 Complex Programme. According to the latest Programme, co-operation is to concentrate upon five main directions of scientific-technical progress:

(i) Electronification. Super computers, personal computers, digital information transfer, optical fibres, satellite systems, sensor-monitoring-and-measuring equipment, and highly integrated circuitry.

(ii) Automation. Flexible production systems, automated scheduling, industrial robots, automated production, standardised components and standardised technical products for transportation, loading and warehousing work.

(iii) Nuclear energy. New nuclear power stations of existing types; better use of fuels; new nuclear heating power stations; equipment for fast-breeder reactors.

(iv) Materials. Production of new high-density, corrosion- and heat-resistant materials; ceramic motors and gas turbines; new polymer materials; amorphous and micro-crystalline materials; new semi-conductor materials; laser, vacuum and high-pressure technology.

(v) Bio-technology. New biologically active substances and medical preparations; micro-biological aids to plant growth;

feed additives, and biologically active substances for use in animal husbandry.

The realisation of this programme is designed to serve, above all, the intensification of production. The aim is, by this means, to achieve a doubling of labour productivity by the year 2000, and a decisive reduction in specific expenditure on energy and raw materials per unit of national income and, thus, economic growth on the basis of technological progress. In order to carry out this programme, the CMEA countries are urged to co-ordinate their activities with other interested members on the basis of equality of rights and mutual acceptability. The instrument of co-ordination is to be a system of mutually co-ordinated agreements and contracts. Because so little time has elapsed since this programme was adopted, as yet no concrete agreements or contracts based on this programme have been announced.

On account of the absence of a market mechanism, the co-ordination of national economic plans is of primary importance for the development of the CMEA economies on the basis of the aims of the integration policy which is now being pursued. Although attempts at plan co-ordination were being made even before the introduction of the 1971 Complex Programme (see Dietz and Grosser, 1981, p. 21; Fallenbuchl, 1974), plan co-ordination in various areas has gained in importance in these particular respects only since the mid-Seventies (see Wienert and Slater, 1986, p. 146). Firstly, the extent of plan co-ordination in the field of investment, investment collaboration and production specialisation has grown considerably. Secondly, plan co-ordination now covers a timespan of ten to fifteen years. Thirdly, there are efforts clearly being made to improve the technique of plan co-ordination. Corresponding to the five-year plan periods, three programmes for the co-ordination of national economic plans have so far been adopted (to date). The focus of co-ordination efforts lies in the area of multilateral specialisation and co-operation, especially in machine building, electro-technology/electronics and the chemical industry. Thus, the proportion of specialised industrial products in GDR exports to the Comecon countries increased from 30 per cent in 1980 to 39 per cent in 1984. Over the same period of time GDR exports of these goods to the USSR increased from 38 per cent to 49 per cent (*Statistisches Taschenbuch der DDR*, 1985, p. 99).

In the energy, raw materials and fuels sector there have been or are being carried out various projects involving joint investment. The GDR is involved in most of these undertakings, which are mainly being realised in the USSR, as regards planning, plant, machinery and deliveries of other commodities, but also where the provision of manpower is concerned. Little is known about the nature and extent of these contributions, apart from indications in value terms. The repayment of these 'credits in kind' takes the form of deliveries of appropriate quantities of the products of these investment projects, supplied on contractually agreed terms. The main objects of GDR investment participation in the 1960s were the cellulose works at Ust-Ilim (USSR), the asbestos combine Kiyembai (USSR) and the metallurgical complex for the mining of the iron ore deposits of the Kursk basin (USSR). Investment projects in which the GDR is also involved are the 'Soyuz' natural gas pipeline from Orenburg to Ozhgorod (USSR) and the 750 kV high-tension line from Vinnitsa (USSR) to Albetirsa in Hungary (Haendcke-Hoppe, 1985).

Other areas of co-operation within Comecon are the so-called 'long-term goal programmes', the contents of which are, however, not known in concrete detail. Time-wise, they cover a period of ten to fifteen years and concern various priority areas, such as raw materials, energy and fuels, agriculture and transport (see Wienert and Slater, 1986, pp. 150 ff.).

SOME ASPECTS OF THE FOREIGN TRADE AND PAYMENTS POSITION OF THE GDR IN COMECON

The utilisation of statistical data concerning the development of the foreign trade of Comecon countries in order to measure the degree of integration in the CMEA that has been achieved is a matter of debate, since it depends on how the concept of integration is defined (Wienert and Slater, p. 179, footnote 3). None the less, such figures can give at least some indication of the economic importance of individual countries. Foreign trade data processed in widely varying ways are commonly used in this connection, and it is probably generally known that Comecon and members' statistical source material (and this is especially true of the GDR) is by no means based on a wealth of documentation such as is usual with Western statistics.

Table 13.1: GDR foreign trade by country percentage shares[a]

	1970	1975	1980	1981	1982	1983	1984	1985
Socialist countries,[b] of which:	71.6	69.7	66.5	66.6	66.0	65.2	65.7	66.1
CMEA[c]	67.0	66.2	62.7	63.5	63.1	62.5	63.0	63.8
USSR	39.1	35.7	35.5	37.5	38.0	37.9	38.6	38.8
Western industrial countries[d]	24.4	25.9	27.4	28.5	28.1	29.4	29.5	29.6
Developing countries	4.0	4.4	6.1	4.9	5.8	5.4	4.7	4.4

Notes: a. Basis actual prices; b. CMEA countries and the People's Republic of China, Yugoslavia, North Korea and Laos (since 1978); c. Albania, Bulgaria, Czechoslovakia, Cuba (since 1972), Mongolia, Poland, Romania, USSR, Hungary and Vietnam (since 1978); d. OECD countries, including inner-German trade.
Source: *Statistisches Jahrbuch der Deutschen Demokratischen Republik* (1985), p. 241; *Neues Deutschland*, no. 15 (1986), 18-19 January; shares calculated. Taken from Plötz, P., 'DDR — Wachstumspfad stabilisiert' in Bolz, K. (ed.) *Die wirtschaftliche Entwicklung in den sozialistischen Ländern Osteuropas zur Jahreswende 1985-86* (Hamburg, 1986), p. 103.

Table 13.1 shows the general structural development of the GDR's foreign trade by country; this is dominated by intra-bloc trade. Since 1980 Comecon has consistently accounted for around 63 per cent of foreign trade turnover. It is noticeable that in 1985 the USSR accounted for the relatively high proportion of 38.8 per cent of the GDR's foreign trade turnover with socialist countries. This, however, at the same time represents almost 61 per cent of the GDR's trade turnover with Comecon countries.

A glance at the figures given in Table 13.2, however, reveals a marked asymmetry in foreign trade within the CMEA, not only in foreign trade turnover as a whole, but also, and yet more clearly, in imports and especially in exports. Thus, in 1984, the USSR accounted for almost 45 per cent of intra-bloc foreign trade turnover. Since 1960 at latest, the GDR has occupied second place both in intra-bloc foreign trade turnover as a whole, and in intra-bloc exports and imports, although the GDR's share under these headings has decreased slightly. By contrast, since 1980 the relevant figures for the USSR have clearly risen. This is a reflection of the fact that, in international trade among Comecon countries, the USSR has strengthened its predominance yet further. This has, moreover, led to a rise in the Soviet Union's share of the GDR's trade with Comecon from some 57 per cent in 1980 to around 61 per cent in 1984,

Table 13.2: Intra-bloc foreign trade turnover: exports and imports of the CMEA (percentage shares)

	1960	1970	1980	1984
	Foreign trade turnover			
Bulgaria	4.5	6.3	5.9	6.4
Hungary	6.9	7.8	9.3	9.9
GDR	16.6	15.4	11.5	12.0
Cuba			3.4	3.7
Mongolia		0.3	0.3	0.3
Poland	10.6	11.7	11.1	8.6
Romania	5.1	6.2	7.4	5.1
USSR	42.2	40.1	42.1	44.9
Czechoslovakia	14.1	12.2	9.0	9.1
	Exports			
Bulgaria	4.3	6.5	6.1	6.2
Hungary	6.6	7.5	9.1	9.8
GDR	16.7	14.8	10.9	12.0
Cuba			3.2	3.0
Mongolia		0.3	0.2	0.3
Poland	10.1	11.4	10.4	8.4
Romania	5.5	6.0	6.8	5.6
USSR	42.2	41.3	44.3	45.9
Czechoslovakia	14.6	12.2	9.0	8.8
	Imports			
Bulgaria	6.5	6.1	5.7	6.6
Hungary	7.8	8.1	9.5	9.9
GDR	18.5	16.0	12.1	12.0
Cuba			3.7	4.4
Mongolia		0.4	0.3	0.4
Poland	11.2	11.9	11.8	8.8
Romania	4.9	6.5	7.9	4.6
USSR	42.1	38.8	39.9	48.8
Czechoslovakia	13.6	12.2	9.1	9.3

Source: *Statisticheskii Yezhegodnik Stran-Chlenov SEV* (Moscow, 1985), p. 329.

at the expense, especially, of the GDR's industrialised European Comecon neighbours, Poland and Czechoslovakia (see Table 13.3). Here, of course, the significance of Poland's well-known economic problems for the negative trend in foreign trade turnover with the GDR should not be overlooked.

The developments above are not surprising, since the USSR has very considerable raw material reserves. The CMEA countries, which are, in the main, poorly endowed with raw materials (and this is especially true of the GDR) are, in the absence of other and more favourable import opportunities, dependent on

Table 13.3: Intra-bloc foreign trade turnover of the GDR with CMEA countries in billion VM (actual prices) and in percentage shares

	1970		1980		1984	
	valuta marks	%	valuta marks	%	valuta marks	%
Bulgaria	1.38	5.1	3.79	5.0	4.9	4.4
Czechoslovakia	3.77	13.8	9.31	12.4	12.83	11.7
Cuba	0.48	1.8	1.01	1.3	2.03	1.8
Mongolia	0.07	0.3	0.1	0.1	1.17	1.1
Poland	2.90	10.6	7.71	10.3	8.74	7.9
Romania	0.95	3.5	3.87	5.2	4.63	4.2
USSR	15.48	56.8	42.61	56.7	67.11	60.8
Hungary	2.05	7.5	6.37	8.6	8.58	7.8
Vietnam	0.17	0.6	0.32	0.4	0.37	0.3
Total	27.25	100	75.09	100	110.36	100

Source: *Statistisches Taschenbuch der DDR* (1985), pp. 101 ff.; shares calculated.

the USSR for the supply of these commodities. The increase in the USSR's share of intra-bloc trade, and the rise in the relevant figures in relation to the GDR, are, however, also attributable to the increases in the prices of raw materials and especially oil, which are connected with the Moscow price formula and which, despite a lagged reaction to world market prices, are nevertheless considerable. Thus, for example, the price of Soviet oil rose from an average of 52 transferable roubles in the period 1976-80 to 183 transferable roubles in 1984. In 1984 Soviet oil supplies to the GDR, reduced in 1982 from 19 million tonnes to the present-day level of 17 million tonnes, absorbed more than 42 per cent of the value of GDR exports to the Soviet Union, compared with an average of little more than 25 per cent in the period 1976-80. At the same time the proportion of the GDR's total imports of oil accounted for by the Soviet Union fell from an average of almost 89 per cent in the period 1976-80 to around 74 per cent in 1984 (see Meier, 1986, p. 33). On account of its low import elasticity *vis-à-vis* deliveries from the USSR, the GDR was unable to match the import values that had risen rapidly in consequence of the price increases in trade with the USSR, either by raising the prices of its own exports or by an appropriate increase in the quantity of its exports to the USSR, so that by 1985 there was a cumulative trade deficit with the Soviet Union of almost four billion transferable roubles

(Meier, 1986, p. 20). Some relief for the GDR would come about if the Moscow price formula were to be modified in such a way that, when there is a fall in world market prices, the relevant CMEA prices would not be held above the level of the respective world market prices, but adjusted accordingly. Machowski, quoting Polish sources, thought this to have been conceded by the USSR for oil during the CMEA summit in the summer of 1984 (Machowski, 1984, p. 344). This would have meant a considerable loss of revenue from the sale of oil to Comecon countries, since conditions on the world market have changed for the worse. The USSR, however, could not agree to the sort of extremely large price reductions seen on world markets being reflected in trade with its CMEA partners, because the Soviet Union itself has suffered considerable reductions in export revenues, not only due to lower world oil prices, but also as a result of reduced volume. This can be confirmed by a comparison between the world price and the probable CMEA price. According to the Moscow price formula, involving calculation of a five-year average, the price of oil in the first quarter of 1986 would have been around 172 transferable roubles a tonne — equivalent, at the Soviet rate of exchange, to a price of $227 a tonne. During the same period of time, however, the average world market price was about $124 a tonne (Haendcke-Hoppe, 1986, p. 27, footnote 2).

The fall in oil prices and the depreciation of the US dollar, especially against the DM, has affected the GDR's external economic relations in a number of ways. Until 1983 the GDR benefited from relatively cheap Soviet oil, since prices reacted to world market levels only with a time lag. As a result, the GDR was able to more than double its exports of oil and oil products to the West from 3 million tonnes in 1980 to 6.6 million tonnes in 1984 (*Statisticheskii Yezhegodnik Stran-Chlenov SEV*, Moscow, 1986, p. 354). In inner-German trade GDR deliveries of oil products to the FRG, in value terms, accounted for a high average of almost 24 per cent of total deliveries during the period 1980-5. Chemical products accounted for more than 13 per cent (*Statistisches Bundesamt Wiesbaden: Warenverkehr mit der DDR und Berlin (Ost), Fachserie 6, Reihe 6, Jahreshefte; Bundesanzeiger*). If the USSR were to make no concessions in respect of the price of its oil, this would mean a considerable weakening of the GDR's competitive position in these products in the markets of the

FRG and other Western countries. The depreciation of the US dollar since the beginning of 1986 has similarly affected the GDR, in that the GDR is now likely to meet increased competition on Western markets for products produced in low-wage countries in the Far East and mostly priced in US dollars (consumer goods, such as textiles and clothing). The fall in the GDR's hard currency earnings alone from oil and oil products between 1985 and 1986, depending on price developments in these products and alternative quantitative adjustment strategies by the GDR, has been estimated as lying in the range $600 million to $1.3-1.5 billion (Stinglwagner, 1986).

Noticeable, moreover, is the marked complementarity of trade relations between the GDR and the Soviet Union; this does not obtain to the same extent *vis-à-vis* any other European member of the CMEA. Whilst the USSR is the chief supplier of raw materials to the GDR, the latter exports to the former mainly machinery, equipment and means of transport, as well as consumer goods of all kinds. In order to reduce its indebtedness to the USSR and to secure its supplies of raw materials from the USSR, the GDR has undertaken, in a 'Programme for co-operation in science, technology and production between the GDR and the USSR to the year 2000', to increase its exports to the USSR by 40 per cent in the case of industrial consumer goods and by 50 per cent for chemical products. Exports of investment goods, moreover, are to be increased quantitatively and qualitatively. In total, the volume of trade with the USSR in the 1986-90 plan quinquennium is to increase by 25 per cent according to GDR data and by 30 per cent according to Soviet figures, whilst GDR exports are to rise more rapidly than imports, indicating an attempt to reduce the trade deficit with the USSR (see Haendcke-Hoppe, 1986, p. 24).

In contrast to the goal mentioned in the 1971 Complex Programme to assimilate the levels of development of the CMEA member countries, the clear differentials in economic performance have, in some cases, not only persisted, but become even more pronounced (Poland, Romania). The GDR can be considered to have the most highly developed economy in the Comecon bloc, including the USSR. Specific export products of the GDR (e.g. machinery, equipment, means of transport, electrical and electronic as well as optical and precision engineering goods), some of which cannot easily be sold for hard currencies on Western markets, due to intense competition in terms of quality and price, are considered desirable imports within Comecon, since here they are of relatively high quality and in any case, for whatever reason, they are either not attainable at all from the West or only on economically worse terms. The GDR thus finds itself in a relatively strong bargaining position *vis-à-vis* its CMEA partners, and especially the USSR, as regards negotiating the conditions relating to bilateral trade (product quantities, prices, delivery dates, lines of credit, compensation etc.). Moreover, the lower oil prices will, even using the Moscow price formula, gradually ease the burden of the GDR's exports of goods as payment for oil deliveries.

As a result of the lower world market price for oil, however, the Soviet Union's hard currency earnings situation has deteriorated. The Soviet Union, therefore, may be forced to rely more on its Comecon partners, especially the GDR, for plant, machinery and equipment in order to promote its own development and the associated exploitation of raw material resources. This, on the other hand, would reduce the possibility of these countries integrating themselves further into the world economy. Such a restrictive development seems likely for the GDR at least.

In contrast to the five-year plan for 1981-85, which envisaged a ratio of 70:30 in the volume of foreign trade with the 'socialist' as against 'non-socialist' countries, the structure of the GDR's foreign trade by regions has shifted to a ratio of 66:34, thus increasing the importance of the 'non-socialist' and especially of the 'capitalist' countries. The intention is that in the current five-year plan for 1986-90 this proportion shall not alter any further. The share of the USSR and of the other socialist countries in the GDR's foreign trade volume is to be stabilised at about two-thirds (*Direktive des XI. Parteitages der SED zum Fünfjahrplan für die Entwicklung der Volkswirtschaft der DDR in en Jahren 1986-1990,* East Berlin, April 1986, p. 57), and under the new five-year plan the volume of trade with the remaining CMEA countries is only to grow at the moderate rate of 2.4 per cent on average, compared to the figure of 5 per cent in relation to the USSR. The fact that the GDR has thus committed itself in regard both to the development of the regional structure of its foreign trade and to the planned priorities in its exports within Comecon and especially to the USSR, is likely to cause the GDR economy considerable problems of adjustment. This applies above all to the GDR's room to manoeuvre in regard to trade policy towards Western industrial countries, which, in view of the commitments outlined above, is likely to be less flexibly deployed in future. It follows from this, however, that the GDR's ability to import Western technology, under licence and/or embodied in machinery and equipment imported from Western industrial countries, will, despite the special status of inner-German trade, be severely limited. It is likely that, in view of the aforementioned obligations of the GDR to the CMEA and especially to the USSR, GDR investment will be increasingly concentrated in those branches producing goods for export. This will leave but little room for the development of the domestic consumer goods industry. In consequence, any substantial increase or qualitative improvement in the domestic supply of consumer goods is scarcely to be expected in the GDR in the next few years.

In the wake of the combine reform and the accompanying intensification efforts, in part through rigorous economy measures (e.g. fuel rationing for transport purposes, reorganisation of the transport system, greater use of domestic lignite as an energy source and as a primary product for the chemical industry), the GDR has reduced the specific input of energy and materials in production, which should save on imports and enhance the competitiveness of its exports, at least within Comecon. Despite the current high degree of integration of research and development in the organisational structure of the combine, the practical application of the results of R&D seems to continue to pose considerable difficulties. This is not so serious a matter in respect to the GDR's export opportunities within Comecon, as long as the partner countries are afflicted with the same sorts of problems. But the GDR's competitiveness in Western markets is certainly negatively affected.

A more effective utilisation and an economically advantageous structure of external economic and especially foreign trade relations for the CMEA partners, however, also depends on whether decisive economic progress is achieved by reforming their economic systems. As far as can be ascertained, the reforms within the Comecon bloc to date, with the exception of Poland and Hungary, have not affected the basic principles of central state management and planning of the economies of these countries and hence the powers of political decision makers within the framework of the state monopoly of foreign trade, payments and exchange. The extent and structure of external economic relations are, thus, determined not only by economic, but also by political factors. Without decisive reform of the national economic systems, as well as the CMEA itself, external economic relations in the Comecon bloc for the partner countries are likely to play only a modest role as a factor in economic progress.

14

Economic Reform in the GDR: Causes and Effects

Hannelore Hamel and Helmut Leipold

THESES CONCERNING THE CAPACITY FOR REFORM OF THE SOCIALIST PLANNED ECONOMY

The economic system of the GDR has, since its introduction after the Second World War, been characterised by a high intensity of reform. At regular intervals, both the system of central planning and management and the enterprise incentive and monitoring structures have been altered. The causes, and in particular the effects, of these institutional reforms are the subject of controversy and of differing evaluations in both West and East. The opposing views can be reduced to two theses which, following Höhmann (1985, pp. 19 ff.), can be described as the 'Popperian thesis' and the 'Krylov thesis'.

The proponents of the 'Popperian thesis' are of the opinion that in the socialist planned economies step-by-step improvements are possible, in a manner analogous to the reform strategy of 'piecemeal social engineering' proposed by Karl Popper for the free societies of the West. In regard to economic reform in the GDR since the beginning of the Eighties this thesis is advanced, for example, in the conclusions of Cornelsen, Melzer and Scherzinger (1984, p. 217), according to whom, 'the multitude of small steps has in the meantime also come to signify a change in the quality of the economic mechanism'. A full-scale statement of this thesis is to be found in 'The Political Economy of Socialism', according to which, from the stage of the construction of socialism, announced in 1952, down to the present stage of 'the formation of developed socialism', the economic system of the GDR has been continually 'creatively developed' and is distinguished by a constant 'perfecting' (*Vervollkommnung*).

Against this 'perfecting thesis' stands the 'Krylov thesis', the proponents of which are sceptical about the possibility of an economically efficient reform of the socialist centrally planned economies. The literary model for this view is supplied by the Russian poet Krylov, in his fable of the four animal musicians who, hoping to improve their sound, keep swapping seats, but in vain. This fable finds its economic counterpart in the thesis of Hensel concerning the 'constant pressure for experimentation in economic policy' and the continually repeated 'cycle of economic reforms' (Hensel, 1977, pp. 173 ff.). This scepticism is expressed in still more drastic terms in the Soviet 'Study of Novosibirsk' (1984, pp. 17), according to which the further development of the economic mechanism is 'impossible, in the sense of gradually replacing the most obsolete elements by more efficient ones'.

In what follows, it is proposed to examine the explanatory value of these two opposed theses in the light of the economic reforms of the GDR. To this end it is necessary to determine the most important causes of the economic reforms. In the next section some fundamental defects with respect to allocation and motivation in the socialist centrally planned economy are analysed and the question examined of whether, and to what extent, these defects can be removed by means of institutional reforms. As examples of concrete reform experiments, the 'New Economic System' of the Sixties and the 'economic strategy of the Eighties' are described in the third section. The evaluation which is to be undertaken in the concluding section, will, at the same time, throw light on the relevance of the two initial theses.

AN EXPLANATION OF THE CAUSES OF THE REFORMS IN TERMS OF THEORIES OF ALLOCATION AND MOTIVATION

The allocation problem

As in every economic system, so in a socialist planned economy, too, certain fundamental problems of economic management have to be solved, including, first of all, the problem of allocation.[1] Scarce resources have to be directed towards those goals which will produce the greatest possible benefit, which includes the requirement to utilise resources sparingly and efficiently. The most important precondition for this is a knowledge of the degree of scarcity of individual categories of goods, including the factors of production, in the economy as a whole. Rational planning and allocation of economic processes is only possible if economic decisions take into account the availability or scarcity of every individual good. Of course, the individual economic entities have, in the nature of things, no overview of the processes at work within the national economy, and hence of the degree of scarcity of particular goods. For this, a system of information and calculation is necessary, which informs the economic entities as to the relative scarcity of goods, and which co-ordinates the individual planning decisions into a consistent system of plans for the economy as a whole.

In market economies this problem of information and co-ordination is solved through the market price mechanism; in centrally planned economies, in contrast, it is by means of physical planning and balancing methods that the solution is found. As Hensel (1977, p. 178) has rigorously shown, in the case of state planning of economic processes:

> The degrees of scarcity in the economy as a whole ... are only discernible in the physical plan balances, which have to be worked out by the central planning authority. In order, therefore, to ensure economic rationality in the steering of the aggregate process by means of planning ..., as many physical plan balances would, theoretically, have to be worked out and co-ordinated with each other, as there are kinds of goods, in other words many millions.

In reality, however, in the GDR, as in other socialist centrally planned economies, the balancing of all the sorts of goods that exist is not possible. In consequence of the restrictions relating to information and organisation, the central planning authorities are only able to draw up a few thousand goods balances, in which key goods of strategic importance to the national economy are balanced in detail; the other goods are balanced in aggregated fashion. In view of these restrictions, recourse to secondary planning and co-ordination procedures is indispensable. To these belong the involvement of enterprises in the national economic planning process, the use of economic policy instruments for steering, and influencing enterprise behaviour by means of continual, discretionary management directives in the process of plan implementation.

Bureaucratic self-interest and departmental segmentation

In the GDR the central planning and management powers are distributed among a considerable number of state bodies. The most important is the Council of Ministers, whose task is to manage the national economy in accordance with the directives of the party leadership and on the basis of the national economic and state budget plans. To this end it makes use of various state bodies. The work of national economic planning and co-ordination devolves upon the State Planning Commission and on a number of functional ministries and state offices. The management of specific economic sectors is the responsibility of the branch ministries. It is supplemented through a territorially based system of management, involving counties, districts and communities. The central planning and management apparatus also, finally, comprises a series of state monitoring authorities.

According to the official blueprint, these state organs should manage and monitor the economic processes in a unitary fashion. In reality, however, the planning process is characterised by negotiations and disputes that are fraught with conflict and plagued with departmental selfishness, which result from the individual bureaucratic interests of the state bodies and from the scarcity of available means.

Each state manager upholds, in the first place, the interests that are directly connected with his particular office and administrative department. In the case of those authorities that are delimited in accordance with the 'production principle' these are economic branch interests, whilst, where bodies demarcated according to the 'territorial principle' are concerned, it is of course the interests of individual regions, counties or districts which take first place. Each of these state organs seeks to further its own interests in the planning process. The party secretary of a county fights, just like any branch minister, for priority allocation both of financial and investment resources and of materials and manpower. The most generous possible allocation of scarce resources allows of ambitious plan targets and hence also personal influence and success.

In view of this conflict of interest on the one hand, and of the scarcity problem on the other, the process of central planning and balancing takes on a pattern which Bahro (1977, p. 251) has characterised as a process of 'bureaucratic rivalry'. This rivalry impairs central plan co-ordination in several ways. Firstly, it results in scarce resources being allocated in accordance with the political power positions of the party and state bodies involved; hence, the allocation of goods laid down in the national economic plan reflects the structure of political power and influence. Secondly, this bureaucratic rivalry stands in the way of a division of labour that is efficient in terms of the national economy. Decisive in this connection is the departmental self-interest on the part of the central management organs. This causes not only fights to secure the largest possible allocations for themselves, but at the same time there is displayed little willingness with regard to co-operation beyond their own boundaries. Since any indication of willingness is taken as an admission of under-utilisation of his own capacities and could lead to a reduction in carefully built-up disposable potentialities, each state manager seeks to create allocation processes with the highest degree of departmental autarky; in other words, to reduce branch- or region- external deliveries and dependencies (see Leipold, 1983).

These departmental segmentations hinder, above all, the planning and balancing of highly complex economic processes. A considerable degree of complexity is especially characteristic of the development and introduction of new products and production procedures, for which, apart from research and development activity, as a rule improved production technology and innovations in utilisation in prior, simultaneous or subsequent economic areas are required. The central system of management is, however, only able to meet these requirements to a very limited extent, given this departmental self-interest. The resultant segmentation of aggregate economic planning and balancing produces a gap in central economic calculation. This is demonstrated by constant complaints from GDR economists about imperfect managerial control over complex economic and innovation processes (see, for example, Krinks *et al.*, 1980) and is an important reason for institutional reforms, which is to be gone into later.

Enterprise self-interest and behaviour conditioned by plan-fulfilment strategy

In drawing up national economic plans, the central planning authorities are dependent upon information concerning the concrete performance capacities of enterprises, since they are able to attain only a very imperfect overview and estimate of these. They lack the knowledge of 'the particular circumstances of place and time' (von Hayek, 1976, p. 107), without which sound decisions concerning the allocation of goods cannot be made. In consequence, the most important role of enterprise plans consists in making the central plan draft more detailed and supplementing it with information. In accordance with centrally prescribed plan tasks, which combine managements are required to disaggregate down to enterprises, the latter must draw up detailed plan drafts and conclude preliminary inter-enterprise contracts. These preliminary contracts are, in this connection, an important co-ordinating instrument of sub-plans, because, through them, enterprise outputs can be legally guaranteed and bottlenecks identified at the earliest possible stage. To that extent the system of contracts forms a sort of substitute for the market, by means of which, however, the prescribed 'unity of plan, balance and contract' is intended to be secured.

As a rule, however, enterprise plans and the contract system furnish information which reveals imperfections caused by the process of aggregation and by vested interests. The enterprise managers know that the data which they submit to their superiors pre-form the later compulsory plan targets, upon the fulfilment of which depend the evaluation of their own performance and the linked bonuses and deductions to funds. For this reason, there is a powerful incentive to transmit information selectively, with an eye to plan targets that will be easy to fulfil; in other words, they tend to exaggerate their requirements for manpower and allocations of materials, energy, investment resources and finance and to understate their production and performance capacities. As a result of this behaviour on the part of enterprises, which is conditioned by plan-fulfilment strategies, the central authorities receive information which is imprecise and of only limited reliability, and which does not give an objective picture of the true performance capacities of enterprises. It follows that the performance targets derived from the finalised national economic plan and prescribed to enterprises in the form of plan targets, indicators and normatives, cannot serve as objective criteria for the evaluation of performance either.

Hence, the interest of enterprise in attaining 'soft' plans means that central plan drafting and co-ordination relies upon data which are not conducive to a rational, scarcity-related economic calculation. The gap in central economic calculation already referred to, which is caused by bureaucratic rivalry between state management authorities is, consequently, worsened by a second one, caused by the involvement of enterprises in the planning process and the resulting information shortfall due to vested interests and motivations (see Hensel, 1977, and Schüller, 1986).

The co-existence of plan- and price-orientated allocation

Despite the participation of enterprises in the detailed planning process, a complete planning and balancing out by the centre of all sub-processes is, as already mentioned, not possible. Beside the 400 or so state plan balances, in which supply and utilisation of 'goods of national economic importance' are determined, the other central balances (approximately 700) comprise only highly aggregated magnitudes, leaving enterprises latitude as regards goods assortment and factor use in the process of plan disaggregation and implementation. Since enterprises seek to utilise this elbow-room to achieve their own goals, the central planning authorities find themselves confronted with the task of harmonising enterprise modes of behaviour with central plan goals by means of 'implicit restrictive regulations' (Gutmann, 1983, pp. 5 ff.).

To this end the quest is to lay down all magnitudes of 'economic accounting' in such a way that, acting as 'economic levers', they bring about the fulfilment of central plan objectives. To these magnitudes belong the prices of goods and factors of production as well as all financial regulations ('normatives'), which influence enterprise profit formation and utilisation. For enterprises these magnitudes in value terms serve as standards on the basis of which they make their decisions. The closest possible linkage of enterprise and central goals can only be brought about if the data system created by means of these 'levers' stimulates enterprises to produce and utilise those goods which are proposed and programmed in the national economic plans, which are imperfectly balanced in detail. What is required, therefore, is that there should be an identity between centrally balanced economic calculation and enterprise economic calculation guided by 'economic levers'. This, however, can only be achieved if prices reflect the same degree of scarcity of goods and factors of production as were ascertained in the physical balancing system in the light of plan balances and upon which the decisions as to allocation were based.

This condition, however, is one which state-fixed prices are not able to meet. As they are cost-related and fixed for a considerable period of time they are, leaving chance aside, not scarcity prices. Nevertheless, enterprise decisions about assortment of goods and use of inputs are guided by prices of this kind. The non-co-ordinated co-existence of plan- and price-orientated allocation of goods thus gives rise to a third gap in the economic calculation of socialist centrally planned economies, in which is to be seen one of the most important causes of economic reform.

The co-existence of balanced planning and discretionary management

The gaps in economic calculation mentioned so far are the cause of numerous disproportions in the process of plan implementation. Deliveries in instalments of materials, raw materials, energy or replacement parts which are not made or not on time, assortment of goods which are poor in quality or do not conform to desired requirements, are often the reason why contracts and plans are not fulfilled. Constant interventions in enterprise activity by the central authorities are therefore necessary to overcome these supply bottlenecks. These interventions are, however, not backed up by plan or balance; they serve, rather, to correct co-ordination defects in the central planning system.

Administrative interventions in enterprise activity that are summed up under the heading of 'management',[2] however, merely succeed in filling shortfalls in delivery and supply in an *ad hoc* and short-term manner. Since the allocation of goods is governed by the general problem of scarcity and interdependence, spontaneous interventions normally give rise to unforeseen repercussions. Administratively decreed reshuffles or special allocations of scarce goods are no longer available at other places, where plan corrections are consequently necessary. Adjustments of individual sub-plans, in turn, produce a chain-reaction in regard to the fulfilment of other sub-plans, so that each current plan revision is bound to require the simultaneous and co-ordinated correction of other plans. This requirement is one which cannot be met by the discretionary intervention of the managing authorities, if only because such interventions are neither keyed into the scarcity-related calculation context, nor co-ordinated with one another.

The enterprises frequently attempt to counter regimentations and administrative actions of this kind by themselves securing the missing goods that are required for plan-fulfilment by means of informal swaps and bypassing the official supply system, whereby personal contacts, bribes and barter deals are used as *ad hoc* levers. From this there arises a widespread network of illegal exchange relationships, through which goods are diverted from the official sector and thus endanger plan-fulfilment there.

From the co-existence of balanced planning, discretionary management and unplanned, partially illegal materials procurement there arises a fourth gap in economic calculation in centrally planned economic systems, the origins of which lie in the three previously mentioned.

If the diagnosis is correct that the above-mentioned gaps in economic calculation are decisive causes for the multiple inefficiencies in the economic system of the GDR, then they will also serve as criteria for the assessment of reform measures and their effects. It is proposed, in what follows, to examine in the light of the reforms of the Sixties and since the beginning of the Eighties to what extent these have narrowed or even closed this or that gap in economic calculation.

ANALYSIS OF THE REFORM MEASURES

The reform concept of the Sixties

The 'Guidelines for the new economic system of planning and management of the national economy', issued after the Sixth

Congress of the SED in 1963, were noteworthy in many respects.

In the first place, the GDR was the first socialist country which, in view of the existing inefficiencies of the centrally administered economic system, combined with considerable dips in economic growth, considered it necessary to make the system more efficient and drew the appropriate conclusions.[3]

Secondly (and contrary to the ideologically postulated harmony of interests), it was admitted for the first time that there existed 'contradictions between the demands of society as laid down in the plan and the actions of individual persons and groups' (*Richtlinie für das neue ökonomische System der Planung und Leitung der Volkswirtschaft vom 11 Juli 1963, GBL der DDR*, Teil II, p. 457); the drawing up of 'soft' plans (p. 467), as well as other shortcomings were 'the symptoms of a type of planning rendered obsolete by political and economic developments ...' (p. 454).

Thirdly, what characterised the proposed changes was not, as in earlier years, individual organisational or procedural policy measures, but an overall concept of structural policy, which included all levels of the vertical economic hierarchy as well as the functioning of the system of planning and management and which, according to Ulbricht (*Richtlinie* 1963, p. 456), was to be uniformly put into effect from 'above' down to the last production unit.

As the actual developments of the years 1963 to 1970 have shown, however, the implementation of this new concept was beset by considerable difficulties (see Beyer, 1972, pp. 129 ff.). In particular, the development of the 'New Economic System' (NES) into the 'Economic System of Socialism' (ESS) which was installed after the Seventh Congress of the SED in 1967 and which was intended to bring about a 'new quality' in national economic planning (Ulbricht, 1968, p. 253), finally encountered stiff resistance within the SED leadership.

What effects did the reforms of those years have upon the gaps in economic calculation diagnosed above and implicitly confirmed in the *Richtlinie* (1963, pp. 482 ff.)?

(1) At the level of the central planning organs there took place, initially, only the transfer of responsibility for balancing from the State Planning Commission, which was to concern itself primarily with perspective planning and co-ordination

tasks, to the industrial ministries formed in 1965, directly subordinate to the Council of Ministers.

In addition to the fact that the number of central material and equipment balances was greatly reduced, and that of the associations of nationally owned enterprises (VVBs) as new 'socialist concerns' was considerably increased, their quality was also altered by a 'fundamental regulation' adopted in 1968: central state planning was concentrated on 'basic questions of the structural development and effectiveness of the national economy'; the 'structure-determining tasks' deriving from the concept of structural policy were to have priority in the perspective plan as the 'chief instrument of guidance', and current processes were to be steered indirectly by means of long-term economic policy 'guiding parameters' (structure-concrete tasks and normatives) (*Beschluss über die Grundsatzregelung für komplexe Massnahmen zur weiteren Gestaltung des ökonomischen Systems des Sozialismus in der Planung und Wirtschaftsführung für die Jahre 1969 und 1970 vom 26 Juni 1968, GBL der DDR*, Teil II, p. 434).

The rivalry among the industrial ministries for the largest possible allocations of resources had thus been limited within the confines of the structure-determining areas, and in part transferred to the 80 or so VVBs as the 'economic leadership bodies' of the industrial branches.

(2) The information shortfall of the central planning bodies, resulting from the enterprises' penchant for 'soft' plans, was similarly increasingly reduced during the course of the Sixties. The enterprises no longer had prescribed for them every detail of production, procurement, sales and financing by means of numerous quantitative plan targets; instead, value indicators with a normative character came to the fore, especially the chief indicator profit, with the aim of increasing the willingness of enterprises to reveal performance reserves and to encourage production orientated towards profit (and therefore also sales), instead of the previous one-sided output-orientation in accordance with the chief indicator 'commodity production'.

The decisive change in this direction was carried through by means of the already mentioned '*Grundsatzregelung*' (1968), which decidedly enhanced the responsibility of enterprises in relation both to planning and to the utilisation of their net profit. In regard to planning, Nick (1970, p. 201), one of the leading reform theorists of that period, clearly set forth the new line in the following words:

> The enterprise plan is no longer the 'disaggregation' of the plan indicators of the VVBs. Rather, the enterprise is required to work out for itself, on the basis of prescribed concrete structural tasks and normatively fixed long-term economic conditions, all concrete objectives, such as the development of profit, commodity production and investment etc., in other words the indicators previously handed down by the management body to which it was subordinate.

The intention was that, by means of a new 'system of plan data', which would have to be set up, the competent superior bodies would be kept informed about current enterprise processes and the 'plan positions for which enterprises are personally responsible' for the coming year (*Grundsatzregelung*, 1968, p. 443).

The objective function of enterprises, therefore, was no longer to fulfil or over-fulfil centrally prescribed plan indicators (i.e. in the highest possible difference between planned and actual figures), but rather the achievement of maximum net profit as the difference between actual revenue and costs. According to the principle of 'earning one's own resources', enterprises could make independent decisions regarding the distribution of retained profit (net profit minus a profit deduction by the state) between the enterprise bonus fund and the 'extended reproduction' fund (for investment, working capital, science and technology, repayment of credit etc.).

The intention of the reform concept was, therefore, to provide enterprises, by means of the linking of the bonus fund and realised profit, with a direct incentive to increase net profit and thus also to achieve cost-efficient production and high market sales. To this extent the second gap in economic calculation (enterprise data falsification, due to self-interest, in the form of 'soft' plans), was no longer relevant conceptually, since allocative decisions were now to be taken primarily by the enterprises, admittedly on the basis of central development planning as well as of a comprehensive steering system for the implementation of economic policy.

(3) What was decisively new about the whole reform con-

cept was the proposal indirectly to orientate the extended rights of action and decision-making accorded to enterprises towards the fulfilment of central goals by means of a 'comprehensive system of economic levers' (*Richtlinie*, 1963, pp. 467 ff.). This system included all magnitudes which influenced the formation and utilisation of enterprise profit. Prices, sales, wage and material costs, credits and interest rates were all to be used as levers to guide profit formation; with regard to profit utilisation, it was a case of normative regulation of state charges and of the distribution of profits between the enterprise fund and the bonus fund for employees.

While in the early years they confined themselves to the revaluation of the capital stock (1963), to adjusting the prices of basic and raw materials, semi-finished products and finished goods (which had remained unchanged for many years) to increased costs (1964-66), and to improving inter-enterprise contractual relationships (1965), it was only from 1967 onwards that the economic levers (such as a capital charge, fund-related prices and the net profit deduction) were introduced (see Chapter 3 and Hamel, 1975, pp. 77 ff. for details).

Overall, the aim was to provide the enterprises, by means of the normative steering of profit formation, with incentives to reduce their labour and capital costs, to increase output, to improve product quality (which made it possible to raise prices) and to increase sales, in order to achieve maximum net profit. By means of normatives relating to enterprise profit utilisation, it was hoped at the same time to achieve the macro-economic proportions of consumption, accumulation and state needs in the interest of the primacy of 'social interests'.

The effects on economic calculation deriving from the *Grundsatzregelung* (1968) consisted, as the years 1969 and 1970 showed, above all in the absence, at both the central and the enterprise level, of scarcity-related standards of measurement for a rational planning of processes. Since central planning was to be restricted to 'basic questions of national economic development' and structure-determining tasks, and hence was no longer the basis for aggregate economic allocation decisions, these were left primarily to enterprises. The centrally ordained data system in the form of economic levers was of prime importance for their decisions, but these levers were based on factor and goods prices which at best reflected the relevant degree of scarcity only by chance. For this reason, there could be no question of a 'comprehensive system of economic levers', nor could a comprehensive economic calculation by means of profit-orientated enterprise decisions be developed.

(4) The administrative interventions by the management bodies in enterprise processes formed one of the main points of criticism when the NES was introduced. Under this system, for many economic and state functionaries, the 'traditional way' of overcoming problems 'normally [consisted] in the intensification of administrative intervention and the application of specific corrective levers' (*Richtlinie*, 1963, p. 483). In the ensuing years, too, there continued to be criticism of the 'interference of central organs in enterprise affairs' and of the frequent changes that accompanied the drawing up and implementation of plans (see Beyer, 1972, pp. 136, ff.). Ulbricht (1968, p. 151) repeatedly demanded the use of *economic* guidance methods instead of 'administrative interventions, which are divorced from the implementation of the plan and sometimes even work against it'; 'petty tutelage over enterprises' should, he argued, be eliminated and the individual responsibility of enterprises strengthened.

At the same time, however, decisions for which enterprises were individually responsible should be subjected to a comprehensive 'social monitoring', especially by the newly established 'Workers' and Peasants' Inspectorate' (*Beschluss des Zentralkomitees der SED und des Ministerates der DDR über die Bildung der Arbeiter-und-Bauern-Inspektion der DDR vom 13 Mai 1963, GBL der DDR*, Teil II, p. 263), in which all party, state and trade union monitoring bodies had been amalgamated. Its task consisted, above all, in monitoring the execution of national economic plans, of uncovering 'all cases of infringement of state discipline ... sloppy work, economic mismanagement, waste' etc., and of taking firm action against 'localism, glossings over and false reporting'.

It was only after the *Grundsatzregelung* of 1968 that the administrative interventions and monitoring no longer seemed to have the desired effect. Thus, Politburo member Günter Mittag declared in June 1970, in reference to the implementation of the national economic plan in 1970, that plan discipline was in many cases being neglected and developments being more or less left to 'run themselves'. Because of enterprise production reorganisations and 'mis-investments' it could already be foreseen that numerous plans would not be fulfilled. State monitoring via superior bodies had failed; even the ministries had not taken action, although the development in the direction of 'self-running', which was becoming apparent in the enterprises, had been pointed out to them (Mittag, 1970).

The pursuit of profit unleashed in the enterprises had led to undesired price increases and to the production of goods which did not serve the fulfilment of central structural goals. The economic levers remained, in part, ineffectual, since enterprises activated material and financial reserves which they had hoarded in previous years with the aim of easy plan-fulfilment (Hensel, 1972, pp. 168 ff.). Finally, in order to regain control over enterprise processes and aggregate economic development, the extension of the reform, already envisaged for the period 1971 to 1975, and most regulations of the preceding years were rescinded. The SED leadership decided to return instead to the centrally administered planning and management system as it had existed before the introduction of the NES. From 1971 onwards there was reinstated the absolute authority of the annual economic plans, with a multitude of obligatory plan indicators, which were to be disaggregated down to the enterprises, whose function was to fulfil them. Although several 'levers' of the Sixties were retained (such as the capital charge and the 'unitary enterprise result' in exporting enterprises), in the first place all measures were aimed at restoring and stabilising the traditionally centrally administered economic system.

This recentralisation of economic processes, however, also led to the re-emergence of all those deficiencies which had been sharply criticised at the introduction of the NES (*Richtlinie*, 1963, pp. 482 ff.): the enterprises' plan-fulfilment strategy in the form of 'soft' plans, their resistance to innovation, the predominantly extensive growth and so on. During the 1970s a deteriorating foreign trade and payments situation added to these systemic deficiencies, especially after the oil crisis of 1973.

The SED leadership sought to counter these difficulties by means of a variety of measures, namely, an improved Order of Planning for 1976-80, several price corrections, a change in the wage system and numerous social policy measures to improve performance. All these (predominantly formal) changes, however, did not resolve the basic economic problems 'of determining objectives, deciding structure, selecting priorities and co-ordinating the performance of the various sectors' (Melzer, 1982, p. 70).

The 'economic strategy' of the Eighties

In order to make progess towards the goal of intensification of economic processes, the end of the Seventies saw the taking up of the discussion about systems, initiated by the Soviet Union, concerning problems of the 'economic mechanism' and revolving around the 'perfecting of the system of management, planning and economic incentives' (Hamel, 1983, pp. 27 ff.). A first step in this direction was the amalgamation of nearly all enterprises in industry and construction into combines as the new 'basic units of material production', which were directly subordinated to one of the eleven industrial ministries. This change in the organisation of management and enterprises was followed from the beginning of the 1980s by a flood of new legal regulations, which were designed to improve the system of central planning and balancing, the economic steering of enterprise modes of behaviour and economic accounting.[4] To what extent was economic calculation in the system as a whole altered by this new 'economic strategy'?

(1) The fundamental principle of combine formation was the setting up of 'reproduction processes with a high degree of comprehensiveness', i.e. the linking up of research and development, of the manufacture and sale of end-products, including raw materials, materials and semi-finished products and of construction capacities. With this it was hoped to achieve two things. Firstly, the idea was, within what had now become a two-level management structure, to transfer a range of decision-making powers from ministries to Directors General of combines, who, at the same time, were endowed with extended planning, balancing, steering and monitoring responsibilities *vis-à-vis* the enterprises. Secondly, industrial ministries were to confine themselves to the co-ordination of national economic cross-sector processes, which exceed the powers of combines, whereas the latter had entrusted to them the management and co-ordination of relatively autarkic longitudinal processes (Leipold, 1984, p. 255).

The growth in the power of combine managements resulting from this, however, was in the meantime to be restricted once again, as the expected intensification effects failed to appear. In 1982 the influence of the central authorities on balancing was, to a certain extent, strengthened; in consequence, over 76 per cent of production is now decided upon at the central level (Cornelsen, Melzer and Scherzinger, 1984, p. 206). For the years 1986 to 1990 'state national economic plans are to be worked out along both ministerial and combine lines' (Rost, 1985, p. 14).

(2) In order to improve the central authorities' data situation, combines have to submit their plan drafts not only to the competent industrial ministries, but also to the State Planning Commission, to the Ministry of Finance and to the State Bank. In order to combat the continuing attempts to achieve 'soft' plans and hence to submit data favourable to plan-fulfilment, a change in the indicator system was introduced from 1980 onwards. What had been the chief indicator, 'industrial commodity production', which had orientated enterprises towards a one-sided concern to increase production (without regard for costs and sales), was initially supplemented by the indicators 'net production' and 'basic materials costs per 100 marks of commodity production'. Since 1984 the following main indicators have applied: net production, net profit, products and services for the population and exports; these, in addition to four 'further important qualitative indicators' (labour productivity, total costs, material costs and the production of goods having national economic importance and of newly developed products) from among a total of more than 90 plan indicators, are above all decisive for the evaluation of the performances of combines and enterprises. With the aid of these chief indicators, which are compulsory, centrally determined target magnitudes and which have to be broken down by combine managements for enterprises and disaggregated right down to enterprise departments, foremen and work collectives, the intention is to orientate more strongly the interests of combines and enterprises in the period 1986-90 'towards a rapid growth of production with decreasing production consumption and falling costs' (Rost, 1985, p. 19).[5]

(3) In 1982 the entire system of 'economic accounting' relating to the central steering of enterprise decision-making was regulated anew. In contrast to the NES of the Sixties, however, the talk was now no longer of 'economic levers', but of 'economic categories, such as costs, price, credit and interest', which are centrally fixed 'on the basis of the national economic

plan'. In this connection, first place went to cost reduction (as the 'core' of economic accounting), by means of which the relationship between expenditure and result was to be improved (*Verordnung über die weitere Vervollkommnung der wirtschaftlichen Rechnungsführung auf der Grundlage des Planes vom 28 Januar 1982, GBL der DDR*, Teil I, pp. 85-9).

To this end, numerous detailed regulations were issued to force enterprises to use their fixed capital, working capital and manpower more rationally, and, at the same time, to raise their interest in exceeding and over-fulfilling the net profit indicator, by means of bonus fund allocations dependent on it (see Chapter 7). Also, the measures for 'perfecting management, planning and economic accounting'[6] prescribed for the period 1986-90 aim primarily at forging a closer link between the economic categories used in economic accounting and planning, in order to 'harmonise more closely national economic benefits and enterprise advantages' (Rost, 1985, p. 81) — a demand first raised by the Soviet economist Liberman and one which has been a permanent feature of all GDR reform programmes ever since.

(4) As the 1986-90 Order of Planning makes clear, the room for manoeuvre of the combine directors as regards decision-making and action is determined centrally by a whole array of detailed regulations. By means of the breakdown of the annual plan into quarterly and monthly plans, introduced in 1984, the central authorities are kept currently informed about the position as regards plan-fulfilment in the individual combines and enterprises; in the case of plan indicators not being adhered to, they are obliged to intervene in enterprise affairs through 'operational decisions' and to ensure a corresponding deployment of resources (*Durchführungsbestimmung zur Verordnung über die Material-, Ausrüstungs- und Konsumgüterbilanzierung — Bilanzierungsverordnung vom 2 Juni 1983, GBL der DDR*, Teil I, p. 162). The 'trend towards economic dirigisme' is unmistakable: 'Instead of the ministries being pushed into a retreat from day-to-day economic life, it is apparent that direct intervention by the state economic administration and by the party apparatus in economic management is becoming more marked' (Schneider, 1985, p. 138).

With the increase in the numerous regulations about planning, balancing and economic accounting, the need for monitoring by the central bodies necessarily increases too. In addition to the already mentioned 'Workers' and Peasants' Inspectorate', the monitoring organ of the Central Committee of the SED and of the Council of Ministers, numerous new state inspectorates and offices have the task of supervising balancing, the carrying out of investment, the use of resources in a way which is economical and in conformity with the plan and the adherence to economic contracts as well as to price and quality regulations.[7] In addition, a comprehensive monitoring of performance is carried on under the 'annual accounting', which was tightened up in 1983, and which is enforced upon the Directors General of combines and of foreign trade enterprises as well as enterprise managers by the body which in each case is superior to them. These are required to monitor adherence to all material and financial plan targets, as well as the fulfilment of financial obligations *vis-à-vis* the state budget, the bank and the co-operating partners and hence to draw the appropriate conclusions for the ensuing plan year.

Evaluation of the effects of the reform

In the light of the allocative inefficiencies in centrally planned economies diagnosed in the second section, it finally remains to assess how far these can be eliminated or at least modified by the numerous measures of the NES concept and also of the present 'economic strategy'. At the same time, possible productive and counter-productive reform effects will be clarified and weighed against one another.

The basic idea behind the Sixties reform was gradually to extend the enterprise's rights of action and to develop indirect steering by means of a system of economic levers. As a consequence of this decentralisation, a reduction occurred in the extent of central planning and balancing. The result was a decrease in the importance of branch and territorial segmentation of the central management system due to bureaucratic self-interest. To this extent, the transition to a greater degree of indirect steering held the promise of a lessening of allocative inefficiencies due to departmentalism.

This positive reform effect was reinforced through the structure of enterprise incentives. Of course, enterprises in the NES phase (1963-68) were still subject to the iron law of plan-fulfilment, but they were given greater freedom of action as regards the allocation of goods and, in particular, the use of funds. Although in this way the motivation to perform of enterprise managers was strengthened, they continued to wish to obtain goods assortments and factor allocations which favoured plan-fulfilment and bonuses. Fundamental changes were only brought about by the '*Grundsatzregelung*' for the years 1969 and 1970, which, with the exception of structure-determining products, provided for the elimination of the plan-fulfilment principle. Rather, under the profit principle now obtaining, enterprises were encouraged to produce assortments of goods which responded to demand and were cost-effective. To this extent, therefore, favourable conditions had been created for overcoming enterprise behaviour coloured by plan-fulfilment strategies and the desire for 'soft' plans and, hence, eliminating the second gap in economic calculation.

The decisive problem with this reform concept lay, however, in the harmonisation of central, structure-determining development planning and enterprise, profit-orientated process planning, which was supposed to be attained by means of the system of economic levers. Here a general problem is posed, namely the economic policy or 'parametric' steering of economic processes in socialist planned economies, which has not as yet been solved. Conceptually, the central authorities were confronted with the task of inducing, by means of a normative steering magnitudes, enterprise behaviour which was in harmony with central plan goals. As has already been shown above, this can only be achieved if the steering magnitudes or parameters are fixed in such a way that the enterprises' price-orientated allocative decisions lead to the fulfilment of central, structural goals. This fundamental functional precondition of a parametric steering system, however, was not met by the regulations of the Sixties, because prices did not convey information (or did so only by chance) on relative scarcities of goods. Since enterprises, nevertheless, took these prices as their guide, there arose errors in steering and, above all, divergences between the actual and the centrally desired assortment of goods.

The increasing neglect of plan discipline and the undesired 'self-running' of enterprise processes finally afforded the central management authorities a welcome pretext for correcting enterprise decisions by way of continuous directives and interventions. As a result, the underlying concept of this economic reform was increasingly undermined. Since the interventions did not take scarcities into account and thus caused errors in the steering of goods, the end of this reform was foreseeable.

In the weighing up of positive and negative effects of the economic reforms of the Sixties it becomes apparent that their failure was preprogrammed. The whole concept of the NES displayed built-in construction errors, as it were, which impaired the positive reform effects. The ESS regulations admittedly provided for a greater incorporation of market elements, but the necessary institutional measures to guide the entrepreneurial initiatives which had been released in the direction deemed desirable by the political leadership, were lacking. The allocative inefficiencies necessitated a fundamental decision regarding the system: either to move over fully to a socialist market economy (as originally envisaged for 1971-5) or to restore the system of central planning and balancing. Clearly the fear of the loss of political power which socialist market economy conditions would entail was decisive, in that the opponents of reform asserted themselves in the SED leadership against Ulbricht and, by rendering him politically powerless, forced a return to the centrally planned economy.

How, by comparison with this, can the effects of the reform strategy since the beginning of the Eighties be evaluated?

With the change in the organisation of management and of the enterprise involving combine formation, which was carried out first of all, the grouping and subordination of enterprises within economic branches was altered. In this organisational reform, the main emphasis needs to be placed on the positive, albeit limited, innovation effects. The amalgamation of the research and development institutes of one product group, of the most important supplier enterprises, of rationalisation and construction resources and of final production capacities, undoubtedly facilitated the development and implementation of new products and processes. The unified and hierarchically organised management of innovation processes internal to the combine reduces, above all, the high costs of reaching agreements in the multitude of synchronisation negotiations previously necessary between the various branch ministries and enterprises outside the branch. In addition, it is more likely to stimulate the tackling of innovations, which are always risky, since individual sub-activities remain under unified monitoring, and successes or failures can more readily be attributed.

There could also be positive effects on state research and development policy, since the targeted promotion of high technologies is facilitated by the concentration of R&D potential in the combines. Moreover, the direct subordination of combine management permits the direct intervention of ministries in planned innovation projects. To this extent, the combines represent an effective organisational means for concentrating productive forces and resources on selected technologies.

These possible positive effects, however, are faced with restrictions on innovations stemming from the combine organisation, which are, above all, evident in the implementation of complex innovations. In this regard, the introduction of new technologies presupposes the parallel development and co-ordination of innovative inputs in earlier or later production stages and also in sectors remote in terms of production technology. This is especially the case with the high technologies (e.g. micro-electronics, new energy technologies, and robotic, office and communications technologies) being pushed by the political leadership. The development and implementation of such complex innovations, however, come up against the constraints imposed by combines. The greater reliance of combine management on their own R&D and production potential, it is true, means that they can avoid the aforementioned barriers to co-ordination across branches and production stages. At the same time, however, this is associated with the loss of specialisation and co-operation effects, which are necessary for the development of high technologies. Thus, the combine organisation stimulates the development of technologically autarkic innovations, which, nevertheless, may be only of limited competitiveness internationally. This problem has also been recognised in the GDR. According to Gerisch and Hofmann (1979, p. 133), the development and implementation of innovations is a question of 'the right relationship between the combination within the large-scale economic units and co-operation as measured in relation to the whole national economy. Only in this way is it possible to prevent the combines implementing their present "striving for autarky"'. The demand that these strivings be countered by means of an improved and stronger co-ordination of innovation processes by state authorities, is surprising in view of the many negative experiences relating to their unwillingness to co-ordinate, which was supposed to be overcome by the combine organisation.

In so far as the combine organisation diminishes branch-related segmentation within the central management system and hence the first gap in economic calculation, there are positive if (measured by international standards) modest innovative effects.

It is doubtful whether, via combine formation, it has proved possible to improve data transmission on the part of the enterprises. The changes in the indicator system served, in the first place, the purpose of solving the acute economic policy problems (more expensive raw materials, a high level of foreign debt and slower economic growth). With the aid of the new indicators, combines and enterprises were to be obligated, above all, to save on costs, to improve earnings and to make greater efforts in regard to exports and in consumer goods production. What is characteristic of the present indicator system is, therefore, the combination of administrative pressure and material incentives. The administrative element is assured by the extension of various state monitoring institutions, whose task it is to ensure that the enterprises behave in a manner orientated towards plan and performance. This has, undoubtedly, made it possible to reduce the consumption of scarce raw materials and materials. This achievement of savings, however, does not in itself constitute proof that a transition to all-round intensification has taken place. For the law of plan-fulfilment means that enterprises continue to be basically interested in 'soft' plans and, hence, in transmitting appropriate false information 'upwards'. The altered structure of incentive and monitoring has thus intensified the pressure on enterprises to behave in a manner more consistent with performance and has improved adaptation to the more urgent scarcity situation. In this way, however, it is merely the symptoms of the second gap in economic calculation which have been attacked by means of an altered therapy, whilst the causes have remained unremedied.

In reference to the third and fourth gaps in economic calculation, the most recent reform experiments do not, at bottom, afford ground for a more favourable evaluation. Admittedly, the prices of production goods have been partially adapted to dearer imports and higher production costs for energy and raw materials. Yet the price system as it now stands does now reflect the objective scarcity relations of goods, so that the uncoordinated coexistence of plan- and price-related allocation, too, remains as a problem that is still to be solved. Moreover, within the two-level management organisation, the subordination of a relatively small number of large combines offers the branch ministers and other central authorities favourable opportunities for continuous direction and intervention, so that the problem of the uncoordinated coexistence of balanced state planning and discretionary management also continues to exist.

The evaluation of the reform strategy of the Eighties thus paints a conflicting picture. The improvements in the state planning and management of complex economic processes, which it is possible to make by means of the combine structure, and the savings in scarce resources brought about through the tighter incentive and monitoring system, may be regarded as positive effects of the reform. On the other hand, the inflated monitoring apparatus, the discrepancy which still remains between plan- and price-orientated allocation, and the discretionary meddling of the state management authorities in enterprise processes, are all plainly counter-productive effects. Partial improvements, therefore, have to be weighed against grave systemic defects, whose remedy in the future will require new reform experiments. That there are no doubts about this in the socialist countries, is clear from the following admission by the Soviet economist Fedorenko (1985, p. 365):

> The root of all evil lies in the fact that in the mechanism as it is at present there exists no harmonisation between the plan targets, which express the overall interests of the state, and the system of economic levers. Because these levers are not harmonised with the plan goals, they work against them at every turn.

Returning to the theses concerning the capacity for reform of the socialist planned economies referred to at the beginning of the chapter, it can be concluded that the positive reform effects may be interpreted as an expression of step-by-step learning and perfecting processes in accordance with the 'Popperian thesis'. As our analysis of the economic reforms has shown, however, such processes come up against systemic barriers. The positive effects achievable through reform experiments are impaired by the 'discord' of counter-productive effects. To this extent the authors' evaluation of the reform tends rather to confirm the 'Krylov thesis'.

NOTES

1. Further fundamental problems of economic management which arise in any system are those of vested interests (power), performance and distribution (Gutmann, 1981, pp. 22 ff.). The solution of these fundamental problems depends on the systemic economic and political conditions.

2. According to Haffner (1985, p. 171) this 'management in the narrower sense' consists in the exertion of direct influence by management bodies on the subordinate units concerned in the form of directives, decisions regarding personnel, plan targets, plan alterations and similar regimentations. On the other hand, the concept of management is regarded in the GDR as an all-embracing concept for all forms of central economic steering.

3. The first proposals to make the economy more efficient had been made as early as 1957 by the GDR economists F. Behrens and A. Benary, but they had been condemned by the party leadership as revisionists. These proposals were taken up again after the Soviet economist E.G. Liberman had, in 1962, put forward similar proposals and thus initiated an official discussion of the reform.

4. A selection of the most important laws and decrees, including 68 issued in 1982 and 1983 alone, is to be found in Cornelsen, Melzer and Scherzinger (1984, pp. 221 ff.). The Order of Planning for 1986-90 (*Anordnung über die Ordnung der Planung der Volkswirtschaft der DDR 1986-1990 vom 7 Dezember 1984, GBL der DDR*, Sonderdruck Nr. 1190 a-r), and the 'General Guidelines' (*Anordnung über die Rahmenrichtlinie für die Planung in den Kombinaten und Betrieben der Industrie und des Bauwesens vom 7 Dezember 1984, GBL der DDR*, Sonderdruck Nr. 1191), for planning in the combines and enterprises based upon it, form the foundation for the present regulations; the two documents together come to more than 1,200 pages.

5. According to this interpretation, the intensification efforts reveal nothing more than the recognition of the general 'economic principle', the operation of which in every economic system is the precondition for rational economic management and, consequently, also for further economic growth (see also Haffner, 1985, p. 167).

6. The inclusion of 'economic accounting' (*wirtschaftliche Rechnungsführung*), in place of the earlier 'economic stimulation' (*ökonomische Stimulierung*), in the system conception of the socialist planned economy, clearly shows the changed function of value categories compared to those used during the NES. By means of a closer linkage with material planning, enterprise behaviour patterns are to be more strictly orientated to the fulfilment of central plan goals.

7. An overview of the most important monitoring organs at central level and in combines and enterprises is to be found in Cornelsen, Melzer and Scherzinger (1984, p. 213).

Contributors

Dr Eleonore Breuning. Department of History and Centre of Russian & East European Studies, University College, Singleton Park, Swansea SA2 8PP.

Professor Phillip J. Bryson. Department of Economics, College of Business and Public Administration, University of Arizona, Tucson, Arizona.

Dr Hannsjörg F. Buck. Gesamtdeutsches Institut, Bundesanstalt für gesamtdeutsche Aufgaben, Adenauerallee 10, 5300 Bonn 1.

Dr Hannelore Hamel. Forschungsstelle zum Vergleich wirtschaftlicher Lenkungssysteme der Philipps-Universität Marburg, Barfüssertor 2, 3550 Marburg 1.

Dr Hanns-Dieter Jacobsen. Stiftung Wissenschaft und Politik, Forschungsinstitut für internationale Politik und Sicherheit, 8026 Ebenhausen.

Dr Ian Jeffries. Department of Economics and Centre of Russian & East European Studies, University College, Singleton Park, Swansea SA2 8PP.

Dr Werner Klein. Staatswissenschaftliches Seminar der Universität zu Köln, Albertus-Magnus-Platz 1, 5000 Köln 41.

Dr Helmut Leipold. Forschungsstelle zum Vergleich wirtschaftlicher Lenkungssysteme der Philipps-Universität Marburg, Barfüssertor 2, 3550 Marburg 1.

Dr Manfred Melzer. Deutsches Institut für Wirtschaftsforschung, Königin-Luise-Strasse 5, 1000 Berlin 33.

Professor Dr Konrad Merkel. Forschungsstelle für gesamtdeutsche wirtschaftliche und soziale Fragen, Stresemannstrasse 90, 1000 Berlin 61.

Professor Arthur A. Stahnke. School of Social Sciences, Southern Illinois University, Edwardsville, Illinois.

Dr Manfred Tröder. Osteuropa-Institut, Freie Universität Berlin.

Glossary

Agrochemisches Zentrum (ACZ) Agro-chemical centre. Supplies and applies chemical fertilisers and plant pest control agents.
Agrar-Industrie-Komplex (AIK) Agro-industrial complex.
Anordnung Regulation. Centrally issued legal ordinance of the lowest order of importance, which every minister is entitled to promulgate.
Arbeiter- und Bauern-Inspektion Workers' and Peasants' Inspectorate.
Aufgaben des Kombinates Minimum state plan targets which reach the combine in the first phase of annual planning and which form the basis of detailed planning for the combine.
Auflagen Obligatory state plan targets (indicators), which emerge after a process of information exchange and adjustment with the ministry.
Beitrag für gesellschaftliche Fonds Contribution for social funds. A form of payroll tax fixed at 70 per cent of the wage fund. At present only incorporated as a cost element in the prices of new products.
Beschluss Resolution.
Betrieb mit staatlicher Beteiligung Semi-state enterprise.
Betriebskollektivvertrag Enterprise collective contract.
Betriebspreis Enterprise price.
Bezirk County.
Brutto-Bodenproduktion Gross crop production.
Christlich-Demokratische Union Deutschlands Christian Democratic Party of Germany.
Delikatläden Special shops, first opened in 1976. Sell high-quality (GDR and Western) foodstuffs and semi-luxuries (such as tea, coffee, beer, wine and tobacco) for GDR marks at high prices.
Demokratische Bauernpartei Deutschlands Democratic Farmers' Party of Germany.
Demokratischer Frauenbund Deutschlands Democratic Women's Federation of Germany.
Deutsche Aussenhandelsbank German Foreign Trade Bank.

Deutsche Handelsbank German Trade Bank.
Effektivitätsnachweis Proof of efficiency.
Eigenbau von Rationalisierungsmitteln In-house manufacture of machinery and equipment, improving, repairing and re-designing, for purposes of rationalisation and innovation.
Einheitliches staatliches Finanzsystem Unitary state financial system.
Einheitliches Betriebsergebnis Unitary enterprise result. In addition to profits from domestic sales, takes into account foreign trade profits and losses on enterprise revenue through the use of existing exchange rates and (unpublished) direction coefficients (see **Richtungskoeffizienten**).
Einheitshaushalt Consolidated budget (combining central, county, district and municipal budgets).
Einzelhandelsspanne Retail trade margin.
Einzelhandelsverkaufspreis Retail price.
Endprodukt Final product.
Erzeugnisgruppen Product groups.
Exquisitläden Shops first opened in 1962. Sell high-value products (for example, ready-made clothes and leatherware goods, often imports from the West) for GDR marks at high prices.
Fondsbezogener Preistyp Capital-related price type.
Freie Deutsche Jugend Free German Youth.
Freier Deutscher Gewerkschaftsbund Free German Trade Union Federation.
Gärtnerische Produktionsgenossenschaft Market gardening producer co-operative.
GBL (Gesetzblatt der DDR) Law Gazette of the GDR.
Gebrauchswerteigenschaften Use-value (utility) properties or characteristics.
Gegenplan Counter-plan.
Gemeinde Community (municipality).
Genex-Geschenkdienst Set up in 1957 to handle gifts from the West to GDR citizens of goods and services produced in the GDR, Comecon or the West and paid for in convertible currencies.
Genussmittel Semi-luxuries, such as tea, coffee, beer, wine, spirits and tobacco.
Getreideeinheitenschlüssel (GE) Grain equivalent key.
Grosshandelsabgabepreis Wholesale price.
Grosshandelsspanne Wholesale trade margin.
Grossmastanlagen Factory farming plants.
Grossvieheinheit (GV) 'Large livestock equivalent'. 1GV =

500 kilogrammes live weight.

Grundfonds Fixed capital assets, such as machines, equipment and construction (buildings).

Grundfondsökonomie Management of fixed capital assets.

Grundfondsreproduktion Replacement of fixed capital assets.

Grundlohn Basic wage.

Grundmaterial Basic materials which form the material substance of a product. It is only a part of the wider term '**Material**' (materials = basic materials plus energy, water, fuel, power and lubricants).

Grundmittel Basic means. Fixed capital assets.

Grund-und Umlauffonds Fixed and working capital.

Handelsfondsabgabe Capital charge applying to trade enterprises.

Hauptaufgabe Chief task.

Industrielle Warenproduktion Industrial commodity (gross) output.

Innerdeutscher Handel Inner-German, inter-German or intra-German trade. So called because in the FRG, in contrast to the GDR, this is not considered to be foreign trade. Note that in this context the term *Lieferungen* (deliveries) is used instead of exports and **Bezüge** (purchases) instead of imports.

Intershop-Läden Shops which sell products similar to those to be found in **Delikat-** and **Exquisitläden** and first opened in 1962. Until 1973 only open to Western visitors using Western currencies. Since 1973 open to GDR citizens, who have to use either 'public cheques' (**Forum-Schecks**) (which they obtain in exchange for their convertible currencies at state banks) or DMs.

Intensivierung Growth achieved mainly through the more efficient use of existing factors of production. This contrasts with 'extensive' growth, which relies largely on increasing inputs.

Intertank Convertible currency service stations.

Kalkulierter Gewinn Profit margin calculated in the price.

Kombinat Combine.

Kombinat industrieller Mast (KIM) Factory farming combine, mostly concerned with poultry and eggs, but some with pork and beef. Literally combine for industrial fattening. Specialised unit for animal production.

Kombinatsspitze Director General of the combine and the board of managers.

Kontrollieren To monitor.
Kooperation Sub-contracting.
Kooperationsleistungen Services and intermediate goods bought in from another production unit.
Kooperative Abteilung Pflanzenproduktion (KAP) Co-operative division for crop production.
Kreis District.
Kreisbetrieb für Landtechnik (KfL) District enterprise for rural technology. Maintains and repairs agricultural machinery.
Kulturbund der DDR League of Culture of the GDR.
Landwirtschaftliche Nutzfläche (LN) Land used for agricultural purposes.
Landwirtschaftliche Produktionsgenossenschaft Agricultural producer co-operative.
Leitidee Leading idea.
Leitsätze Guiding principles.
Leitung Management. In the GDR this term is used in the broad sense, encompassing all forms of central economic steering.
Leitziel Main goal.
Liberal-Demokratische Partei Deutschlands Liberal Democratic Party of Germany.
Material Materials (= basic materials plus energy, water, fuel, power and lubricants).
Material-, Ausrüstungs- und Konsumgüterbilanzen Material, equipment and consumer goods (MAK) balances.
Materialverbrauch Materials consumed (used up).
Mehrleistungslohn Extra-performance wage.
Messe der Meister von Morgen Young innovator exhibitions.
Ministerrat Council of Ministers.
National-Demokratische Partei Deutschlands National Democratic Party of Germany.
Nettogewinn Net profit: unitary enterprise result of the enterprise or combine plus additions corresponding to statutory provision minus the capital charge minus impermissible profit (e.g. due to violations of price and quality regulations) minus profit gained from exceeding the manpower plan minus fines going to the state budget.
Nettogewinnabführung Net profit deduction (deducted by the state).
Nettoproduktion Net production: commodity (gross output)

minus materials consumed (see **Materialverbrauch**) minus productive services consumed (bought-in services, repairs, transport and storage costs and other productive services) minus rents and leases minus depreciation.

Normen des Materialeinsatzes Norms of materials use are determined at the enterprise level and are the basis for the fixing of normatives (see below).

Normative des Materialeinsatzes Upper limits for use of specific materials. Normatives of material consumption are obligatory state plan targets. They determine the upper limit for the specific production use of economically important materials and raw materials for a plan period and are disaggregated by the individual management levels in plan formulation. (*Normative,* in a broader sense, apply not only to materials use, but also to such things as profit deductions into incentive funds, profit utilisation and the size of the wage fund.)

Ökonomische Hebel Economic levers, such as prices, taxes and interest rates.

Ordnungsmittel Regulatory methods such as the Order of Planning, but also employees' and occupational classifications, production classifications for enterprises, key lists and subdivisions (e.g. lists for cost groups according to accounting categories).

Pflichtenhefte Duty dossiers, the necessary basis for the start and implementation of a research project. They have to show the costs and benefits associated with a project by means of a variety of technical-economic data, e.g. production cost ceilings, foreign currency profitability and work stages.

Planungsordnung Order of Planning.

Preis-Leistungs-Verhältnis Price-performance relationship. Analogue pricing, operative between 1976 and 1983. Pricing in accordance with the improvement in use value characteristics, compared to an analogous product.

Prinzip der Eigenerwirtschaftung der Mittel Principle of earning one's own resources. The principle not only that production units should cover current expenditure from their own revenue, but also that investment is not to be financed exclusively from budgetary grants, but out of profit, depreciation allowances and interest-bearing credits.

Prinzip der Einzelleitung Principle of individual management (one-man responsibility and control).

Produktgebundene Abgabe Product-related levy.

Produktgebundene Preisstützung Product-related subsidy.
Produktionsfondsabgabe Production fund levy. Capital charge.
Produktionsgenossenschaft des Handwerks Handicraft producer co-operative.
Produktionsstätten Production plants.
Produktionsverbrauch Raw materials and intermediate goods used up in the course of production plus depreciation (capital consumption). Productive consumption.
Produziertes Nationaleinkommen Produced national income.
Rat für Gegenseitige Wirtschaftshilfe (RGW) Comecon (CMEA). Council for Mutual Economic Assistance.
Rechtsvorschrift Legal ordinance. Statutory regulation or provision.
Rechentechnik Computer technology.
Richtungskoeffizienten Direction coefficients, differentiated by country (or groups of countries) and commodity groups in order to correct exchange rates and promote the politically desired trade flows.
Rückflussdauer Recoupment period.
Rückkoppelung Feedback.
Selbstkosten Production costs.
Soll-Ist-Vergleich Should-be/is comparison. Objective compared to performance. Planned compared to actual figures.
Soll-Sätze Prescriptive principles, such as those guiding the tasks of various levels of management, and the participation of workers in the drawing up of the plan.
Sonderkonto 'S' Special account 'S' for inner-German trade (held by the FRG's **Bundesbank**), which enables the GDR to make purchases outside the normal clearing accounts by means of payments in DMs.
Sowjetische Aktiengesellschaft (SAG) Soviet joint-stock company.
Sozialistische Einheitspartei Deutschlands (SED) Socialist Unity Party of Germany.
Staatliche Plankommission State Planning Commission.
Staatsrat der DDR State Council of the GDR.
Stammbetrieb Parent enterprise.
Steuerungs-, Regel-, und Robotertechnik Steering, automation and robot technology.
Strukturbestimmende Aufgaben Structure-determining tasks.
Swing Interest-free overdraft facility, set up in 1949, which permits both the FRG and the GDR to overdraw their clearing

accounts up to a certain limit. The original aim was to prevent obstacles to bilaterally balanced trade flows resulting from time lags in settling claims. In reality, however, this facility has almost always been used by the GDR, in order to save on interest payments.

Tonnenideologie Tonnage ideology (ideology of tons).

Transparenz Openness (glasnost').

Valuta Mark Foreign currency mark, used in the presentation of the GDR's foreign trade results. The official rate of conversion to the domestic mark is not published. The VM corresponds to the value of the DM before the 1961 revaluation. (1982: 1VM=0.71 DM. 1984: 1VM=0.74 DM.)

Vered(e)lung Increasing value added by more processing, greater refinement and improved quality of products. Note that the term '**höhere Vered(e)lung**' is also used, meaning greater refinement/transformation and higher quality/utility.

Vereinbarungspreis Contractually agreed price. Price agreed upon by producer and purchaser on the basis of calculation guidelines and without confirmation by pricing authorities. The rate of profit may be higher or lower than that laid down. Especially applicable to special or one-off products, special machines, complete plants and R&D services.

Vereinigung volkseigener Betriebe (VVB) Association of nationally owned enterprises.

Verflechtungskoeffizienten Input-output coefficients.

Vermögensplanung Fixed capital planning procedures.

Verordnung Decree.

Verrechnungseinheit (VE) Clearing (settlement, accounting) unit. Clearing unit of account used in trade between the FRG and the GDR. Its value corresponds to that of the DM. Note, however, that the VEs earned by the GDR can only be used for purchases in the FRG, and not in other Western countries.

Versorgung Consumer supply.

Vervollkommnung Perfecting (of planning, management and economic accounting).

Verwendetes Nationaleinkommen Utilised national income. (Produced national income minus exports plus imports.)

Volkseigener Aussenhandelsbetrieb (AHB) Nationally owned foreign trade enterprise (FTE).

Volkseigener Betrieb (VEB) Nationally owned enterprise.

Volkseigenes Gut State farm.

Volkseigenes Kombinat Nationally owned combine.

Volkskammer People's Chamber.
Volkswirtschaftlich erforderlicher Aufwand Economically necessary expenditure.
Volkswirtschaftsrat National Economic Council.
Vollarbeitskräfte (AK) 'Full-time manpower'. Permanent agricultural employees multiplied by the constant factor 0.9.
Vorgaben Targets.
Vorleistungen Raw materials, materials and semi-finished products.
Währungsordnung Currency system.
Warenproduktion Commodity (gross) output.
Werkstoffe Various kinds of materials, such as wood and metal.
Wirtschaftliche Rechnungsführung Economic accounting. Management methods by means of which central goals are to be attained and production unit activity geared to the fulfilment of state tasks. Hence a measuring, incentive and monitoring function.
Zahlungs-und Verrechnungsverkehr Payments and clearing system.
Zielfunktion Objective function.
Zentralkomitee der DDR Central Committee of the GDR.
Ziel-Mittel-Gefüge Goal-means structure (implying that means are needed to implement goals).
Zwischenbetriebliche Einrichtung (ZBE) Inter-enterprise organisation.
Zwischenbetriebliche Einrichtung Pflanzenproduktion Inter-enterprise organisation for crop production.
Zwischenbetriebliche Einrichtung Tierproduktion Inter-enterprise organisation for livestock production.
Zwischengenossenschaftliche Einrichtung (ZGE) Inter-cooperative organisation.
Zwischenbetriebliche Grossmastanlagen Inter-enterprise factory farming plants.

References

Åslund, A., *Private Enterprise in Eastern Europe* (Macmillan, London, 1985).
Authors' Collective, *Das Finanzsystem der DDR* (Verlag Die Wirtschaft, East Berlin, 1962).
—— *Leistungsorganisation in den Betrieben und Kombinaten* (East Berlin 1976).
—— *Planung in Industriebetrieben und Kombinaten* (East Berlin 1977).
—— led by König, E., *Das sozialistische Finanzwesen der DDR (Fachschullehrbuch)* (Verlag Die Wirtschaft, East Berlin, 1978).
—— led by Friedrich, G. and Koziolek, H., *Zur Vervollkommnung der Leitung, Planung und Organisation der Kombinate,* (East Berlin, 1981).
—— *Sozialistische Finanzwissenschaft (Hochschullehrbuch)* (Verlag Die Wirtschaft, (East Berlin, 1981).
—— *Handbuch der Planung für Kombinate und Betriebe* (East Berlin, 1982).
—— led by Finger, H. and Gertich, W., *Stimulierung in Industriebetrieben und Kombinaten* (East Berlin, 1982).
—— *Aussenwirtschaftsrecht der DDR* (East Berlin, 1985).
—— *Planungsordnung 1986 bis 1990, Blickpunkt Wirtschaft* (Verlag Die Wirtschaft, East Berlin, 1985).
—— *Wirtschaftsrecht-Lehrbuch* (Staatsverlag der DDR, East Berlin, 1985).
—— led by Rost, H., in *Blickpunkt Wirtschaft,* vol. 3 (East Berlin, 1985).
Bahro, R., *Die Alternative. Zur Kritik des real existierenden Sozialismus* (Cologne and Frankfurt, 1977).
Beyer, A., '*Die Reformpolitik der DDR in den Parteibeschlüssen*', in Bress, Hensel *et al.* (1972).
Boot, P., 'Continuity and Change in the Planning System of the German Democratic Republic', *Soviet Studies,* vol. 35, no. 3 (1983).
Bornstein, M., 'Economic Reform in Eastern Europe' in US Congress Joint Economic Committee, *East European Economies Post-Helsinki* (1977).
Bottesi, V. and Hummel, G., *Kombinatsplanung und Leistungssteigerung* (Dietz Verlag, East Berlin, 1984).
Bress, L., Hensel, K.P. *et. al., Wirtschaftssysteme des Sozialismus im Experiment–Plan oder Markt* (Frankfurt, 1972).
Brückner, D. in *Neues Deutschland,* 22 October, 1985.
Bryson, P.J., *The Consumer under Socialist Planning: The East German Case* (Praeger, New York, 1984).
Buck, H.F., in *DDR Handbuch* (1979).
—— in *Deutschland Archiv,* vol. 11 (1981).
—— *Steuerpolitik im Ost-West-Systemvergleich* (Berlin Verlag,

Berlin, 1982).
—— 'Forschungs- und Technologiepolitik in der DDR. Ziele, Lenkungsinstrumente, Mobilisierungsmittel und Ergebnisse' in Gutmann (1983).
—— in *DDR Handbuch* (1985).
Burian, W., in *Wissenschaftliche Zeitschrift der Hochschule für Ökonomie*, vol. 3 (1978).
Cassel, D., *Wirtschaftspolitik im Systemvergleich* (Verlag Franz Vahlen, Munich, 1984).
Childs, D., *The GDR: Moscow's German Ally* (George Allen and Unwin, London, 1983).
—— (ed.), *Honecker's Germany* (George Allen and Unwin, London, 1985).
Cornelsen, D., 'GDR: Industrial Reforms' in NATO (1980).
—— in *Wochenbericht des DIW*, no. 31 (1981).
—— in *Wochenbericht des DIW*, no. 5 (1982a).
—— in *Wochenbericht des DIW*, no. 32 (1982b).
—— in *Wochenbericht des DIW*, no. 5 (1983).
—— in *Wochenbericht des DIW*, no. 50 (1983).
—— in *Wochenbericht des DIW*, no. 5 (1984).
—— in *Wochenbericht des DIW*, no. 5 (1985).
—— in *Wochenbericht des DIW*, no. 5 (1986).
—— in *Wochenbericht des DIW*, no. 31 (1986b).
—— Melzer, M. and Scherzinger, A., in *Vierteljahrshefte zur Wirtschaftsforschung des DIW*, no. 2 (1984).
DDR Handbuch (Federal Ministry for Inner-German Relations, Cologne, 1979).
—— (Federal Ministry for Inner-German Relations, Cologne, 1985).
Debardeleben, J., 'Marxism-Leninism and Economic Policy. Natural Resource Pricing in the USSR and the GDR', *Soviet Studies*, vol. 1 (1983).
—— *The Environment and Marxism-Leninism. The Soviet and East German Experience* (Westview Press, Boulder and London, 1985).
Dennis, M., 'An Objective Necessity? Shift Working in an Advanced Socialist Society', *GDR Monitor*, vol. 9 (1983).
Dietz, R. and Grosser, I., 'Comecon Energy Perspectives and the Long-Term Target Programmes', *Forschungsbericht*, vol. 58 (Wiener Institut für internationale Wirtschaftsvergleiche, 1981).
DIW, *Handbuch DDR-Wirtschaft* (Rowohlt Verlag, Hamburg, 1984).
Drewnowski, J. (ed), *Crisis in the East European Economy* (Croom Helm, London, 1982).
Dyker, D.A., *The Future of the Soviet Economic Plannng System* (Croom Helm, London, 1985).
Ebert, G. and Opel, G. in *Einheit*, vol. 4 (1982).
Edwards, G.E., *GDR Society and Social Institutions* (Macmillan, London, 1985).
Ehlert, W., Hunstock, D. and Tannert, K. (eds), *Geld und Kredit in der DDR* (Verlag Die Wirtschaft, East Berlin, 1985).
Ellman, M., *Socialist Planning* (Cambridge University Press, Cambridge, 1979).

Erdmann, K., in *Deutschlande Archiv*, vol. 4 (1982).

—— 'Wirtschaftliche Rechnungsführung im Kombinat–Betriebswirtschaftliche Aspekte und Konsequenzen', in Gutmann (ed.) (1983).

—— and Melzer, M., in *Deutschland Archiv*, vol. 13, Parts I and II, nos. 9 and 10 (1980).

Fedorenko, N.P., in *Sowjetwissenschaft. Gesellschaftswissenschaftliche Beiträge*, vol. 4 (1985).

Freris, A., *The Soviet Industrial Enterprise: Theory and Practice* (Croom Helm, London, 1984).

Friedrich, G. *et al.*, *Leitung der sozialistischen Wirtschaft* (Verlag Die Wirtschaft, East Berlin, 1983).

Frowen, S., 'The Economy of the German Democratic Republic' in Childs (ed.) (1985).

Fünfjahrplan, 'Gesetz über . . .', in *Gesetzblatt der DDR*, Teil I, *Band* 35 (1981).

Gabler, U. and Wichler, E., in *Wirtschaftswissenschaft*, *Band* 27, no. 5 (1979).

Garland, J., 'FRG-GDR Economic Relations', in Joint Economic Committee of the Congress of the United States (1986).

Gebhardt, G. *et al.*, *Finanzen und Finanzsystem im Sozialismus* (Dietz Verlag, East Berlin, 1981).

Gerisch, R. and Hofmann, W., in *Wirtschaftswissenschaft*, no. 2 (1979).

—— Rosenkranz, R. and Siefert, A., in *Wirtschaftswissenschaft*, July (1983).

—— and Wagner, W., in *Die Wirtschaft*, vol. 5 (1982).

Gesetzblatt der DDR, 'Verordnung . . .' Teil I, *Band* 38 (1979).

—— 'Anordnung . . .', Sonderdruck, no. 1020 (1980).

Gorbachev, M., in *Neues Deutschland*, 13 June 1985.

Granick, D., *Enterprise Guidance in Eastern Europe* (Princeton University Press, Princeton, New Jersey, 1975).

Gregory, P.R. and Leptin, G., 'Similar Societies under Differing Economic Systems: the Case of the Two Germanys', *Soviet Studies*, vol. 4 (1977).

—— and Stuart, R.C., *Soviet Economic Structure and Performance* (3rd edn), (Harper and Rowe, New York, 1986).

Groschoff, K., 'Zur weiteren Verringerung der wesentlichen Unterschiede zwischen Stadt und Land in der DDR' in *Intensivierung der landwirtschaftlichen Produktion* (East Berlin, 1979).

Gurtz, J. and Kaltofen, G., *Der Staatshaushalt der DDR* (Verlag Die Wirtschaft, East Berlin, 1982).

Gutmann, G., *Volkswirtschaftslehre. Eine ordnungstheoretische Einführung* (Stuttgart, Berlin, Cologne and Mainz, 1981).

—— (ed.), *Das Wirtschaftssystem der DDR* (Fischer Verlag, Stuttgart, 1983).

—— and Haendcke-Hoppe, M., *Die Aussenbeziehungen der DDR, Schriften der Gesellschaft für Deutschlandforschung e.V., Jahrbuch 1980* (Heidelberg, 1981).

—— and Mampel, S. (eds), *Probleme systemvergleichender Betrachtung* (Berlin, 1986).

Haase, H.E., in *Berichte des Osteuropa-Instituts an der Freien Universität Berlin*, vol. 117 (1978).
—— 'GDR: Prospects for the 1980s', in NATO (1980).
—— *Hauptsteuern im sozialistischen Wirtschaftssystem* (Osteuropa-Institut an der Freien Universität Berlin, Berlin, 1980).
Haberland, F. and Rosenkranz, R., in *Einheit*, vol. 7 (1984).
Haendcke-Hoppe, M., in *FS-Analysen*, vol. 3 (1978).
—— in *East Central Europe*, vol. 11, nos. 1-2 (1984).
—— in *FS-Analysen*, vol. 1 (1985a).
—— in *FS-Analysen*, vol. 5 (1985b).
—— in *FS-Analysen*, vol. 2 (1986).
Haffner, F., in *FS Analysen, DDR-Reformbemühungen in Theorie und Praxis*, vol. 6 (1980).
—— in *18. Tagung zum Stand der DDR-Forschung in der Bundesrepublik Deutschland* (Cologne, 1985).
Haker, R., in *Die Wirtschaft*, vol. 1 (1983)
Hamel, H., *Das sowjetische Herrschaftsprinzip des demokratischen Zentralismus in der Wirtschaftsordnung Mitteldeutschlands* (Berlin, 1966).
—— 'Sozialistische Marktwirtschaft in der DDR? Hinwendung und Abkehr' in Leipold (1975).
—— (ed.), *Systemvergleich als Aufgabe* (Stuttgart and New York, 1977).
—— 'Sozialistische Unternehmenskonzentration und Managerverhalten. Die Kombinatsbildung in der DDR als Effizienzproblem', in Hedtkamp, G. (ed.), *Anreiz- und Kontrollmechanismen in Wirtschaftssystemen*, vol. I (Duncker & Humblot, 1981).
—— 'Reformen des Wirtschaftsmechanismus', in Gutmann (1983).
Hanson, P., 'Success Indicators Revisited: The July 1979 Soviet Decree on Planning and Management', *Soviet Studies*, vol. 1 (1983).
Hare, P.G., Radice, H.K. and Swain, N. (eds), *Hungary: A Decade of Economic Reform* (George Allen and Unwin, London, 1981).
Heinrichs, W., in *Wirtschaftswissenschaft*, no. 8 (1978).
—— in *Wirtschaftswissenschaft*, no. 7 (1984).
Hensel, D. and Kuciak, G., in *Wirtschaftswissenschaft*, vol. 32, no. 3 (1984).
Hensel, K.P., 'Zyklus der Reformen in der DDR', in Bress, Hensel *et al.* (1972).
—— 'Der Zwang zum wirtschaftspolitischen Experiment in zentral gelenkten Wirtschaften', in Hamel (1977).
—— *Grundformen der Wirtschaftsordnung — Marktwirtschaft — Zentralverwaltungswirtschaft*, 3. Auflage (Verlag C.H. Beck, Munich, 1978).
Heuer, U-J., in *Wirtschaftsrecht*, no. 4 (1979).
—— in *Neue Justiz*, no. 9 (1982).
—— in *Wirtschaftsrecht*, no. 4 (1985).
Hinkel, U. and Langendorf, G., in *Einheit*, vol. 7 (1985).
Hinze, H.H., Knop, H. and Seifert, E., *Sozialistische Volkswirtschaft* (Verlag Die Wirtschaft, East Berlin, 1983).
Hochbaum, H-U., in *Wirtschaftsrecht*, no. 1 (1975).

Höhmann, H-H., Kaser, M. and Thalheim, K.C. (eds), *The New Economic Systems of Eastern Europe* (Hurst, London, 1975).
—— (ed.), *The East European Economies in the 1970s* (Butterworth, London, 1982).
—— in *Berichte des Bundesinstituts für ostwissenschaftliche und internationale Studien (Köln)*, vol. 41 (1985).
Honecker, E., in *Neues Deutschland*, 4 October 1981.
—— in *Neues Deutschland*, 14 December 1979.
Hoss, P., in *Wirtschaftswissenschaft*, no. 2 (1984).
Jacobsen, H-D., 'Foreign Trade Relations of the GDR', in Von Beyme and Zimmerman (1984).
—— 'Sonderfall innerdeutsche Beziehungen', in Rode and Jacobsen (1984).
Jeffries, I. (ed.), *The Industrial Enterprise in Eastern Europe* (Praeger, New York, 1981).
Joint Economic Committee of the Congress of the United States, *East European Economies. Slow Growth in the 1980s Vol. 3: Country Studies on Eastern Europe and Yugoslavia* (Washington, 1986).
Junker, W., in *Neues Deutschland*, 4 October 1973. [Wolfgang Junker is the Minister for Construction.]
Jurk, H. *et al.*, in *Blickpunkt Wirtschaft*, vol. 2 (Verlag Die Wirtschaft, East Berlin, 1985).
Keren, M., 'The New Economic System in the GDR: An Obituary', *Soviet Studies*, vol. 24 (1973).
—— in *Europaeische Rundschau*, 2.
Klein, W., 'Das Kombinat: eine organisationstheoretische Analyse', in Gutmann (1983).
Klinger, G., in *Staat und Recht*, vol. 2, no. 3 (1980).
Krakat, K., in *FS-Analysen*, vol. 3 (1980).
—— in *FS-Analysen*, vol. 6 (1984).
Krinks, V., Oberländer, K. and Rouscik, L., in *Wirtschaftswissenschaft*, no. 7 (1980).
Kühnau, K-H., in *Staat und Recht*, vol. 1 (1979).
Ladensack, K., in *Sozialistische Arbeitswissenschaft*, vol. 3 (1980).
Lambrecht, H., in *Aus Politik und Zeitgeschichte. Beilage zur Wochenzeitung Das Parlament*, October, 40/82 (1982).
Lane, D., *Soviet Economy and Society* (Basil Blackwell, Oxford, 1985).
Langendorf, G., Review in *Wirtschaftswissenschaft*, May 1983.
Leipold, H., 'Der Einfluss von Property Rights auf hierarchische und marktliche Transaktionen in sozialistischen Wirtschaftssystemen', in Schüller (1983).
—— in *Jahrbuch für neue politische Ökonomie (Tübingen)*, vol. 3 (1984).
—— (ed.), *Sozialistische Marktwirtschaften — Konzeptionen und Lenkungsprobleme* (Munich, 1985).
Leptin, G., 'Das neue ökonomische System Mitteldeutschlands', in Thalheim, K.C. and Höhmann, H-H (1968).
—— and Melzer, M., *Economic Reform in East German Industry* (Oxford University Press, Oxford, 1978).
Liehmann, P., *Wirtschaftswissenschaft*, vol. 32, no. 2 (1984).

Machowski, H., in *DIW-Wochenbericht*, vol. 29 (1984).
McCauley, M., *The German Democratic Republic since 1945* (Macmillan, London, 1983).
Meier, Ch., in *Berichte des Bundesinstituts für ostwissenschaftliche und internationale Studien (Köln)*, vol. 6 (1986).
Melzer, M., in *Vierteljahrshefte zur Wirtschaftsforschung des DIW*, vol. 1 (1977).
—— in *FS-Analysen*, vol. 6 (1978).
—— in *Vierteljahrshefte zur Wirtschaftsforschung des DIW*, vols. 3-4 (1980).
—— 'Combine Formation in the GDR', *Soviet Studies*, vol. 33, no. 1 (1981a).
—— 'Combine Formation and the Role of the Enterprise in East German Industry', in Jeffries (ed.) (1981b).
—— 'The GDR — Economic Policy Caught between Pressure for Efficiency and Lack of Ideas', in Höhmann (ed.), (1982).
—— 'Wandlungen im Preissystem der DDR', in Gutmann (1983a)
—— (with the assistance of W. Steinbeck), in *Beiträge zur Strukturforschung des DIW*, vol. 74 (1983b).
—— 'Wirtschaftspolitik der administrativen Reformen', in Cassel (1984a).
—— in *Berichte des Bundesinstituts für ostwirtschaftliche und internationale Studien*, vol. 35 (1984b).
—— in *FS-Analysen*, vol. 7 (1984c).
—— 'Die Rolle der Kombinate und Betriebe im Wirtschaftssystem der DDR', in Gramatski, E. and Nutzinger, G. (eds), *Betrieb und Partizipation in Osteuropa* (Campus Verlag, Frankfurt and New York, 1986).
—— and Erdmann, K., in *FS-Analysen, Die Kombinatsbildung der DDR in Theorie und Praxis*, vol. 8 (1979).
—— Scherzinger, A. and Schwartau, C., in *Vierteljahrshefte zur Wirtschaftsforschung des DIW*, vol. 4, (1979).
—— and Stahnke, A., 'The GDR faces the Economic Dilemmas of the 1980's: caught between the Need for New Methods and Restricted Options', in Joint Economic Committee of the Congress of the United States (1986).
Michalsky, H., 'Social Policy and the Transformation of Society', in Von Beyme and Zimmerman (1984).
Ministerium der Finanzen, *Besteuerung des Arbeitseinkommens* (Staatsverlag der DDR, East Berlin, 1981).
Mittag, G., in *Neues Deutschland*, 11 and 12 June 1970.
—— in *Einheit*, vol. 5 (1982).
—— *Ökonomische Strategie der Partei: klares Konzept für weiteres Wachstum* (Dietz Verlag, East Berlin, 1983).
—— in *Wirtschaftswissenschaft*, vol. 32, no. 1 (1984).
—— *Mit höchsten Leistungen den XI. Parteitag vorbereiten* (Dietz Verlag, East Berlin, 1985).
—— in *Berliner Zeitung*, 12 September 1986.
Müller, R., in *Abhandlungen der Akademie der Wissenschaften der DDR*, vol. W3 (1985).

Musgrave, R.A., *Fiscal Systems* (Yale University Press, New Haven and London, 1969).

Naor, J. 'How Dead is the GDR?' in *Soviet Studies*, vol. 25 (1973).

—— Review of Leptin, G. and Melzer, M., (1978) in *Soviet Studies*, vol. 32 (1980).

NATO, Economics Directorate. Proceedings of Annual Colloquium, Brussels. *Economic Reforms in Eastern Europe and Prospects for the 1980s* (1980).

Nick, H., *Gesellschaft und Betrieb im Sozialismus. Zur zentralen Idee des ökonomischen Systems des Sozialismus* (East Berlin, 1970).

—— in *Tribune*, 2 November 1982.

Nove, A., *The Soviet Economic System* (2nd edn, George Allen and Unwin, London, 1980).

—— *The Economics of Feasible Socialism* (George Allen and Unwin, London, 1983).

Rembel, E., *Ökonomie der Landwirtschaft und Nahrungsgüterwirtschaft der DDR* (VEB Deutscher Landwirtschaftsverlag, East Berlin, 1983).

Richter, H., in *Wirtschaftsrecht*, vol. 1 (1979).

—— 'Zu Aspekten der Entwicklung leistungsfähiger Kombinate in der Industrie der DDR', in Sachse, E. (ed.), *Zu Grundfragen der Betriebswirtschaft in der DDR und in Japan* (Hochschule für Ökonomie 'Bruno Leuschner', East Berlin, 1981).

—— *et al.*, *Aus- und Weiterbildung sozialistischer Leiter* (Verlag Die Wirtschaft, East Berlin, 1981).

Rind, K., in *Blickpunkt Wirtschaft*, vol. 1 (Verlag Die Wirtschaft, East Berlin, 1985).

Ritzschke, G., in *Abhandlungen der Akademie der Wissenschaften der DDR*, vol. W3 (1985).

Rode, R. and Jacobsen, H-D., *Wirtschaftskrieg oder Entspannung? Eine politische Bilanz der Ost-West-Wirtschaftsbeziehungen* (Bonn, 1984).

Roesler, J., in *Jahrbuch für Wirtschaftsgeschichte* (East Berlin, 1983).

Rohde, E. and Fengler, H., *Der Staatshaushalt der DDR* (Verlag Die Wirtschaft, East Berlin, 1959).

—— and Siebenhaar, H., *Haushalts- und Finanzwirtschaft der Städte und Gemeinden* (Staatsverlag der DDR, East Berlin, 1975).

Röse, G., in *Wirtschaftsrecht*, vol. 3 (1974).

Rost, H., in *Die Wirtschaft*, vol. 4 (1982).

—— *et al.*, *Planungsordnung 1986-1990: Wichtiges Instrument zur Verwirklichung der ökonomischen Strategie* (East Berlin, 1985).

Rzesnitzek, F., *Theorie und Entwicklung der Staatseinnahmen in der DDR* (Verlag Die Wirtschaft, East Berlin, 1959).

Salecker, W., in *Wirtschaftswissenschaft*, no. 3 (1984).

Scharf, C.B., *Politics and Change in East Germany: an Evaluation of Socialist Democracy* (Frances Pinter, London, 1984).

Schmidt, E., in *Wirtschaftsrecht*, vol. 11, no. 1 (1980).

Schmidt, P-G., 'Internationale Währungspolitik im sozialistischen Staat, theoretische Grundlegung und empirische Überprüfung am Beispiel der DDR', in *Schriften zum Vergleich von Wirtschaftsordnungen*,

vol. 36 (Gustav Fischer Verlag, Stuttgart and New York, 1985).
Schmidt, R., in *Einheit*, vol. 7 (1985).
Schneider, E., *The GDR* (Hurst, London, 1978).
Schneider, G., in Schneider and Tröder, in *Berichte des Osteuropa-Instituts an der Freien Unversität Berlin (Wirtschaft und Recht)*, no. 137 (1985).
Schroeder, G., 'Soviet Economic Reform Decrees: More Steps on the Treadmill', in *Joint Economic Committee of the Congress*, Part I (Washington, 1983).
Schüller, A. (ed.), *Property Rights und ökonomische Theorie* (1983).
—— 'Der theoretische Institutionalismus als Methode des Systemvergleichs', in Gutmann and Mampel (1986).
Seiffert, W., *Das Rechtssystem des RGW* (Baden-Baden, 1982).
Smith, A.H., *The Planned Economies of Eastern Europe* (Croom Helm, London, 1983).
Steeger, H., 'Das Wachstums- und Effektivitätskonzept des Fünfjahrplanes 1981 bis 1985 und die weitere Vervollkommnung der Planung und wirtschaftlichen Rechnungsführung', *in Leistung-Wachstum-Effektivität im Kombinat und Betrieb* (Verlag Die Wirtschaft, East Berlin, 1982).
Stinglwagner, W., in *Analysen und Berichte*, vol. 7 (1986).
Stolper, W.F., *The Structure of the East German Economy* (Harvard University Press, Cambridge, Massachusetts, 1960).
Strassburger, J., 'Economic System and Economic Policy', in von Beyme and Zimmerman (1984).
—— in *DDR Handbuch* (1985).
Studie von Nowosibirsk, in *Osteuropa*, vol. 34, nos. 1 and 3 (1984).
Thalheim, K.C., 'Die DDR im RGW', in Gutmann and Haendcke-Hoppe (1981).
—— in *FS-Analysen*, vol. 5 (1984).
—— *Stagnation or Change in Communist Countries* (Centre for Research into Communist Countries, London, 1986).
—— and Höhmann, H-H. (eds), *Wirtschaftsreformen in Osteuropa* (Wissenschaft und Politik, Cologne, 1968).
Thiele, H. *et al.*, *Handbuch der Planung für Kombinate und Betriebe* (Verlag Die Wirtschaft, East Berlin, 1982).
Thieme, H.J., 'Probleme der Definition und Messung von Inflationen in Systemen zentraler Planung', in Schenk, K-E. (ed.), *Lenkungsprobleme und Inflation in Planwirtschaften* (Schriften des Vereins für Sozialpolitik, NF, vol. 106, Berlin, 1980).
Tillack, P., in *Internationäle Zeitschrift der Landwirtschaft*, vol. 1 (1983).
Ulbricht, W., *Zum ökonomischen System des Sozialismus in der DDR*, Band 2 (East Berlin, 1968).
—— *Zum ökonomischen System des Sozialismus in der DDR*, 2 vols (Dietz Verlag, East Berlin, 1968).
Uschakow, A., *Integration im RGW, Dokumente* (2nd edn, Baden-Baden, 1983).
Vankai, T.A., 'Agricultural Performance and Prospects in the German Democratic Republic during the Eighties', in Joint Economic Com-

mittee of the Congress of the United States (1986).
Volze, A., in *Deutsche Studien*, vol. 21, p. 83 (1983).
Von Beyme, K., 'Output Policy in the GDR in Comparative Perspective', in Von Beyme and Zimmerman (1984).
—— and Zimmerman, H., *Policymaking in the German Democratic Republic* (Gower, Aldershot, 1984).
Von Grumbkow, G. (ed.), *Sozialistische Finanzkontrolle* (East Berlin, 1984).
Von Hayek, F.A., *Individualismus und wirtschaftliche Ordnung* (Salzburg, 1976).
—— 'Die Verwertung des Wissens in der Gesellschaft', in von Hayek (1976).
Vortmann, H., in *DIW Handbuch — Wirtschaft* (1984).
Wädekin, K-E., *Agrarian Policies in Communist Europe* (Allanheld, Osmun and Co., New Jersey, 1982).
Wahl, G., in *Die Wirtschaft*, vol. 22 (1975).
Weidauer, R. and Wetzel, A., *Kombinate erfolgreich leiten* (Verlag Die Wirtschaft, East Berlin, 1981).
Wenzel, M., in *Wirtschaftswissenschaft*, vol. 32, no. 8 (1984).
Wenzel, S., in *Abhandlungen der Akademie der Wissenschaften der DDR*, vol. W3 (1985).
Wienert, H. and Slater, J., *East-West Technology Transfer. The Trade and Economic Aspects* (OECD, Paris, 1986).
Wilkens, H., *The Two German Economies* (Gower, London, 1981).
Wittich, G. *et al.*, *Leitung der Sozialistischen Wirtschaft* (Verlag Die Wirtschaft, East Berlin, 1983).
Zimmerman, H., 'The GDR in the 1970s', *Problems of Communism*, March-April 1978.
—— 'Power Distribution and Opportunities for Participation: Aspects of the Socio-Political System of the GDR', in von Beyme and Zimmerman (1984).

Index